THE
PRYDAIN
COMPANION

❖

Lloyd Alexander. Photo by Alexander Limont.

THE PRYDAIN COMPANION

A Reference Guide to
Lloyd Alexander's Prydain Chronicles

⁜

MICHAEL O. TUNNELL

Foreword by

LLOYD ALEXANDER

HENRY HOLT AND COMPANY · NEW YORK

Henry Holt and Company, LLC
Publishers since 1866
115 West 18th Street
New York, New York 10011
www.henryholt.com

Library of Congress Cataloging-in-Publication Data
Tunnell, Michael O.
The Prydain companion : a reference guide to Lloyd
Alexander's Prydain chronicles / Michael O. Tunnell ;
foreword by Lloyd Alexander.
p.   cm.
Summary: A reference guide in dictionary format to the characters,
places, objects, and themes in Lloyd Alexander's five-book series,
the Chronicles of Prydain. Includes bibliographical references.
1. Alexander, Lloyd. Chronicles of Prydain—Dictionaries.
2. Children's stories, American—Dictionaries.   3. Fantasy fiction,
American—Dictionaries.   [1. Alexander, Lloyd. Chronicles of
Prydain—Dictionaries.]   I. Alexander, Lloyd. Chronicles
of Prydain.   II. Title.
PS3551.L35698 C4838 2003   813'.54—dc21   2002027552

ISBN 0-8050-7271-3
First published in hardcover in 1989 by Greenwood Press
Reissued in hardcover in 2003 by Henry Holt and Company
Printed in the United States of America on acid-free paper. ∞

1   3   5   7   9   10   8   6   4   2

ACKNOWLEDGMENTS

✜

The author and publisher are grateful to the following for granting use of their material:

Excerpts from Lloyd Alexander's books, *The Book of Three* (1964/1999), *The Black Cauldron* (1965/1999), *Coll and His White Pig* (1965/as part of *The Foundling and Other Tales of Prydain* reissue, 1999), *The Castle of Llyr* (1966/1999), *Taran Wanderer* (1967/1999), *The Truthful Harp* (1967/as part of *The Foundling and Other Tales of Prydain* reissue, 1999), *The High King* (1968/1999), and *The Foundling and Other Tales of Prydain* (1973/1999), courtesy of the publisher Henry Holt and Company, LLC.

Jacket illustrations from *The Book of Three*, *The Black Cauldron*, *Coll and His White Pig*, *The Castle of Llyr*, *Taran Wanderer*, *The Truthful Harp*, and *The High King*, and the map of Prydain from *The High King*, courtesy of the Estate of Evaline N. Bayard, Arnold A. Bayard, Executor.

The jacket illustration from *The Foundling and Other Tales of Prydain*, courtesy of Sasha Meret.

The photograph of Lloyd Alexander by Alexander Limont, courtesy of the photographer.

Excerpts from James S. Jacobs's 1978 dissertation entitled "Lloyd Alexander: A Critical Biography," courtesy of James S. Jacobs.

Excerpts from "Classic Hero in a New Mythology" by Marion Carr. *The Horn Book Magazine*, October 1971. Reprinted by permission of The Horn Book, Inc., Boston, MA.

Excerpts from *The White Goddess* by Robert Graves, courtesy of Farrar, Straus & Giroux, LLC, and Carcanet Press Limited, copyright © 1948, renewed 1975 by Robert Graves.

For Lloyd, Jim, and Glenna

✤

CONTENTS

✤

FOREWORD BY LLOYD ALEXANDER

✜

Some while ago, the Children's Book Council asked me to name my favorite childhood book. Unwilling to hurt the feelings of such old and dear friends as William Shakespeare, Charles Dickens, or Mark Twain by singling out one above another, I chose the dictionary: a book encompassing all that has ever been or ever will be written.

This was more than a fanciful way to wriggle out of answering a difficult, even impossible, question. From as far back as I can remember, the dictionary has indeed been one of my favorites. The dictionary—no, I should say "dictionaries" so as to include dictionaries of foreign words and phrases, etymological dictionaries, biblical concordances, indices of first lines of poems, dictionaries of familiar quotations, musical dictionaries, dictionaries of fictional characters, and all such treasure troves. For me, they can be as exciting as a great many novels, sometimes more so.

If we use a dictionary only as a household drudge, now and then prodding it to give a quick answer on spelling or definition, I think we miss out on one of life's great pleasures and entertainments: browsing. It is, of course, hazardous. One word leads us to look up another; one allusion or bit of etymology can set us on such a long trail of associations that we forget why we consulted the dictionary in the first place. The dictionary can put us under a spell (no pun intended), but it is a happy enchantment. We come out richer than we were before, and we can always go back again.

The joys of browsing are easily available to young and old. Yet, I balk at the word "browsing." To me, it evokes herbivorous ruminants wandering around nibbling on blades of grass. While I have the deepest affection for herbivorous ruminants, "browsing" suggests something a little too passive, too peacefully bucolic instead of active adventuring and thrilling discovery.

It is this sense of adventure that I hope readers will find in *The Prydain Companion*. Here, I must immediately admit to a great lack of impartiality.

Few authors have had their work honored by such a volume; my comments are unashamedly tinged with personal bias, but I hope they are no less valid because of that.

To begin with, *The Prydain Companion* is accurately entitled. It is indeed a companion; a traveling companion, say, or a friendly guide who well knows the country and its inhabitants, who can lead us on a journey of exploration in which we observe strange, surprising places and people.

For this, *The Prydain Companion* is more than a quick reference or handy glossary, though it is all of that as well. Instructive, certainly. But, like any good companion, a pleasure to be with over a long period of time.

This is not to overlook its practical utility. For one thing, it gives pronunciations for the names of people and places. Though authentic, ancient (the *Companion* details their sources), and to me very beautiful, those Welsh names have baffled a number of readers, who will be baffled no longer.

On that subject, I have to smile a little to myself. Having grown so familiar with them during my research, the names—exotic to anyone else—became, to me, quite ordinary and not at all difficult. In the early stages of *The Book of Three,* my editor Ann Durell despaired of them. She urged me to change many; but, by then, they had become so entwined with the characters in my mind that I could no more change their names than I could change my own. Ann agreed they should be kept, but warned me that I would be haunted ever after by readers trying to puzzle them out.

My attitude was, and is, simply to have fun with them. I have always urged readers to pronounce those peculiar names as seemed best to their own ears and tongue. It has worked pretty well. Still, many readers are curious about the "real" pronunciations. So, here they are in the *Companion*, pronounced not as a native Welsh speaker might say them, but simplified and made more comfortable for English speakers.

The Prydain Companion does a great deal more. On a level of scholarship, it offers librarians and teachers—and, above all, readers—a unique resource. For those unfamiliar with Prydain, it is a most enjoyable kind of orientation, touching on the nature of fantasy, of mythology, and the interplay between them. Those who have already journeyed through that imaginary realm will meet old friends again and see them in a new light, realizing connections and contexts that might previously have gone unnoticed.

One fascinating aspect: The entries show how ancient source materials became transformed into a work whose mythological roots are recognizable yet elaborated into something highly personal and qualitatively different.

One case in point: The entry on that outrageous and exuberant bard, Fflewddur Fflam, details the genesis of his harp whose strings break whenever he stretches the truth. The origins, in this instance, are not mythological but personal. Fflewddur's harp derives from a very real instrument: my own, still standing on the mantelpiece in my living room. It has a number of broken strings which I have deliberately left unmended—but I won't spoil a good story by condensing it here.

Likewise with Gurgi. The *Companion* notes the sketchy mythological and archetypal forebears of this half-human, half-animal creature. It also gives an account of the Prydainian Gurgi suddenly springing to life, complete with crunchings and munchings, in the author's own poor tender head.

Much of this behind-the-scenes material resulted from extensive and enjoyable conversations and correspondence with Dr. Michael Tunnell. I was grateful for the opportunity to talk at length—ramble might be more accurate—about my own hopes and motivations underlying the Chronicles of Prydain. Recollections are not always reliable; hindsight is clearer than foresight; memory tends to get readjusted; some things are simply forgotten. If readers find omissions or inconsistencies, they are the fault of the author, not of the lexicographer.

The Castle of Llyr is dedicated to the "Friends of the Companions." I hope this present volume will be a companion to the friends of Prydain.

Lloyd Alexander

How to Use the Companion

✠

Major Characters, Places, Objects, and Themes

The following major terms, which are also listed as entries in *The Prydain Companion,* are mentioned frequently throughout the Prydain series or are basic to the story. Therefore, their treatment within the texts and references of various entries differs from that of other terms that also serve as entry headings. Please refer to "Reading an Entry" for further explanation.

Achren	Dyrnwyn
Annuvin	Eilonwy
Arawn	Fflewddur Fflam
Assistant Pig-Keeper	Gurgi
bard	Gwydion
bauble	Hen Wen
the Black Cauldron	the High King
The Book of Three	House of Llyr
Caer Dallben	Kaw
cantrev	Lluagor
Cauldron-Born	Llyan
Coll	Melynlas
Companions	Prydain
Dallben	Taran
Doli	the truthful harp

The titles of the ten major references (see below) and the series titles, Chronicles of Prydain or Prydain Chronicles, are also considered major terms.

List of Abbreviations for the Ten Major Sources

The books of the Prydain series are abbreviated as follows, and refer to both the most current and to the original editions (see *Reading an Entry* for further detail):

BT   *The Book of Three* (© 1999/© 1964)
BC   *The Black Cauldron* (© 1999/© 1965)
CL   *The Castle of Llyr* (© 1999/© 1966)
TW   *Taran Wanderer* (© 1999/© 1967)
HK   *The High King* (© 1999/© 1968)
F   *The Foundling* (including *The Truthful Harp* and *Coll and His White Pig*, © 1999/original © 1973)
CWP   *Coll and His White Pig* (in *The Foundling*, © 1999/as picture book, © 1965)
TH   *The Truthful Harp* (in *The Foundling*, © 1999/as picture book, © 1967)

Coll and His White Pig and *The Truthful Harp* were originally published as individual picture books. Both stories have been added as chapters in the reissue of *The Foundling* (© 1999).

Other frequently used reference sources are abbreviated as follows:

M   Guest, Lady Charlotte. *Mabinogion*. 1877 ed. Chicago: Academy, 1978.
WG   Graves, Robert. *The White Goddess*. First American revised and enlarged edition. New York: Farrar, Straus and Giroux, 1966.

Finding an Entry

Entries are arranged in alphabetical order. Characters are listed by first name. Honorifics or titles are ignored. For example, King Smoit is listed under "S" for Smoit, Fflewddur Fflam is listed under "F" for Fflewddur, and the Horned King is found under "H" for Horned. Places, objects, or themes are listed by first word. Caer Dallben is listed under "C" for Caer, and mounds of honor is found under "M" for mounds.

Reading an Entry

Ten books are used as major references for this work. Abbreviations (see above) with accompanying page numbers are used for these titles when they are referenced within the body of an entry. The page numbers refer to both the current and the original editions, respectively (e.g., BT 8–10/ 23–25). In this example, 8–10 indicates the page numbers in the 1999 edition of *The Book of Three*, and 23–25 refers to the original (1964) edition. For *The Truthful Harp* and *Coll and His White Pig*, the first page number refers to *The Foundling* (© 1999) and the second to the original picture book (e.g., CWP 75–76/8). Quotes from the Prydain books may vary slightly from one edition to another. Some minor changes were made in the new editions. Sources other than the ten major reference sources will be noted in parentheses in the text of each entry as needed: (Alexander, 1978:248), Alexander (1978:248) or Alexander (1978). The full reference may then be found at the back of this book in the section entitled "References." This bibliography is arranged alphabetically by author's last name, and then chronologically if there is more than one source by an author. In the case of Alexander where there are multiple references listed for some years, the parenthetical notation within an entry will refer to the particular source as 1986a, 1986b, and so on, corresponding to its placement in the "References" list.

At the conclusion of each entry a summary of page references for the ten major reference sources is listed in parentheses. The page numbers given will note the first page of each occurrence of the character or other term (e.g., WG 49, 341) unless at some point the terms begin to appear repeatedly throughout the rest of the chapter or book. Then the page number will be followed by a "+" (e.g., WG 49, 74+).

However, if an entry is a *major* character, place, object, or theme (see above), no page references will be given for any of the eight Prydain books. Such terms are basic to the Prydain series and are mentioned so frequently that noting each page reference would be cumbersome. Two asterisks (**) preceding the entry heading will remind the reader that the entry is major (e.g., **Taran). Sometimes an entry will have a synonymous name or title used infrequently in its place (e.g., "Prince of Don" for "Gwydion"). Though the synonymous name or title is listed as an entry, it will usually do little more than refer the reader to its counterpart.

A single asterisk (*) is used within the body of each entry to indicate words or phrases that are themselves entries, whether major or other terms. However, only the first occurrence of such words or phrases within each entry will be noted with an asterisk. The asterisk precedes the first letter of the word under which this item is entered (excluding "the" in titles; e.g., *The High King). Both singular and plural forms will be noted in this manner (e.g., *barrow and *barrows). Other cross references not listed within the text are given at the conclusion of each entry (e.g., *See also* Dorath, Fantastic objects).

Pronunciation Guides

The pronunciation of Welsh words in entry headings is given in parentheses [e.g., **Achren (AHK-ren)]. The pronunciation aids were provided by Lloyd Alexander, who advises us that they are not necessarily true to the Welsh tongue. Many sounds in the Welsh language are simply not available in English. Alexander (1985b) does not want the Welsh words to be a stumbling block for readers of the Prydain Chronicles and has therefore made the pronunciations as simple as possible.

THE
PRYDAIN
COMPANION

✣

❖

**Achren (AHK-ren): Prince *Gwydion describes Achren as being "as dangerous as *Arawn himself; as evil as she is beautiful" (BT 24/41). Achren once wore the *Iron Crown of Annuvin as *Queen of Prydain but made the mistake of teaching her consort Arawn the secrets of her enchantments. "And he betrayed me," says Achren. "He robbed me of my throne and cast me aside" (HK 17/28–29). However, in *The Book of Three she still seems to be in league with Arawn, for it is the *Death-Lord's *Cauldron-Born who capture Gwydion and *Taran and deliver them to her. When the reader first meets Achren, she is described in this manner:

> Her long hair glittered silver in the torchlight. Her face was young and beautiful; her pale skin seemed paler still above her crimson robe. Jeweled necklaces hung at her throat, gem-studded bracelets circled her wrists, and heavy rings threw back the flickering torches. (BT 45/63)

Achren's power as an enchantress is exhibited immediately upon her first appearance. She touches Taran's wounds and his pain is replaced by a comforting warmth. Angry when Gwydion scorns the offer to join forces with her, Achren resorts to dark *magic in this powerful scene:

> Achren raised [Gwydion's] sword above her head and smote with all her force against a stone pillar. Sparks flashed, the blade rang unbroken. With a scream of rage, she dashed the weapon to the ground.
> The sword shone, still undamaged. Achren seized it again, gripping the sharp blade itself until her hands ran scarlet. Her eyes rolled back into her head, her lips moved and twisted. A thunderclap filled the hall, a light burst like a crimson sun, and the broken weapon fell in pieces to the ground.
> "So shall I break you!" Achren shrieked. (BT 47–48/65)

It is in Achren's stronghold, *Spiral Castle, that Taran meets *Eilonwy. Eilonwy believes Achren to be her aunt. However, Gwydion later explains that "Achren stole Eilonwy and brought her as a child to Spiral Castle" (CL 130/157). The sorceress had recognized Eilonwy's *bauble as the *Golden Pelydryn, a powerful magical object that could unlock the secrets of the *enchantresses of Llyr. Because the Golden Pelydryn loses its power if taken forcibly from its rightful owner, Achren found it necessary to "take" its owner. However, Achren loses Eilonwy and her bauble when the girl escapes from Spiral Castle with Taran. Achren also loses Spiral Castle. It tumbles into a mountainous heap of stone because Eilonwy and Taran remove the magic sword, *Dyrnwyn, from the stronghold's maze of subter-ranean chambers. The reader learns at the conclusion of *The Book of Three* that Achren has taken Gwydion to another of her castles, *Oeth-Anoeth, just before the destruction of Spiral Castle. From his prison cell, Gwydion fights the evil spells of Oeth-Anoeth, and his willpower destroys this stronghold as well. We do not see Achren in *The Black Cauldron* and assume she may have perished when Oeth-Anoeth fell.

Achren surfaces in *The Castle of Llyr*. Her power has steadily waned, Gywdion tells us, since the day she broke with the *Lord of Annuvin. She therefore makes one final bid to gain back what she has lost. For this she needs Eilonwy and the Golden Pelydryn. With the girl in her power, Achren need only find the *book of spells recorded by the *daughters of Llyr to fulfill her desire. Only a daughter of Llyr (and Eilonwy is the last remaining) can use these spells, which are only visible by the light of the Pelydryn. Robed in black now, Achren returns with a bewitched Eilonwy to the ruins of *Caer Colur, the ancestral home of Llyr. "Caer Colur shall rise more glorious than ever," she says with passion. "The Lord of Annuvin himself shall kneel in homage to me. . . . Arawn of *Annuvin shall cower and beg for mercy. . . . He betrayed me and now he shall suffer my vengeance" (CL 148/177).

Finally Achren acquires the Golden Pelydryn and the book of spells, both of which had been lost. But again her plans are frustrated. Eilonwy is able to free herself momentarily from Achren's spell and touch the Pelydryn to the pages of the book. The book of spells is destroyed and with it Achren's power forever. Unable to face her loss, Achren uses the last of her magic to conjure a dagger from a piece of driftwood and tries to kill herself. Gwydion stops her and says, "Your enchantments have ever been the enchantments of death. . . . Seek life, Achren" (CL 163/193). She does then agree to come with the *Companions to *Caer Dallben and accept Gwydion's offer of refuge.

By her own choice, Achren accepts the role of a commoner. At Caer Dallben she toils as a scullery maid and will sleep only upon a pallet of straw in the granary. Her time with *Coll and *Dallben seems to mellow Achren. She is more civil and even welcomes Taran home from his wanderings. However, she still harbors a deep hatred for Arawn and has sworn an oath of revenge. Achren betrays Arawn by revealing the Death-Lord's most closely guarded secret. She explains that the Lord of Annuvin can shape-change to any form and that this is the time when he is most vulnerable. "Once he assumes a shape, his strength and skill are no greater than that of the guise he wears. Then he can be slain, like any mortal thing" (HK 17/28). Gwydion will not, however, allow Achren to leave Caer Dallben to seek vengeance against Arawn, even though she may know best where the Death-Lord would hide the stolen sword Dyrnwyn.

Achren will not be denied and leaves secretly for Annuvin. It is not until near the end of *The High King that she reappears. Near the gates of Annuvin, *Kaw and his band of crows save her from death at the talons of the *gwythaints. Taran and his Companions bind her wounds. For the first time, Achren offers words of humility and thanks. "Forgive me. . . . I am grateful to you for my life and shall repay you far beyond its worth" (HK 205/237–238). Achren then shows them the shortest route into Annuvin—a secret roadway that winds over *Mount Dragon and up to the *Iron Portals.

Making good on her promise to repay the Companions, Achren sees through Arawn's final shape-changing guise and throws herself upon his serpent shape. The serpent sinks its fangs deep into Achren's throat, but the moment of distraction allows Taran to cleave the snake in two.

Achren has received her death wound. "'Have I not kept my oath, Gwydion?' she murmured, smiling vaguely. 'Is the Lord of Annuvin slain? It is good. My death comes easily upon me.' Achren's lips parted as though she would speak again, but her head fell back and her body sagged in Gwydion's arms" (HK 222/257).

It is with some regret that we see Achren die. Yet it is best, for there is no future for her in the new Prydain. Achren is laid to rest in the *Great Hall of Annuvin. As the Companions leave her there, the stronghold bursts into flame and the walls crumble. It seems fitting that Annuvin, the kingdom she once ruled, becomes both her pyre and her *barrow.

> In death the face of Achren, no longer bitterly haughty, was at last tranquil. Shrouding the woman in her tattered black cloak, the companions bore the body to rest in the Great Hall, for she who had once ruled Prydain had died not without honor. (HK 224/259)

The name of Achren was gleaned by Alexander from *Celtic mythology. In her notes to the *Mabinogion, *Lady Charlotte Guest recounts the tale of "The Battle of the Trees," which served as Alexander's inspiration for *The Book of Three. The story tells of a battle fought between Amathaon, brother to Gwydion, and Arawn, King of Annuvin (Hell). In the tale there appears a powerful woman named Achren. In fact, the battle is often referred to as the Battle of Achren. Not only was there a man in this battle who could not be overcome unless his name were known (as with the *Horned King) but "there was on the other side a woman called Achren, and unless her name were known her party could not be overcome" (M 280). As eventually occurs in the *Prydain Chronicles, this Achren was apparently aligned with Gwydion and his brother.

Elizabeth Lane (1973:26) states a strong case for similarities between another figure in Celtic tales and Alexander's Achren. This character, Arianrhod, appears in several stories, primarily "Math the Son of Mathonwy" in the Mabinogion.

> One senses an affinity [of Achren] with Arianrhod, however, in various small ways: both share castles with well-known dungeons, for one thing. . . . The similarity is borne out in Robert Graves's book The White Goddess. The names of Achren's two strongholds, Spiral Castle in The Book of Three and Caer Colur in The Castle of Llyr, do not occur anywhere in the Mabinogion, but both appear in Graves's work—and in connection with Arianrhod and her castle. All are death symbols and labyrinthine fastnesses associated with the Ariadne myth, according to Graves. Alexander's Spiral Castle is just such a maze . . . , and his ruined Caer Colur lives up to its meaning, which Graves gives as "gloomy castle."

Lane (1973:26) points to another similarity. "Throughout the Prydain books Achren and Gwydion show a solicitude for each other that would be a little shocking if the old brother-sister relationship didn't come to mind." Arianrhod and Gwydion are indeed brother and sister in the Celtic myths of the Welsh Triads (WG 56).

See also Characters—fantasy, Magic.
(M 280; WG 49, 341)

Adaon (ah-DAY-on): Adaon is the son of the *Chief Bard, *Taliesin. He is introduced in *The Black Cauldron with this description:

> Adaon . . . was tall, with straight black hair that fell to his shoulders. Though of noble bearing, he wore the garb of an ordinary warrior, with no ornament save a curiously shaped iron *brooch at his collar. His eyes

were gray, strangely deep, clear as a flame, and *Taran sensed that little was hidden from Adaon's thoughtful and searching glance. (BC 11–12/23)

"He is one of the bravest men I know," says *Fflewddur of Adaon. "That and more, for he has the heart of a true *bard. Someday he will surely be our greatest, you can mark my words" (BC 12/24).

Adaon is a gentle man, yet firm. His wisdom, a mark of greatness in Alexander's books, is evident in statements such as this one to the quarreling Taran and *Ellidyr: "We hold each other's lives in our open hands, not in clenched fists" (BC 22/36). Repeatedly, Adaon speaks against rash action with wise words. "I have learned there is greater honor in a field well plowed than in a field steeped in blood" (BC 27/43). It is this statement that Alexander (1964b) feels is "a perfect expression of one theme of [the story]."

As Taran comes to know Adaon, he sees a truly well-rounded man.

There was little Adaon had not seen or done. He had sailed far beyond the *Isle of Mona, even to the northern sea; he had worked at the potter's wheel, cast nets with the fisherfolk, woven cloth at the looms of the cottagers; and, like Taran, labored over the glowing forge. Of forest lore he had studied deeply, and Taran listened in wonder as Adaon told the ways and natures of woodland creatures. . . . (BC 27–28/43)

The *Brooch of Adaon, given him by his beloved and betrothed *Arianllyn, gives power to dream prophetic dreams and see all things more clearly. However, when Taran is bequeathed the brooch and experiences similar visions, he says that Adaon's greatness was surely not because of the clasp alone. Adaon understood things without the aid of the brooch, but it probably served to heighten his already keen awareness. Adaon sees in a dream the "black beast" on Ellidyr's shoulder, the consuming beast of pride that destroys him. He also foresees his own death, which will occur as he rides with Taran to search for the *Black Cauldron in the *Marshes of Morva. Yet, Adaon does not try to dissuade Taran from this quest and dies from a *Huntsman's dagger in his breast. The dagger was meant for Taran; Adaon chooses to take the blow instead.

Adaon leaves all his possessions to Taran—his brooch, healing herbs, and his horse *Lluagor—along with a final word of wisdom. "Is there not glory enough in living the days given to us? You should know there is adventure in simply being among those we love and the things we love, and beauty, too" (BC 75/99). Adaon is laid to rest in the glade in which he perishes.

The Brooch of Adaon becomes Taran's most prized possession, though the gift of "seeing" is a heavy burden. It is the brooch that makes possible the acquisition and eventual destruction of the *Black Crochan, *Arawn

*Death-Lord's *cauldron of death. Taran must trade the witches *Orddu, *Orgoch, and *Orwen the brooch for the *Crochan.

The figure of Adaon appears in the story, "The Dream of Rhonabwy," in the *Mabinogion. He is called "the most eloquent and wisest youth that is in this island [Britain]; Adaon the son of Taliesin" (M 304). *Lady Charlotte Guest speaks of Adaon in her notes following the story.

> Adaon or Avaon, son of the chief of the bards, and a bard himself, was also celebrated for his valour. He was one of those three daunt-less chieftains who feared nothing in the day of battle and strife, but rushed onwards regardless of death. This courage and daring supported him through all the dangers of war. He fell at length by the hand of an assassin. . . .
>
> The bold and determined character of Avaon appears to have con-tinued even after death. . . . Avaon is spoken of as one of the grave-slaughtering ones, so called from their having avenged their wrongs from their graves. (M 325)

See also Characters—fantasy.
(BC 11+/23+; HK 12/23; M 304, 325)

Adaon's (ah-DAY-on) brooch: See Brooch of Adaon.

Aedd (EED): Aedd was the father of the farmer, *Aeddan. The name Aedd appears in the *Mabinogion various times: Odgar the son Aedd, king of Ireland; *Prydain ab Aedd Mawr; Prydain son of Aedd the Great.
(TW 25/39; M 238, 386, 390)

Aeddan (EE-dan): Aeddan is one of the first new faces *Taran meets as he begins his journey in *Taran Wanderer. The old but stout farmer of *Cantrev Cadiffor wields his oak staff in Taran's defense, driving off Lord *Goryon's henchmen. Alexander describes Aeddan as "a man in a sleeve-less jacket of coarse wool girt with a plaited rope. His bare arms were knot-ted and sinewy, and his back bent, though less by years than by labor. A shock of gray, uncropped hair hung about a face that was stern but not unkind" (TW 25/39). Aeddan has the look of honesty and good nature in his weathered face.

His farm does not yield much, so Aeddan must also work in a neighbor's field. He admits to Taran that he lacks the knowledge to be productive and explains that the knowledge and skills of husbandry were stolen years ago by *Arawn *Death-Lord. In fact, Aeddan's crops have failed two years in a row. He has lost his ox and his cow. But worst of all, his son *Amren was killed in a battle against raiders. Now Aeddan or his wife *Alarca must pull the plow themselves, and they have only planted one field. "Indeed, it must not [fail]. This season our livelihood hangs on it" (TW 28/43).

Taran works for a while on Aeddan's farm, and the kindly farmer offers him a home. Though Taran is grateful, he must go on to seek his parentage.

Aeddan's field is later destroyed by the feuding Lords, *Gast and Goryon, in a battle over the prize cow, *Cornillo. Taran urges King *Smoit, the angry chieftains' monarch, to restore Aeddan's losses. Gast and Goryon relinquish Cornillo to the farmer and must labor in Aeddan's field to mend the damage.

In the final battles to be waged against the *Death-Lord, Aeddan is one of the first to throw his lot in with Taran. Taran is grateful but points out that Aeddan owes his allegiance to King Smoit. When Taran is crowned *High King of *Prydain, Aeddan is among the throng that comes to hail their new leader.

The name of Aeddan appears in the *Mabinogion, though briefly, and is spelled Aedan or Aeddon.
(TW 25/39, 33/49, 52/70, 56/74; HK 82/100, 247/285; M 125, 281, 437)

Alarca (ah-LAR-kah): Alarca is the farmer *Aeddan's wife. She is described as a tall, work-hardened farm wife with features as lined as her husband's.

See also Amren.
(TW 26/41, 58/77)

Alaw (AH-law), River: The River Alaw is located on the *Isle of Mona. *Taran and the *Companions are directed by *Kaw to follow the Alaw in order to find the abducted Princess *Eilonwy. *Caer Colur, where Eilonwy is imprisoned, is on an island located just offshore where the Alaw empties into the sea.

The River Alaw is mentioned in *Celtic mythology. It was upon the banks of the Alaw where the mythical Branwen, *daughter of Llyr, was buried.
(CL 43/62, 73/95; M 382, 387)

Amren (AHM-ren): Amren was the son of the farmer *Aeddan and his wife *Alarca. "He was of your years," Alarca tells *Taran, when "he rode with the battle host" (TW 28/42–43). Amren died fighting to drive away the raiders who sought to plunder *Cantrev Cadiffor.
(TW 28/42)

Amrys (AHM-riss): Amrys is an old shepherd who lived in the days before *Taran. His sheepfold gate is broken by King *Rhitta during a royal hunt. The *King of Prydain promises to mend it, for Amrys is too weak to do it himself. When the king forgets, Amrys's sheep stray and a lamb dies. Repeatedly, Amrys comes to Rhitta's court to ask that the gate be mended. In a fit of temper, Rhitta slays the shepherd with the sword *Dyrnwyn for questioning his honor. It is Amrys's blood that slowly stains the blade of Dyrnwyn black.

Amrys's murder corrupts Rhitta's ability to rule. He guards his possessions jealously and wars with his own trusted nobles. The ghost of Amrys appears on the battlefield and later in the king's bedchamber. Clutching the dead lamb, the ghost warns Rhitta of his fate. "Remember the lost sheep. The path you follow leads you, too, astray" (F 59/69). Again he appears and pleads with the king to "find yourself before you lose yourself" (F 60/71).

To escape the ghost, King Rhitta hides himself in the maze of passages below *Spiral Castle. Amrys appears once more, expressing pity for the king, and Rhitta draws Dyrnwyn to strike the shepherd. But he is no longer of noble worth, and fire from the *magic blade destroys him and all his guards.

No one in the kingdom knows of Rhitta's fate, and "only the shepherd Amrys ever grieved for him" (F 62/74). Alexander (1985b) finds Amrys's grief from beyond the grave "a very poignant thought." "In fact," he says, "[it gave me] a sort of shock when I thought of [it]."
(F 53+/63+)

Angharad (an-GAR-ad): Angharad's existence predates the story of *Taran. *The Foundling tells us the first part of her story. Angharad was a *Princess of Llyr in the days when *Caer Colur still stood as the *House of Llyr's stronghold. With her red-gold hair and sea-green eyes, she was considered the most beautiful of all the Princesses of Llyr. Her physical characteristics were passed on to her daughter, *Eilonwy.

When Angharad came of age to be married, her mother, Queen *Regat, sent throughout the land to find an appropriate suitor. *Daughters of Llyr were enchantresses and therefore were only allowed to marry enchanters. The enchanters, *Gildas and *Grimgower, came to vie for Angharad's hand. To prove themselves each was asked to perform a feat of *magic: Gildas turned day to night, and Grimgower conjured monsters. As imperturbable as her daughter, Angharad was neither impressed nor alarmed by Grimgower's horrible beasts. And displaying the same wit so familiar in Eilonwy, she said to Gildas:

"My dear enchanter, I don't doubt for a moment you've gone to a great deal of work and strain. I only hope you haven't done yourself harm. Not to say anything against your spells, you understand, but frankly, I don't see the point of going to such trouble for the sake of turning day into night. All anybody needs to do is to be patient a little while and night will come along very nicely by itself, with a far better quality of darkness than yours—much more velvety. Not to mention the moon and a whole skyful of stars for good measure." (F 32/36)

A third enchanter, *Geraint, was then brought into the *Great Hall. But he only posed as a wizard. He produced magical effects by sleight of hand and through the art and power of storytelling. Angharad fell instantly in love with the handsome young impostor. Queen Regat refused to let them marry, but Angharad defied her mother. The two star-crossed lovers ran away together. Gildas and Grimgower tried spells to bar their leaving, but the love of Geraint and Angharad for one another overcame the enchantments.

Angharad's decision was as ill fated as that of Romeo and Juliet, and her story ends as tragically. *Gwydion explains that "Caer Colur was abandoned and fell into ruins after Angharad Daughter of Regat fled the castle to marry against her mother's wishes. The *book of spells, which she carried away with her, was believed lost" (CL 129/157). The book of spells and the *Golden Pelydryn, keys to the enchantments of *Llyr, were both in Angharad's possession when she left with Geraint. Perhaps with these secrets gone it was impossible to sustain the House of Llyr and Caer Colur.

More is revealed of Angharad's fate when *Morda, the evil enchanter, explains to Taran how he came to possess the emblem of the House of Llyr. He says that "the Princess Angharad is long dead" and the secrets of her emblem are now his. It was he who received the book of spells (though he never understood its use) and the emblem with its magic gem when Angharad wandered into his keep. She begged refuge on a winter's night as she searched for her stolen infant daughter. Angharad was weak and "did not live out the night" (TW 91–92/112–114). In her wretched condition, Angharad barters the emblem, a bright gem held in the horns of a *crescent moon, for food and lodging. It becomes the source of Morda's power.

Of the intervening years between Angharad's departure from Caer Colur and her death, nothing more is written. There is no clue concerning the fate of Geraint. But we do know that Angharad's infant girl, Eilonwy, was stolen from her by the evil enchantress, *Achren, and that the Golden Pelydryn was the cause of the abduction. Gwydion explains that "the Golden Pelydryn was not lost" as was believed. "What better way to hide it than to put it as a shining toy in the hands of a child?" (CL 130/157). Eilonwy's *bauble was recognized by Achren. She knew it to be a key to the enchantments of Llyr. But she needed a daughter of Llyr to make the Pelydryn operate; therefore, she took both bauble and child.

The name of Angharad is one that Alexander borrowed from *Celtic mythology. In the story "Peredur the Son of Evrawc" from the *Mabinogion, Angharad Law Eurawc is a lady in Arthur's court at Caerlleon. She and Peredur, one of Arthur's knights, pledge their love to one another and stay to live with the King.

See also Angharad's gem, Llyr Half-Speech.
(BT 55/73; CL 129/157; TW 91/112; HK 17/28, 163/192, 229/265; F 29+/33+; M 100, 131)

Angharad's (an-GAR-ad) gem: This magical gem was originally from the *Fair Folk realm. "We always honored the *House of Llyr and gave the stone to Princess *Regat as our wedding gift," says *Doli of the Fair Folk. "She must have handed it down to her daughter [*Angharad]" (TW 109/133).

All *daughters of Llyr wear the emblem of the House of Llyr, a silver *crescent moon. However, the emblem worn by Angharad was unique because of the stone. "The horns of the crescent held a strangely carved gem, clear as water, whose facets sparkled as though lit by an inner fire" (TW 91/112).

The evil enchanter *Morda possesses the emblem and stone in the *Prydain Chronicles. He obtains it when Angharad, Regat's daughter and *Eilonwy's mother, seeks refuge one winter's night in Morda's keep. She offers him the crescent moon and its stone in exchange for food and shelter. Weak and unhealthy, Angharad dies before morning, but not before she tells Morda that "the gem would lighten burdens and ease harsh tasks" (TW 93/115). Morda discovers the gem's secrets and uses it to dwindle "the heaviest fagots to no more than piles of twigs," raise the *wall of thorns around his cottage, and locate a hidden spring (TW 93/115).

Morda then discovers how to use the gem in evil ways. The jewel leads the sorcerer to a Fair Folk treasure trove. It is with Angharad's gem that he is able to turn *Fflewddur Fflam into a hare, *Gurgi into a field mouse, and nearly reduces *Taran to an earthworm. Morda even turns Doli into a frog, and no enchanter before has possessed the power to bewitch the Fair Folk. But the most shocking enchantment accomplished with the gem is evidenced when Taran plunges a sword into the sorcerer's breast. Unharmed, Morda mocks Taran, explaining that with the jewel he was able to draw out his life and hide it safely away. If *Kaw had not discovered the hiding place, the *Companions would yet be forest animals.

When Morda is defeated, Taran willingly gives the jewel to Doli. Gratefully, Doli acknowledges that the stone is much too dangerous in other hands and returns it to the *Realm of the Fair Folk.

See also Fantastic objects.

(TW 91/112, 97/119, 109/132)

Annlaw (AHN-law) Clay-Shaper: The reader first hears of Annlaw when *Fflewddur Fflam discovers a wine bowl of his making in Lord *Gast's treasure store. "I recognize the work from the hand of Annlaw Clay-Shaper, a master craftsman, the most skilled potter in *Prydain," says Fflewddur. "I swear his wheel is enchanted" (TW 42/59).

Later, as Taran wanders the *Free Commots, he chances upon "a hale old man" digging soil from the bank of a stream in *Commot Merin. "Beside him stood a pair of wooden buckets on a yoke, and into these he carefully poured spadefuls of pale brown earth. His iron-gray hair and beard were cropped short; despite his age, his arms seemed as brawny as those of *Hevydd the Smith" (TW 189/221–222). As soon as Taran sees racks of earthenware in the old man's cottage, he knows from its workmanship that this is Annlaw Clay-Shaper.

Though Annlaw's pottery is prized like treasure outside the Free Commots, he himself has no care for riches. In fact, Annlaw sends most of his work to other small *Commots without potters in exchange for food. "Treasure is what I need the least," explains Annlaw. "My joy is in the craft, not the gain. Would all the fortunes in Prydain help my fingers shape a better bowl?" (TW 192/225).

Annlaw denies any enchantments in his potter's wheel and tells Taran the story of *Govannion the Lame, who created the enchanted implements and discovered the high secrets of all crafts. These, of course, were all stolen by *Arawn. "A lifetime have I striven to discover them [the secrets] again," says Annlaw. "The deepest lore yet lies beyond my grasp" (TW 192–193/226).

Annlaw's dedication to his craft is best exemplified during the time Taran apprentices with him. "Craftsmanship isn't like water in an earthen pot, to be taken out by the dipperful until it's empty," he says. "No, the more drawn out the more remains. The heart renews itself . . . and the skill grows all the better for it" (TW 194/228). Annlaw's philosophy allows no compromise; every detail is important. Taran must learn painstakingly of the nature of clay, pigments for coloring, and methods of firing before he is allowed to touch the wheel. Annlaw also rarely repeats a pattern in any of his work. "Stale water is a poor drink. Stale skill is worse," he says. "And the man who walks in his own footsteps only ends where he began" (TW 197/230).

Unfortunately, Taran does not have the gift to master the one craft he most wants. Wisely, Annlaw tells his apprentice that it is fortunate he has discovered this early, rather than spending years in "vain hope" (TW 198/232).

Alexander, who learned to make pottery from his sister Florence during the 1940s, related to that experience when creating the Annlaw sequences (Jacobs, 1978:492). But the figure of Annlaw was probably inspired by Alexander's violin teacher, Lucius Cole (Alexander, 1985b). More than anything, Alexander wanted to learn to play the violin, but he started too late in life to master it. After a few years of lessons and hard work, Alexander was gently told by Lucius Cole that though he had done amazingly well, there was no point in continuing the lessons (Jacobs, 1978:304). He and Taran shared similar feelings of disappointment. Yet Alexander learned well enough to continue playing the violin for great personal pleasure. In spite of the similarity between Lucius Cole and Annlaw, Alexander is still not certain if he thought consciously of the violin lessons as he wrote *Taran Wanderer. He does say that the emotions of the experience certainly translated to the story of Annlaw Clay-Shaper (Alexander, 1985b).

While Taran is in the Commot Merin raising an army for the *House of Don, marauders attack, and Annlaw Clay-Shaper is killed. His body is found among the shattered remains of his work. Taran anguishes over Annlaw's death, for the potter is his dearest Commot friend.

See also Fernbrake Stream.

(TW 42/59, 189/221, 208/243; HK 6/16, 100/120, 105/126, 110/131, 237/273)

Annuvin (ah-NOO-vin): Annuvin is *Arawn *Death-Lord's realm that lies in the west of *Prydain. It is a barren wasteland surrounded by craggy mountain peaks. Annuvin is called the *Land of Death. Little plant life will grow and all but the evil will languish within its boundaries. The race of the *Fair Folk will die if kept in Annuvin but a few days. (This nearly happened to *Doli.) Annuvin's inhabitants are largely Arawn's *Cauldron-Born, lifeless warriors who slaughter and destroy at the Death-Lord's command. It is from this mountain stronghold that Arawn makes his bid to take all of Prydain.

Though Annuvin is mentioned with dread throughout the *Chronicles of Prydain, it is not until late in *The High King that the reader gets a glimpse of it. Description of the jagged and barren peaks prefaces *Taran's view of the stronghold.

Suddenly the dark towers of Arawn's fastness were below him. Beyond the high walls, beyond the massive *Iron Portals, ugly and brooding, he glimpsed the spreading courtyards, the *Hall of Warriors where once the *Black Cauldron had stood. Arawn's *Great Hall rose, glittering like black, polished marble, and above it, at the highest pinnacle, floated the Death-Lord's banner. (HK 209/242)

Alexander purposely did not describe the Death-Lord nor his kingdom in much detail. For instance, he never tells us what symbols are on Arawn's banner, only that it is black. The element of mystery and horror are better preserved in one's imagination, explains Alexander (1985b):

I think, particularly when you're dealing with terrible villains—in other words . . . monstrous, awful, terrible [beings]—the less description specifically, the better. Because once you've described something you have its measure. . . . If there is some way you can express or suggest to the imagination awful things—much stronger.

Concerning the symbol on Arawn's banner, Alexander (1985b) says, "I never described it, and I never drew it on a piece of paper. And I never clearly spelled it out or envisioned it in my own mind." In fact, he says he still doesn't know what the symbol is but expects it is some ancient symbol of death—something terrible to look at.

Annuvin is introduced early in *The Book of Three as *Dallben instructs a young Taran. The ancient enchanter explains that "Annuvin is more than a land of death. It is a treasure-house, not only of gold and jewels but of all things of advantage to men. Long ago, the race of men owned these treasures. By craft and deceit, Arawn stole them, one by one, for his own evil uses" (BT 7/21). As a part of his effort to destroy Prydain, Arawn has stolen knowledge from its people and stores these secrets, unused, in the treasure chambers of Annuvin. It seems his "evil uses" are to deprive mankind of enlightenment and progress, thus weakening Prydain.

However, Arawn's plans are frustrated, and he himself is destroyed. When Taran and his *Companions leave Annuvin after the final battle, the dark banner bursts into flame and the walls of the stronghold tremble and fall.

Underworlds, or lands of the dead, such as Annuvin, are common to most mythologies. For example, in Greek mythology Hades is the home of the dead and was thought to be located beneath the earth. In *Celtic mythology, Annuvin (often spelled Annwn or Annwvyn) is referred to as "the Lower Regions" or "Hell" (M 363).

Alexander borrowed Annuvin and its ruler, Arawn, from the *Mabinogion. In a few instances, Annuvin is described as a sort of underworld with broods of devils (M 241). Annuvin is mostly portrayed as a magical and beautiful land and Arawn as an honorable enchanter/king. Annuvin plays a role in many of the Celtic tales, either in the *Mabinogion* or other sources noted by *Lady Charlotte Guest. For example, "The Battle of the Trees," an ancient Celtic tale that was Alexander's inspiration for *The Book of Three*, tells of a battle waged because Amathaon, *Gwydion's brother, stole a white roebuck and a whelp from Annuvin. Alexander (1965f) writes that Annuvin was traditionally thought to have actually existed in the Prescelly Mountains in Wales.

See also Achren, Dark Gate, Iron Crown of Annuvin, Mount Dragon. (M 241, 280, 340, 363. WG 30, 49+, 118, 216, 291)

Antlered King: *See* Horned King.

**Arawn (ah-RAWN), King: Arawn, also known as the *Death-Lord and the *Lord of Annuvin, is the worst of villains, the embodiment of evil. He is a powerful enchanter and has increased his strength through evil wizardry and deception. Arawn has long desired to rule *Prydain by destroying it. From his mountain stronghold, *Annuvin, he directs a campaign to gain total domination.

The *Lord of Death did not always possess such power. *Gwydion explains to *Taran that "indeed, it was *Achren who gave Arawn his power in the days when she herself ruled Prydain" (CL 23/39). As her consort, Arawn was taught the secrets of Achren's enchantments. When he had learned what Achren had to offer, he wrested Annuvin from her. If the *Sons of Don had not come from the *Summer Country to stand as some protection against Arawn, he would have gained dominion over all of Prydain (BT 7/22).

The reader is first introduced to Arawn as *The Book of Three* begins. As *Dallben instructs the young *Taran, he tells us that "by craft and deceit, Arawn stole" all things of advantage to men "for his own evil uses" (BT 7/21). Taran learns more of what this means when he meets *Aeddan the farmer. Aeddan tells of a time when the now meager *Hill and *Valley Cantrevs produced richly from their farms and ranches. There even existed plows and tools that worked by themselves. Arawn stole them all, says the farmer, but the most severe blow was his theft of the secrets of making the earth yield richly (TW 27/41–42). Later, *Hevydd the Smith informs Taran that the Lord of Death has stolen the deepest secrets of shaping metal (TW 176–177/208). Arawn even steals *Hen Wen, *Coll's oracular pig, in order to discover the many deep secrets she knows (CWP 76–77/11). The

Death-Lord has weakened Prydain primarily by removing knowledge from the people. Because Prydain is no longer a prosperous and enlightened land, it can be more easily defeated in battle.

In *The Foundling ("The Smith, the Weaver, and the Harper"), the reader is told how Arawn uses trickery and enchantments to steal implements from the craftsmen of Prydain. He takes the hammer of *Iscovan which "could work any metal into whatever shape its owner wished" and the shuttle of *Follin that "could weave quicker than the eye could see, with never a knot or a tangle" (F 65/77). It is important to note that the Death-Lord could not deceive *Menwy the *bard. Therefore, bardic knowledge and enchanted harps are still present in Prydain (F 70–72/84–87).

Probably Arawn's most useful possession, and certainly the most deadly, is the *Black Crochan or *Black Cauldron. The *cauldron rejuvenates the bodies of lifeless warriors, and the Death-Lord maintains an ever-increasing army of the invincible and ghastly soldiers. In order to keep the ranks of the *Cauldron-Born from swelling, the *Sons of Don lead a quest that sees the cauldron destroyed. *Gwydion tells the people of Prydain that the destruction of the Black Cauldron "is one of the gravest defeats Arawn has ever suffered" (BC 174/217).

The Lord of Death obtained the cauldron from the three witches, *Orddu, *Orwen, and *Orgoch. Orddu tells Taran that Arawn so desired the cauldron that he "paid dearly for the use of it" (BC 107/139). But what was the price? Alexander (1985b) says, "I never specified what he paid, deliberately so. Because once you specify something, it is minimized. . . . We can only guess what it was." However, Alexander does say that the cauldron cost Arawn "something painful" and because of this he was "more vulnerable." Orddu also says that "even Arawn had to be allowed to have his chance" to possess the Black Crochan, despite its fearful uses (BC 107/138). "He [Arawn] had to have a chance, in effect, to make his bid and take over the kingdom," says Alexander (1985b). "It is only fair" that Arawn has the opportunity to decide right from wrong and to live with the consequences of his decisions.

Besides his legions of Cauldron-Born, Arawn also commands his deadly *Huntsmen of Annuvin. Unlike the Cauldron-Born, these fearsome men of the forest may be killed. However, when one of their band is struck down, the remaining members gain in strength. "Even as their number dwindles, their power grows" (BC 34/50). The *gwythaints, birds giant and ruthless, are also servants of the Death-Lord. He speaks their language and sends them forth to serve as spies and messengers. Gwydion speaks of Arawn's power to manipulate even the men of Prydain into his service.

"Arawn does not long abandon Annuvin . . . but his hand reaches every-where. There are chieftains whose lust for power goads them like a sword point. To certain of them, Arawn promises wealth and dominion, play-ing on their greed as a bard plays on a harp. Arawn's corruption burns every human feeling from their hearts and they become his liege men, serving him beyond the borders of Annuvin and bound to him forever." (BT 19/34)

Both *Morgant and *Pryderi are examples of Arawn's seductive powers. Tempted by promises of power, they relinquish their honor by turning against their own people.

One of Arawn's chief characteristics is the ability to change shape. In *The High King Arawn leaves Annuvin to steal the *magic sword *Dyrnwyn. He changes shape to appear as Taran, thus luring Gwydion into a trap. Achren explains that the Death-Lord does not alter his form with-out risk.

"Arawn dares not pass the borders of Annuvin in his true form. . . . To do so would mean his death. But he commands all shapes, and they are both shield and mask. . . . Now you glimpse one of Arawn's subtlest powers. But it is a power used only when none other will serve him. . . . Arawn has many secrets, but this one is most deeply guarded. Once he assumes a shape, his strength and skill are no greater than that of the guise he wears. Then can he be slain, like any mortal thing." (HK 16–17/27–28)

Alexander (1985b) likes the idea that this may be the price Arawn paid for acquisition of the cauldron. In other words, he relinquished to the witches his invulnerability when in another form. Indeed, this weakness proves to be Arawn's undoing.

When it is clear that Annuvin has fallen, Arawn, in a final effort to sur-vive, changes shape twice. First he appears to Taran in the shape of Gwydion. He commands Taran to sheath the flaming Dyrnwyn and relin-quish it to him. But Arawn is unable to disguise himself fully, for he cannot speak the honest words of Gwydion. Taran sees through the ruse and tries to strike him down. "Before the blade struck home, the Death-Lord's dis-guised shape blurred suddenly and vanished. A shadow writhed along the corridor and faded away" (HK 216/250). Later, the Death-Lord changes into a serpent. Cleaving the snake in two, Taran deals Arawn his death blow. The serpent's body shimmers, writhes and blurs.

In its place appeared the black-cloaked figure of a man whose severed head had rolled face downward on the earth. Yet in a moment this shape too lost its form and the corpse sank like a shadow into the earth; and where it had lain was seared and fallow, the ground wasted, fissured as though by drought. (HK 222–223/257)

Arawn no longer exists, and it seems fitting that he ends his life in the form of a serpent, the ancient symbol of evil.

Arawn remains a mystery. We see him only in shapes not his own or as dark shadows writhing along corridors. When Alexander allows us a fleeting glimpse at Arawn's true shape, he turns the features of the severed head against the ground. "When you're dealing with terrible villains—in other words . . . monstrous, awful, terrible [beings]—the less description specifically, the better." Alexander (1985b) works hard to keep Arawn Death-Lord a mysterious, unseen horror.

> If there is some way you can express or suggest to the imagination awful things—much stronger. . . . [Writers] have made this mistake: they have tried to describe something that is so monstrous, and the more they try to describe it in detail the less monstrous it becomes.

Alexander borrowed the name of Arawn and his kingdom, Annuvin, from *Celtic mythology. In the *Mabinogion, the story "*Pwyll Prince of Dyved" tells of a magical but not evil kingdom called Annwvyn ruled by the honorable King Arawn. This Arawn is also a shape-changer and enchanter (M 340–344). Other sources noted by *Lady Charlotte Guest in her translation of the Mabinogion indicate that Arawn was king of the underworld, Annuvin being synonymous with "Hell" or "the Lower Regions" (M 363). "The Battle of the Trees," an ancient Celtic tale that was Alexander's inspiration for The Book of Three, recounts a great battle waged because a white roebuck and a whelp were stolen from Arawn by Amathaon, Gwydion's brother (M 280).

See also Characters—fantasy, Good versus evil.
(M 61, 280, 340; WG 30, 49+, 118, 216, 291)

Arianllyn (ah-ree-AHN-lin): Arianllyn is the betrothed of *Adaon. She lives in the *northern domains and there awaits Adaon's return. It is Arianllyn who gives Adaon the *magic *brooch. The brooch offers its wearer clearer understandings and dreams of prophecy.

Originally, Arianllyn was not to be included in *The Black Cauldron. Though she never appears in the story, Alexander feels the mention of Arianllyn is a perfect story element. To his editor, Ann Durell, he writes, "Your suggestions about Adaon's betrothed worked perfectly and made things even more heartbreaking." However, her inclusion caused a problem. When Adaon dies, wouldn't he be more apt to leave the brooch to

Arianllyn than to *Taran? And Taran must have it later to trade for the *Black Cauldron. In the same letter to Ann Durell, Alexander (1964c) says, "In the passage where he [Adaon], in effect, makes his will, I was stumped for a while, figuring he should leave her something valuable (he obviously wouldn't leave her his horse, etc.). But I think this does it—by making his betrothed the one who gave him the brooch in the first place!"

See also Brooch of Adaon.
(BC 28/44, 75/99, 80/106)

Ash-Wing: In the days before *Taran, the owl Ash-Wing helps *Coll retrieve *Hen Wen from the *Land of Death. During his search for the white pig, Coll rescues an owlet trapped in a tree trunk. Ash-Wing, the owlet's father, thanks Coll, who is surprised that owls can speak. Ash-Wing explains that all animals speak, but "until now, it is you who have not understood" (CWP 76/11). The owl's understanding is deep, however. He knows Coll has recently eaten of the *Hazel Nuts of Wisdom which have enabled the farmer to understand the speech of animals. It is Ash-Wing who informs Coll that Hen Wen has been stolen by *Arawn *Death-Lord because "she knows many deep secrets" (CWP 77/12). This is the first Coll knows of Hen Wen's oracular abilities.

With help from his keen night eyes, Ash-Wing leads Coll to *Annuvin and helps him find Hen Wen. Because the effects of the Hazel Nuts of Wisdom are temporary, they must hurry or be unable to communicate. Ash-Wing finds a hidden passage into Annuvin and then lures away the *gwythaints guarding Hen Wen so that Coll may take her.

Ash-Wing has a counterpart in the *Mabinogion. The Owl of Cwm Cawlwyd, one of the oldest and wisest of the animals, helps lead Arthur's knights to the secret prison of Mabon in the tale of "Kilhwch [*Kilhuch] and *Olwen" (M 247).

See also Oak-Horn, Star-Nose.
(CWP 76+/10+; M 247)

ash-wood: Both *Dallben's staff and the *letter sticks are made of ash. According to *Celtic mythology, ash is a tree of magical properties and represents the third letter in the Druid alphabet (Nion). The Druidical wands were made of ash. In ancient Wales oars and coracle slats were also made of ash, as were rods for urging on horses. Ash was considered the tree of sea power (WG 168–169). All knowledge and science was supposedly inscribed upon three ash rods by the great prophet and *bard, Einigan Gawr (M 269).

See also Fantastic objects, Magic.
(BT 12/27; HK 25/36, 183/213, 188/218, 229/264; WG 168; M 269)

**Assistant Pig-Keeper: *See* Taran.

Avren (AHV-ren): *See* Great Avren River.

Avren (AHV-ren) Harbor: Avren Harbor is a shipping port built where the *Great Avren River empties into the sea. It is from this harbor that the *Companions sail to the *Isle of Mona in *The Castle of Llyr.
(CL 4/18, 8/22; HK 42/56, 53/68, 225/260)

Avren (AHV-ren) valley: *See* Great Avren River.

B

⟐

banner of the White Pig: Embroidered by *Eilonwy, this piece of cloth becomes *Taran's standard around which he rallies the men of the *Free Commots in the battle against *Arawn (HK 93/112). Eilonwy binds her embroidery to a spear, calling it Taran's "battle flag," and *Gurgi becomes Taran's standard bearer (HK 83/101). The banner shows a blue-eyed *Hen Wen (the oracular pig actually has brown eyes) on a field of green (HK 10/20). The banner of the White Pig is "slashed almost beyond recognition" when *Caer Dathyl falls to *Pryderi and the *Cauldron-Born (HK 129/154). (HK 9+/20+)

**bard: Bards seem to be an integral part of society in *Prydain. They are often a wandering lot who bring news and entertainment to the *cantrevs of the land. "It's so usual for a bard to drift in and sing for his supper," says *Fflewddur (HK 58/73). They are musicians—the harp is their instrument—and storytellers.

Of the bardic tradition in ancient Wales, Robert Graves says:

> It seems that the Welsh minstrels, like the Irish poets, recited their traditional romances in prose, breaking into dramatic verse, with harp accompaniment, only at points of emotional stress. . . . The most famous Welsh collection [of romances] is the *Mabinogion, which is usually explained as "Juvenile Romances," that is to say those that every apprentice to the minstrel profession was expected to know. (WG 27)

However, bards are much more than traveling entertainers. They are historians and scholars. Alexander (1985b) is quick to make the distinction between minstrels and true bards. He points out that bards historically were thought to be wise and to harbor knowledge concerning all things: medicine, philosophy, mathematics, history, music, and so on. When

*Taran shows Fflewddur the *Old Writing on *Dyrnwyn's scabbard, he says, "Bards are supposed to understand these things" (BT 85/107). Knowledge of ancient script and story was part of bardic training. Had Fflewddur been a true bard, he would have been able to read the Old Writing. *Taliesin, the *Chief Bard, is the epitome of this bardic image. Taran senses in Taliesin an "authority far greater than a war-leader's and more commanding than a king's" (HK 111/133). Though he is called bard, Fflewddur Fflam, who did not pass the bardic exams, may be considered more of a wandering minstrel.

The history learned by bards is often acquired and passed on in the form of poems or ballads sung to the accompaniment of the harp. For example, *Gwydion tells Taran that *Coll's rescue of *Hen Wen from *Annuvin is famous in bardic lore. "The bards of the north still sing of it" (BT 24/40). It is the supreme honor to perform some deed that is recorded in the bardic lore. "The bards will sing our praises forever!" says Fflewddur as he contemplates battling the foes of the *House of Don (BT 82/103). Even *Gurgi is conscious of the immortality one can achieve through the bards. "Oh, bards will sing of clever Gurgi with rantings and chantings!" he says (TW 58/76).

The *bardic symbol represented on *Adaon's brooch, three lines arranged "like a sort of arrowhead," symbolizes knowledge, truth, and love (BC 89/117). "I sometimes think it's hard enough to find any one of them [knowledge, truth, love], even separately," says Fflewddur. "Put them all together and you have something very powerful indeed" (BC 90/117).

*Lady Charlotte Guest writes of the bardic symbol in her notes to the *Mabinogion*. According to *Celtic mythology, the bardic symbol is exactly as described by Alexander, three radiating lines (arranged like an arrowhead) which are supposed to represent the three diverging rays of light seen originally by the bard Einigan Gawr. These rays had inscribed upon them all knowledge and science. The knowledge was inscribed by Einigan Gawr upon three ash rods. The tale tells that the people who saw the ash rods deified them. This so grieved Einigan "that he broke the rods and died" (M 269). Later, *Menwy "saw three rods growing from the mouth of Einigan" (M 269). Menwy took the rods, learned all that was written upon them, and taught the knowledge to others. The three lines of the bardic symbol contain all the elements of the bardic alphabet, "as there is not a single letter in it that is not formed from them" (M 269). The alphabet is alleged to have been used only upon wood, so it was constructed to avoid horizontal or curved lines, "which could not be cut on wooden rods without splintering or running, on account of the grain of the wood" (M 270).

A tribute to bards is found in the last sentence of the *Prydain Chronicles. "Yet long afterward, when all had passed away into distant memory, there were many who wondered whether King Taran, Queen *Eilonwy, and their *companions had indeed walked the earth, or whether they had been no more than dreams in a tale set down to beguile children. And, in time, only the bards knew the truth of it" (HK 248/285).

See also Adaon, ash-wood, Council of Bards, truthful harp.
(M 269; WG 17+)

bardic symbol: See bard.

barrow: A barrow is a burial place or tomb. *Taran and *Eilonwy stumble upon the barrow of King *Rhitta among the passages beneath *Spiral Castle. It is there that they find the *magic sword *Dyrnwyn, still in the dead king's grasp.

However, a barrow is usually a hillock or mound of stones or earth marking a burial spot. For example, a barrow is raised in *Ellidyr's memory in *The Black Cauldron.
(BT 34+/51+; BC 174/217; WG 102+)

battle horn: In *The Castle of Llyr, the *Companions barely escape death when *Caer Colur is washed into the sea. Later, the sea gives up a silver-bound battle horn that must have hung in the halls of the ancient castle. *Eilonwy plucks it from the surf and bestows it upon *Taran as a pledge that she will not forget him while she is away on the *Isle of Mona learning to be a lady.

Taran carries the battle horn with him on his quest to find his parentage. *Doli later identifies the horn as being of *Fair Folk craftsmanship. After examining it carefully, Doli determines there is only one call left in the horn. "This was crafted long ago, when men and Fair Folk lived in closer friendship and each was glad to help the other. The horn holds a summons to us" (TW 113/137). Doli whistles the notes "of a pitch and sequence strange to Taran" (TW 113/137). He tells Taran to sound the notes on the horn just that way, and the nearest Fair Folk will come to aid in whatever way possible. Taran chooses to use the one remaining call to save *Craddoc, the shepherd who pretended to be his father. The Fair Folk pull Taran and Craddoc from an icy mountain crevice.

See also Fantastic objects.
(CL 169/200; TW 8/21, 112/136, 116/140, 122/147, 128/154, 155/184, 159/188; HK 3/13, 10/21)

**bauble: *Eilonwy's bauble is "a ball of what seem[s] to be gold" (BT 50/68). She reveals some of its magical power early in *The Book of Three* when she causes it to shine, thus lighting *Taran's cell in *Spiral Castle. Later *Gwydion reveals that the bauble is actually one of the great treasures of *Llyr. It is the *Golden Pelydryn, an enchantment "handed down from mother to daughter" in the *House of Llyr (CL 129/157). The Golden Pelydryn was thought to have been lost. Instead, it had been hidden by Eilonwy's mother, Princess *Angharad. "What better way to hide it," says Gwydion, "than to put it as a shining toy in the hands of a child?" (CL 130/157). Both the Golden Pelydryn and the *book of spells were taken from *Caer Colur by Angharad when she left to marry against her mother's wishes. The enchantments in the book of spells are visible only under the light of the Pelydryn.

The child, Eilonwy, was kidnapped by *Achren because the sorceress recognized the Golden Pelydryn. She knew its power and knew that only a *daughter of Llyr would be able to work its *magic and use the spells from the book. She also realized that the Pelydryn would lose its power if forcibly taken from its owner. Therefore, Achren stole both the bauble and Eilonwy, the last of the daughters of Llyr. Later, in *The Castle of Llyr, Achren kidnaps a more mature Eilonwy to try to gain power over *Prydain through the magic of Llyr. She bewitches Eilonwy and eventually is able to bring the Golden Pelydryn and the lost book of spells together again. But the Pelydryn alone held also the power to destroy the book, and Eilonwy regains her senses long enough to touch the bauble to its pages. The book of spells erupts into a pillar of fire, consuming itself.

The bauble is lost twice during the *Prydain Chronicles. Both instances occur in *The Castle of Llyr.* First, Eilonwy drops it by the River *Alaw as *Magg carries her to Achren at Caer Colur. Taran and the *Companions find it and then have unknowingly in their possession both the Golden Pelydryn and the book of spells, which they found in *Glew's cottage. The second loss seems more permanent. When Caer Colur is buried by the sea, the bauble apparently sinks with it. However, *Kaw somehow rescues, and later returns, the bauble to the Princess Eilonwy.

In *The Book of Three,* Eilonwy tosses the bauble to Taran as they make their way through the tunnels of Spiral Castle. Though it continues to shine in this instance, the bauble winks out immediately when Prince *Rhun handles it early in *The Castle of Llyr.* Later, when the Companions are trapped in Glew's cavern, they try to light the bauble without Eilonwy. None has success until Taran turns his thoughts away from his plight to that of the kidnapped Eilonwy. Then the bauble begins to glow in his hand.

Even the "feckless" Rhun is able to make the bauble blaze, blinding the giant Glew and saving the Companions from death. Rhun's willingness to sacrifice his life for his friends gave power to the bauble. Taran asks of *Fflewddur, "Can that be its [bauble] secret? To think more for others than ourselves?" (CL 123/150). Fflewddur replies, "That would seem to be one of its secrets, at least. Once you've discovered that, you've discovered a great secret indeed—with or without the bauble" (CL 123/150).

In *The Black Cauldron*, Eilonwy offers the bauble to the witches *Orddu, *Orwen, and *Orgoch, in exchange for the *Black Cauldron. Of course, the witches prefer to take the *Brooch of Adaon from Taran.

It is the bauble Eilonwy uses in *The High King* to warn Taran of the approaching *Huntsmen of Annuvin. The bauble shines so brightly that the night turns bright as noon, revealing the danger. This also fulfills a part of *Hen Wen's prophecy concerning how *Dyrnwyn might be recovered from *Arawn *Death-Lord. The prophecy states that Dyrnwyn will not be regained until "Night turn to noon" (HK 31/43). The bauble also makes clear the unreadable inscription on Dyrnwyn's scabbard, just before the *Old Writing fades forever.

As the Prydain Chronicles come to an end, Eilonwy offers the bauble to Taran as a remembrance of her. Taran is going to stay in Prydain, and she must go to the *Summer Country with the *Children of Don. When *Dallben tells Eilonwy she may give up her powers as an enchantress and thus stay in Prydain with Taran, she gladly does so. The moment the spell removing her powers is completed, the light of the bauble winks out, its enchantments gone.

See also Dorath, Fantastic objects.

Belin (BELL-in): Belin, the *King of the Sun, was the consort of the *Lady Don. The *Children of Don or the *Sons of Don are the progeny of these two. Though the Children of Don voyaged from the *Summer Country to *Prydain, Alexander (1985b) says that Belin and the Lady Don did not make the journey.

The name Beli appears in *Celtic mythology, and Robert Graves in *The White Goddess* feels the name is associated with Belin, the English or British god of the sun (WG 58–60). Alexander (1985b) confirms that this Belin mentioned by Graves became the King of the Sun in *The Book of Three*. Belin is also known as a sea god in some myths (WG 59).

Fflewddur Fflam frequently uses the expression "Great Belin" as an oath or exclamation. As Fflewddur has the blood of *Don in his veins, it seems appropriate that he refer to his patriarch.

(BT 7/22, 74/94, 104/126; BC 41/59, 102/132, 108/139, 139/178; CL 17/32, 42/60, 50/70, 57/77, 64/85, 65/86, 71/92, 77/99, 83/106, 90/114, 99/123, 102/128, 104/129, 111/136, 113/139, 118/144, 125/152, 160/189; TW 48/66, 57/76, 66/85, 70/90, 77/97, 82/103, 94/116, 107/130, 114/138, 121/146, 125/150, 141/168, 143/171, 158/187; HK 12/23, 30/42, 56/71, 61/76, 62/78, 66/82, 66/83, 76/94, 104/125, 140/166, 150/177, 172/201, 173/202, 177/207, 195/227, 226/261, 231/267, 241/278; M 224; WG 58)

black bear: The black bear is the emblem of the *House of Smoit. The bear is displayed on a crimson banner.
   See also Smoit.
(TW 45/62; HK 44/59, 55/70)

**Black Cauldron: The reader is first introduced to the Black Cauldron in *The Book of Three* when *Gwydion tells *Taran of *Arawn's *Cauldron-Born. The *Death-Lord uses this *cauldron to rejuvenate the corpses of soldiers and has created an army of the ghastly, lifeless warriors. Taran also calls it the cauldron of Arawn and the cauldron of *Annuvin. However, the witches *Orddu, *Orgoch, and *Orwen reveal its true name: the *Black Crochan.

The *Sons of Don undertake a quest in *The Black Cauldron to destroy Arawn's cauldron. However, they discover that it has already been taken from the *Lord of Annuvin. *Gwystyl of the *Fair Folk reluctantly informs the *Companions that the cauldron had been taken into the *Marshes of Morva. When they find the marshes and the dwelling of the three witches, they also find the Black Cauldron.

The witches (Orddu, Orwen, and Orgoch) explain that the Black Crochan was theirs to begin with; they lent it to Arawn. When *Eilonwy asks indignantly how they could have done such a thing, Orddu answers tolerantly, "Even Arawn had to be allowed to have his chance," and he "paid dearly for the use of it, very dearly indeed" (BC 107/138–139). But Arawn did not return it when the time came. "He broke his oath to us, as might be expected" (BC 108/139). So, the three retrieved it from Annuvin.

*Gurgi uncovers the *Crochan in the witches' chicken roost. The Companions are stunned by its appearance.

> It was squat and black, and half as tall as a man. Its ugly mouth gaped wide enough to hold a human body. The rim of the cauldron was crooked and battered, its sides dented and scarred; on its lips and on the curve of its belly lay dark brown flecks and stains which Taran knew were not rust. A long, thick handle was braced by a heavy bar; two heavy rings, like the links of a great chain, were set in either side. Though of

iron, the cauldron seemed alive, grim and brooding with ancient evil. The empty mouth caught the chill breeze and a hushed muttering rose from the cauldron's depths, like the lost voices of the tormented dead. . . . [Taran] well understood Gurgi's terror, for the very sight of the cauldron was enough to make him feel an icy hand clutching his heart. (BC 114/145–146)

Alexander continues to hint that the Black Cauldron may be a living entity. It mutters defiance when the Companions try to dislodge it from a river, and *Fflewddur swears that it purposely broke his arm. "The wretched thing struck at me deliberately, I'm sure!" he says (BC 139/177).

Orddu tells the Companions that "the Crochan is useless—except for making Cauldron-Born. Arawn has spoiled it for anything else" (BC 121/155). Considering its awful appearance and its aura of evil, what other uses could the Black Cauldron have had? "Just use your imagination," says Lloyd Alexander (1985b). "It could have been used for any number of marvelous things." Before it was "spoilt" it could well have been used for positive, helpful purposes. Alexander (1985b) suggests some such uses:

To be ridiculous, it could have been a source of constant food and drink. . . . I think it could have rejuvenated anything. Just for the sake of argument, you could put dead trees in there, and they would have bloomed again. . . . It could do all kinds of marvelous regenerations, whatever they may be. . . . Maybe it could have regenerated people who turned out to be good people. Maybe it was like the fountain of youth. . . . Sick people, lame people can bathe in its water and come out whole. . . . [Yet] steeping it in blood "corrupted it."

Taran and the Companions try to destroy the Crochan with bars and hammers, but it remains undented. Orddu then explains the only way to destroy it.

"A living person must climb into it. When he does, the Crochan will shatter. But, there's only one disagreeable thing about that, the poor duckling who climbs in will never climb out again alive. . . . Not only that, but whoever gives up his life to the Crochan must give it willingly, knowing full well what he does." (BC 129/165)

Orddu, Orwen, and Orgoch offer the Crochan to the Companions in trade for something of value. They will not accept Fflewddur's *truthful harp, Gurgi's *wallet of food, or Eilonwy's *bauble. They do settle for Taran's most prized possession, the *Brooch of Adaon. But the cauldron is soon wrested from the Companions by *Ellidyr, and then King *Morgant takes it from him. Morgant has been corrupted and plans to use the

Jacket illustration by Evaline Ness

Crochan to create his own armies of Cauldron-Born. Captured by the traitor king, the Companions are in danger of becoming the first of his deathless host.

Repenting his harsh deeds, Ellidyr chooses to sacrifice his life to destroy
the Black Cauldron. He breaks free and fights his way to the Crochan,
flinging himself inside.

> The Crochan shuddered like a living thing . . . in another instant a
> sharp clap, louder than thunder, rang above the clearing. The leafless
> trees trembled to their roots; the branches writhed as if in agony. Then,
> while echoes ripped the air and a whirlwind screamed overhead, the
> cauldron split and shattered. The jagged shards fell away from the lifeless
> form of Ellidyr. (BC 172/214–215)

*Gwydion later explains that the destruction of the Black Cauldron
"is one of the gravest defeats Arawn has ever suffered" (BC 174/217).

"The cauldron that brings the dead back to life has its counterparts in
other mythologies, too, even in the story of Jason and Medea," says Lloyd
Alexander (Jacobs, 1978:268). However, Alexander found the prototype
for his Black Cauldron in the *Mabinogion*. In the story "Branwen the

*Daughter of Llyr," Bendigeid Vran, brother of Branwen and king of the Island of the Mighty (Britain), atoned for an insult to Matholwch, king of Ireland and husband to Branwen, by giving him many gifts. One of the gifts was a cauldron, "the property of which is, that if one of thy men be slain to-day, and be cast herein, to-morrow he will be as well as ever he was at the best, except that he will not regain his speech" (M 373). Alexander's Cauldron-Born are also mute.

Later in the story of Branwen, some of Matholwch's men were killed by the British. He then "kindled a fire under the cauldron of renovation" and cast the bodies into it "until it was full" (M 381). The next day they came forth as fighting men, as good as before but unable to speak. Evnissyen, the quarrelsome brother of Branwen, who caused the war between England and Ireland, was deeply grieved. So he cast himself among the dead bodies and was flung into the cauldron. The cauldron was then rent into four pieces, and the heart of Evnissyen was burst.

*Lady Charlotte Guest's notes to the *Mabinogion* tell of another cauldron of rejuvenation. A race of necromancers called the Tuatha de Danann invaded Ireland and brought with them a cauldron they obtained in Asia. This cauldron would resuscitate their dead warriors by sending demons to animate their corpses (M 391).

See also Fantastic objects.
(M 373, 381, 391)

Black Cauldron, The: The second volume of the *Prydain Chronicles, The Black Cauldron,* was originally to be entitled *The Book of the Cauldron.* Alexander had thought of repeating "book" in each title of the Prydain series (then conceived as a trilogy). Later, he decided that the *"Book of Three" was an object, not a book about three. So the repeated use of "book" was inconsistent (Jacobs, 1978:279–280).

Alexander says that *The Black Cauldron* was one of the easiest of his books to write. "Something about the book simply clicked early on, resulting in the book almost writing itself" (Jacobs, 1978:280).

The Black Cauldron is the story of the quest to destroy the *Black Crochan, thus preventing *Arawn *Death-Lord from creating more of his *Cauldron-Born. Walt Disney Productions released a 1985 film using the title *The Black Cauldron.* However, the film was loosely based on the Prydain Chronicles in general. *The Black Cauldron* was a Newbery Honor Book in 1966. This is a runner-up award to the most prestigious American prize for children's literature, the Newbery Medal, which is presented annually by the American Library Association.

Black Crochan (CROH-kahn): *See* Black Cauldron.

black dagger: The black dagger carried to *Caer Dallben by *Pryderi is the only weapon that can take *Dallben's life. Pryderi receives it from the hand of *Arawn with instructions to kill the enchanter and take *The Book of Three. Pryderi was told that Dallben may not take a life and will be unable to stop the blade from piercing him. When Pryderi learns he has been told only half-truths concerning Dallben's vulnerability and his safety, he does not use the black dagger.

See also Fantastic objects.

(HK 188/219)

Black Lake: The black lake is a trap that snares anyone who ventures too near the *Kingdom of Tylwyth Teg or the *Realm of the Fair Folk. Those who enter the lake waters cannot escape. For example, *Taran and the *Companions are pulled downward through a tremendous whirlpool into King *Eiddileg's underground kingdom.

Mountains rise sharply from half the lake's shoreline. When the Companions descend to the shore, Taran notices that the water is indeed black, not in reflection of a sky choked with storm clouds, but "the water itself was dark, flat, and as grim and heavy as iron" (BT 131/156).

The proper noun, Black Lake, is not used until *Doli speaks of it in *Taran Wanderer (TW 80/100). Before then it is simply called the black lake.

*Lady Charlotte Guest mentions a black lake in her notes to the *Mabinogion. Llyn (lake) Dulyn is located in the Snowdon Mountains in Wales. It is situated "in a rugged valley encircled by high, steep rocks. This lake is extremely black, and its fish are deformed and unsightly, having large heads and small bodies. No wild swans are ever seen alighting upon it . . . nor ducks, nor any bird whatever" (M 77). Alexander (1985b) says that *Guest's notes were his inspiration for Black Lake. However, in a letter to Ann Durell, his editor, Alexander (1965f) says that "Black Lake and Eiddileg's realm would be around Lake Bala." He was advising Ann to watch for certain Prydainian landmarks during her trip to Wales.

See also Fair Folk, Fantastic objects.

(BT 130/155, 137/162; TW 80/100; M 77)

book of spells: The book of spells was the greatest treasure of the *House of Llyr. In it were recorded the spells of the *enchantresses or *daughters of Llyr. The book appears to be blank, but the spells become visible under the light of the *Golden Pelydryn (*Eilonwy's *bauble). The spells can only be used by a daughter of Llyr.

The Princess *Angharad took with her the Golden Pelydryn and the book of spells when she left *Caer Colur, the stronghold of *Llyr, to marry against her mother's wishes. The book and the Pelydryn, along with Angharad, disappeared and were considered lost. In *The Castle of Llyr, the book resurfaces in *Glew's humble cottage on the *Isle of Mona. Readers learn from Glew that he was given the book of spells by a wizard. Neither he nor the wizard understood what they possessed. Later, in *Taran Wanderer, the evil wizard *Morda reveals that Angharad died in his cottage years earlier. She had with her the blank book and her powerful jewel. The jewel was of great use to Morda, but he sold the book to the gullible Glew.

It is with the Princess Eilonwy (the last of the daughters of Llyr), the Golden Pelydryn, and the book of spells that *Achren makes her final bid to overthrow *Arawn and rule *Prydain again. Though she has bewitched the Princess Eilonwy to do her bidding, Achren does not account for the power of love and friendship. The princess is able to momentarily shake off Achren's spell as she watches *Taran and the *Companions suffer because of her misguided power. Standing within the ruins of Caer Colur, she touches the Golden Pelydryn to the pages of the book of spells.

> The Golden Pelydryn flared brighter than he had ever seen it and Taran flung up his hand to shield his eyes. Light flooded the Hall. . . .
>
> Suddenly Eilonwy cast the book to the flagstones. From the pages burst a crimson cloud that spread into a sheet of fire, leaping upward to the vaulted ceiling of the *Great Hall. Even as the book of spells consumed itself in its own flames, the blaze did not dwindle but instead rose ever higher, roaring and crackling, no longer crimson but blindingly white. The shriveled pages swirled in a fiery whirlwind to dance within the shimmering heart of the flame, and as they did, the whispering voices of Caer Colur groaned in defeat. . . . Now the book had vanished utterly, but still the flames mounted unappeased. (CL 155–156/185)

The touch of the Pelydryn is the only way the book of spells could be destroyed. Eilonwy's opportunity to become a true enchantress and Achren's chance to rule again are both destroyed along with the book.

See also Fantastic objects, Magg, Rhun.
(CL, 57/76, 96–97/121, 118/144, 129/156+; TW 92/114)

Book of Three, The: This magical book, possessed by *Dallben, is "a ponderous, leather-bound volume" sometimes used by the enchanter to instruct *Taran of *Prydain's history (BT 6/21). But it is much more than a mere his-

Jacket illustration by Evaline Ness

tory book; within its pages are also "Dallben's deepest secrets" (BC 13/24). We learn of the tome's power as the *Prydain Chronicles begin. Taran attempts to peek inside it while Dallben naps, and his fingers are "stung" as if by hornets. The power of the book is so great that *Arawn *Death-Lord sends *Pryderi to steal it. But Dallben warns him not to touch the book, for within its pages Pryderi is marked for death. Unheeding, Pryderi grasps its cover and is struck dead by a bolt of lightning that springs forth from the ancient tome.

In *The High King* we learn that *The Book of Three* is "thus called because it tells all three parts of our lives: the past, the present, and the future" (HK 239/275). In *Coll and His White Pig* Dallben offers *Coll the opportunity to read about one day of his future life, saying that "in it [*The Book of Three*] is set down all that will happen in the days to come" (CWP 82/28). As it foretold Pryderi's death, the book also hinted at Taran's destiny to become the *High King. It foretold that "when the *Sons of Don departed from Prydain the High King would be one who slew a serpent, who gained and lost a flaming sword, who chose a kingdom of sorrow over a kingdom of happiness." He also "would be one of no station in life" (HK 240/276). Taran matched these qualifications. However, Dallben says that *The Book* *of Three* "could as well be called a book of 'if'" (HK 239/275). *If* Taran had failed at his tasks or chosen a different path, say one of evil, then things would have worked out differently. "For the deeds of a man, not the words of a prophecy, are what shape his destiny," Dallben explains (HK 239/276). In spite of the book's prophetic attributes, it does not tell how the sword *Dyrnwyn is to be retrieved from Arawn.

When the Sons of Don depart for the *Summer Country Dallben gives Taran *The Book of Three* after he writes in it one last sentence: "And thus did an *Assistant Pig-Keeper become High King of Prydain" (HK 244/281). It has become merely a history book at this point in the story but is a valued heritage.

The story of how Dallben acquired *The Book of Three* is told in *The Black Cauldron* by the witch, *Orddu, and also in more detail in *The Foundling*. Orddu, *Orwen, and *Orgoch find Dallben, a deserted infant, and raise him. When Dallben is a young boy, he is stirring a potion for the weird sisters. Some of it splashes, burning his fingers. When Dallben sucks his fingers to cool them he inadvertently tastes a concoction that causes him suddenly to know as much as the witches. The three feel they can no longer keep him but decide to send him away with some gift of power. Dallben is allowed to choose from among a harp that would make him the world's greatest *bard, a sword that would give him the power to rule Prydain, and *The Book of Three*. Of the book, Orddu says, "Yet whoever owns this book shall have . . . [wisdom] and more, if he likes. For the odd thing about wisdom is the more you use it the more it grows; the more you share, the more you gain" (F 11/10).

Dallben chooses *The Book of Three*. Unable to curb his curiosity, he stops soon after leaving his surrogate mothers to read the book. Within its covers, Dallben finds "knowledge he had never dreamed of: the pathways of the stars, the rounds of the planets, the ebb and flow of time and tide. All secrets of the world and all its hidden lore unfolded to him" (F 11–12/11). The book also shows him a sadder side of the world: cruelty, suffering, and death. "He read of greed, hatred, and war. . . . Each page he read pierced his heart" (F 12–13/13). It is the weight of all this knowledge, specifically the unhappy things, that ages Dallben overnight. Yet before Dallben finishes his reading, he finds within the book reason for hope, for it tells "not only of death, but of birth as well" and "how things lost may be found again" (F 13/14).

> He learned that the lives of men are short and filled with pain, yet each one a priceless treasure, whether it be that of a prince or a pig-keeper. And, at the last, the book taught him that while nothing was certain, all was possible. (F 14/14)

The Book of Three is also the title of the first of the *Prydain Chronicles. However, the first volume of the Chronicles was originally to be named *The Battle of the Trees* (Jacobs, 1978:273). "The Battle of the Trees" is a fragment from *Celtic mythology that tells of a battle between Amathaon, *Gwydion's brother, and Arawn, King of *Annuvin (Hell). Alexander says that the following lines from "The Battle of the Trees" gave him the plot framework for his book (Jacobs, 1978:268–269).

> And therefore Amathaon ab *Don, and Arawn, King of Annwn (Hell), fought. And there was a man in that battle, unless his name were known he could not be overcome; and there was on the other side a woman called *Achren, and unless her name were known her party could not be overcome. And Gwydion ab Don guessed the name of the man. (M 280; WG 49)

Initially, the scene with the battle took place in the first fifty pages of Alexander's book. The eventual omission of these pages and the fact that no one at Holt, Rinehart and Winston liked the title *The Battle of the Trees* prompted Alexander's editor, Ann Durell, to suggest *The Assistant Pig-Keeper*. Alexander then suggested several other titles, such as *The Black Sword*, *The Burning Blade*, *The Flame in the Sword*, *The Master of the Sword*, *The Children of Don*, and *The Sons of Don*. The title *The Book of Three* was eventually suggested by Nonny Hogrogian, art director at Holt (Jacobs, 1978:274).

See also Fantastic objects, Taliesin.
(M 280; WG 27+)

Bran-Galedd (bran-GAHL-ed): *See* Hills of Bran-Galedd.

Briavael (bree-AH-vel): This she-wolf is smaller than her mate, *Brynach, and has a white blaze on her breast. She and Brynach live with *Medwyn in his hidden valley. Briavael may have made an appearance in *The Book of Three* when the *Companions are barred from entering *Medwyn's valley by wolves. However, these wolves are not given names.

In *The High King*, Medwyn sends Briavael and Brynach to warn all forest creatures of the rise of *Annuvin. The two wolves rally the animals to battle against the *Death-Lord.

Briavael and her mate, along with an army of wolves, save *Eilonwy and *Gurgi from shame and death at the hands of *Dorath. All of *Dorath's Company are slain. The wolves then lead Eilonwy and Gurgi to *Taran.

The name Briavael appears in the *Mabinogion. However, it is the name of a wood that was the burial place of the mythic character Gwrthmwl Wledig.
(BT 112/135; HK 89/108, 165/194; M 335)

brooch: *See Brooch of Adaon.

Brooch of Adaon (ah-DAY-on): *Adaon, the son of the *Chief Bard *Taliesin, wears on his collar a curiously shaped iron *brooch. It was given to him by his betrothed, *Arianllyn. The true power of the brooch is not revealed until *Taran becomes its owner. Adaon wills the brooch and his other possessions to Taran should he perish, and indeed Adaon receives his death wound from the *Huntsmen of Annuvin. Just before he dies, he removes the brooch and gives it to Taran, saying, "Take this. . . . Guard it well. It is a small thing, but more valuable than you know" (BC 81/106).

As with Adaon, Taran begins to have unusual dreams as he wears the brooch. He sees hints of the future and is shown the "black beast" that plagues *Ellidyr. "I feel pity for Ellidyr," says Taran. "Adaon once told me he saw a black beast on Ellidyr's shoulders. Now I understand a little what he meant" (BC 83/109). The brooch also heightens Taran's awareness. He sees "not so much with his eyes but in a way he had never known before" (BC 84/110). Even the air he breathes bears special scents he never before noticed.

Taran's visions and dreams guide him and the *Companions, keeping them from danger. In one instance, he recognizes from his dreams a meadow and a marsh bird circling in the sky, and suddenly "with fear and excitement" he begins to understand the brooch's power. As the Companions search for the *Marshes of Morva, Taran's visions provide direction like a map. Taran says of the brooch, "All I know is that I *feel* differently somehow. I can see things I never saw before—or smell or taste them. I can't say exactly what it is. It's strange, and awesome in a way. And very beautiful sometimes" (BC 87/113). Taran is also able to foresee the location of a much needed stream, the coming of a rain storm, and the collapse of the hillside under which the Companions were camped.

*Eilonwy realizes that the brooch has changed Taran. "You don't even sound quite like yourself," she says. "Adaon's clasp is a priceless gift. It gives you a kind of wisdom . . . which, I suppose, is what *Assistant Pig-Keepers need more than anything else" (BC 87/114). But Taran's dreams are often troubled and unhappy; the brooch may be as much a burden as a boon.

Through the power of the brooch, Taran is able to see the places where they may safely tread in the treacherous Marshes of Morva. The Huntsmen of Annuvin are not so fortunate and perish in the quagmire. The Companions are guided to the cottage of the three witches, *Orddu, *Orwen, and *Orgoch. Here they find the goal of their quest: the *Black Cauldron. But in order to obtain the deadly *cauldron, Taran must trade the Brooch of Adaon.

Orddu tells the Companions that they recognized the brooch immediately. "Yes, we know the brooch well. *Menwy Son of *Teirgwaedd, first of the *bards, fashioned it long ago" (BC 127/162). Taran asks why then they did not simply slay the Companions and take the clasp.

> Orddu smiled sadly. "Do you not understand, poor chicken? Like knowledge, truth, and love themselves, the clasp must be given willingly or its power is broken. And it is, indeed, filled with power. This, too, you must understand. For Menwy the bard cast a mighty spell on it and filled it with dreams, wisdom, and vision. With such a clasp, a duckling could win much glory and honor. Who can tell? He might rival all the heroes of *Prydain, even *Gwydion *Prince of Don.
>
> "Think carefully, duckling," Orddu said. "Once given up, it shall not come to you again." (BC 127/162)

Taran weeps at the loss of the brooch, even though he willingly parts with it. Much later, Eilonwy compares Taran's decision to relinquish the brooch to the decision she makes to give up the chance of becoming a true enchantress (CL 166/197).

See also Fantastic objects.
(BC 11+/23+; CL 166/197; TW 16/30; HK 114/136)

Brynach (BRIN-ack): When *Kaw drops into *Medwyn's valley, injured from an attack by *gwythaints, it is Brynach who finds him. "Beside the old man [*Medwyn], the wolf Brynach sat on his haunches. Lean and gray, with yellow eyes, he wagged his tail and grinned up at the crow" (HK 89/108).

He and his mate *Briavael may have been the wolves that subdued the *Companions when they inadvertently wandered too near Medwyn's secret valley in *The Book of Three*. However, those wolves, who also lived with Medwyn, were not named.

Brynach and Briavael are sent to spread word of *Annuvin's rise to the wolves, bears, stags, and all other forest dwellers of *Prydain. They are to rally them into an army to fight against *Arawn. Brynach and Briavael and a pack of wolves save *Eilonwy and *Gurgi from shame and death at the hands of *Dorath and his band. The wolves kill all of *Dorath's Company and then lead Eilonwy and Gurgi to find *Taran.

Brynach appears in "The Rascal Crow," a tale in *The Foundling. The wolf organizes others of his kind to protect the forest creatures from the *Chief Huntsman of *Annuvin, who has been commanded to enslave all animals. He must endure the peevish torments of *Kaw's father, *Kadwyr.

The name Brynach is found in the *Mabinogion. However, it is the name of the man (Brynach Wyddel) who received a wolf cub from *Henwen, the marvelous sow of Dallpenn (Dallben).

(BT 112/135; HK 88/106, 166/194; F 43/50; M 268)

Caer (KARE) Cadarn (KAH-darn): Caer Cadarn is located in the
*Cantrev Cadiffor and is the stronghold of King *Smoit. It stands in a
woodland clearing that is a three-day ride from the western border of
Cantrev Cadiffor. Its description seems to fit its rough-edged but lovable
owner. "Smoit's castle was a fortress with walls of hewn stone and iron-
studded gates thick enough to withstand all attack; the chips in the stones
and the dents in the portal told *Taran the castle had indeed thrown back
not a few assaults" (TW 45/62). From Caer Cadarn's main tower flies the
crimson banner with the *black bear emblem of the *House of Smoit.

In the *Mabinogion, Cadarn appears as a man's name: Nerth the son of
Kadarn.
(BC 20+/34+; TW 22/36, 32/47, 38/54, 45/62, 63/82; HK 34/46, 87/105,
105/126; M 312)

Caer (KARE) Colur (KOH-loor): Caer Colur was once the stronghold of
the *House of Llyr. It fell into ruin when Princess *Angharad left its court
to marry against her mother's (Queen *Regat) wishes. The princess took
with her the *Golden Pelydryn (*Eilonwy's *bauble) and the *book of
spells of the *daughters of Llyr. The loss of these items caused the eventual
downfall of Caer Colur (Alexander, 1986b).

We first learn of Caer Colur from the wistful giant, *Glew. "Long ago,
Caer Colur was part of [the *Isle of] Mona. But it broke from the mainland
during a flood. Now it's no more than a speck of island" (CL 97/121–122).
This island with the ruins of Caer Colur (the *Castle of Llyr) stands just off
the shore of the Isle of Mona at the mouth of the River *Alaw. According
to Alexander (1986a), it is reasonable to assume that *Mona was originally
the kingdom of *Llyr.

In *The Castle of Llyr, *Achren kidnaps the Princess Eilonwy, the last of the daughters of Llyr, and takes her to what is left of her ancestral home. Achren plans to use Eilonwy's latent power as an enchantress in conjunction with the Golden Pelydryn and the book of spells to regain control of *Prydain. She then plans to rule Prydain from a restored Caer Colur.

The *Companions and *Gwydion discover that Eilonwy is being held on the island. The following description of Caer Colur is the setting for their night-rescue attempt.

> The pinnacles of Caer Colur rose black against a dark sky. Mist rolled around the columns of stone which once had been, *Taran guessed, proud and lofty towers, but were now crumbled and jutting ruins thrusting upward like the shards of broken swords. As they came closer, he saw the heavy, iron-bound portals, reminders of a day when Caer Colur had been a fortress rooted on the mainland. The gates faced the sea, but, since the castle had sunk lower, they stood half-submerged in the restless water. . . .
>
> Near the massive portals wind and water had gouged a cavelike hollow. . . . *Kaw had already flown to the walls, and Taran envied the crow his wings as he saw the sheer facing of stone and the broken parapets brooding high above. *Gwydion led them along the base of the wall toward the heavy lintels of the gates. The bastion was cleft as though by a sword stroke, and loose rubble had fallen into the breach. (CL 131–132/159–160)

Achren's plans are thwarted, and her servant and steward, *Magg, opens the gates to the sea, flooding Caer Colur and utterly destroying it. The Companions barely escape drowning in the rush of seawater. Later, on shore, they see that the flood has torn the castle apart, and now "Caer Colur lies at the bottom of the sea" (CL 161/190–191).

According to Robert Graves, Caer Colur ("gloomy castle") in *Celtic mythology is another name for Caer Sidi or Caer Arianrhod, the "revolving castle." These three names are also synonymous with *Spiral Castle, a mythic place of death. Graves feels, however, that the castles may actually have been separate places (WG 106).

Caer Arianrhod is also a submerged town off the coast of Caernarvon (WG 98). In her notes to the *Mabinogion, *Lady Charlotte Guest quotes the Rev. P. B. Williams: "There is a tradition that an ancient British town . . . called Caer Arianrhod, was swallowed up by the sea, the ruins of which, it is said, are still visible during neap tides, and in fine weather" (M 438). Alexander (1985b) readily admits that the submersion of Caer

Arianrhod provided the "raw material" for the inundation of Caer Colur in his story.
(CL 96+/121+; HK 229/265; M 438; WG 98, 106)

Caer (KARE) Dallben (DAHL-ben): Caer Dallben is *Coll's farm where both he and *Dallben dwell. It is in the south of *Prydain below the *Great Avren. It is called "the little farm" and is nestled in a forest clearing (BT 5/19). Caer Dallben is a humble dwelling consisting of little more than a cottage, stable, and fields. Yet it is a place of great power. It is here where the oracular pig *Hen Wen lives, not to mention the most powerful enchanter in Prydain, Dallben. So powerful a spot is Caer Dallben that it is "the one place *Arawn *Death-Lord dares not attack" (BC 18/32). It is Caer Dallben where *Taran is raised. It is also the site of *Pryderi's death when he comes to kill Dallben and take *The Book of Three.

Before the story of Taran begins, Dallben comes to Coll's farm to warn him of a threat to Hen Wen. He arrives too late for Coll has already left for *Annuvin to rescue the kidnapped pig. But Dallben stays on to tend the garden until Coll returns. It is here that Dallben and Coll first meet and decide to stay together on the farm. Dallben's decision to stay pleases Coll greatly (CWP 82–83/30). Soon the farm became known as Caer Dallben.

In *Lady Charlotte Guest's notes to the *Mabinogion, Coll ab Collfrewi kept the swine of Dadweir Dallpenn (Dallben) in a valley called Dallwyr. Dallwyr is located in what is now Cornwall.
(M 268)

Caer (KARE) Dathyl (DATH-il): During *Taran's time, Caer Dathyl is the place where the *High King of *Prydain, *Math Son of *Mathonwy, dwells. "The *Sons of Don built their stronghold at Caer Dathyl, far north in the *Eagle Mountains. From there, they helped regain at least a portion of what *Arawn had stolen, and stood as guardians against the lurking threat of *Annuvin" (BT 7/22). When the *Companions visit the stronghold, the following description is given:

> Standing high on a hill, the fortress alone was big enough to hold several *Caer Dallbens. Taran saw armorers' shops, stables for the steeds of warriors, breweries, weaving rooms. Cottages clustered in the valleys below, and clear streams ran golden in the sunlight. (BT 180/210)

*Gwydion explains that this golden-towered citadel was built by the Sons of Don "not only as a shield against Arawn but as safeguard for the wisdom and beauty of Prydain" (HK 121/145). It is also a place of memory.

Within its bastions . . . grew a living glade of tall hemlocks, and among them rose *mounds of honor to ancient kings and heroes. Halls of carved and ornamented timbers held panoplies of weapons of long and noble lineage, and banners whose emblems were famed in the songs of the *bards. In other buildings were stored treasures of craftsmanship sent from every *cantrev and *Commot in Prydain. (HK 109–110/131)

The *Council Chamber of the Bards is located at Caer Dathyl. *Taliesin, the *Chief Bard, dwells there and oversees the *Hall of Lore and the *Hall of Bards wherein much of Prydain's ancient learning is stored.

Though the armies of Prydain struggle to defend it, Caer Dathyl is destroyed by the traitorous *Pryderi and legions of Arawn's *Cauldron-Born. The Cauldron-Born use a battering ram to breach the gates of Caer Dathyl and then turn the rams to the walls. Pryderi's warriors set fire to the Hall of Lore and other buildings as the banner of the *crimson hawk (Pryderi) and Arawn's black banner fly from the Middle Tower.

Caer Dathyl (sometimes spelled Caerdathal) appears in Celtic tales. In the *Mabinogion, the story "Math the Son of Mathonwy" explains that "Math lived always at Caer Dathyl, in Arvon" (M 413). The remains of Caer Dathyl are today called Pen y Gaer. In her notes to the Mabinogion *Lady Charlotte Guest says, "They [the ruins] are on a hilltop about a mile from Llanbedr in Caernarvonshire, midway between Llanrwst and Conway. It appears to have been well defended by deep moats, which yet surround it" (M 435).

Alexander (1965f) envisions the location of Caer Dathyl as the Snowdonia region of Wales near Mount Eryni (Eagle Mountain).

See also Hall of Thrones.

(BT 7+/22+; BC 178/221; TW 9/22; HK 80+/98+; TH 88/11, 89/14, 93/26; M 224, 413, 435)

cantrev (kantrev): "Prydain is a land of many cantrevs—of small kingdoms—and many kings" (BT 6/21). The word cantrev is also used similarly in the *Mabinogion.
(M 227, 339, 390, 398, 413)

Cantrev (kantrev) Cadiffor (ka-DIF-for): Cantrev Cadiffor is the largest of the *Valley Cantrevs. It is the realm of King *Smoit whose major stronghold is *Caer Cadarn. This region of wooded land and meadows is where the bickering Lords *Goryon and *Gast dwell and is where the farmer *Aeddan and his wife *Alarca maintain their small farmhold.
(BC 14/26, 18/32; TW 22/36, 53/71, 63–64/83, 217/253; HK 33/45, 205/237)

Cantrev (kantrev) Dau (dow) Gleddyn (GLED-in): This kingdom of southern *Prydain supports the *Horned King and provides troops for his campaign against the *Sons of Don. With a variation of spelling, Cantrev Dau Gleddyv is mentioned in the *Mabinogion. It is one of the *cantrevs of Dyved, the kingdom of *Pwyll and then later of his son, *Pryderi. (BT 39/56; M 362)

Cantrev (kantrev) Mawr (MAUER): This kingdom of southern *Prydain supports the *Horned King and provides troops for his campaign against the *Sons of Don. In *The Book of Three, King *Eiddileg's *Children of Evening are scheduled to sing in the forest of Cantrev Mawr. The giant, *Glew, mentions this *cantrev as the spot where he found a dragon.

    In *Lady Charlotte Guest's notes to the *Mabinogion, Cantrev Mawr is listed as a cantrev that *Pryderi adds to his father's kingdom of Dyved. The name is used in three other instances: Lluefer Mawr (the second of the three blissful Rulers of the Island), Prydain ab *Aedd Mawr, and Traeth Mawr. The first two are names of people, and the third of a place. (BT 39/56, 138/164; CL 95/120; M 362, 385, 386, 418)

Cantrev (kantrev) Rheged (REG-ed): This kingdom of southern *Prydain supports the *Horned King and provides troops for his campaign against the *Sons of Don. The name Rheged appears in the *Mabinogion. For example, Owain, one of Arthur's knights, was the son of Urien Rheged. Rheged is never used to name a place, however. (BT 39/56; M 3, 34, 229, 312)

**Castle of Llyr (LEER): *See* Caer Colur.

**Castle of Llyr (LEER), The: *The Castle of Llyr* is the third book in the *Chronicles of Prydain. This novel came about as Lloyd Alexander was starting into what originally was to be the third book of a *Prydain trilogy. He realized suddenly that there would have to be another book, which at this point made the Chronicles a four-book series (Jacobs, 1978:281). Ann Durell, Alexander's editor, suggested the title *The Castle of Llyr* as he was working on the novel (Alexander, 1965d). He liked it and immediately adopted it.

    The Castle of Llyr tells the story of growing mutual affection between *Taran and *Eilonwy. Eilonwy travels to the *Isle of Mona to be schooled as a lady. Though she is accompanied by Taran and the other *Companions, she is kidnapped by *Achren. Achren plans to use Eilonwy's latent

Jacket illustration by Evaline Ness

power as an enchantress to regain control of Prydain and then rule from the princess's ancestral home, *Caer Colur (the *Castle of Llyr).

See also Angharad, book of spells, Golden Pelydryn, Llyr Half-Speech, Regat.

cauldron: *See* Black Cauldron.

**Cauldron-Born: Early in the *Prydain Chronicles, *Gwydion explains the Cauldron-Born to *Taran.

> "They were [men], once. . . . They are the dead whose bodies Arawn steals from their resting places in the long *barrows. It is said he steeps them in a *cauldron [the *Black Cauldron] to give them life again—if it can be called life. Like death, they are forever silent; and their only thought is to bring others to the same bondage." (BT 35/51)

These deathless warriors are *Arawn's guards within *Annuvin and do not often leave because though "the Cauldron-Born cannot be slain, yet their power dwindles if they journey too far, or stay too long beyond Arawn's realm" (HK 40/53). Gwydion explains that the *Death-Lord does, however, send them forth from time to time to do "his most ruthless tasks. . . . These Cauldron-Born are utterly without mercy or pity . . . for Arawn has worked still greater evil upon them. He has destroyed their remembrance of themselves as living men. They have no memory of tears or laughter, of sorrow or loving kindness" (BT 35/51). The Cauldron-Born have "been deprived of their humanity," says Lloyd Alexander (1985b). "A fate, in my opinion, considerably worse than death. The risk of dehumanization—of being manipulated as objects instead of being valued as living people—is, unfortunately, not confined to the realm of fantasy."

When Taran first encounters the deathless warriors they are described as follows:

> Their faces were pallid; their eyes like stones. Heavy bands of bronze circled their waists, and from these belts hung the black thongs of whips. Knobs of bronze studded their breastplates. They did not bear shield or helmet. Their mouths were frozen in the hideous grin of death. (BT 42/59–60)

Yet Taran is most terrified by their "ghostly silence" (BT 43/60). Even when Gwydion drives his sword into the heart of a Cauldron-Born, the warrior makes no outcry. He does not bleed and only shakes himself once before renewing his attack.

In *The High King, the Cauldron-Born are sent to aid *Pryderi in the destruction of *Caer Dathyl and the murder of the *High King. However, the mute warriors stop when confronted by the aged King *Math "as if at the faint stirring of some clouded memory" (HK 127/152). But then they push forward, striking down the High King and marching over his lifeless body.

The secret to the destruction of the Cauldron-Born lies in the sword, *Dyrnwyn. Taran finds the stolen sword hidden atop *Mount Dragon, overlooking Annuvin. He rips the blade from its scabbard and plunges it into the heart of a deathless warrior.

> The Cauldron-Born stumbled and fell; and from his lips long mute burst a shriek that echoed and re-echoed from the Death-Lord's stronghold as though rising from a thousand tongues. . . .
>
> Along the path and at the *Iron Portals the Cauldron warriors toppled as one body. (HK 214/247)

This event marks the end of Arawn's power over *Prydain.

A cauldron of rejuvenation like the Black Cauldron of Arawn is told of in the *Mabinogion. A slain man would be restored when cast into it, and he would be "as well as ever" except, as with the Cauldron-Born, "that he will not regain his speech" (M 373). The Irish, who briefly possessed this cauldron in the story "Branwen the *Daughter of Llyr," used it to restore many of their dead warriors.

See also Black Crochan, Characters—fantasy.
(M 373, 381)

Celtic mythology: See Mabinogion.

Characters—fantasy: In modern fantasy literature characters may be drawn from three sources: the world of men, the legendary past, and the imaginary present (Madsen, 1976:95–97). The world of men is comprised of typical human beings. *Taran, *Rhun, and *Coll represent such characters in the *Prydain series. *Fflewddur Fflam has a bit of magical blood in his veins (he is a distant relation to the *Sons of Don), but he is too far removed to be considered anything more than human.

Characters from the legendary past include beings, mythical and legendary, from our ancient stories, particularly the fairy tale—such characters as pixies, fairies, dwarves, dragons, trolls, witches, and wizards. Examples from *Prydain include *Doli and all the *Fair Folk, *Dallben, *Arawn, *Morda, *Medwyn, *Achren, the Sons of Don, and perhaps the *Cauldron-Born. Even the Princess *Eilonwy could be considered a character of the legendary past until she chooses to relinquish her enchantress blood (HK 246/284). Of course, it can be argued that Taran, Eilonwy, and the other "men" in the Prydain stories became part of our legendary past. "Yet long afterward, when all had passed away into distant memory, there were many who wondered whether King Taran, Queen Eilonwy, and their *companions had indeed walked the earth, or whether they had been no more than dreams in a tale set down to beguile children" (HK 248/285). However, Taran must be judged within the context of the tale—he was but a man.

Characters from the imaginary present are the wonderful creations of the present-day authors. Tolkien created his hobbits, ents, and orcs. Alexander brought to life the *gwythaints, *Huntsmen of Annuvin, and *Gurgi. Many of these creative characters still have links to legend and myth—the Cauldron-Born, for example. However, Alexander's Cauldron-Born are nothing like the rejuvenated dead in the *Mabinogion and are therefore more like characters from his imagination. The same is true for *Hen Wen, *Llyan, and the three weird sisters, *Orddu, *Orwen, and *Orgoch. Even *Gurgi has a counterpart (half-man, half-animal) in Welsh stories, but the similarities are so scanty that Gurgi may easily be called a character type created exclusively by Alexander.

Alexander has been compared to many of his Prydain characters. For example, readers often claim a similarity between Alexander and Fflewddur Fflam. But a friend of Alexander's saw it a different way.

A friend reading *The Black Cauldron* remarked to me: "Oh, I see you've done a very interesting self-portrait here."

I answered that he must obviously be referring to the brave, kind, wise, noble, handsome Prince *Gwydion.

"Hell, no," he said. "I mean that wretched, miserable *Gwystyl!"

Reluctantly, I admitted he was right, that I was more qualified, even in my own book, to play hypochondriac instead of hero. (Jacobs, 1978:493)

More seriously, Alexander explains that he does not identify with his characters of great power, specifically the legendary characters.

I identified with the nonheroic figures, the fallible humans: Fflewddur Fflam, for instance. I think we all have many personalities—an infinite number perhaps; and all these characters, Gwystyl, Fflewddur Fflam, Gurgi—are refractions of myself. I've been as scared of things as Gurgi, stretched the truth as much as Fflewddur and whined as much as Gwystyl. (Jacobs, 1978:493)

However, Alexander does say that he identifies with his hero Taran. "I have been racked up by indecision just as much as poor Taran, and I certainly have physically gone through, to some small extent, the same kinds of miseries." But Taran emerged a "shining hero, and I did not" (Jacobs, 1978:494).

See also Heroism.

Chief Bard: *See* Taliesin.

Chief Giant: *See* Yspadadden.

Chief Huntsman: *See* Huntsman, Chief.

Chief Mole of Prydain: *See* Star-Nose.

Chief Steward: *See* Steward, Chief.

Children of Don (DAHN): *See* Sons of Don; Daughters of Don.

Children of Evening: It is not plain in *The Book of Three* just what sort of creatures the Children of Evening are. They are a part of the *Fair Folk realm but, according to Alexander (1985b), are not dwarves. He explains that the Children of Evening are exclusively singers. When the *Companions are held captive in *Tylwyth Teg, the kingdom of the Fair Folk, King *Eiddileg complains that the Children of Evening ("another ridiculous name thought up by humans") are scheduled to sing that very evening in the forest of *Cantrev Mawr. But they have not practiced, two are sick, and one cannot be found. Apparently the Children are in such a state of upset that they try to push into Eiddileg's throne room, and the reader gets a brief glimpse of them. "Some were tall, slender, with white robes; others were covered with glistening scales, like fish; still others fluttered large, delicate wings" (BT 138/163).

Later, Taran hears the Children of Evening practicing. He had "never in his life heard such beautiful singing. He listened, enchanted, forgetting, for the moment, all but the soaring melody" (BT 139/165). "The Children of Evening have evidently got together again," says Eiddileg (BT 139/165).

*Lady Charlotte Guest in her notes to the *Mabinogion describes a race of "beneficent and joyous beings" called the Tylwyth Teg or the Family of Beauty. They are beings "who dance in the moonlight on the velvet sward, in their airy and flowing robes of blue or green, or white or scarlet, and who delight in showering benefits on the more favored of the human race" (M 263). Guest's note was an inspiration for Alexander's Children of Evening.

See also Characters—fantasy; Lake Sprites.
(BT 138/163; M 263)

**Chronicles of Prydain (prih-DANE), The: Alexander (1968a) states that the Chronicles of Prydain, his five-book fantasy classic, "began by accident." He had been researching some material for another book, *Time Cat*, which was to have one of its episodes set in Wales. The wealth of mythic material he found prompted him to change the setting in *Time Cat* to Ireland and save Wales for a new project. Originally, Alexander conceived the Chronicles as a retelling of stories from *Celtic mythology. Later, as he completed further research, Alexander decided to write an original fantasy trilogy, though inspired by the Celtic stories. It was to be called *The Sons of *Llyr. The three books of the trilogy were to be entitled *The Battle of the Trees*, *The Lion with the Steady Hand*, and *Little Gwion* (Jacobs, 1978:279–280).

As the first volume neared completion, Alexander groped for a new and better title. *The Book of Three, suggested by Nonny Hogrogian (art director at Holt, Rinehart and Winston), was finally adopted. Just before The Book of Three was released, Alexander established the series name: the Chronicles of Prydain (Jacobs, 1978:278–280).

The second book, *The Black Cauldron, was nearly named The Book of the *Cauldron. Alexander thought he might begin the titles of all three books with "the book of . . ." However, because The Book of Three is also an object in the stories, he decided the use of "book" in each title would not be consistent (Jacobs, 1978:280).

As Alexander began work on the third and supposedly final volume of the series, he knew another book was needed. The *Prydain story then became a four-book series. He also envisioned some related books, and his editor suggested writing the text for some picture books (Jacobs, 1978: 281–282). Two were eventually produced: *Coll and His White Pig and *The Truthful Harp. The art was done by Evaline Ness, who also did the dust jackets for the hardback copies of the five Prydain novels. The stories pre-date the story of *Taran but still tell of the mythical land of Prydain. *The Castle of Llyr became the third book of the series and *The High King (work-ing title The High King of Prydain) the fourth (Jacobs, 1978:284).

However, Ann Durell, Alexander's editor, was troubled by book four until she suddenly realized that yet another book was needed to make the story complete. Though The High King alluded to Taran's experiences dur-ing his maturing years, Durell felt more needed to be known about this period of the hero's life. *Taran Wanderer, though written last, became the fourth book in the series (Jacobs, 1978:286–287). Of course, The High King needed some rewriting to adjust it to the new fourth volume.

"Coming to the last page of The High King was a sad moment for me," says Lloyd Alexander, "a feeling more akin to loss than liberation; as if something one had loved deeply for a long time had suddenly gone away" (Jacobs, 1978:291). He explains his attachment to Prydain: "I don't want to imply that I didn't like writing adult books, or wasn't interested, or didn't do my best. But I found this writing [Prydain] to be the deepest form of art I had ever come across" (Jacobs, 1978:305–306).

Alexander decided to write nothing more about Prydain when The High King was published (Jacobs, 1978:288). However, he later changed his mind and wrote a series of Prydain short stories (Jacobs, 1987:314). These stories predate the story in the Chronicles, as did the picture books, and are bound in a volume called *The Foundling, which was published five years after *The High King*. Later, when the picture books went out of print, their stories were added to *The Foundling*.

The books of the Prydain series have all been American Library Association "Notable Books" and/or School Library Journal "best books." These highly respected yearly lists note the outstanding books published for children and young adults. The most prestigious prize given for children's literature in America is the John Newbery Medal, awarded annually by the American Library Association. Alexander was presented this award in 1969 for *The High King*. *The Black Cauldron* was a runner-up for the award in 1966 (Newbery Honor) (Jones, 1983:186). *The High King* also was a National Book Award Finalist (children's category) in 1969 (Jones, 1983:186) and a National Book Award Finalist in the paperback fiction category in 1981 (Weiss, 1983:420). For information concerning each book in the series, see the entries listed under individual book titles.

**Coll (KAHL) Son of Collfrewr (KAHL-frure): Coll of *Caer Dallben had been a dauntless warrior in his youth. In the tales of *Prydain, Coll is "grown . . . stout around the middle, and much lacking in hair on the crown of his head" (CWP 75/7). Yet, "not even *Dallben, the most powerful enchanter in Prydain, had greater skill in plowing, planting, or harvesting than Coll. No man was as good-natured with a garden, as tender-hearted with a tree, or as agreeable with animals" (CWP 75/8).

Before the story of *Taran begins, Coll defies death to rescue his beloved white pig, *Hen Wen, from *Annuvin. He is aided in his quest by three animals. The first, *Ash-Wing the owl, offers his help because Coll stops to rescue his owlet from a tree trunk. From this incident Coll learns that he can understand the speech of animals. Ash-Wing informs him that this understanding, though temporary, results from Coll's eating the *Hazel Nuts of Wisdom. It is interesting to note that the word Coll, the name of a letter in the Druid alphabet, means hazel tree (WG 181).

Ash-Wing also tells the farmer that Hen Wen is "no ordinary pig. She knows many deep secrets" (CWP 77/11). This is the first Coll knows of Hen Wen's oracular abilities, and he realizes why *Arawn stole her.

Coll rescues *Oak-Horn the stag from entanglement in a thorn bush and *Star-Nose the mole from Arawn's *gwythaints. When Coll arrives at Annuvin, Ash-Wing lures the gwythaints away from Hen Wen's prison. Oak-Horn does the same with the *Huntsmen of Annuvin, leaving Coll free to descend into the pit where the oracular pig is kept. The guards return before Coll escapes, but Star-Nose and an army of moles open the floor of the pit, providing a tunnel to freedom.

When Coll returns to his farm, he finds Dallben, who had come to warn of danger to Hen Wen, waiting for him. This is their first meeting, yet Dallben stays permanently at Coll's farm which then becomes Caer Dallben.

Coll is the perfect example of a humble man. He is not concerned with power, wealth, or glory. Coll even declines Dallben's offer to see one day of his future life by peering into *The Book of Three. He says there is no need—except perhaps to know if his turnips will fare well that year. For that Dallben does not need to consult the book to answer yes. Later, in *The High King, Taran calls Coll a true warrior. Coll replies, "Do you mean to honor me? Then say, rather, I am a true grower of turnips and a gatherer of apples" (HK 98–99/119). *Taliesin says of Coll that his wisdom is of a good and kindly heart, like *Gurgi, "and added thereto the wisdom of the earth, the gift of waking barren ground and causing the soil to flourish in a rich harvest" (HK 113/135).

As the forces build for the final battle against Arawn, Coll rides with Taran to rally the *Commot Folk under the *banner of the White Pig. "Taran was grateful for Coll's wisdom and gladly sought his counsel" (HK 98/118). When Taran's command is sent to delay the deathless warriors in their march to Annuvin, Coll advises Taran as to strategy for slowing the *Cauldron-Born. The stout farmer saves Taran's life during the battle against *Pryderi's host.

As Taran's troops defend the old wall that crosses the *Red Fallows, Coll sees the Cauldron-Born striving to clamber through an undefended breach. Almost single-handedly he beats them back, but he receives his death wound. "Coll was bleeding heavily from the head; his fleece-lined coat, bloodsoaked, was slashed and tattered by the blades of the Cauldron-Born" (HK 141/167–168). Coll recognizes his imminent death though Taran tries to dismiss the obvious in hopes he will survive. But *Gwyn the Hunter sounds his horn. Coll's last words are "See to our plantings, my boy" (HK 142/169).

Coll's death is an emotional moment in the *Prydain Chronicles. He is a father-figure to Taran, a pillar of strength and stability. He hates war and strife, yet gives his life in the battle against evil. Taran hollows a grave in the harsh soil of the Red Fallows with his hands, and the *Companions raise a humble mound with tumbled stones from the old wall. He sends the others on and mourns alone for a time at Coll's graveside.

In *Guest's notes to the *Mabinogion, Coll ab Collfrewi is mentioned as one of the three powerful swineherds of the Island of Britain. Coll kept the swine of Dadweir Dallpenn (Dallben), and one of Dallpenn's sows was called Henwen, an extraordinary pig. Coll is said to have been a powerful enchanter and is listed as "one of the chief enchanters of this island"

(M 269). In one instance Coll is said to have taught *Rhuddlum the Giant, another principal enchanter of Welsh myth, his illusions. Another note tells that Coll learned from Rhuddlum. Such confusion is not unusual in Guest's *Mabinogion*. "These are corrupted texts . . . and there's really no way of sorting them out," says Alexander (1985b). The names could easily have been transposed. Coll is also credited with introducing wheat and barley in Britain. It is said only oats and rye were cultivated before his time.

See also Characters—fantasy, Collfrewr.
(M 213, 269; WG 181, 221)

Jacket illustration by Evaline Ness

**Coll (KAHL) and His White Pig: This is the first of two *Prydain picture books. It was illustrated by Evaline Ness, who also did the hardback dustcovers for the *Prydain Chronicles. The story predates the story of *Taran and is the tale of *Coll rescuing *Hen Wen from *Annuvin.

The picture book is no longer in print, but the story of *Coll and His White Pig* has been added to the collection of Prydain short stories in the current edition of *The Foundling*.

See also The Truthful Harp.

Collfrewr (KAHL-frure): Collfrewr is the father of *Coll. The name Colfrewr appears in the *Mabinogion* but is spelled "Collfrewi" (Coll ab Collfrewi).
(BT 24/40; BC 19/32; HK 113/135, 125/149, 142/169; M 213, 269; WG 221)

Commot (KOM-ot) Cenarth (KEN-arth): Commot Cenarth is the southernmost of the *Free Commots and the home of *Hevydd the Smith. It is the first of the Free Commots to rally around the *banner of the White Pig. Cenarth is a Welsh town according to *Lady Charlotte Guest's notes to the *Mabinogion.
(TW 175/206; HK 91/110; M 362)

Commot (KOM-ot) folk: This is the term used to describe the people living in the *Free Commots of *Prydain. The word "folk" is not capitalized in *Taran Wanderer but becomes a proper noun in *The High King.
(TW 175/206; HK 91/110, 225/260, 235/271, 247/285)

Commot (KOM-ot) Gwenith (GWEN-ith): Commot Gwenith is north of *Commot Cenarth along the *Valley of Great Avren. *Dwyvach Weaver-Woman dwells there.
(TW 181/213, 187/220; HK 95/114)

Commot (KOM-ot) Isav (IS-av): This is the smallest *Commot that *Taran visits, with "fewer than half-a-dozen cottages and a little grazing plot for a handful of sheep and cattle" (TW 200/234). The Commot Isav does not have its own potter; therefore, *Annlaw Clay-Shaper makes wares for its people. Taran makes the one-day journey to Isav to deliver for Annlaw and stays to help the Commot defeat a band of raiders (*Dorath's Company). He devises a plan to overcome the raiders by using the element of surprise. The shepherd, *Drudwas, and his son, *Llassar, dwell in the Commot Isav.

   In her notes to the *Mabinogion, *Guest mentions that a commot named Isav was where *Gwydion supposedly stored his treasure (booty).
(TW 197/231, 200/234, 207/242, 213/249; HK 96/116; M 436)

Commot (KOM-ot) men: The men from the *Free Commots who rallied under the *banner of the White Pig are called Commot men throughout *The High King. Many of them perished in the conflict between *Arawn and the *Sons of Don. It is recorded that in the battle to protect *Caer Dathyl "the enemy had taken cruel toll of the Commot men" (HK 129/154).
(HK 91+/111+)

Commot (KOM-ot) Merin (MEHR-in): Commot Merin is north of *Commot Gwenith. It is the "fairest *Commot . . . [*Taran] had ever seen. A tall stand of firs and hemlocks circled broad, well-tended fields, green and abundant. White, thatch-roofed cottages sparkled in shafts of sunlight. The air itself seemed different . . . cool and touched with the sharp scent of evergreens" (TW 188/221). Merin is the home of *Annlaw Clay-Shaper.

The name Merin appears in the *Mabinogion: Clis, the son of Merin. (TW 188/221, 195/229, 200/234, 208/243, 211/246, 218/254; HK 99/ 119–120, 237/273; M 221)

Commots (KOM-ots): *See* Free Commots.

**Companions: When *Taran, *Eilonwy, *Gurgi, and *Fflewddur Fflam band together to travel to *Caer Dathyl in *The Book of Three*, a fellowship is established. At first, the four do not get on well together. At this point Alexander calls them either a group or travelers. Slowly Taran begins to view them as his companions. But the real turning point occurs when Taran realizes he could never have reached Caer Dathyl alone. "I see now that I wouldn't have got even this far without help. It is a good destiny that brings me such brave companions" (BT 107/129). From this time forward, throughout the *Chronicles, this fellowship is known as "the companions."

Other characters are inducted into the fellowship as the story unfolds. *Doli of the *Fair Folk, Prince *Rhun, and perhaps even *Coll may be considered a part of this companionship. The animals—*Kaw, *Llyan, *Melynlas, *Lluagor—also are included.

Cornillo (kor-NILL-oh): When we first hear of the black cow Cornillo, she is in the possession of Lord *Gast of *Cantrev Cadiffor. She is "the finest cow in all the land!" says Gast (TW 42/59).

> "Gentle as a lamb! Strong as an ox! Swift as a horse and wise as an owl! . . . She leads my cattle . . . better than any herdsman can. She'll pull a plow or turn a grist mill, if need be. Her calves are always twins! As for milk, she gives the sweetest! . . . So rich the dairy maids can scarcely churn it!" (TW 43/59–60)

Cornillo is a constant source of dispute between Lord Gast and Lord *Goryon. *Taran witnesses a skirmish between the two when Goryon steals Cornillo. King *Smoit, *Cantrev Cadiffor's supreme ruler, clarifies the matter of Cornillo for Taran. "His [Gast's] cow indeed! Gast stole her from Goryon himself last year. And before that, the other way around. Neither of them knows whose beast it rightly is" (TW 48/65).

Gast and Goryon destroy the field of *Aeddan the farmer as they battle for possession of Cornillo. At Taran's suggestion, King Smoit grants

Cornillo to Aeddan as partial compensation for his losses. Goryon and Gast are allowed to have her next calves.

Cows were a standard of currency among the ancient Welsh, according to *Lady Charlotte Guest (M 261). A large, well-bred herd was a mark of wealth, and herdsmen held places of distinction. Guest's notes to the *Mabinogion* tell of Llawnrodded Varvawc, who was "one of the three Tribe Herdsmen of the Island of Britain" (M 273). Though he tended the cattle of Nudd Hael (some 21,000 milk cows), his own cow was named Cornillo, "and was one of the three chief cows of the Island" (M 273).

A similar story to that of Goryon and Gast bickering over Cornillo is recounted in Guest's notes. Nynniaw and Peibiaw, quarreling kings, fight over possession of fields and flocks until they begin to destroy the land. As with Smoit, *Rhitta, the giant king of Wales, finally puts a stop to their feuding and punishes them for their carnage (M 283). (TW 42/59, 48/65, 56/74; M 273)

Council Chamber of the Bards: *See* Council of Bards.

Council of Bards: Called the High Council of Bards in *The Truthful Harp*, this examination committee has the responsibility of accepting or rejecting candidates who wish to become *bards. *Taliesin is the head of the committee and is therefore known as the *Chief Bard. It is this committee that rejects *Fflewddur Fflam when he fails the bardic test and yet presents him with the *truthful harp. The *Council Chamber of the Bards was located at *Caer Dathyl before its destruction.

In *Guest's notes to the *Mabinogion*, the Council of Bards is listed under three peculiar names: the Impulsive Stocks of the baptismal bards of Britain, the nine superinstitutionalists of the baptismal chair, and the Chair of the Round Table. Taliesin was their "chair-president," and there were nine members of the council: Taliesin, Madog, Merddin Emrys, Saint Talhaiarn, Merddin ab Madog, Meugant Hen, Balchnoe, Saint Cattwg, and Cynddylan (M 498–499). (BT 89/110, 129/153; TH 88/8, 88/11; M 498)

Craddoc (KRAD-ok) Son of Custennin (kus-TEN-in): As *Taran searches to discover his identity, he meets Craddoc the shepherd in the *Hill Cantrevs. Craddoc is "a tall, broad-shouldered man" with dark eyes (TW 133/159–160). Gray streaks his hair and beard, and scars crease his wide brow. "Unarmed save for a long hunting knife in his leather belt, he wore the rude garb of a herdsman; his cloak was rolled and slung over his back; his jacket was tattered at the edges, begrimed and threadbare" (TW 134/160). What Taran first thinks is a shepherd's staff turns out to be a roughly fashioned crutch. Craddoc's right leg is badly lamed.

The *Companions discover that Craddoc was crippled defending his land and that of his neighbors from "certain lords" (TW 136/162). Only Craddoc stayed to work the ruined land; he wished to retain his freedom, laboring for no other man. His farmstead is little more than a tumbledown cottage in a dale among the steep hills. Its stone walls, partly fallen away, are made of rocks delved from the fields. Rusted farm implements lie in an open-fronted shed.

Upon hearing Taran's tale of unknown parentage, Craddoc excitedly claims to have placed his infant son, after his wife died in childbirth, in the hands of a wayfarer named *Dallben, who promised him his son would one day return. "The promise has been kept," Craddoc says to Taran. "My son has come back" (TW 139/166).

Taran is deeply disappointed and struggles to accept his station in life. All thoughts of marrying the Princess *Eilonwy must be abandoned now that he is proven a commoner. Craddoc's land becomes a prison for him, but he labors nevertheless to rebuild the farmhold. Craddoc is proud of his son and of their work. The cottage is restored, fences and walls mended, ground cleared. Yet, Taran is unable to call Craddoc "father."

When winter grips the hill country, Craddoc falls into an icy crevice and is grievously wounded. To rescue him from the bottom of the pit is almost impossible, and Taran feels a terrible surge of relief at the prospect of freedom. But anguish floods in to drown the dishonorable and wicked thoughts, and Taran cries, "What man am I?" (TW 153/181). The question is answered as he leaps into the crevice to sacrifice his life, if need be, to save Craddoc.

As he lies in what may be an icy grave, Craddoc admits to Taran that he lied about their kinship. Dallben did indeed come by years earlier, but Craddoc's son had died before that time. "Even as I spoke the lie, I was ashamed, then more ashamed to speak the truth. . . . At first I leaned upon you as on my crutch, because you served my need, but no father came to love a son more dearly" (TW 155/184). Craddoc tells Taran not to risk his life but to go away and leave him. Taran instead uses the last call in the *battle horn given him by Eilonwy to summon the *Fair Folk to Craddoc's rescue. As he blows the horn, Taran drops to the ledge that holds Craddoc and loses consciousness.

When Taran awakes, he is in the cottage, his wounds tended. The Fair Folk had come, but Craddoc still had not survived. Craddoc's death affects

Taran deeply. Instead of rejoicing in his freedom to seek noble parents, he is burdened with guilt.

> "I was ashamed to be base-born, so ashamed it sickened me. I would have left Craddoc to his death. Yes, left him to die!" he burst out. "Because I believed it would have set me free of him. I was ashamed to be the son of a herdsman. But no longer. Now my shame is for myself." (TW 159/188–189)

The *Mabinogion* only briefly uses the name Craddoc, spelled Cradawc (Cradawc son of Iaen).

See also Custennin.
(TW 133/159, 140/167, 149/177, 159/188, 198/232, 210/245; M 223)

crescent moon: The crescent moon is the emblem of the *House of Llyr.
See also Angharad, Angharad's gem, Eilonwy, Morda.
(BT 54/72; CL 3/17, 136/164; TW 90/112; HK 5/15)

crimson hawk: The crimson hawk is the emblem of the *House of Pwyll.
See also Pryderi.
(HK 116/138, 128/153)

Crochan (CROH-kahn): See Black Crochan.

Crugan-Crawgan (kroogan-KRAW-gan): Crugan-Crawgan is a heavy, plodding turtle who appears in the story "The Rascal Crow" from *The Foundling*. This turtle is so slow (but steady!) that in a race against a snail he only managed a draw.

Crugan-Crawgan offers the other animals and *Medwyn the help of all turtles in battling the *Chief Huntsman of *Arawn. But he is so slow and faltering in his speech that *Kadwyr, the impudent crow, ridicules him by saying, "And we'll be well into next week by the time you're done telling us" (F 44/52). Kadwyr laughs at Crugan-Crawgan's offer and tells him the best thing he could do would be to pull his head into his shell and hide. Yet it is Crugan-Crawgan who trips the Chief Huntsman, who thinks he is vaulting a rock not a turtle, and sends the villain over a cliff to his death. Kadwyr's life is saved, for he was nearly in the grasp of Arawn's henchman.

See also Brynach, Edyrnion, Gwybeddin, Nedir.
(F 44/51, 49/57)

Custennin (kus-TEN-in): Custennin was the father of *Craddoc, the herdsman who claimed to be *Taran's father. There are two characters in the *Mabinogion who bear this name. In the story, "Geraint the Son of Erbin," one of King Arthur's pages is named Goreu, the son of Custennin. However, the more notable Custennin is a herdsman in the story of "Kilhwch [*Kilhuch] and *Olwen." He is also a brother to Yspaddaden (*Yspadadden), Olwen's father.

(TW 134/160; M 143, 231)

D

✚

Dallben (DAHL-ben): The three weird sisters *Orddu, *Orwen, and
*Orgoch found Dallben floating in a wicker basket among the tall grasses of
the *Marshes of Morva. He is "the foundling" for which the collection
of *Prydain short stories is named. The crones gave Dallben his name and
raised him to boyhood, as they explain both in *The Black Cauldron
and *The Foundling. Then one day the sisters left young Dallben alone to
stir a cauldron of brew, warning him not to taste the liquid. When the brew
came to a boil, some of it bubbled up and splashed on Dallben's fingers. "It
burned his poor dear fingers," says Orddu. "But he didn't cry, no indeed. He
just popped his fingers into his mouth, the brave little starling. Of course,
some of the potion was still there, and he swallowed it" (BC 104/135). "As
soon as he did that," Orwen goes on to explain, "he knew every bit as much
as we did. It was a magical brew, you understand, a recipe for wisdom" (BC
105/135). Dallben's mind was suddenly opened, and he looked about the
hags' cottage with new insight.

> Now he understood that the leather bellows lying by the hearth com-
> manded the four winds; the pail of water in the corner, the seas and
> oceans of the world. The earthen floor of the cottage held the roots of all
> plants and trees. The fire showed him the secrets of its flame, and how
> all things come to ashes. (F 8/6)

Dallben's beginnings relate to those of other mythic and biblical characters. Moses, for example, was also found floating in a wicker basket. However, Alexander (1985b) says that he was not necessarily alluding to Moses
when creating this facet of Dallben's life because "the specific idea of a
child found floating [in a basket] is a common mythological motif." Robert
Graves in The White Goddess also points out that the myths of Moses,
*Taliesin and Llew Llaw Gyffes (from *Celtic mythology), and Romulus all

involve the child being found in a basket (WG 158). Dallben's acquisition of knowledge and power also parallels that of Gwion Bach in the *Mabinogion* story, "Taliesin." Gwion Bach (who later becomes Taliesin) burns his fingers while mixing a cauldron of brew for the hag Caridwen. The brew is one of Inspiration and Science, and when Gwion sucks his scorched fingers, he also gains the "knowledge of the mysteries of the future state of the world" (M 472).

Dallben is not allowed to stay longer with the enchantresses. "You can't have that many people knowing that much all under the same roof," says Orddu (BC 105/136). But they let Dallben choose a gift from many powerful objects stored about the cottage. Dallben could have taken a certain sword that would have made him the greatest warrior in Prydain. He might have ruled Prydain through its power. He also might have owned a golden harp and become "the greatest *bard in Prydain" (F 10/9; BC 105/136). But Dallben chooses *The Book of Three*. "It holds everything that was ever known, is known, and will be known," Orddu explains (F 10/9).

Dallben departs from the witches and soon after stops to read from the ancient tome. At first, the pages reveal wonderful secrets. "For here was knowledge he had never dreamed of: the pathways of the stars, the rounds of the planets, the ebb and flow of time and tide" (F 11–12/11). Dallben's joy is unbridled until the pages begin "to grow dark and stained with blood and tears" (F 12/13).

> For now the book told him of other ways of the world; of cruelty, suffering, and death. . . .
>
> Each page he read pierced his heart. The book, which had seemed to weigh so little, now grew so heavy that his pace faltered and he staggered under the burden. (F 12–13/13)

He spends a night of agony, and the next morning he is shocked to see his reflection in a puddle.

> His fair, bright curls had gone frost-white and fell below his brittle shoulders. His cheeks, once full and flushed with youth, were now hollow and wrinkled, half hidden by a long, gray beard. His brow, smooth yesterday, was scarred and furrowed, his hands gnarled and knotted, his eyes pale as if their color had been wept away. (F 13/13)

The cost of wisdom is great; Dallben ages in a single night. He finishes *The Book of Three* and finds that there is hope that good may yet prevail. Then Dallben begins his journey through life as protector of all that is good against the forces of evil. This is the Dallben we meet as the *Chronicles of Prydain* begin, more than three hundred years later.

Shortly before *Taran's story begins, Dallben travels to *Coll's farmstead to warn him that *Arawn *Death-Lord is about to kidnap the oracular pig, *Hen Wen. Though he arrives too late (Coll is already attempting Hen Wen's rescue), the enchanter stays to tend Coll's garden and orchard. Even though he and Coll had not met before, Dallben stays on after Coll and Hen Wen return so that he may help protect the marvelous sow. Coll's farm becomes *Caer Dallben (CWP 82/30).

*The Book of Three introduces Dallben as the 379-year-old enchanter who is Taran's guardian. His appearance has not changed since he was aged in a night. Dallben is tall yet bent, with bony knees and withered limbs. "His beard covered so much of his face he seemed always to be peering over a gray cloud" (BT 5/19). Alexander explains that Coll and Taran tend to the fields and flocks, and Dallben undertakes "the meditating" (BT 5/19). In spite of his frail appearance, "Dallben is the most powerful enchanter in Prydain" (BC 18/32).

Dallben's *magic is evidenced sparingly but convincingly throughout the Chronicles. He turns the *Horned King and his men away from Caer Dallben with a ring of fire in The Book of Three. In *The Castle of Llyr, he foresees danger to Princess *Eilonwy on the *Isle of Mona and counsels *Gwydion to turn his attention there. In *The High King, he restores *Glew to his normal size and interprets Hen Wen's reading of the *letter sticks, the prophecy concerning the recovery of *Dyrnwyn.

More about Dallben's powers is revealed in The High King when Lord *Pryderi comes to kill the enchanter. Dallben hears Pryderi's band coming before any other ears are able to detect sound and is able to determine that there are twenty riders. He repels Pryderi's attack upon Caer Dallben first by blowing out his breath "as if he were puffing at thistledown" (HK 184/215). A biting gale roars across the field and batters the riders with lashing branches. Next he strikes his staff on the frozen turf and the field heaves "like a restless sea" (HK 185/215). The warriors who have not already fled are sent scurrying by a crimson flame that leaps from the enchanter's outstretched hand. Pryderi alone presses forward. His sword shatters on Dallben's *ash-wood staff, but the traitorous king pulls forth a *black dagger given him by Arawn. It is the one weapon that can penetrate Dallben's magic and take his life. Pryderi reveals that Dallben has one weakness: he may not kill or his life is forfeit. Though this is true, Dallben tells the warlord that he still will not leave Caer Dallben alive. "You have believed half-truths," says Dallben. "No man has ever suffered death at my hands. But those who scorn my spells do so at their own peril" (HK 189/220). A crimson glow pours in the window as a broad belt of flames springs up to circle

Caer Dallben. "Slay me, Lord Pryderi, and the flames you see will sweep over Caer Dallben in an instant" (HK 189/220). The black dagger is never tested. Pryderi flings it away in doubt and fear. He grasps *The Book of Three* in hopes of escaping with it. Lightning leaps from the ancient tome, killing the once noble lord.

Of Dallben's ban against taking life Alexander (1985b) says, "No individual has placed a ban on him. . . . [No] mighty power says, 'You may never kill. . . .' It was his own knowledge, compassion . . . that prevented him from it. It was his conscience." However, Alexander makes it plain that Dallben literally cannot break this ban. The enchanter *must* allow himself to be killed before magic will work to destroy Pryderi.

Alexander often expresses his views of life through Dallben. The enchanter offers his wisdom in council to Taran and others, and we benefit from his lessons. A smattering of examples is given below:

"There are times when the seeking counts more than the finding." (BT 185/215)

"Nothing we do is ever done entirely alone. There is a part of us in everyone else—you [Taran], of all people, should know that." (BT 185/215)

"But it is not Caer Dallben which has grown smaller. You [Taran] have grown bigger. That is the way of it." (BT 186/216)

"My dear boy [Taran], this [sword] is a bit of metal hammered into a rather unattractive shape; it could better have been a pruning hook or a plow iron. Its powers? Like all weapons, only those held by him who wields it." (BC 23/37–38)

"Child, child [Eilonwy], do you not see? For each of us comes a time when we must be more than what we are." (CL 4/18)

"It takes as much strength of heart to share the one [honor] as to face the other [shame]." (TW 6/18)

"Ah, Princess [Eilonwy] . . . a crown is more discomfort than adornment. If you have learned that, you have already learned much." (HK 9/20)

"You [Pryderi] have steeped your hands in blood, and in your pride sought to pass judgment on your fellow men. Was it your concern to serve Prydain? You chose an evil means to do it. Good cannot come from evil." (HK 189–190/220–221)

"For the deeds of a man, not the words of a prophecy, are what shape his destiny." (HK 239/276)

Dallben had long searched for the *High King who would rule when the *Sons of Don returned to the *Summer Country. *The Book of Three* told of the signs by which the new king would be recognized. He would be one who slew a serpent, who gained and lost a flaming sword, who chose a kingdom of sorrow over one of happiness, and who was of no station in life. Taran fulfills these requirements by slaying Arawn in serpent form, gaining possession of Dyrnwyn just as its magical powers disappear, and choosing to stay in Prydain rather than travel with the Sons of Don to the Summer Country. But Dallben does not reveal the truth of Taran's parentage until the Chronicles are about to conclude. He tells of finding the infant Taran hidden in the trees next to a field where a battle had raged. Everyone else was dead, so there was no way to determine this child's heritage. Therefore, he could surely be considered one of "no station in life." Alexander (1985b) explains Dallben's reasoning:

> How often are you going to come across an infant whose parentage is unknown? You can find an orphan . . . but there's going to be someone who'll say, "His grandpa was so and so, and his parents are dead." In other words, this was a case where it was not possible to find out anything about him.

Alexander (1985b) also feels that Dallben may well have felt a tingle of inspiration to confirm Taran's destiny. "I think he [Dallben] must have recognized this situation is quite rare, that there's no way anyone can ever know [the child's parentage], and I think that clicked. Call it inspiration or sensation, or whatever it may be."

Dallben, as "caretaker of Prydain," tests the new High King one last time when Taran reveals that he will not travel to the Summer Country. The old enchanter tries to shake Taran's resolve by saying, "Once taken, your choice cannot be recalled. Will you dwell in sorrow instead of happiness? Will you refuse not only joy and love but never-ending life?" (HK 236/273). Taran nevertheless decides to stay, and Dallben then reveals that the *Assistant Pig-Keeper is indeed the new High King. Dallben explains that the time of enchantments in Prydain is over, and now "men unaided guide their own destiny" (HK 229/264). He presents Taran with *The Book of Three*, now merely a history book, though an important heritage. The enchanter writes one last sentence in the book. "And thus did an Assistant Pig-Keeper become High King of Prydain" (HK 244/281).

Dallben also keeps the secret of Eilonwy's destiny until the story is nearly finished. It seems the Princess is bound to travel with the Sons of

Don to the Summer Country. But when she decides she is tired of other people deciding things for her, Dallben reveals that the Princess has a choice. By twisting the ring Gwydion once gave her one full turn and wishing fervently to no longer have powers of enchantment, Eilonwy may become fully human. She gladly does so and stays in Prydain to rule with Taran. As his final official act in Prydain, Dallben performs a ceremony sealing their betrothal. "Come, clasp hands the two of you, and pledge each other your troth" (HK 246/284).

Dallben surfaces in the *Mabinogion. The name Dadweir Dallpenn appears in the story of "Kilhwch [*Kilhuch] and *Olwen." But *Guest's notes following the story reveal more concerning this figure from Celtic mythology. Dadweir Dallpenn was to have possessed the marvelous sow named Henwen, and Dallpenn's swineherd was none other than Coll ab Collfrewi, considered one of the three powerful swineherds of the Island of Britain (M 268).

Alexander's research uncovered a source that told of Dadweir Dallpenn as a blind Druid. However, he was unable, after more than twenty years, to remember where he found this information.

> My card file note simply says, "Dallwyr—Blindmen, followers of the mystic Dallben, owners of Hen Wen, the sow tended by Coll."
>
> Surely I got that from somewhere—but where? Davies? Some other source? I distinctly remember my source referred to Dallben as being blind . . . the symbolic meaning being that he was gifted with inner vision. . . . (Dall means "blind" in Welsh.)
> (Alexander, 1986a)

Alexander (1986a) toyed with the idea of making Dallben blind in the *Prydain Chronicles. But as he thought about it, he decided it would present terrible problems as he developed the story.

See also *Characters—fantasy, *Magic.
(M 223, 268)

Dark Gate: The twin mountain peaks guarding the southern approach to the *Land of Death are known as Dark Gate. They are not as mighty as *Mount Dragon to the north of *Annuvin but are nevertheless treacherous, with sharp crags and hidden drops.

Dark Gate is briefly mentioned in *Lady Charlotte Guest's notes to the *Mabinogion. In relation to the kingdom of Dyved (realm of *Pwyll and *Pryderi), the notes read, "And the centre of this kingdom was the Dark-

Gate, in Carmarthen" (M 362). Graves in *The White Goddess* explains that this was the entrance to the Underworld (WG 385). The relation between Annuvin, the Land of Death, and the mythic Underworld, also a land of the dead, makes Alexander's use of Dark Gate most appropriate.
(BC 19/32, 30/45, 72/96, 106/136, 157/198; HK 210/242, 214/247; CWP 79/18; M 363; WG 385)

Daughter of Angharad (an-GAR-ad): *See* Eilonwy.

Daughters of Don (DAHN): The phrase "Daughters of Don" is used only once in the *Prydain Chronicles. We are told at the conclusion of *The High King* that the Daughters of Don journeyed from the *eastern strongholds to accompany the *Sons of Don to the *Summer Country. Alexander (1985b) explains that the Daughters of Don "were evacuated . . . [from *Caer Dathyl to the eastern strongholds], the way people were evacuated from London during World War II. They were sent into the country . . . to be relatively safe" during the great battle with *Arawn, the *Lord of Death. Because *Caer Dathyl fell to the forces of Arawn and *Pryderi, it is fortunate that the wives and daughters of the *House of Don were removed to the eastern regions of *Prydain.
    See also Belin, Children of Don, Lady Don, the.
(HK 235/271)

Daughters of Llyr (LEER): *See* House of Llyr.

Death-Lord: *See* Arawn.

Dinas (DEEN-as) Rhydnant (RID-nant): Dinas Rhydnant is the stronghold and capital city of the *House of Rhuddlum. It is located on the *Isle of Mona by a crescent-shaped harbor with steep cliffs rising from almost the edge of the water. On the highest cliff stands the tall castle of King *Rhuddlum and Queen *Teleria. The harbor (*Mona Haven), with its piers and clusters of ships, is protected somewhat by jetties and a stone seawall. Dinas Rhydnant is also the home of Prince *Rhun, who becomes one of the *Companions.
    *Lady Charlotte Guest explains in her notes to the *Mabinogion that Dinas is the Welsh word "in actual use for a city" (M 188). Also from her notes comes a brief piece of verse from the *Myvyrian Archaiology,* a manuscript containing ancient Welsh tales, which includes both Rhydnant and Rhun.

Whose is the grave on the banks of the Rhydnant?
Rhun was his name, of the steady progress,
He was a king; Rhiogan slew him. (M, 332)

(CL 13+/28+; HK 20/31, 237/273; M 332)

Doli (DOH-lee): The dwarf, Doli, first appears when King *Eiddileg of the *Fair Folk assigns him to lead the *Companions from *Tylwyth Teg, the *Realm of the Fair Folk, to *Caer Dathyl.

> Doli, short and stumpy, almost as broad as he was tall, wore a rust-colored leather jacket and stout, knee-high boots. A round cap covered his head, but not enough to conceal a fringe of flaming red hair. An axe and short sword hung from his belt; and over his shoulder, he wore the stubby bow of the Fair Folk warrior. (BT 147/174)

Doli also has bright red eyes to match his hair. Like all dwarves, he is little taller than a man's knee. He is ill-tempered, but, like King Eiddileg, he is truly kindhearted. Initially, his bad temper results from his inability to make himself invisible. Doli grumbles and rants between stints of holding his breath, which is supposed to activate invisibility.

> "I'm *supposed* to be invisible," snapped Doli. "My whole family can do it. Just like that! Like blowing out a candle. But not me. No wonder they all laugh at me. No wonder Eiddileg sends me out with a pack of fools. If there's anything nasty or disagreeable to be done, it's always 'find good old Doli.'" (BT 149–150/176)

"Good old Doli" becomes Doli's standard form of complaint when he's called upon to do difficult, unpleasant, or dangerous tasks.

*Eilonwy sees through Doli's rough exterior quickly. "Doli means well. . . . He's like a porcupine, all prickly on the outside, but very ticklish once you turn him over" (BT 159/187). And the dwarf proves to be very skillful, leading the Companions unerringly and speedily toward their destination.

Doli proves to be a faithful comrade and indeed becomes one of the Companions. As *The Book of Three concludes, Doli is rewarded by *Gwydion and King *Math along with the others. He is granted the power of invisibility. Yet, whenever he makes himself invisible, his ears ring terribly. In one instance, he reappears with "his ears trembling and rimmed with blue" (BC 68/91).

In *The Black Cauldron, Doli rescues the other Companions from King *Morgant's tent just before they are slain and made into *Cauldron-Born.

In *Taran Wanderer, Doli is turned into a frog by the evil wizard, *Morda. *Llyan finds him, dehydrated and near death, in the forest. Though he is drenched in water, he sickens from an ague. Fortunately, *Taran is able to defeat the wizard, and Doli returns to his proper form. He regains "his long frown and short patience," but "the occasional flicker of a grin" betrays "his delight at seeing the companions again" (TW 111/135).

Because Doli knows the craft and secrets of his Fair Folk heritage, he is often able to solve difficult problems for the Companions. In *The Black Cauldron*, he locates *Gwystyl and his Fair Folk *way post when the Companions need sanctuary. It is through Gwystyl that they learn where the *cauldron is being kept. In *Taran Wanderer*, Doli recognizes Taran's *battle horn and explains its use to him. Later, the one call left in the horn summons Fair Folk to the rescue of *Craddoc and Taran. In *The High King, Doli finds the Fair Folk mine that could have been a shortcut through the *Hills of Bran-Galedd had not *Glew caused a cave-in. It is also Doli's plan to start fires on a frozen lake, melting the ice and causing a flood that destroys the *Huntsmen of Annuvin. This fulfills *Hen Wen's prophecy that rivers would burn with frozen fire before the sword *Dyrnwyn would be regained from *Arawn.

Fair Folk may not tarry long within the borders of *Annuvin. The strong presence of evil will cause death. In *The High King* when the other Fair Folk warriors are forced to turn back, Doli tries to continue the journey. Because he has spent so much time above ground with humans, he thinks his resistance to the *Land of Death may be greater. Yet, he soon becomes so weak that he is unable even to ride *Melynlas. "Doli's usually ruddy face had grown mottled and he breathed only in painful gasps" (HK 192/223). Taran is about to send him back to safety when Doli turns invisible. He discovers that invisibility is a protection against this evil influence and is able to continue the journey.

Doli is present when Arawn is finally slain, and *Prydain is freed. Undoubtedly, the Companions and Prydain would not have weathered the storm without Doli's assistance. But as the age of enchantments ends in Prydain, Doli and all Fair Folk must return forever to Tylwyth Teg. *Dallben explains that King Eiddileg will bar all passages into the realm. Doli grumbles about being glad that dealings with mortals will be finished. Yet, there are tears in his bright red eyes as he must say good-bye to Taran and the others. He presents Taran, the new *High King, with his axe as a remembrance.

Doli also appears in *The Foundling. He is the dwarf in a tale called "The Stone." Doli is freed from a fallen tree by a cottager named *Maibon and therefore must grant him a wish. Maibon wishes never to grow older. Though Doli tries to dissuade the man, he eventually gives Maibon a stone that will stop him from aging. However, the stone also keeps all his possessions from growing older: cows will not calve, eggs do not hatch, fields never ripen. No matter where Maibon throws the stone, it always returns. Doli eventually comes to help the cottager rid himself of the curse.

See also Characters—fantasy.

Don (DAHN): *See* Sons of Don; Daughters of Don.

Don (DAHN), the Lady: *See* Lady Don, the.

Dorath (DOH-rath): Dorath is a pitiless mercenary who says of his work, "My trade is to spill another's blood, not waste my own" (TW 127/152). When Dorath first appears in *Taran Wanderer*, he is introduced in this manner:

> Closest to the fire, stretched at his ease, a heavy-faced man leaned on one elbow and toyed with a long dagger, which he tossed and twirled. . . . He wore a horsehide jacket whose sleeves had been ripped out; his muddy boots were thick-soled and studded with iron nails. His yellowish hair fell below his shoulders; his cold blue eyes seemed to measure the three *companions with an unhurried glance. (TW 117/141)

*Taran, *Gurgi, and *Fflewddur unfortunately wander into Dorath's camp as they travel to the *Llawgadarn Mountains in search of Taran's parentage. Dorath and his band of brigands are convinced the Companions seek treasure and try forcing upon them their "services" as guides and protectors. "We serve any who pay us to serve: a weak lord who craves a strong war band, or three wayfarers who need protection against the dangers of their journey" (TW 120/145). In order to be free of the scoundrels, Taran must fight a hand-to-hand battle with Dorath. If Taran wins, Dorath will consider the fee for "services" paid. If not, Taran will relinquish his sword. Dorath shows his true lack of honor when he pulls a dagger from his boot during what is to be a weaponless match. Employing other dirty fighting techniques, the brigand wins and takes from Taran the sword *Dallben had given him. "The getting pleased me, swineherd," says Dorath. "The taking pleases me all the more" (TW 131/157).

Finally rid of *Dorath's Company, though shamed, Taran travels onward in search of his identity. But he meets with Dorath again. As Taran delivers the pottery of *Annlaw Clay-Shaper to the *Commot Isav, he learns a band of brigands has been raiding the surrounding area. He stays with the people of Commot Isav and devises a plan to surprise and defeat the raiders, who indeed are Dorath's Company. Though some of his Company perish, Dorath makes his escape on his sorrel mare.

Taran has another encounter with Dorath before *Taran Wanderer* ends. When Taran finally locates the *Mirror of Llunet, an oracular pool that may tell him of his parents, Dorath suddenly appears. The brigand is certain Taran has led him to treasure and is angered to find nothing. He stamps his foot in the shallow basin that holds the magical waters, emptying it. Because the water collects so slowly, the Mirror of Llunet is destroyed. Dorath flees when his sword, acquired from Taran, shatters against the blade Taran wrought himself in the forge of *Hevydd the Smith.

The villain surfaces again in *The High King*, capturing *Eilonwy and Gurgi as they wander lost in the *Hills of Bran-Galedd. Dorath thinks Eilonwy is a boy (because of her attire) and strikes her across the face. The *bauble drops from the folds of her jacket, and Dorath greedily snatches it from the ground. Then the brigand recognizes Gurgi and discovers Eilonwy's relationship to Taran. He decides to settle his score with Taran by violating his beloved. Gurgi tries to prevent the rape, and Dorath swings his sword downward to slay the defenseless creature. But before the blade tastes Gurgi's flesh, a gray shape throws Dorath to the earth. The wolves, *Brynach and *Briavael, sent from *Medwyn's valley to aid in the battle against *Arawn, rescue Eilonwy and Gurgi. Their wolf pack kills all of Dorath's Company (HK 165/194).

The name of Dorath appears in the text of the *Mabinogion, but is not associated with a villain. In the story, "Kilhwch and *Olwen," Kilhwch (*Kilhuch) requests the aid of Ruawn *Pebyr the son of Dorath in his quest to win the hand of Olwen (M 223).

See also Drudwas, Gloff, Llassar.
(TW 117/141, 201/235, 213/248; HK 97/117, 162/190, 179/209; M 223)

Dorath's (DOH-rath) Company: This band of mercenaries is composed of common thieves and murderers. *Fflewddur deems them "ruffians and loot-ers" (TW 121/146). Their leader, *Dorath, is a despicable villain who battles several times with *Taran and also tries to violate *Eilonwy.

When Dorath's Company is not in someone's "service," they make sport and profit by pillaging defenseless *commots and farmholds. The brigands raid the *Commot Isav but are turned away by Taran's plan to intercept them.

Dorath's Company captures Eilonwy and *Gurgi as they wander lost in the *Hills of Bran-Galedd in *The High King*. But before any harm comes to them, the wolves, *Brynach and *Briavael, and their pack kill every member of the mercenary band.

See also Drudwas, Gloff, Llassar.
(TW 118/142, 201/235; HK 165/193)

Drudwas (DRUD-was) Son of Pebyr (PEH-bir): Drudwas is a shepherd of the *Commot Isav who informs *Taran that *Dorath's Company has been raiding the local area. Drudwas and the other men of Commot Isav accept Taran's plan to surprise the raiders and thereby defeat them.

Drudwas's son, *Llassar, is a courageous youth who stands by Taran during the battle against *Dorath. When Taran revisits the *Free Commots to rally troops for the *Sons of Don, Llassar sadly reports that "the winter took . . . [Drudwas] from us" (HK 97/116). Undoubtedly, had Drudwas lived he would have followed Taran into battle against *Arawn as does Llassar.

In the *Mabinogion, Drudwas is a knight in the Court of Arthur. "There were three golden-tongued Knights in the Court of Arthur: Gwalchmai the son of Gwyar, Drudwas the son of Tryffin, and Eliwlod the son of Madog ap Uthur" (M 57).
(TW 201/235; HK 97/116; M 57, 223, 270)

Dwarf King: *See* Eiddileg.

Dwyvach (DWIH-vahk) Weaver-Woman: In *Taran Wanderer*, when *Taran first happens upon Dwyvach's cottage in the *Commot Gwenith, he sees a "cluster of sheds, stables, chicken roosts, and storehouses seeming to ramble in all directions" (TW 181/213). However, he soon sees order in the arrangement, for the maze of buildings is carefully linked by covered walkways or flagstone paths. Taran and *Gurgi are invited into the main dwelling by a voice that crackles "like twigs in a fire" (TW 181/213).

> Taran saw a bent old woman cloaked in gray beckoning him to the hearth. Her long hair was white as the wool on the distaff hanging from her belt of plaited cords. Below her short-girt robe, her bony shins looked thin and hard as spindles. A web of wrinkles covered her face; her cheeks were withered; but for all her years she gave no sign of frailty, as though time had only toughened and seasoned her; and her gray eyes were sharp and bright as a pair of new needles. (TW 181–182/213–214)

Then Taran notices a high *loom "standing like a giant harp of a thousand strings in the corner of the cottage" (TW 182/214).

Around it were stacked bobbins of thread of all colors; from the rafters dangled skeins of yarn, hanks of wool and flax; on the walls hung lengths of finished fabrics, some of bright hue and simple design, others of subtler craftsmanship and patterns more difficult to follow. Taran gazed astonished at the endless variety. (TW 182/214)

Dwyvach is a master at the art of weaving. When Taran asks how such intricate and beautiful work is done, the *Weaver-Woman answers wisely. "Thus is it done, *Wanderer, as all things are, each in its own way, thread by thread" (TW 183/215). She then consents to teach Taran her craft. To begin with, she suggests weaving a cloak for "Taran Threadbare" (TW 183/215).

Dwyvach teaches Taran the craft from the beginning of the process. The apprentice must tease thorns and cockleburs from the mountains of wool needed for a cloak. Then he must comb and card the wool. Next Taran must spin the wool into thread, dye it, and thread it on the loom. "The aged weaver-woman, Taran soon learned, had not only a tart tongue but a keen eye. Nothing escaped her; she spied the smallest knot, speck, or flaw, and brought Taran's attention to it with a sharp rap from her distaff to his knuckles" (TW 184/216). In frustration Taran says that *Hevydd the Smith once told him that life is a forge. His apprenticeship to Dwyvach shall certainly temper him like fine steel if his cloak is to be finished. "Life a forge?" answers the Weaver-Woman. "A loom, rather, where lives and days intertwine; and wise is he who can learn to see the pattern" (TW 185/218).

Taran discovers that the shuttle is "heavier" than the hammer, anvil, and tongs of Hevydd's forge combined. Dwyvach smiles and says, "It's not the shuttle that burdens you . . . but lack of skill, a heavy burden, Wanderer, that only one thing can lift" (TW 186/218). The one thing? Patience. But Taran finds he can never outwork the Weaver-Woman. She never seems to tire even after a full day's labor.

The task becomes easier with practice, but Taran is not pleased with his pattern and unravels his first attempt to start anew. When the cloak is completed, Dwyvach is pleased with Taran's skill and product. She asks him to stay, and she will teach him to be one of the finest weavers in *Prydain. But Dwyvach knows it is not in Taran's heart to be a weaver. In parting, she says, "But mind you, if life is a loom, the pattern you weave is not so easily unraveled" (TW 188/220).

In *The High King, Taran returns to the *Free Commots to rally forces for the *Sons of Don. Happily, he meets again with Dwyvach Weaver-Woman and briefly tries his skill at the loom once more. Dwyvach also meets *Eilonwy and gives her a beautiful cloak. "Take this as a gift from a

crone to a maiden," says Dwyvach, "and know there is not so much difference between the two. For even a tottering granddam keeps a portion of
girlish heart, and the youngest maiden a thread of old woman's wisdom"
(HK 96/115). Then she consents to weave garments for the army of *Commot men who will follow Taran under the *banner of the White Pig.

We do not see Dwyvach again in the *Chronicles of Prydain. However,
it is possible that she is among the *Commot Folk who come to hail Taran,
their new *High King. If not, Dwyvach surely sits at her loom in Commot
Gwenith awaiting another visit from her former apprentice.

Alexander's childhood experiences prepared him for creating the
sequences with Dwyvach Weaver-Woman. "Lloyd's sister, Florence, inadvertently helped prepare him for *Taran Wanderer* in those lean years in the
late 1940s when she taught him how to weave and make pottery" (Jacobs,
1978:492). Though Florence taught him to weave, Alexander (1985b) says
the image of Dwyvach was, of course, that of an older woman. "I think I can
say [with] hindsight, and maybe I was even thinking of it when I did it, that
[Dwyvach] could well have been my old Aunt Annie."
(TW 181/213, 193/226, 196/230, 217/253; HK 6/16, 95/115)

**Dyrnwyn (DURN-win): The history of the sword Dyrnwyn is clouded
in mystery throughout the *Prydain Chronicles. It is only in *The High
King* and in the subsequent publication, *The Foundling*, that Dyrnwyn's
background and qualities are fully revealed.

As the Prydain Chronicles begin, Dyrnwyn has long been lost. It is
found by *Eilonwy as she and *Taran wander through the passages beneath
*Spiral Castle. In their effort to escape *Achren, she and Taran stumble
upon a *barrow. Dyrnwyn is in the grasp of a dead king, and for the want of
a weapon, Eilonwy takes it from him. Later, Eilonwy points out the *Old
Writing on the sword's scabbard as well as a symbol of power. She interprets
the runes as best she can. "It says *Dyrnwyn*, first. I don't know whether
that's the name of the sword or the name of the king. Oh, yes, that's the
name of the sword; here it is again: *Draw Dyrnwyn, only thou of royal blood,
to rule, to strike the . . .*" (BT 86/107). Eilonwy is unable to make out the rest
of the message for the words seem to have been scratched away.

Eilonwy guards the sword because of its obvious power. She does not
even allow Taran to carry it. However, when later confronted by the
*Horned King, Taran draws Dyrnwyn.

> The blade would not come free. He pulled with all his strength. The
> sword moved only a little from its sheath. The Horned King raised his
> own weapon. As Taran gave a final wrench, the scabbard turned in his

hand. . . . Lightning seared his arm and he was thrown violently to the ground. The sword Dyrnwyn, blazing white with flame, leaped from his hand. (BT 169–170/198)

The flaming sword nearly takes Taran's life. *Gwydion later explains that Dyrnwyn is a weapon of great power, so ancient he almost believed it to be a legend. The removal of the sword from Spiral Castle is what caused the stronghold to crumble; indeed, Taran and Eilonwy barely escaped being buried in the rubble. The discovery of Dyrnwyn is also a severe blow to *Arawn *Death-Lord, says the *Prince of Don. Gwydion is able to unsheathe the blade without harm. He temporarily becomes its possessor.

After *The Book of Three, Dyrnwyn seems to be no longer of great importance. It is mentioned briefly in *The Black Cauldron. In *The Castle of Llyr, Gwydion states that the removal of the sword from Spiral Castle was Achren's "most grievous defeat" (CL 23/39), and when the *Companions attempt Eilonwy's rescue from Achren, the blazing of Dyrnwyn sends the enchantress's few warriors fleeing in fear.

Dyrnwyn does not assume further importance in the story until *The High King. Arawn, changing shape in order to appear to Gwydion as Taran, lures the Prince of Don into a trap, and the *Huntsmen of Annuvin strip him of Dyrnwyn. The loss of the sword to Arawn precipitates the great final battle of *good versus evil. "Its loss is fatal," says Gwydion (HK 22/33).

Gwydion reveals more of Dyrnwyn's history to the Companions as they prepare to seek its return. He explains that much of its history has been forgotten or destroyed.

> "*Taliesin *Chief Bard is wisest in the lore of *Prydain, but even he could tell me only that *Govannion the Lame, a master craftsman, forged and tempered Dyrnwyn at the behest of King *Rhydderch Hael, as a weapon of greatest power and protection for the land. To safeguard it, a spell was cast upon the blade and a warning graven on the scabbard." (HK 22/33–34)

Gwydion clarifies the meaning of the runes that are still readable. Instead of "Draw Dyrnwyn only thou of royal blood," it reads "only thou of noble worth."

> "The enchantment forbade the sword to all but those who would use it wisely and well. The flame of Dyrnwyn would destroy any other who sought to draw it. But the writing on the scabbard has been marred. The full message, which might have told more of the sword's purpose, is unknown.
>
> "King Rhydderch bore the blade throughout his life," Gwydion continued, "and his sons after him. . . . King *Rhitta, grandson of Rhydderch,

was the last to hold the blade. He was lord of Spiral Castle before it became the stronghold of Queen Achren. He met his death, in a way unknown, with Dyrnwyn clutched in his hands. From that time the sword was seen no more, forgotten as it lay buried with him in Spiral Castle's deepest chamber." (HK 22–23/34)

In order to understand how Dyrnwyn may be recovered, *Dallben consults the oracular pig *Hen Wen. Though frenzied with fear, Hen Wen points to the runes engraved on the *letter sticks. But the sticks shatter before the message is complete. Nevertheless, what is told Dallben is grim and disheartening.

> Ask, sooner, mute stone and voiceless rock to speak.
> Quenched will be Dyrnwyn's flame;
> Vanished, its power.
> Night turn to noon
> And rivers burn with frozen fire
> Ere Dyrnwyn be regained. (HK 31/43)

The message that came through Hen Wen is eventually proven a prophecy. Each of the stipulations comes to pass. Night is turned to noon when Eilonwy uses the light from her *bauble to warn Taran of approaching Huntsmen. "The beams spread and rose toward the clouds, as though the sun itself were bursting from the mountainside" (HK 171/200). Rivers burn when *Doli of the *Fair Folk engineers an idea to destroy the Huntsmen of Annuvin by creating a flood. Taran's band lights brush fires on a frozen lake, and when the ice melts, a torrent of water cascades into the ravine where Arawn's forces are camped.

When the Companions reach *Annuvin, Taran stumbles upon Dyrnwyn's hiding place under an odd-shaped rock atop *Mount Dragon. The wind keening past the rock's irregularities speaks as if with a voice, drawing Taran's attention to it and Dyrnwyn. As Taran puts it, "The voiceless stone spoke clearly" (HK 221/256). The last part of the prophecy is fulfilled when Arawn is finally slain by Dyrnwyn. The blade flickers, and the white brilliance fades. "Faster then the glow faded, no longer white but filled with swirling colors which danced and trembled. In another moment, Taran's hand held no more than a scarred and battered weapon" (HK 223/257). Light from Eilonwy's bauble reveals the rest of the Old Writing on Dyrnwyn's scabbard just before the message fades forever. "*Draw Dyrnwyn, only thou of noble worth, to rule with justice, to strike down evil. Who wields it in good cause shall slay even the *Lord of Death*" (HK 223/258). "Dyrnwyn's task is ended," says Gwydion as the sword's power vanishes (HK 224/258).

Also, Dyrnwyn held the power to slay Arawn's deathless warriors. Taran pulls the sword from its hiding place and plunges the flaming blade into the heart of an attacking *Cauldron-Born. "The Cauldron-Born stumbled and fell; and from lips long mute burst a shriek that echoed and re-echoed from the *Death-Lord's stronghold as though rising from a thousand tongues" (HK 214/247). As one body, the entire army of deathless warriors topples and lies motionless. Perhaps the cry of the mute warriors also fulfilled the prophecy concerning mute stone speaking.

As Taran's story ends, everything concerning Dyrnwyn has still not been revealed. In *The Foundling, the tale titled "The Sword" completes the *magic blade's story. King Rhitta uses the blade unwisely and for evil purposes. He slays an innocent shepherd named *Amrys; then continues to use the blade in selfish, unclean exploits. Guilt and fear drive the cursed king to his doom. Because he does not repent, Rhitta watches the blood of Amrys slowly stain the shining blade to deep, dark black. Try as he may, Rhitta cannot clean Dyrnwyn. He is the one who mars the Old Writing on the scabbard, for the words mock him. Finally, Rhitta builds the maze of passages under Spiral Castle to escape both real and imagined dangers. The ghost of Amrys, who continues to plague the king, visits Rhitta in his secret chamber. The king draws Dyrnwyn to strike the spirit. No longer worthy to draw the blade, Rhitta and all his guards are immediately slain by Dyrnwyn's fire. The chamber became Rhitta's barrow and remained hidden until Eilonwy and Taran stumble upon it.

Dyrnwyn is mentioned in *Lady Charlotte Guest's notes to the *Mabinogion. Dyrnwyn, the sword of Rhydderch Hael, was one of the thirteen precious things of the Island of Britain. If any drew it except Rhydderch, "it would burst into a flame from the cross to the point, and all who asked it received it; but because of this property all shunned it" (M 285). This brief note became Alexander's inspiration for Dyrnwyn in the *Chronicles of Prydain.

See also Fantastic objects.
(M 285)

E

❖

Eagle Mountains: This mountain range is located in northern *Prydain. *Caer Dathyl, the stronghold of the *Sons of Don and home of *Gwydion and King *Math, is nestled among these peaks. The foothills of the Eagle Mountains is where *Medwyn dwells. Also, the Eagle Mountains hold the source of the *Great Avren.

Alexander (1965f) visualizes the Eagle Mountains as being located in the Snowdonia region in Wales. The most noteworthy of the peaks is called the Eagle in *The Book of Three and is described as "tall and serene . . . towers of sun-flecked ice and black stone" (BT 152/179). Alexander (1965f) also pinpoints its Welsh counterpart. "Eagle Mountain is Mount Eryri—or, I think they call it something like yr Wydfa (or Gwydfa?) now." (BT 23/39, 36/52, 108/131, 152/179; HK 103/124)

eastern strongholds: The *Daughters of Don are sent to the eastern strongholds of *Prydain, apparently a place of relative safety, during the great final battle against *Arawn *Death-Lord. The eastern strongholds are located in the northeastern section of Prydain and are sheltered from *Annuvin by the *Realm of the Fair Folk, *Medwyn's hidden valley, and the *Eagle Mountains. (HK 235/271)

Edyrnion (eh-DIR-nee-on): This noble bird, first described in *The High King as "an enormous eagle," dwells in *Medwyn's hidden valley (HK 89/108). He is introduced while perching on the back of Medwyn's chair. Edyrnion is sent to rally the eagles of *Prydain against *Arawn *Death-Lord.

In *The Foundling, Edyrnion pledges support from all eagles in battling against the *Chief Huntsman of *Annuvin. Though he is ridiculed by the impudent *Kadwyr, Edyrnion later bears the wounded crow to *Medwyn's valley to be cared for and sheltered.

The *Mabinogion tells of a wise eagle much like Edyrnion. The Eagle of Gwern Abwy appears in the story of "Kilhwch [*Kilhuch] and *Olwen." He is the oldest animal in the world and because of his wisdom is able to help King Arthur's knights locate the secret prison of Mabon. Finding Mabon is an important step in Kilhuch's quest to win Olwen's hand in marriage (M 247).

The name Edyrnion (spelled Edeyrnion) also appears in the Mabinogion. However, it is apparently the name of a town in Merionethshire, Wales (M 377).

See also Characters—fantasy.

(HK 89/108; F 42/49, 45/53, 49/58; M 247, 377, 387)

eggs, magic: Acquired from a reluctant *Gwystyl, these *Fair Folk eggs produce great clouds of smoke when thrown or cracked. The eggs are used by *Eilonwy, *Fflewddur, and *Rhun in a plan to rescue *Taran and *Gwydion from the evil *Magg. Creating a diversion with the eggs and magical *mushrooms that explode, they hope to reach the prison cells and free their friends. It is the diversion created by King *Rhun, however, that proves most successful in the rescue attempt.

See also Fantastic objects.

(HK 64/80, 70/87, 75/92)

Eiddileg (eye-DIL-eg): Eiddileg is the King of the *Fair Folk, sometimes called the *Dwarf King (BT 139/165). His kingdom, the *Kingdom of Tylwyth Teg or the *Realm of the Fair Folk, is located in the *Eagle Mountains of northern *Prydain. *Taran and the *Companions are captured by Eiddileg and the Fair Folk when they wander into a snare designed to catch anyone coming too close to *Tylwyth Teg. A whirlpool in *Black Lake pulls the Companions down into Eiddileg's realm. Dripping and befuddled, the Companions are brought before "a dwarfish figure with a bristling yellow beard," who is wearing "a robe of garish red and green" with rings sparkling from his plump fingers (BT 136/161).

Eiddileg has magical powers, as illustrated not only by his "whirlpool," but also by his ability to freeze Taran and *Fflewddur when they threaten to draw their blades. He is blustery and tries to be intimidating, but the Dwarf King is actually softhearted and kind. He is, however, overly dramatic in his speech and his actions. When *Eilonwy calls him conceited, stubborn, and selfish, Eiddileg explodes into wild dramatics.

"Conceited!" shouted Eiddileg, his eyes popping. "Selfish! You won't find anyone more openhearted and generous. How dare you say that? What do you want, my life's blood?" With that, he tore off his cloak and threw it in the air, pulled the rings from his fingers and tossed them in every direction. "Go ahead! Take it all! Leave me ruined! What else do you want—my whole kingdom? Do you want to leave? Go, by all means. The sooner the better! Stubborn? I'm too soft! It will be the death of me! But little you care!" (BT 142/168)

*Gurgi discovers that Eiddileg has found *Hen Wen, the object of Taran's search. The king had never planned to tell the Companions that the oracular pig is in Tylwyth Teg. Eilonwy tells Eiddileg that he should be ashamed of himself for keeping such a secret, but he still refuses to turn Hen Wen over to them. "'Finders keepers,' the Dwarf King snapped" (BT 144/170). However, Eiddileg's rough exterior suddenly dissolves when Taran mentions that there is a question of honesty and honor to be considered.

Eiddileg blinked and looked sideways. He took out his orange kerchief and mopped his brow again. "Honor," he muttered, "yes, I was afraid you'd come to that. True, the Fair Folk never break their word. Well," he sighed, "that's the price for being openhearted and generous. So be it. You shall have your pig." (BT 145/171)

In his weak moment, Eiddileg also consents to giving the Companions supplies, weapons, and even a guide to help them complete their quest. He reacts to the requests as though they are too much to tolerate. But his blustery front erodes when Eilonwy steps up to his throne, bends, and kisses the king on the top of his head.

"Thank you," she whispered, "you're a perfectly lovely king."
"Out! Out!" the dwarf cried. As the stone door closed behind him, Taran saw King Eiddileg fondling his head and beaming happily. (BT 146/172)

Though Eiddileg only appears in *The Book of Three, he is mentioned often in the other books of the Prydain series, mostly by *Doli. Doli of the Fair Folk is the guide Eiddileg assigns to the Companions, and he becomes one of their fellowship. As *The High King concludes, *Dallben informs Taran that the age of enchantments is over, and therefore Eiddileg and all Fair Folk will return forever to their own realm. Eiddileg commands the barring of all passages to his kingdom (HK 229/264).

*Lady Charlotte Guest's notes to the *Mabinogion include an entry about Eiddilig the Dwarf. Eiddilig is said to have taught his illusions to

Rhuddlwm (*Rhuddlum) the Giant, one of the principal enchanters in Welsh legend (M 213).

See also Characters—fantasy.
(BT 136+/161+; BC 10/21, 50/69, 58/78, 65/87, 158/199; TW 78/99, 110/134, 115/139; HK 61/77, 67/83, 80/98, 151/178, 177/206, 229/264; M 213)

**Eilonwy (eye-LAHN-wee): Eilonwy, the irrepressible heroine of the *Prydain Chronicles, appears early in *The Book of Three*. She meets *Taran in the dungeon of *Spiral Castle where he is being held prisoner by *Achren. Because Eilonwy is supposedly Achren's niece, she wanders the evil castle in relative freedom. She drops her *bauble, a golden light-producing sphere, into Taran's cell and asks him to hand it to her. From the moment Eilonwy speaks, her strong-willed, straightforward personality is revealed. She talks nonstop to Taran through the cell bars and chastises him for not paying attention to what she has told him.

> "Haven't I just been and finished telling you? Are you slow-witted? I'm so sorry for you. It's terrible to be dull and stupid. What's your name?" she went on. "It makes me feel funny not knowing someone's name. Wrong-footed, you know, or as if I had three thumbs on one hand, if you see what I mean." (BT 51/69)

Eilonwy is quick to express her opinion on matters. She immediately disclaims any kind feelings toward Achren and states grandly her true lineage. "'I am Eilonwy. Daughter of *Angharad. Daughter of *Regat. . . . My ancestors,' she said proudly, 'are the *Sea People. I am of the blood of *Llyr Half-Speech, the *Sea King'" (BT 54–55/73).

According to a description of Angharad in *The Foundling*, she and her daughter must have shared similar appearances (F 29/33). The initial description of Eilonwy is as follows:

> Eilonwy . . . had, in addition to blue eyes, long hair of reddish gold reaching to her waist. Her face, though smudged, was delicate, elfin, with high cheekbones. Her short, white robe, mud-stained, was girdled with silver links. A *crescent moon of silver hung from a fine chain around her neck. She was one or two years younger than he [Taran], but fully as tall. (BT 54/72)

Though Taran thinks Eilonwy a scatter-brained child at first, she soon proves her resourcefulness and intelligence. She leads *Fflewddur Fflam, *Melyngar, and Taran out of Spiral Castle by way of the maze of tunnels beneath the stronghold. When she and Taran are making their way to freedom, they stumble upon the secret *barrow of King *Rhitta, and Eilonwy takes from the dead king the sword of legend, *Dyrnwyn. The removal of Dyrnwyn destroys Spiral Castle, and Eilonwy and Taran barely escape its collapse.

Assuming the *Prince of Don perished in the destruction of Spiral Castle, Eilonwy, Taran, and Fflewddur band together to finish as best they can *Gwydion's quest to find *Hen Wen and warn *Caer Dathyl of the *Horned King. Though the fellowship is tenuous at first, and even more so when *Gurgi joins the group, this is the beginning of a companionship that will endure. Taran, however, trusts no one at the onset, and makes the tough-minded Eilonwy cry when he calls her a traitor and a liar. He suspects her of purposely leaving Gwydion to die in Spiral Castle. But the *Companions come to depend on one another, and Taran and Eilonwy plant the seeds for an eventual romance.

Eilonwy's sharp tongue is evidenced repeatedly throughout *The Book of Three*. For example, when Taran suggests Fflewddur escort Eilonwy to her relatives, she retorts quickly. "If *you* [Fflewddur] . . . try to conduct me to my mean, stupid kinsmen—and they're hardly related to me in the first place—that harp will be in pieces around your ears!" (BT 92/113). Later, when the Companions stumble into the *Realm of the Fair Folk, she chastens King *Eiddileg. "You should be ashamed of yourself," she says (BT 144/170), and then tells him flatly, "If you . . . [keep us here,] you *are* a thief and a wretch!" (BT 145/171).

Eilonwy is also given to making comparisons, many of which do not seem applicable considering the circumstances. She says to Taran, for example, "I'm not sure I'm going to help you any more at all, after the way you've behaved; and calling me those horrid names, that's like putting caterpillars in somebody's hair" (BT 77/97–98). Later in *The Book of Three*, when Taran finds the lost Hen Wen, Eilonwy gaily observes that "it's always nice to see two friends meet again. It's like waking up with the sun shining" (BT 147/173–174). And when *Doli can't make himself invisible, the princess counsels that "it's silly . . . to worry because you can't do something you simply can't do. That's worse than trying to make yourself taller by standing on your head" (BT 150/177). "I can't stand people who say 'I told you so,'" she says at one point in the story. "That's worse than someone coming up and eating your dinner before you have a chance to sit down" (BT 159/187).

Courage is another of Eilonwy's traits. She refuses to run from *Arawn's deathless warriors, the *Cauldron-Born, when Taran commands her to flee. She stands with the others against them. At this point, we also glimpse Eilonwy's latent magical powers. She murmurs a phrase over an arrow and shoots it into the air above the Cauldron-Born. The arrow produces a great silvery web that settles over their foes. Unfortunately, the spell is weak, and the net is too flimsy to hold the warriors captive (BT 104/126–127). But Taran later compliments her "enchantment." Eilonwy blushes but quickly recovers by saying, "You were more interested in that [the enchantment]; you didn't care whether *I* was in danger" (BT 106/128). Poor Taran, yet to understand women and especially one such as this, is at a loss for words. Soon after, he tries to express his true feelings.

> "What I meant was: I really was worried about you. But the web surprised me so much I forgot to mention it. It was courageous of you to stand up against the Cauldron warriors. I just wanted to tell you that."
>
> "You took long enough getting around to it," said Eilonwy, a tone of satisfaction in her voice. (BT 107/129)

This marks the point at which Eilonwy and Taran begin to develop their feelings of love for one another. Though they argue and grumble at each other throughout the series, their spats become much more like lovers' quarrels. For example, Eilonwy will often say to Taran, "I'm not speaking to you," but she always does (CL 170/201; HK 95/114; etc.).

As *The Book of Three* concludes, the Companions successfully complete their quest and are rewarded by Gwydion and King *Math. Eilonwy receives a ring from Prince Gwydion that will later prove to have much-wanted magical powers. *Dallben also reveals at this time that Eilonwy is indeed a true *Princess of Llyr.

As *The Black Cauldron* begins, Eilonwy and Taran quarrel again because Taran is so clumsy in his "advances." Dallben presents him a sword, and he wants Eilonwy to gird it on him.

> "Look!" he cried. "Dallben gave me this! Gird it on me—I mean, if you please. Say you will. I want you to be the one to do it."
>
> Eilonwy turned to him in surprise. "Yes, of course," she said, blushing, "if you really . . ."
>
> "I do!" cried Taran. "After all," he added, "you're the only girl in *Caer Dallben."
>
> "So that's it!" Eilonwy retorted. "I knew there was something wrong when you started being so polite. Very well, Taran of Caer Dallben, if that's your only reason you can go find someone else and I don't care how long it takes you, but the longer the better!" (BC 23–24/38)

Taran makes amends, and Eilonwy buckles on the sword. But then she discovers that she will be left behind on the quest to destroy the *Black Cauldron. True to her character, the princess goes anyway. She follows

Taran and appears beneath the shadows of the *Dark Gate of *Annuvin—just in time to share the grandest part of the adventure.

When Doli and Fflewddur return from a scouting mission within Annuvin and report that the *cauldron is missing, Eilonwy's self-assured, take-charge nature immediately surfaces. "You didn't lose it!" Eilonwy cries. "No! Oh, you pack of ninnies! Great heroes! I knew I should have gone with you from the beginning" (BC 42/60).

The Black Cauldron was taken before Doli and Fflewddur entered Annuvin. The Companions then discover that the cauldron is in the *Marshes of Morva and set out to find it. Eilonwy will hear nothing of being sent back to Caer Dallben and rides with the rest of them. When they locate the cauldron, Eilonwy again exhibits her budding powers of enchantment. She is able to discern that food offered by the witches *Orddu, *Orwen, and *Orgoch is neither poisoned nor enchanted.

The witches will not part easily with the cauldron and seek a fair trade. In a true spirit of sacrifice, Eilonwy offers her most prized possession, her bauble. The witches decline her offer, wanting instead something more personal. They ask for one of Taran's summer days, the recollection of which they could take from him. Instead, Taran relinquishes the *Brooch of Adaon, bequeathed him only days before by the son of *Taliesin. Eilonwy had hoped the offer of her bauble would keep Taran from parting with the *brooch, which had given him the gift of premonition. Her sacrifice would have been not only for *Prydain but for Taran as well.

Taran parts with the brooch, making an extreme sacrifice to obtain the cauldron. Eilonwy exhibits her solid sense of wisdom when she consoles him.

> "I realize it's no consolation to you," she said, "but if you look at it in one way, you didn't give up a thing to the enchantresses, not really. You did exchange the clasp and everything that went along with it. But, don't you see, all those things came from the clasp itself; they weren't inside of you.
>
> "I think," she added, "it would have been much worse giving up a summer day. That's part of you, I mean. I know I shouldn't want to give up a single one of mine. Or even a winter day, for the matter of that. So, when you come right down to it, Orddu didn't take anything from *you*; why, you're still yourself and you can't deny that!" (BC 132/168–169)

With the impetus of Eilonwy's spunk, the Companions see the cauldron destroyed. She stands against *Ellidyr, who nearly succeeds in wresting the credit from Taran for finding and winning the cauldron. Her courage, insight, and optimism are greatly responsible for maintaining the Companions throughout the ordeal of this quest.

*The Castle of Llyr is Eilonwy's story. Alexander says that what befalls the heroine in this book is "as important, and perilous, as the hero's own quest" (CL viii/15). He also notes that "The Castle of Llyr is, in a sense, more romantic than the preceding chronicles—Taran is noticeably aware of his feelings toward Eilonwy" (CL viii/15).

Eilonwy is sent to live on the *Isle of Mona to learn from King *Rhuddlum and Queen *Teleria how to be a lady and a princess. "I don't care about being a princess," she says bluntly. "And since I'm already a young lady, how else could I behave? That's like asking a fish to learn how to swim!" (CL 4/18).

Dallben surveys the princess-turned-farm-girl and replies, "I have never seen a fish with skinned knees, torn robe, and unshod feet. They would ill become him, as they ill become you" (CL 4/18).

Taran and Gurgi escort Eilonwy to the Isle of Mona. When the Companions meet the "feckless" and clumsy Prince *Rhun, son of King Rhuddlum, Taran states bluntly that the prince's birthright cannot be enough to make him worthy of his rank. Eilonwy shows her innate wisdom when she replies, "It seems to me that if an *Assistant Pig-Keeper does the best he can, and a prince does the best he can, there's no difference between them" (CL 10/26). Eilonwy, realizing Taran is jealous, retorts with one of her wonderful comparisons. "I really believe you're jealous. And sorry for yourself. And that's as ridiculous as—as painting your nose green!" (CL 11/26). But Taran soon learns that Rhuddlum plans to wed Rhun to Eilonwy, and he is crestfallen. Eilonwy knows nothing of the king's plans and certainly would not agree to the arrangement. But Taran is so convinced of his destiny to be merely a common pig-keeper that he does not question the royal decision.

Eilonwy's independent spirit is no less dampened by the ladies of Rhuddlum's court. "I've never met such silly women!" she says. "Why, I don't think there's one of them that's ever drawn a sword" (CL 27/44). She has much more interest in adventuring and wants to explore the island.

Taran is to return to Caer Dallben once Eilonwy has been welcomed on Mona. But then both Fflewddur Fflam and Prince Gwydion (disguised as a shoemaker) appear on the Isle of Mona. Gwydion has been directed by Dallben to turn his attention toward the island and Eilonwy, for the princess may be in danger. The source of the danger seems to come from the evil enchantress Achren. In spite of the warning, Eilonwy is abducted by

*Magg, *Chief Steward of Rhuddlum, secretly in Achren's employ. Taran stays to search for the princess.

The Companions finally discover that Achren is keeping Eilonwy in the ruins of *Caer Colur just off the coast of the Isle of Mona. Before Gwydion and the others attempt her rescue, the Prince of Don explains why the evil enchantress is holding the princess captive.

Eilonwy is the last Princess of Llyr. For generations the daughters of the *House of Llyr were the most skillful enchantresses, using powers with wisdom and kindness. Eilonwy's mother, Angharad, fled Caer Colur, the ancient seat of the House of Llyr, to marry against her mother's wishes. Presumably, the young man (*Geraint) who took Angharad away was Eilonwy's father (F 35–38/40–44).

Angharad carried a *book of spells and the *Golden Pelydryn away from Caer Colur with her. Both objects are items of great power, but the spells may only be read by the light of the Pelydryn and only be worked by a Princess of Llyr who has reached womanhood. The Golden Pelydryn was placed in Eilonwy's hands when she was a child. Angharad thought the bauble would be hidden as a child's toy.

But Achren recognized the Pelydryn. Understanding its powers, she kidnapped the child Eilonwy and the bauble in hope that someday she could use them to possess even greater power. Eilonwy and the bauble slipped from Achren's grasp, but she knows the time is ripe for her to abduct the princess again. Though the evil enchantress has lost much of her power, she hopes to use Eilonwy, the Pelydryn, and the book of spells to recapture her days of glory. She plans to rule all Prydain from Caer Colur. Fate, however, has placed both the Golden Pelydryn and the book of spells into the hands of the Companions.

Achren holds Eilonwy under a deep spell. When Taran reaches her tower "cell," the princess does not recognize him. Achren controls her so completely that she can direct the princess to inflict enchantments of pain upon her friends. "[Eilonwy's] hand, pointing straight at the baffled Gurgi, suddenly tensed. With a sharp cry of pain, Gurgi stiffened and clutched his head" (CL 146/175). Using the princess as a weapon, Achren is able to coerce the Golden Pelydryn and the book of spells from Gwydion and the Companions. With all the missing pieces coming together, Achren seems to have gained ultimate control. But she overlooks the power of love.

With the Pelydryn and the book in hand, Eilonwy is commanded by Achren to "read out the spells" (CL 155/184). But the princess is not so easily manipulated.

Eilonwy, Taran realized in a surge of hope, was struggling against all that held her. The anguished girl was beyond all threats of Achren, beyond all help from the companions.

Then, suddenly, her lonely combat ended. Taran cried out in despair as Eilonwy raised the glowing sphere and in a quick motion brought it close to the empty pages.

The Golden Pelydryn flared brighter than he had ever seen it and Taran flung up his hand to shield his eyes. Light flooded the Hall. . . .

Suddenly Eilonwy cast the book to the flagstones. From the pages burst a crimson cloud that spread into a sheet of fire, leaping upward to the vaulted ceiling of the *Great Hall. (CL 155/184–185)

Once the book is destroyed, Magg opens the gates that hold back the sea, and Caer Colur is flooded. Eilonwy, unconscious from her ordeal, is dragged by Taran toward the shore of Mona. Both are finally pulled ashore by the great cat, *Llyan. Eilonwy is slow to regain consciousness and lies close to death. When she finally recovers, the princess tells Taran that even while entranced, the decision to relinquish her powers as an *enchantress of Llyr was a difficult one.

"Yet, it was as though there were two of me. One did and one didn't want to give up the spells. I knew it was my only chance to become an enchantress, and if I gave up my powers then that would be the end of it. I suppose," she said softly to Taran, "I felt a little the way you did long ago in the Marshes of Morva, when you had to decide to give up *Adaon's magic brooch." (CL 167/197)

True to her character, Eilonwy chooses to sacrifice her heritage for the love of her friends and her land. It seems her bauble is sacrificed as well, but *Kaw somehow retrieves it from the waves, returning it to the princess.

Eilonwy and Taran must part as originally planned. Eilonwy stays on Mona to be trained as a lady, but there are no longer any misconceptions concerning her betrothal to Rhun. She and Taran make a pledge not to forget one another while they are apart. An ancient *battle horn that washes to shore from the submerged ruins of Caer Colur serves as Eilonwy's token of her pledge to Taran.

Eilonwy does not appear in *Taran Wanderer, but she is always in Taran's thoughts during the story. Taran's quest to find the secret of his parentage is prompted by his wish to marry Eilonwy. He is certain they may not marry if he cannot prove his noble lineage.

In *The High King, Eilonwy returns to Caer Dallben. She arrives before Taran returns from his wanderings. Her head is encircled by a gold band,

and she looks every bit a princess and a lady. Yet, she complains bitterly about the tedious training on Mona.

> "And if you think living in a castle is pleasant," Eilonwy went on, without a pause for breath, "I can tell you it isn't. It's weary and dreary! They've made me sleep in beds with goosefeather pillows enough to stifle you; I'm sure the geese needed them more than I did—the feathers, that is, not the pillows. And servitors to bring you exactly what you don't want to eat. And washing your hair whether it needs it or not. And sewing and weaving and curtsying and all such I don't even want to think about. I've not drawn a sword for I don't know how long." (HK 5/15–16)

Then Eilonwy removes the golden circlet from her brow, complaining that it has rubbed a blister and makes her head ache, "like someone squeezing your neck, only higher up" (HK 9/20). "'Ah, Princess,' Dallben said with a furrowed smile, 'a crown is more discomfort than adornment. If you have learned that, you have already learned much'" (HK 9/20).

Immediately, Eilonwy notices a change in Taran. "That's odd," she tells him. "There's something different about you. . . . I mean, unless you told someone they'd never guess you were an Assistant Pig-Keeper" (HK 5/16). Much of what she senses is maturity and peace of mind. Still impressed by the difference, Eilonwy unfurls an embroidered cloth she has created for Taran. It is a picture of Hen Wen on a green background. Taran points out that Hen's eyes are brown not blue, though he assures the princess he values it greatly. It becomes Taran's banner (the *banner of the White Pig) around which he rallies the *Commot Folk to battle against Arawn.

Indomitable as ever, Eilonwy will not stay behind when the quest to retrieve Dyrnwyn from Annuvin begins. She informs the Companions, Dallben, and Gwydion that she won't insist on riding with everyone. However, she may get the urge to go out picking wildflowers. "I might, by accident, lose my way, and mistakenly happen to catch up with you. By then, it would be too late for me to come home, through no fault of my own" (HK 34/46). Eilonwy is allowed to ride as far as *Caer Cadarn, the stronghold of King *Smoit.

On the way to Caer Cadarn, Eilonwy detours to *Avren Harbor with Fflewddur and Rhun. The Companions plan to meet at Smoit's castle. When Eilonwy and her traveling companions arrive at Smoit's, she immediately senses that something inside the stronghold is amiss. Indeed, Taran and the others, including King Smoit, have been taken captive by Arawn's forces under the command of Magg. Eilonwy's sharp reasoning and acute sense of awareness are ignored by Fflewddur who is sure nothing is wrong. But the princess forces Fflewddur and Rhun to heed her warning. When they discover that Eilonwy is right, Fflewddur and Rhun willingly follow her lead in formulating a plan to rescue their friends. Without the resourceful leadership of Eilonwy in Chapters 5 and 6 of *The High King*, the quest to save Prydain would have come to an abrupt end.

After their escape from Magg's clutches, Eilonwy accompanies Taran to the *Free Commots to rally an army for the *Sons of Don. She binds to a spear her embroidered cloth showing Hen Wen and deems it Taran's "battle flag" (HK 83/101). She dons rough warrior's garb while in the *Commots and wears nothing else until Arawn is defeated. Eilonwy even refuses to change when Taran's troops arrive at Caer Dathyl and the court of the *High King. She barely consents to washing her hair and will *not* join the women in their spinning and weaving chambers. "Listening to their giggling and gossiping—why it's worse than having your ears tickled with feathers" (HK 106/127). When the traitorous *Pryderi attacks Caer Dathyl, Eilonwy ignores the order to stay in the castle. On the battlefield, Taran sees the princess suddenly rush forward on *Lluagor, her plaited hair under a leather helmet and a lance in her grasp. "Go back," Taran shouts at her. "Have you lost your wits?" Eilonwy smiles and retorts, "I understand you're upset, but that's no cause to be rude" (HK 125/149).

After Caer Dathyl falls, Taran and his troops are sent to slow the progress of the Cauldron-Born as they march back to Annuvin. In a battle with the deathless host, Eilonwy and Gurgi are separated from Taran's army. Wandering in the *Hills of Bran-Galedd, the two are captured by *Dorath's Company, a ruthless band of marauders. *Dorath and Taran had clashed in *Taran Wanderer*, and unfortunately the mercenary recognizes Gurgi. Though Eilonwy is at first taken for a boy because of her attire, Dorath soon discovers not only that she is a young woman but that she is Taran's beloved. He decides to take his revenge against Taran by raping the princess. Though Gurgi tries to stop Dorath, it is the wolves, *Brynach and *Briavael, sent by *Medwyn to rally the animals against Arawn, who prevent the unholy act. The wolves kill all of Dorath's Company. Eilonwy discovers the ability to understand the wolves by "hearing with the heart" (HK 167/195), and Brynach and Briavael lead Eilonwy and Gurgi to Taran.

From high ground, Eilonwy finally spots Taran's troop, but she also sees they are on a collision course with the *Huntsmen of Annuvin. She raises her bauble into the night sky, and it erupts with light that makes the mountain country as bright as day. Taran sees the danger and also recognizes Eilonwy has returned. This occurrence also fulfills part of

Hen Wen's prophecy. "Night turn to noon . . . Ere Dyrnwyn be regained" (HK 31/43; 180/210).

As Arawn is destroyed and the tale of Prydain comes to an end, the Princess Eilonwy is required to leave with the Sons of Don for the *Summer Country. The age of *magic is over, and all with the blood of enchantment must depart. Taran is invited to travel with them, and he asks Eilonwy to marry him. In typical fashion Eilonwy answers, "Well, indeed . . . I wondered if you'd ever get round to asking. Of course I will, and if you'd given half a thought to the question you'd have already known my answer" (HK 230/266). But Taran is guided by his destiny, and knows he must stay in Prydain. It breaks his and Eilonwy's hearts that they must part. It seems impossible to the princess that Taran would sacrifice her to stay in a world of sorrow. Then Dallben reveals that Taran is to be the new High King of Prydain. *The Book of Three had prophesied that the new High King would indeed choose a kingdom of sorrow (Prydain) over a kingdom of happiness (Summer Country).

Eilonwy offers Taran her bauble, the Golden Pelydryn, as a remembrance of her. But as she is about to leave with the Sons of Don, the princess rebels. "It's not fair!" she cries, stamping her foot. "I didn't ask for magical powers. That's worse than being made to wear a pair of shoes that doesn't fit! I don't see why I have to keep them!" (HK 245/282–283). Then Dallben reveals yet another secret. The ring Gwydion gave Eilonwy long ago has the power to remove her enchantments. "Turn the ring once upon your finger," says Dallben. "Wish with all your heart for your enchanted powers to vanish" (HK 246/283).

> Wondering and almost fearful, Eilonwy closed her eyes and did the enchanter's bidding. The ring flared suddenly, but only for a moment. The girl gave a sharp cry of pain. And in Taran's hand the light of the golden bauble winked out. (HK 246/284)

Dallben's final official act in Prydain seals together Eilonwy and Taran. "Come, clasp hands the two of you, and pledge each other your troth" (HK 246/284). King Taran and Queen Eilonwy rule Prydain for many happy years. Their lives are the stuff from which stories are made.

As pointed out by Elizabeth Lane (1973:26), Eilonwy has no direct counterpart in the *Mabinogion, but combines the qualities of many of its heroines. The most notable example comes from the story, "*Pwyll Prince of Dyved." When Pwyll pursues on horseback the beautiful and mysterious Rhiannon, he can never get any closer to her. Finally he calls to her, asking the maiden to please stop and wait for him. "'I will stay gladly,' said she, 'and it were better for thy horse hadst thou asked it long since'" (M 346). Eilonwy's sharp wit and tongue are reminiscent of Rhiannon (Lane, 1973:26).

Another interesting link to Welsh tradition is evident in Eilonwy's superstition about ghosts. In *The Book of Three,* Eilonwy wonders if the wind wailing from King Rhitta's barrow is a ghost. "I don't have any beans to spit at them," she says, "and that's about the only thing that will really do for a ghost" (BT 70/89). Robert Graves, in *The White Goddess,* explains that "the bean is traditionally associated with ghosts—the Greek and Roman homoeopathic remedy against ghosts was to spit beans at them" (WG 42). Much Roman tradition was transmitted to the British Isles during their occupation.

Eilonwy's strong, independent personality was somewhat unusual for a female character in a book for young readers in the 1960s, when girls were often portrayed in more passive roles. However, Eilonwy is probably in character for a woman of ancient Celtic heritage. History records that Celtic women held important positions of leadership in their tribes. But Lloyd Alexander attributes Eilonwy's personality to something other than his knowledge of ancient Celtic politics.

> . . . I did know that Celtic women, like those in many ancient societies, held leadership and influential positions. Still, this historical fact was not really in my thoughts when Eilonwy emerged.
>
> Quite simply, her personality . . . reflects my own attitude. It really comes from my personal observations and experiences. From as far back as I can remember, my mother, and all the women family members, my women teachers, girl friends, and my daughter, and certainly Janine [Alexander's wife] were strong, active, competent. Not one of them fit the passive stereotype! In short, my own accumulated experience tells me that it's merely a fact, my heroines are—well, that's how I know women to be. (Alexander, 1986d)

In the early stages of writing the Prydain cycle, Alexander received a suggestion from Ann Durell, his editor, that Taran and Eilonwy should have different names. She suggested the name Branwen be substituted for Eilonwy. Branwen is easier to decode and pronounce and comes directly from the *Mabinogion.* Alexander wrote to Ann saying he had been thinking seriously about the changes and explained carefully why he wanted to leave the names unchanged. The letter ends with a postscript that expresses Alexander's emotional attachment. "P.S. Checked with Taran and Eilonwy themselves. For once, they both agree: 'Don't change our names!'" (Jacobs, 1978:277)

See also Characters—fantasy.

Ellidyr (ELLI-deer) Son of Pen-Llarcau (pen LAHR-kow): Ellidyr appears in *The Black Cauldron* as the *Sons of Don organize a quest to destroy *Arawn's *cauldron of death. He is only a few years older than *Taran. His hair is tawny and his eyes black and deep-set in his pale face (BC 5/15–16).

Ellidyr's arrogance and pride are evidenced immediately upon his arrival at *Caer Dallben. He calls rudely to Taran, "You, there! Pig-boy!" and then, soon after, is angry when *Dallben does not give him the deference he feels his rank deserves. Dallben explains at least part of the reason the young prince flaunts his heritage:

> "He is the youngest son of old *Pen-Llarcau in the northern lands; his elder brothers have inherited what little there was of family fortune, and even that is gone. Ellidyr has only his name and his sword, though I admit he uses them both with something less than wisdom." (BC 22/36)

Ellidyr's lack of a kingdom to go with his title also accounts for his less than regal appearance. "Though of excellent quality, his garments had seen much wear, and his cloak was purposely draped to hide his threadbare attire" (BC 5/16).

Ellidyr's pride stabs his soul like a poisoned dagger. *Adaon, the son of the *Chief Bard *Taliesin, sees in a vision that the prince carries a "black beast" on his shoulder—the beast of pride and arrogance that shall eventually devour him. It does not improve Ellidyr's nature when *Gwydion assigns him to guard the pack animals and secure the retreat of the other warriors from *Annuvin. He and Taran are thrown together under the command of Adaon.

As the quest proceeds, Ellidyr becomes more sullen and bitter. His feelings toward Taran deteriorate continually. Early in the story, he forces past Taran on a narrow, treacherous trail, causing Taran's horse (*Melynlas) to fall over the steep embankment. Though the prince shows momentary concern, he masks it quickly, claiming concern only for the horse. Ellidyr exhibits superhuman strength at this point in the story by lifting Melynlas until he is able to clamber back onto the trail.

When Adaon's band discovers that the *Black Cauldron has already been taken from Arawn, they set out anew to find it. From *Gwystyl of the *Fair Folk, they discover it has been taken to the *Marshes of Morva. Ellidyr, seeking personal glory, deserts the band to search on his own. Adaon is killed by the *Huntsmen of Annuvin shortly after Ellidyr vanishes, and Taran adds Adaon's death to the list of Ellidyr's sins, for they sorely needed his help during the battle.

Taran and the *Companions sacrifice greatly to obtain the Black Cauldron from the witches, *Orddu, *Orwen, and *Orgoch. As they struggle to take the evil instrument to Caer Dallben, it slips into the *River Tevvyn. Ellidyr suddenly appears as they try unsuccessfully to remove it from the water. It seems as if the "black beast" has nearly eaten away his soul, for Ellidyr accuses Taran of stealing his justly deserved glory. "'Have you cheated me once more?' His faced darkened with rage. 'Do I risk my life again so that a pig-boy may rob me of my prize?' His eyes were frenzied and he made to seize Taran by the throat" (BC 145/184).

The beast tightens its grip on the *Prince of Pen-Llarcau. He will not help remove the cauldron unless every member of the band swears an oath first. They must consent to give Ellidyr full credit for finding and winning the Black Cauldron. "I care for my honor," Ellidyr shouts (BC 147/188). He is pitifully unaware that he has instead relinquished any honor he may have once had. The Companions agree to Ellidyr's terms only because it is imperative to get the cauldron to safety. However, when the cauldron is freed from the river, Ellidyr's madness suddenly envelops him. Deciding the Companions will betray him, the prince tries to kill Taran, who falls into the river, and then chases the others into the forest. He escapes with the Black Cauldron.

Ellidyr and the Companions soon meet again—prisoners of the traitorous King *Morgant. Morgant has succumbed to evil influences, deciding to use the cauldron to create his own armies of *Cauldron-Born. In Morgant's prison tent, Ellidyr—battered, bloody, and near death—exhibits humility for the first time. "I would make up the ill I have done all of you," he says (BC 168/210). When Taran challenges his sorrow, Ellidyr replies, "I stole the cauldron out of pride, not evil. I swear to you, on whatever honor remains to me, I would not have used it. Yes, I would have taken your glory for my own. But I, too, would have borne the *Crochan to Gwydion and offered it for destruction. Believe this much of me" (BC 168/210).

*Doli of the *Fair Folk comes to rescue the Companions. As Doli unties Ellidyr's bonds, the prince says, "I had not strength enough to break my own bonds, but I can still serve you" (BC 171/213). Summoning the last of his remaining strength, he runs from the tent toward the *Black Crochan. Though pierced by the sword of one of Morgant's warriors, he fights his way forward and flings himself into the cauldron. The only way the cauldron can be destroyed is if a living man knowingly and willingly sacrifices his life by climbing within it.

The Crochan shuddered like a living thing. In horror and dismay, Taran cried out again to Ellidyr. He fought his way toward the cauldron, but in another instant a sharp clap, louder than thunder, rang above the clearing. The leafless trees trembled to their roots; the branches writhed as if in agony. Then, while echoes ripped the air and a whirlwind screamed overhead, the cauldron split and shattered. The jagged shards fell away from the lifeless form of Ellidyr. (BC 172/214–215)

Ellidyr in part redeems himself by giving his life for *Prydain.

Upon the Prince of Pen-Llarcau's death, his steed, *Islimach, leaps over a cliff to her death. Her devotion indeed honors Ellidyr. Gwydion honors the rebellious prince as well. "We shall raise a *barrow to his memory. Islimach, too, shall rest with him, for they are both now at peace" (BC 174/217).

The name Ellidyr is used numerous times in the *Mabinogion, though the spelling varies (Elidyr, Eiladyr), as does the character. Eiladyr, the son of Pen Llarcau, is mentioned briefly in the story "Kilhwch [*Kilhuch] and *Olwen" (M 228). However, the character of Evnissyen in the story "Branwen the *Daughter of Llyr" is much like Alexander's Ellidyr. Evnissyen is the quarrelsome half-brother of Branwen. Like Ellidyr, he is prideful and arrogant. He also repents of grievous crimes against his friends and family by sacrificing himself to destroy a cauldron of rejuvenation, which is much like the Black Crochan. This cauldron is also being used by the enemies of Evnissyen's family to create renewed warriors from dead bodies. Evnissyen hides himself among the dead and is flung into it. The same rules apply as in Prydain—a living man must give his life to destroy the cauldron. "And he [Evnissyen] stretched himself out in the cauldron, so that he rent the cauldron into four pieces, and burst his own heart also" (M 381).
(BC 5+/15+; M 227, 228, 334, 381)

enchantresses of Llyr (LEER): *See* House of Llyr.

Eyes of Annuvin (ah-NOO-vin): *See* gwythaint.

F

❖

Fair Folk: The Fair Folk are generally a race of small beings who live in the *Kingdom of Twylyth Teg or the *Realm of the Fair Folk. Their ruler, the *Dwarf King *Eiddileg, holds in disgust the "insipid, irritating names" given to their race by humans, including "Happy Family," "Little People," and "Fair Folk" (BT 137/162). *Doli and *Gwystyl, both of whom play important roles in the Chronicles, are Fair Folk.

Though the Fair Folk seem to be primarily dwarves, *Taran spots other types of creatures in the Kingdom of Twylyth Teg. "Looking closer, Taran saw not all were dwarfs; some were tall, slender, with white robes; others were covered with glistening scales, like fish; still others fluttered large, delicate wings" (BT 138/163). Alexander explains that there are several "branches" of the Fair Folk community. *Lake Sprites are one branch; the singers, *Children of Evening, are another. The dwarves are yet another branch. "In my own mind," says Alexander (1985b), "the categories are mutually exclusive . . . a dwarf wouldn't be a Child of Evening . . . a dwarf wouldn't be a Lake Sprite or anything else."

The Kingdom of Twylyth Teg, a subterranean realm, is located in northern *Prydain amid the *Eagle Mountains. The *Black Lake, with its whirlpool for snagging alien intruders, is but one of its many entrances. The Fair Folk also maintain many *way posts, such as Gwystyl's near *Annuvin (BC 96/72–73).

The Fair Folk are the only inhabitants of Prydain who did not lose their treasures of knowledge and magical tools to *Arawn *Death-Lord. "Even Arawn might think twice before trifling with them [Fair Folk]," says *Fflewddur Fflam (TW 67/86). Indeed, magical Fair Folk objects (*Angharad's gem, Taran's *battle horn) surface throughout the *Prydain Chronicles. Fair Folk gems, for instance, are noted for giving longer life spans (TW 92/113).

Though tremendously powerful, the inhabitants of the Kingdom of Twylyth Teg are unable to venture too near Annuvin. In *The High King, Doli's army is forced to turn back as the troop nears the evil domain. "That close to Arawn's realm, Fair Folk would die," Doli explains (HK 181/212).

Though the Fair Folk have intervened in the lives of men, they prefer to remain to themselves. But without their aid, Taran would likely have not succeeded in his quests. The Fair Folk rescue Taran and *Craddoc from an icy grave. They lead Taran's troops through the *Hills of Bran-Galedd toward Annuvin. Many times, Doli and even the reluctant Gwystyl rescue the *Companions when death seems assured. But as the Chronicles draw to a conclusion, Eiddileg calls all Fair Folk home. The age of enchantments ends, and no longer will Fair Folk come above ground. The passages to the Kingdom of Twylyth Teg are barred forever (HK 229/264).

In *Lady Charlotte Guest's notes to the *Mabinogion, *Twylyth Teg is explained as a race of "beneficent and joyous beings" often called "Family of Beauty" (M 263). They "dance in the moonlight on the velvet sward, in their airy and flowing robes of blue and green, or white or scarlet, and . . . delight in showering benefits on the more favoured of the human race" (M 263). Gwyn ab Nudd (perhaps *Gwyn the Hunter?) is their sovereign (M 263). Though this description does not match the likes of Doli and the dwarves, it certainly approximates some of the other branches of the Fair Folk, namely the Children of Evening and perhaps the Lake Sprites.

See also Characters—fantasy.
(BT 137/162+; BC 12/23, 19/33, 50/68, 53/72, 158/199, 176/219; CL 17/33, 86/110; TW 67/86, 77/97, 92/113, 109/133, 130/155, 141/168, 155/184; HK 5/15, 9/19, 60/75, 61/77, 80/98, 151/178, 173/202, 181/212, 191+/222+; F 19/22; M 263)

Fantastic objects: According to Madsen (1976:56–57), one of the six basic motifs of high fantasy is the use of fantastic objects. The characters of high fantasy tales may employ numerous magical props in accomplishing their heroic (or dastardly) deeds. Often these fantastic objects explain otherwise unexplainable occurrences.

Such an object in the *Prydain Chronicles is the *magic sword *Dyrn-wyn. It is used to destroy *Arawn's deathless warriors, the *Cauldron-Born. The event of their "death" is only explainable through the enchantments of Dyrnwyn.

Numerous other fantastic objects are in the Chronicles. *Eilonwy's *bauble, the *Black Cauldron, *The Book of Three, the *Brooch of Adaon, the *book of spells, *Angharad's gem, *Morda's finger bone, and *Gwystyl's magic *eggs and *mushrooms are but a few.

Fernbrake Stream: This shallow stream flows through the *Commot Merin and passes near the dwelling of *Annlaw Clay-Shaper. It is from the banks of Fernbrake that Annlaw digs much of the clay he uses in his craft.

In the story of "Kilhwch [*Kilhuch] and *Olwen" in the *Mabinogion, the Hill of the Black Fernbrake is a landmark located in North Britain (M 227).
(TW 189/222; M 227)

**Fflewddur (FLEW-der) Fflam (FLAM) Son of Godo (GOH-doh): Though Fflewddur Fflam is one of the *Companions and is humble in appearance, he is in truth a king. He is a distant kinsman to Prince *Gwydion: "In the veins of a Fflam flows royal blood of the *Sons of Don!" (TW 67/86). Fflewddur's kingdom, which is "several days' journey east of *Caer Dathyl," is unbelievably tiny (BT 88/110).

> Fflewddur Fflam ruled a kingdom so small he could almost stride across it between midday and high noon. The fields and pastures grew so near his castle that sheep and cows ambled up to gaze into his bed-chamber; and the cottagers' children played in his *Great Hall, knowing he would sooner join their games than order them away. (TH 87/7)

Though at first glance Fflewddur appears to be a comic character, he is also one of wisdom, courage, and compassion. In *The Truthful Harp, a story that occurs before *Taran's tale, Fflewddur wanders away from his kingdom to become a *bard. He seems a silly chaser of dreams. Certainly he is unable to keep from stretching the truth. When he appears before the *Council of Bards, Fflewddur miserably fails to pass the bardic exam. Yet, the *Chief Bard (*Taliesin) presents the would-be bard with the *truthful harp before sending him on his way.

As Fflewddur travels away from the Council and Caer Dathyl, he happens upon an old man who is cold and ill-clad. In an act of true compassion, Fflewddur gives the man his cloak. As he turns blue from the cold, the bard says, "Take it and welcome. For the truth of the matter is, I find the day uncomfortably hot!" (TH 89/14). Barely have the words left his lips when the truthful harp shudders "as if it were alive, [bends] like an overdrawn bow" and snaps a string (TH 90/17). Throughout the *Prydain Chronicles, the truthful harp continues to remind Fflewddur when he is coloring the facts.

Fflewddur saves a child from drowning, though he himself cannot swim, and fights beside a lord who has treated him badly. The Chief Bard greets Fflewddur upon his return to Caer Dathyl and says of his recently performed deeds of kindness, "Yet those deeds were far more worthy than all your gallant fancies, for a good truth is purest gold that needs no gilding. You have the modest heart of the truly brave; but your tongue, alas, gallops faster than your head can rein it" (TH 94/30).

Fflewddur Fflam continues to travel as a "bard" at least part of each year. He is at his bardic wanderings when he visits *Spiral Castle, the stronghold of *Achren, and is promptly cast into her dungeon. He shares the dungeon with Taran *Assistant Pig-Keeper and is accidentally rescued because *Eilonwy assumes he is Prince Gwydion.

Shocked and angry to find a stranger waiting outside the castle, Taran is slow to trust Fflewddur, even though he claims to be a kinsman of Gwydion. Taran's initial assessment of Fflewddur Fflam, who introduces himself as "a bard of the harp at your service," leaves him puzzled (BT 75/95):

> The bard was tall and lanky, with a long, pointed nose. His great shock of bright yellow hair burst out in all directions, like a ragged sun. His jacket and leggings were patched at knees and elbows, and sewn with large, clumsy stitches—the work, Taran was certain, of the bard himself. A harp with a beautiful, sweeping curve was slung from his shoulder, but otherwise he looked nothing at all like the bards Taran had learned about from *The Book of Three. (BT 78/98)

Taran's assessment is accurate. Fflam is somewhat of a charlatan, and he is soon revealed when Eilonwy asks him to use his bardic training to read the *Old Writing on *Dyrnwyn's scabbard. Instead of admitting he can't decipher the runes, Fflewddur makes up a meaning. The truthful harp snaps a string. Later, Fflewddur admits he is not an "official bard" but a king who would really rather be a bard. When he describes his kingdom as "a vast realm," the harp loses two strings (BT 88/110). Finally, Fflewddur explains to his new companions the properties of his harp. "I might, ah, readjust the facts slightly," Fflewddur says, "purely for dramatic effect, you understand" (BT 89/111).

Besides Fflewddur's weakness for readjusting the facts, several other of his personality traits are introduced at his initial appearance. Fflam repeatedly uses the oath or expression "*Great Belin" (BT 74/94). *Belin, *King of the Sun, is the ancestral father of the Sons of Don and Prince Gwydion. Therefore, Fflewddur is also related to the legendary Belin. Fflewddur uses the expression "Great Belin" nearly sixty times throughout the Chronicles.

Fflewddur Fflam's sense of valor is revealed when he speaks of aiding Taran in his quest to warn the Sons of Don about the *Horned King. "'And if the hosts of the Horned King overtake me . . .' The bard slashed and thrust at the air. 'They shall know the valor of a Fflam!'" (BT 91/112). His exuberance is shown in much the same manner. When Taran suggests returning to Spiral Castle to look for Gywdion, Fflewddur reacts with a boyish vigor that becomes one of his trademarks. "'By all means,' cried the bard, his eyes lighting up. 'A Fflam to the rescue! Storm the castle! Carry it by assault! Batter down the gates!'" Of course, Spiral Castle lies in ruins, so there are no gates to batter.

As Fflewddur and his new (and lasting) Companions struggle toward Caer Dathyl to warn the Sons of Don, the bard proves that his brave words are not embellishments of the truth. He stands with *Doli and *Gurgi against the foot soldiers of the Horned King, for example, in order to allow Taran and Eilonwy to reach the *High King. Later, Fflam is given a gift for his valor by Gwydion and the *House of Don—a harp string that will never break. "Its tone shall be the truest and most beautiful," Gwydion tells him (BT 181/211).

Fflewddur is a charter member of the fellowship known as the Companions and is with Taran virtually throughout the *Chronicles of Prydain. In *The Black Cauldron, he assists Taran in acquiring the deadly *Black Crochan from the witches, *Orddu, *Orwen, and *Orgoch. Another element of Fflewddur's character is exhibited when he offers his most cherished possession, the truthful harp, in exchange for the *Black Cauldron. Fflewddur hopes that he may sacrifice not only to save *Prydain but to keep Taran from trading the *Brooch of Adaon (BC 124/158–159). This gesture of true friendship binds bard and Pig-Keeper even more strongly.

Fflewddur labors with the others to move the *cauldron to *Caer Dallben for safekeeping and breaks his arm in the effort. He accuses the Black Crochan of harming him purposely. But true to the cause, Fflewddur sees the quest through to the end. Undoubtedly, had it been necessary, he would have thrown his own body into the cauldron to destroy it.

Fflewddur Fflam surfaces on the *Isle of Mona in *The Castle of Llyr. He is supposed to be back in his kingdom ruling his people.

> "I had decided, this time, really to make a go of being a king. And so I did, for the best part of a year. Then along came spring and the barding and wandering season, and everything indoors began looking unspeakably dreary, and everything outdoors began somehow pulling at me, and next thing I knew I was on my way." (CL 17/32–33)

When the *Chief Steward of *Dinas Rhydnant (stronghold of *Mona) discovers Fflewddur is not a true bard, he is moved to the stables. Taran asks why Fflewddur didn't just tell the Chief Steward he was a king. "'No, no,' said Fflewddur, shaking his head. 'When I'm a bard, I'm a bard; and when I'm a king, that's something else again. I never mix the two'" (CL 19/34).

Fflewddur joins Taran in the search for Eilonwy, who has been kidnapped by Achren. Their quest takes them across the Isle of Mona. In their travels, they encounter the great cat, *Llyan. Fflewddur bravely stays behind to soothe the savage beast with his harping while the others escape (CL 65–66/86–87). Llyan so loves the harp that he tracks the bard across Mona and is there to save the Companions from drowning in the sea when *Caer Colur is flooded. The giant cat (so large Fflewddur rides her in place of a horse) becomes devoted to the bard.

> "I've grown quite fond of her myself. It's not often one finds such a good listener, and I think I shall keep her. Or," he added, while Llyan nuzzled her whiskers on his neck and gripped the bard in her powerful paws, "perhaps I should put it the other way around." (CL 160/189–190)

Fflewddur Fflam often displays another personality trait. He can be an optimist and a pessimist in the same breath. An example occurs when the Companions are trapped in *Glew's cavern as they continue their search for the Princess.

> "A Fflam never despairs!" cried Fflewddur. "But," he added dolefully, "I'm coming rapidly to believe this pit will be our grave, without even a decent mound to mark the spot. A Fflam is cheerful—but this is a disheartening situation, no matter how you look at it." (CL 85/108–109)

Fflewddur is also extremely nervous about meddling with enchantments and always recommends that enchanted things be left alone. When the Companions discover that the book (*book of spells) found in Glew's hut is magical, Fflewddur suggests they drop it in the river immediately. "I'd rather not even look at it, if you don't mind. Not that it frightens me. Yes, it makes me feel acutely uneasy; and you know my views on meddling" (CL 121/147). In *Taran Wanderer, when the Companions find *Morda's enchanted finger bone, Fflewddur reacts instantly. "Away with it!" he cries (TW 73/93). Later, the bard is turned into "a dun-colored hare" by the wicked Morda (TW 95/118). Even when he is finally returned to his proper shape, Fflewddur continues to be upset about having been an object of enchantment. He feels his ears, complains that his nose still twitches. "Enchantment is enchantment, and if you'd been through what I've been through, you'd want no part of it. . . . I'll never be the same, that's sure!" (TW 114/138).

Nevertheless, Fflewddur Fflam does understand something of enchantments. He is able to explain why Taran and *Rhun were finally able to light Eilonwy's *bauble when before they had been unsuccessful. The secret is to think more of others than yourself. "'That would seem to be one of its secrets, at least,' replied Fflewddur. 'Once you've discovered that, you've discovered a great secret indeed—with or without the bauble'" (CL 123/150). Fflewddur's wisdom is reflected by this observation. Though the bard seems impulsive and childlike, he actually possesses great intuitive wisdom.

Further examples of Fflewddur's wisdom appear in *Taran Wanderer*. Taran uses the last call left in his enchanted *Fair Folk *battle horn to summon help for the shepherd *Craddoc. Craddoc dies in spite of the Fair Folk rescue party, and Taran feels the call was wasted. "I think not," says Fflewddur. "Since you did your best and didn't begrudge using it, I shouldn't call it wasted at all" (TW 159/188). Anguished, Taran explains he momentarily thought of abandoning Craddoc. Fflewddur comforts him by saying, "Well, now . . . each man has his moment of fear. If we all behaved as we often wished to there'd be sorry doings in Prydain. Count the deed, not the thought" (TW 159/188).

As *The High King begins, the valiant Fflewddur Fflam again exhibits his fearsome fighting skills by rescuing Gwydion from the *Huntsmen of Annuvin. He attacks wildly and drives off the band single-handedly. Though this feat seems too much even for a Fflam, Alexander (1985b) explains that "he caught them [Huntsmen] unawares."

> I've read articles [such as] "Advice If You're About to Be Mugged. . . ." One of the things is do something that is absolutely unexpected and crazy—stand on your head or jump up and down. I think psychologically it's sound. I think that the arrival of Fflewddur, who must have been beside himself, [must] have been a sight to see—this wild yellow head with his harp dangling behind. . . . [The Huntsmen] were confronted with something they didn't expect, and [in] the precious moments that they lost reestimating the situation, Fflewddur grabbed [Gwydion] and saved him.

When the Huntsmen escape with *Dyrnwyn, Gwydion's enchanted sword, Fflewddur joins the quest to retrieve the blade and defeat Arawn. As a wandering bard, Fflewddur may gain access to dangerous strongholds and volunteers as a spy in The High King. He is also a dangerous fighting man, as illustrated by his rescue of Gwydion from the Huntsmen. Fflewddur rides with Taran, now a war leader, to rally troops in the *Free Commots and then to delay the *Cauldron-Born in their march back to *Annuvin. He serves as an advisor to Taran, and his wisdom proves invaluable. It is Fflewddur who helps Taran see that as a war leader his first concern must be his command. Taran longs to leave his post and search for Eilonwy and Gurgi, lost in a skirmish with the deathless warriors.

Before the destruction of Caer Dathyl, Fflewddur meets again with the Chief Bard, Taliesin. It has been a long time since Taliesin gave Fflewddur the truthful harp, and the Chief Bard admits he feels a little guilty for giving him such an instrument. Fflewddur starts to say the harp has been no trouble, but two strings snap. When Taliesin offers to exchange the truthful harp for any other of his harps, Fflewddur declines. "Telling the truth has harmed no one, least of all myself," Fflewddur says. "You have learned no small lesson," Taliesin replies (HK 112/133).

Fflewddur may also be learning the ways of a true bard. He finds a number of his songs have been recorded in the books of the *Hall of Lore.

Though the truthful harp and Fflewddur seem inseparable, Fflewddur is forced to sacrifice it for his friends. In one of the most deeply moving segments of the Chronicles, Fflewddur decides to burn the harp to keep the Companions from freezing, for Eilonwy and Gurgi have already slipped into the deadly sleep that precedes a frozen death. "For a long moment he held the harp lovingly in his hands and gently touched the strings, then with a quick motion raised the beautiful instrument and smashed it across his knee" (HK 201/233).

Taran cries that it is foolish to destroy the harp "for sake of a moment's warmth," but when it is lit, the *magic wood burns and never seems to be consumed. Great quantities of instantaneous heat revive Eilonwy and Gurgi. Eilonwy weeps when she learns of the bard's sacrifice, but Fflewddur says, "Don't give it a second thought. . . . The truth of the matter is that I'm delighted to be rid of it. I could never really play the thing, and it was more a burden than anything else" (HK 201–202/234). Sadly, there is no resounding twang to punctuate his untruth. "'But it gives a foul smoke,' Fflewddur muttered, though the fire was burning clear and brilliant. 'It makes my eyes water horribly'" (HK 202/235). The harp sings its most beautiful music as it slowly dies. In the morning, only the harp string given Fflewddur by Gwydion remains.

The sacrifices and bravery of Fflewddur Fflam were instrumental in the victory over *Arawn *Death-Lord. But when the struggle is ended, Fflam must travel with the Sons of Don, his kindred, to the *Summer Country. No vestige of enchantment may remain in Prydain, and all Sons of Don have enchantment in their blood. Taliesin tells Fflewddur that in the

Summer Country he will become a bard. "Your heart has always been the heart of a true bard. . . . Until now, it was unready" (HK 228/264).

Fflewddur presents Taran, the new High King, with the melted harp string as a token of remembrance, for Taran and Eilonwy remain behind to rule Prydain. Though it is a difficult parting, the optimistic reader can't help feeling that Taran and Eilonwy will one day be with Fflewddur, *Dallben, and the others once again.

Though some of Alexander's characters were reluctant to be developed (Gurgi, for instance), Fflewddur Fflam "loped into *The Book of Three as if he had always lived there and was impatient to get on with it" (Jacobs, 1978:271). Of Fflewddur Alexander says, "We seemed to know each other immediately. (I disregarded the suggestion advanced by certain friends and relatives that Fflewddur and I share the habit of outrageous exaggeration. I never lie—unless, of course, it seems absolutely necessary)" (Jacobs, 1978:271).

However, Alexander did struggle with one part of Fflewddur's character development. He realized "that Gurgi's speech pattern unmistakably identified him," and that Fflewddur also needed a "badge" of his own (Jacobs, 1978:271). Carrying a harp would not be enough.

> Chewing over this problem, I thought of my antique Welsh harp on the mantelpiece. I had bought it years before and had never been able to play it. The instrument was too brittle and fragile, the strings were in bad condition. The strings, in fact, had begun breaking from the day I brought it into the house. That first night, Janine and I were roused from a sound sleep by the loud twang of a snapping string. Next night, another string gave way with a crack that brought me bolt upright in bed. . . .
>
> It suddenly dawned on me that Fflewddur's harp stood in my own living room. The strings would break each time the eager bard stretched the truth. From that moment, Fflewddur's harp became as active a character as its owner. (Jacobs, 1978:271–272)

Alexander's editor, Ann Durell, points out that Alexander is a little like all his Prydain characters. However, "most Prydain fans, on meeting him [Alexander] for the first time, think he is most like Fflewddur Fflam; indeed they are both great storytellers who cannot resist the temptation to make a good tale better even at the risk of stretching the truth to the breaking point" (Durell, 1969:384).

In *Lady Charlotte Guest's notes to the *Mabinogion, Fflewddur Fflam son of *Godo is listed as one of the three sovereigns of the Court of Arthur (M 191). Sovereigns were so chosen because they were princes possessing territory and dominion, yet preferred to remain as knights in Arthur's

Court. This was considered "the chief of honour and gentility in the opinion of the Three Just Knights" (M 191). In the story "Kilhwch [*Kilhuch] and *Olwen," Kilhwch requests the aid of Fflewddur Fflam in his quest to obtain Olwen's hand in marriage (M 223).

See also Characters—fantasy, Ellidyr.
(M 191, 223, 266, 313)

Flyspeck, Prince: Prince Flyspeck is the derisive name *Kadwyr, the impudent crow, uses for *Gwybeddin, a gnat who offers help in the battle against the *Chief Huntsman of *Annuvin.
(F 43/50, 47/55)

Follin (FAHL-in): Follin is a master weaver during the time *Arawn is stealing the knowledge of craftsmanship. Follin's shuttle knows the secrets of his craft and is as skilled as its master. It can weave quicker than the eye can see with no knots or tangles.

However, Arawn *Death-Lord devises a plan to cheat Follin out of his enchanted shuttle. Coming to Follin's cottage dressed in a golden cloak of the finest workmanship, Arawn pretends that the cloth in his garment is shabby and needs replacing. Amazed that such material could be considered worn, Follin admits he could never weave any so fine. Then Arawn shows him a shuttle that can produce the golden cloth, and it works even faster and better than his own. Though Follin is not normally a greedy man, the thought of weaving gold is too much of a temptation. When Arawn offers to trade shuttles, Follin hastily agrees. But the shuttle and the cloth are only illusions. As soon as Arawn is gone, the shuttle splits asunder and the cloth of gold turns to cobwebs.

Follin never replaces his wonderful shuttle and must drudge at his *loom the rest of his days. Arawn adds Follin's shuttle to his treasure hoard.

See also Iscovan, Menwy.
(F 65/77)

Forest of Idris (ID-riss): The Forest of Idris is a grim woodland lying south of *Annuvin. The *Companions carry the *Black Cauldron from the *Marshes of Morva through the Forest of Idris as they struggle toward *Caer Dallben (BC 135/172). It is above the Forest of Idris that *Kaw is attacked and injured by *gwythaints (HK 84/102).

The name Idris is mentioned in *Guest's notes to the *Mabinogion as one of ancient Britain's great astronomers (M 436).
(BC 19/32, 29/45, 72/96, 135/172; HK 84/102; M 436)

Jacket illustration by Sasha Meret

Foundling, The: Alexander had originally envisioned writing two books (besides the picture books) that would relate to the Prydain cycle. But when he completed the series and *The High King* won the Newbery Medal, Alexander abandoned the idea of doing more with *Prydain. "We [Alexander and his editor] decided then that the last thing I should do is to write anything with Prydain for a long, long time, if ever. To write another book about Prydain, almost on the heels of *The High King*, would tend to give the impression that I was trying to cash in on something" (Jacobs, 1978: 291–292). However, five years and a few books later, Alexander returned to the original idea of writing a collection of "Pre-Prydain short stories," and, in 1973, *The Foundling and Other Tales of Prydain* was published (Jacobs, 1978:314).

The first version of *The Foundling* contained six tales that predate the story of *Taran. The first tale, "The Foundling," gives the book its title and tells of *Orddu, *Orwen, and *Orgoch finding and raising *Dallben. *Doli of the *Fair Folk appears in "The Stone," the story of a foolish cottager who wishes to live forever. "The True Enchanter" tells the tale of *Angharad, mother of *Eilonwy, and clarifies why she left *Caer Colur. The fourth tale,

"The Rascal Crow," takes place in and about *Medwyn's valley. *Kaw's father, the impudent crow *Kadwyr, receives a lesson in humility. "The Sword" explains the mystery of King *Rhitta's death and further explains the properties of the *magic sword *Dyrnwyn. The final story, "The Smith, the Weaver, and the Harper," shows how *Arawn stole the secrets of craftsmanship from the people of Prydain.

Some time after the Prydain picture books fell from print, their stories were added to *The Foundling*. The newer editions include "The Truthful Harp" and "Coll and His White Pig."

Free Commots (KOM-ots): The Free Commots are hamlets and small villages located in the southeastern part of *Prydain between the *Hill Cantrevs and the *Great Avren, with the *Llawgadarn Mountains to the north. The most notable of the *Commots are *Commot Isav, *Commot Merin, *Commot Gwenith, and *Commot Cenarth. Fflewddur Fflam describes the Commots:

> "The land itself is the pleasantest in Prydain—fair hills and dales, rich soil to farm, and sweet grass for grazing. There's iron for good blades, gold and silver for fine ornaments. *Annlaw Clay-Shaper is said to dwell among the *Commot folk, as do many other craftsmen: master weavers, metalsmiths—from time out of mind their skills have been the Commots' pride." (TW 46/63–64)

King *Smoit sees another side of the Free Commots. "A proud folk they are," he says. "And a stiff-necked breed. They bow to no *cantrev lords, but only to the *High King *Math himself" (TW 47/64). Yet, Smoit acknowledges that they rule themselves quite well and are strong and steadfast. "And, by my beard, I'm sure there's more peace and neighborliness in the Free Commots than anywhere else in Prydain" (TW 47/64).

Even the *Fair Folk are on best terms with the Commot folk, as *Doli explains to *Taran.

> "They respect us and we respect them. You'll not find many in Prydain to match their stout hearts and good will, and no man lords it over his fellows because he had the luck to be born in a king's castle instead of a farmer's hut. What matters in the Free Commots is the skill in a man's hands, not the blood in his veins. But I can tell you no more than that, for we have few dealings with them. Oh, we keep a *way post open here and there, just in case they might need our help. But it seldom happens. The Commot folk would rather count on themselves, and they do quite well at it." (TW 111–112/135–136)

When Taran finally visits the Free Commots, he discovers his friends have described it and its people accurately. He sees "cottages clustering in loose circles, rimmed by cultivated fields and pastures," and he finds "the Commot folk courteous and hospitable" (TW 175/206). It is among the Commot folk that Taran does a great deal of his maturing, which prepares him to accept his destiny as High King of Prydain. He apprentices under several master craftsmen: *Hevydd the Smith, *Dwyvach Weaver-Woman, and *Annlaw Clay-Shaper. In the process he learns much about life and grows in wisdom under their tutelage.

In *The High King, Taran is sent back to the Free Commots to rally forces for the *Sons of Don. The Commot folk willingly follow Taran's command and march to war against *Arawn under the *banner of the White Pig.

The term commot is used in the *Mabinogion with much the same meaning. "And Madawc took counsel with the men of Powys, and they determined to place an hundred men in each of the three Commots of Powys to seek for him" (M 299).

See also Commot men, Drudwas, Llassar.
(TW 46/63, 111/135, 161/190, 175/206, 217/253; HK 6/16, 39/52, 81–82/ 100, 91/110, 109/130, 247/285; M 299, 373, 416)

Gast (GAST), Lord: Though Lord Gast does not appear until *Taran
Wanderer*, his name is mentioned earlier in the *Chronicles by the *giant,
*Glew (CL 94/119). The cowardly Glew tells of once joining the hosts of
Lord *Goryon to battle Lord Gast (except that he couldn't stand the sight
of blood). As *Taran later discovers, the two lords are continually feuding
with one another.

In his travels seeking his parentage, Taran stops at Lord Gast's stronghold in *Cantrev Cadiffor. The *Companions find the *cantrev lord to be
"a heavy-featured warrior with a beard the color of muddy flax" (TW
39/55). And though Gast is a minor lord, a subject of King *Smoit, he
dresses extravagantly: "A handsome collarpiece dangled from his neck;
rings glittered on fingers stout enough to crack walnuts; and bands of
beaten silver circled his arms" (TW 39/55). Taran notices that even though
Gast's clothes are "costly and well-cut," they bear spots and spatters of
many a feast (TW 39/56).

Lord Gast calls himself "Gast the Generous" and brags of his willingness
to share his wealth. In reality, Gast is a miserly glutton, as the Companions
soon discover.

> "Eat your fill," cried Gast to Taran and *Gurgi, pushing a small hunch of
> gravy-spotted bread toward them and keeping the rest for himself. "Gast
> the Generous is ever openhanded! A sad fault that may turn me into a
> pauper, but it's my nature to be free with all my goods; I can't fight
> against it!" (TW 41/57)

Lord Gast's guests never have their plates and drinking horns filled more
than half way. "So passed the meal, with Gast loudly urging the companions to stuff themselves, yet all the while grudgingly offering them no more
than a few morsels of stringy meat from the heaped platter" (TW 41/58).

Gast speaks disparagingly of Lord Goryon during Taran's visit. It is a pre-lude to another of the neighboring lords' violent feuds. King Smoit later explains to Taran that Gast and Goryon have been arguing and fighting over the marvelous black cow, *Cornillo, for years. They have quarreled so long neither remembers whose beast she was in the beginning. Now, Goryon has raided Gast and stolen Cornillo once more. Taran rides with Smoit to put an end to the ensuing battle.

Lord Gast and Lord Goryon destroy the farmer *Aeddan's only productive field as they skirmish. Smoit would throw them in the dungeon and keep Cornillo for himself. But Taran suggests that Cornillo be given to Aeddan as partial payment for damages, and that Gast and Goryon be required to labor in the field with Aeddan to undo the damage. The lords are also allowed to take the next of the twin calves (Cornillo always bears twins) born to Cornillo. Other cows have also been stolen by Goryon. The herds of Gast and Goryon are so mixed that Taran suggests that one of the lords divide the cows into two groups and then the other lord choose of the two groups first.

With this disagreement settled, we hear little of Lord Gast until *The High King. Gast and Goryon put aside their differences to fight *Arawn *Death-Lord by the side of King Smoit. As Arawn is destroyed, the two come to hail Taran, the newly crowned *High King (HK 247/285).

The name Gast (Gast Rhymhi) is used briefly in the *Mabinogion (M, 249). However, *Lady Charlotte Guest recounts another myth in her notes to the Mabinogion that is similar to the story of the feuding lords. The Kings Nynniaw and Peibiaw (Gast and Goryon) argue over fields and flocks until their feud erupts into full-scale war. They begin to destroy the country-side as they battle. *Rhitta (here comparable to Smoit), the giant king of Wales, intervenes to stop their warring and severely punishes the two dis-obedient lords (M 283). Alexander (1985b) acknowledges that the figures of Gast and Goryon were inspired by the story of Nynniaw and Peibiaw.

See also Steward, Chief.
(CL 94/119; TW 38/54, 48/65, 59/79, 172/203, 191/225, 197/231; HK 50/65, 82/100, 247/285; M 249, 283)

Geraint (GEHR-aint): Geraint is the third suitor for the hand of Princess *Angharad. "He came with no servants or attendants; he bore no *magic wand or golden staff; his garments were plain and unadorned. Yet this youth was the fairest Angharad had ever seen" (F 35/40).

*Daughters of Llyr are only to marry enchanters. When challenged to show his powers, Geraint murmurs no spells. Instead, he speaks in common quiet words "of waters and woodlands, of sea and sky, of men and women, of childhood and old age; of the wonder and beauty of living things" (F 35–36/42). As he speaks, the court falls silent and from his open hands appear flights of doves, blooming flowers, and above them all, stars.

Angharad loves Geraint from the first moment and chooses him. But the other suitors, *Gildas and *Grimgower, challenge Geraint's qualifications as an enchanter, calling him "a hoaxer" (F 36/43). Geraint admits he has not true, inherited powers for sorcery. He fashioned the illusions himself from bits of white parchment, dry grass, tinted leaves, and a handful of pebbles. "I only helped you imagine these things to be more than what they are. If this pleased you for a few moments, I could ask nothing better" (F 37/43). Geraint is the master storyteller.

Gildas and Grimgower have vied for Angharad's hand because they seek power through the *House of Llyr. Geraint has come because of love for the Princess. Queen *Regat, Angharad's mother, will still not allow the union because Geraint is not truly a wizard. Yet, Angharad calls him "the only true enchanter" (F 37/43).

Defying custom, Geraint and Angharad run away together. Gildas and Grimgower try to stop them with enchantments, but the power of Geraint and Angharad's love disarms the spells.

Geraint does not appear except in *The Foundling. He and Angharad become a mystery of sorts. Readers never know of his fate and only learn of Angharad's miserable death in a brief description given by the evil sorcerer, *Morda. Geraint is presumably *Eilonwy's father.

In the *Mabinogion, Geraint is one of Arthur's young knights and is described as "a fair-haired youth, bare-legged, and of princely mien, and a golden-hilted sword was at his side" (M 144). Geraint the son of Erbin avenges a dishonor to Gwenhwyvar by defeating the knight who insulted her and at the same time reclaims lands and possessions for the elderly Earl of Ynywl (M 151).

See also Castle of Llyr, Caer Colur.
(F 35/40; M 142, 223)

giant: See Yspadadden; Glew; Llyan.

Giant, Chief: See Yspadadden.

Gildas (GHIL-das): The balding enchanter, Gildas, was the first suitor to compete for the hand of *Angharad, the *Princess of Llyr. "He was paunchy, with fleshy cheeks shining as if buttered. His garments were embroidered with gold thread and crusted with jewels" (F 30/33–34).

Gildas holds himself in high esteem, assuming the agreement for betrothal should take place without question. However, since *daughters of Llyr must marry enchanters, Angharad forces Gildas to prove his skill. With great effort, the enchanter turns *Caer Colur's *Great Hall as dark as midnight. But Angharad is unimpressed. "Is that all there is to it?" she says. Angharad thinks it a useless bother to turn day into night when nature already does a superior job. Gildas is dismissed, mumbling as he leaves. "It is against my principles to criticize my colleagues. . . . But I can assure Your Majesty [Queen *Regat] in advance: No enchantments can rival mine" (F 32/37).

Gildas and his colleague and fellow suitor, *Grimgower, do not win Angharad. She chooses *Geraint, a young storyteller who is not an enchanter at all. Angharad's mother, Queen Regat, forbids the union, and the two lovers run away together. Gildas and Grimgower attempt to stop them with enchantments. Gildas turns the forest inky black with his spell of darkness and later conjures a fearful blizzard. But the spells fail to conquer true love; Geraint and Angharad escape.

*Guest's notes to the *Mabinogion make mention of a Gildas (M 499). He was known as Gildas the prophet and was a *bard who received his privileges or initiation rites from *Taliesin and the Chair of the Round Table (*Council of Bards).

See also Castle of Llyr, Characters—fantasy.
(F 30/33; M 499, 503)

Glessic (GLES-sik), Prince: When first confronted by the witches of the *Marshes of Morva, *Taran tries to cloak the *Companions' identities by using false names. Taran introduces *Fflewddur Fflam as Prince Glessic. However, *Orddu, *Orwen, and *Orgoch only giggle at his useless effort to hide the truth.

In the *Mabinogion, Glessic is the name of a unique sword. It was one of the three swords known as the "three grinding gashers" and belonged to the brothers Bwlch, Kyfwlch, and Sefwlch. The brothers and their swords were recruited by Kilhwch (*Kilhuch) to aid in his quest to win the hand of *Olwen in marriage (M 228).
(BC 100/130; M 228, 242)

Glew (GLUE): Glew receives a mysterious introduction in *The Castle of Llyr. As *Taran and the *Companions search for a kidnapped *Eilonwy, they stumble upon a windowless abandoned hut with a conical thatched roof and sagging door. Amid the scattered and dust-layered furnishings, the Companions find a little book with blank pages and a sheaf of parchments bearing Glew's name. The blank book is the lost *book of spells of the *House of Llyr, although for some time no one realizes this. The parchments are a diary of sorts containing Glew's spells.

From the notes, they discover that Glew, a tiny individual, had been dabbling with *magic concoctions in order to make himself larger. He had captured a small mountain cat he named *Llyan on which to try his potions. It seems he treated her well, except for the "feedings." Soon she began to grow, and Glew was forced to build a new cage to hold the cat. There the parchment ends, nibbled away by mice. Glew and Llyan have simply disappeared, and the Companions suspect Llyan has eaten her little caretaker (CL 59/79). However, the cat—a *giant larger than a horse—returns to the hut. The Companions are barely able to escape Glew's creation. Llyan later becomes *Fflewddur's dedicated companion, tamed by the *bard's harping.

Readers do not meet Glew until later in the Companions' search for Eilonwy. A cave-in near the bank of the River *Alaw deposits them in a system of caverns, a beautiful place with colorful stone formations and pools of differing hues. A strangely shaped rock catches their attention, and as they examine it, the egg-shaped stone begins to move.

> Two colorless eyes appeared, in a face pale as a dead fish; the eyebrows glittered with flecks of crystal; moss and mold edged the long, flapping ears and spread over the beard that sprouted below a lumpy nose.
>
> Swords drawn, the companions huddled against the jagged wall. The huge head continued to rise and Taran saw it wobble on a skinny neck. A choking noise bubbled in the creature's throat as it cried, "Puny things! Tremble before me! Tremble, I tell you! I am Glew! I am Glew! . . ."
>
> The creature threw a long, spindly leg over the ledge and began slowly drawing himself upright. He was more than thrice as tall as Taran, and his flabby arms dangled below a pair of knobby, moss-covered knees. With a lopsided gait he shambled toward the companions. (CL 89–90/113–114)

Unsure of himself and a coward at heart, Glew peers down on his captives. "'Are you *really* trembling?' he asked in an anxious voice. 'You're not doing it just to be obliging?'" (CL 90/114). Then the "fearsome" giant breaks into great sobs of loneliness and sadly explains how he hid in the caverns to escape Llyan. Once inside, he swallowed the potion, hoping to grow large enough to stand a chance against the cat. But it worked so quickly that his head bumped into the ceiling, and he was forced to squirm deeper into the cavern in order to avoid being wedged among the rocks. Soon Glew was trapped within the cavern's deepest reaches, with rooms large enough to accommodate him but passages too small to grant him freedom. Glew is afraid of bats and crawly things, so living underground has been a nightmare. He has dwelt so long beneath the surface that toadstools grow in his beard.

Glew always wished to be important. He tried to become a warrior, a bard, a king, an enchanter, and a fearsome giant. All efforts failed. Still, he asks the Companions if they might not call him King Glew (*King of Stones). But Fflewddur finds the giant so pitiful that he calls him "a repulsive little grub" and says that "for a giant . . . [Glew is] remarkably small-natured" (CL 117/143).

Glew plans to use one of the Companions as an ingredient for his latest brew: a shrinking potion. He apologizes repeatedly for having to kill one of them and expects the apology to make his captives cooperative. The Companions are able to escape, leaving the wretched giant in his dark and lonely world.

True to a promise he makes to the treacherous Glew, Taran asks *Dallben to make a shrinking potion for him. As Taran travels in search of his parentage in *Taran Wanderer, *Kaw brings him word that Glew has now been returned to normal size (TW 68/87).

More about Glew surfaces when the Companions stumble upon the evil wizard *Morda. Morda acquired both the *book of spells and *Angharad's gem when the hapless Princess *Angharad wandered sick and dying into Morda's keep. After her death, Morda used her powerful gem to cultivate his evil enchantments. But he did not recognize the book of spells and thought the seemingly empty book useless.

> "In time a whining weakling found his way to me. Glew was his name, and he sought to make an enchanter of himself. Little fool! He beseeched me to sell him a magic spell, an amulet, a secret word of power. Sniveling upstart! It pleased me to teach him a lesson. I sold him the empty book and warned him not to open it or look upon it until he had traveled far from here lest the spells vanish." (TW 92/114)

Unknowingly, Glew brings the long-lost treasure of *Llyr back to the *Isle of Mona, the place of its origin. The ruins of *Caer Colur, ancestral home of the *House of Llyr, lies just off *Mona's shores. It is with Eilonwy, the book of spells, and Eilonwy's *bauble (the *Golden Pelydryn) that the sorceress *Achren plans to take control of all *Prydain (CL 148/177).

In *The High King, Taran returns from his wanderings to find Glew at *Caer Dallben. This time Glew appears as a "pudgy little man" with a "flabby nose" and a "scraggly fringe of hair" on his bulbous head. He shows no gratitude to Taran or Dallben for rescuing him. Instead, he talks end-lessly of his days of glory as a giant. When he isn't talking he is eating. Because of his cowardly nature, Glew has no use for adventures and will not consider joining the battle against *Annuvin. But when he discovers there may be treasure to be had at Annuvin, Glew hastily changes his mind.

Glew's greed is a driving force that carries him through the danger and death of the great final battle against evil. Preferring horses to ships (*Gwydion travels to Annuvin by sea), Glew chooses to travel with Taran to Annuvin. Taran's assignment is to slow the progress of the *Cauldron-Born, and many lives are lost in the struggle. Through all this, Glew sur-vives, clinging to the hope of riches.

Glew's true nature is fully exposed when Taran's troops are being led through an old *Fair Folk mine by *Doli. Though the place has been aban-doned, a few low-quality gems are still lying about. Lapsing into a greedy fit, Glew pounces on the first stone he sees. "'It's mine!' he squealed. 'None of you saw it. If you had, you'd have kept it for yourselves'" (HK 156/184). Glew is allowed to retain the worthless gem, but he finds more and more of them, stuffing his pouch beyond capacity. Taran notices that Glew has the same look about him as when he is enjoying a meal. Frenzied with greed, the ex-giant climbs a rickety platform to reach another stone. The structure collapses, and the tunnel caves in, blocking the shortcut to Annuvin. The troops must go back, and critical time is lost. But all Glew is worried about is the "fortune" he lost.

> "Days wasted?" he wailed. "Cauldron-Born? Blocked-up tunnels? But has any one of you stopped to consider I've just lost a fortune? My gems are gone, all of them, and you don't give it a second thought. I call that self-ish. Selfish! There's no other word for it." (HK 160/188)

Throughout the quest to regain *Dyrnwyn and overthrow *Arawn, Glew only thinks of himself and bemoans his ill treatment. "Oh, when I was a giant I'd not have stood for such high-handed treatment!" he says. And when the armies of Prydain finally take Annuvin, his only thought is for his own safety until he and *Gurgi stumble upon Arawn's treasure hoard. Immediately, his greed supplants his anxiety. But Arawn's treasure room is protected by traps, and Glew is nearly burned alive as he tries to line his pockets. Gurgi pulls him to safety (HK 220/254).

Apparently Glew has learned nothing from his experiences. When Dallben invites the Companions to travel with the *Sons of Don to the *Summer Country, Glew complains once again.

Glew snorted. "That's all very well, bestowing never-ending life right and left. Even on a pig! But no one's given a thought to me. Selfishness! Lack of consideration! It's plain that if that Fair Folk mine hadn't come tumbling down—robbing me of my fortune, I might add—we'd have taken a different path, we'd never have gone to *Mount Dragon, Dyrnwyn would never have been found, the Cauldron-Born never slain . . ." For all his indignation, however, the former giant's brow puckered wretchedly and his lips trembled. "Go, by all means! Let me stay this ridiculous size! I assure you, when I was a giant . . ." (HK 230–231/266)

Gurgi takes Glew's side, and Dallben agrees that the pudgy little man served the cause, even though unwittingly. "His reward shall be no less than yours. In the Summer Country he may grow, if he so desires, to the stature of a man," says the enchanter (HK 231/267). At this time, Glew admits freely that Gurgi saved his life in Annuvin. Gurgi had reversed the story to help Glew's case. "At least you've told the truth, giant," says Fflewddur. "Good for you! *Great Belin, I think you've already grown a little taller!" (HK 231/267). Glew even offers Taran, who stays in Prydain, a gem he has carried with him since leaving his cavern on Mona. The blue crystal is to be a remembrance of the little giant.

Though Glew is a colorful character in the *Prydain Chronicles, the characters sharing his name in the *Mabinogion are only bit players. The name is used briefly on two occasions: Glew the son of Ysgawd, Unic Glew Ysgwyd (M 254, 372).

See also Characters—fantasy.

(CL 57/77, 89/113; TW 5/17, 68/87, 92/114; HK 7+/18+; M 254, 372, 377)

Gloff (GLAHF): Besides *Dorath himself, Gloff is the only named member of *Dorath's Company, a band of ruthless mercenaries who make sport of preying upon defenseless farmers and craftsmen. Gloff is marked by a badly scarred face.

When *Taran first encounters Dorath's Company, Gloff wishes to wager that his mare ("an evil-tempered brute and a killer born") can stand against *Llyan (TW 118/142). Unfortunately, *Dorath will not allow it.

Gloff nearly kills Taran during a subsequent raid on the *Commot Isav. As the two struggle, *Llassar, the young shepherd, plunges between them, saving Taran's life. Llassar takes a vicious blow, but his father, *Drudwas, intervenes, chopping Gloff down with his blade and killing him.

This unsavory character shares his name with two characters in the *Mabinogion. Neither of these two, Tegvan Gloff and Arwystli Gloff, is mentioned more than briefly (M 225; M 260).
(TW 118/142, 205/240; M 225, 260)

Godo (GOH-doh): Godo is the father of *Fflewddur Fflam.
(BT 75/95; BC 19/33; HK 81/99, 110/132, 228/263)

Goewin (GOH-win): Goewin is the wife of *Llonio, a happy-go-lucky fellow who relies on providence coupled with creativity to provide his livelihood. She and Llonio have six children.

In the *Mabinogion, Goewin is the maiden who holds the feet of King *Math the son of *Mathonwy. Math "could not exist unless his feet were in the lap of a maiden, except only when he was prevented by the tumult of war" (M 413). Because Gilvaethwy loves Goewin, he and *Gwydion, *sons of Don and nephews to Math, devise a plan to take Goewin from the king. They steal swine from *Annuvin and thereby begin a war that draws Math from his chamber. While the king is away battling *Pryderi, Gilvaethwy and Gwydion steal the maiden. For their treachery, Math, who is also an enchanter, turns them into various wild animals. Gwydion and Gilvaethwy live as animals over a period of several years.
(TW 163/193, 165/195; M 413)

Gold Crown of Don (DAHN): The Gold Crown of Don is the symbol of authority worn by the *High King *Math Son of *Mathonwy. As *Arawn's power in *Prydain grows, the Gold Crown seems to become "a cruel burden" for Math.
(HK 107/128)

Golden Pelydryn (PELL-ih-drin): See bauble.

golden ships: These are the ships on which the *Children of Don traveled to *Prydain from the *Summer Country. The same ships, kept in a hidden harbor near the mouth of the *Kynvael River, are used to take the Children of Don and their friends back to the Summer Country as the *Chronicles of Prydain conclude.

See also Sons of Don
(HK 108/129, 132/157, 227/263)

Golden Sunburst of Don (DAHN): The Golden Sunburst is the emblem of the *House of Don.
(HK 55/70, 105/126)

Good Llyr (LEER): Queen *Teleria of the *Isle of Mona commonly uses the expression, "Good Llyr!" As *Mona is the ancestral home of the *House of Llyr, it can be assumed this expression refers to *Llyr Half-Speech, the ancient *Sea King who is probably considered a sea god.
(CL 15/30, 26/42)

Good versus evil: "Good cannot come from evil," *Dallben tells the once noble *Pryderi, and with this statement he summarizes one of the most basic motifs of high fantasy literature (HK 190/220–221). Alexander, himself "a solid believer in justice" (Jacobs, 1978:88), explains that "the conflict between good and evil is standard in any heroic fantasy" (Alexander, 1968a:172).

While referring to other experts in the field of literature, Linda L. Madsen states that good versus evil is really what myth is all about and that modern high fantasy generally has a strong mythological base. "Fantasies are concerned with how good and evil manifest themselves in individuals" (Madsen, 1976:49). Quoting Sullivan, Madsen strengthens her point.

> Humanity is an idea, a concept . . . a motion toward light or dark, a selection between the will to destroy and the will to save. The more times such selection tends toward the Good, the more human we say that being is becoming. (Sullivan, 1972:1314)

The plot of the *Prydain Chronicles is basically organized around the motif of good versus evil. The forces of light (good) are represented by the *Sons of Don while the dark forces (evil) are centered around *Arawn *Death-Lord. As Madsen (1976:49) points out, characters who represent evil lack not only human characteristics of compassion and kindness but also often lack human form. The more evil the character the less human or, at least, the more nebulous the form. Arawn, for example, is never really viewed but lurks mysteriously as the true essence of evil. The *Horned King, Arawn's champion, appears in full view, but is not fully in the form of a man.

> Astride the foam-spattered animal rode a monstrous figure. A crimson cloak flamed from his naked shoulders. Crimson stained his gigantic arms. Horrorstricken, Taran saw not the head of a man but the antlered head of a stag.

The Horned King! *Taran flung himself against an oak to escape the flying hoofs and the heaving, glistening flanks. Horse and rider swept by. The mask was a human skull; from it, the great antlers rose in cruel curves. The Horned King's eyes blazed behind the gaping sockets of whitened bone. (BT 15/30)

Other evil characters such as *Achren and *Morda retain human countenances but the evil has begun to alter their forms ever so slightly. Achren retains a youthful appearance despite her age, yet her skin is deathly pale and her hair strangely silver. Morda is emaciated, almost skeletal. Other characters who have given in to the temptations of evil are changed primarily in the way they behave. For example, *Pryderi and *Morgant become proud and haughty, thinking themselves wiser and more intelligent than the rest of *Prydain. The lust for power has lured them toward evil.

It is common in fantasy that ultimate evil may be controlled if one can discover its true name. This stems from the ancient belief that power lies in the ability to name objects and people (Madsen, 1976:51). *Gwydion is able to conquer the Horned King by learning his true or secret name. Merely speaking the name causes the evil being to disintegrate. This idea represents the power of knowledge and the weakness spawned from ignorance. Gwydion expresses this principle when instructing the young Taran: "Once you have courage to look upon evil, seeing it for what it is and naming it by its true name, it is powerless against you, and you can destroy it" (BT 179/209).

The age-old theme of good versus evil, religious in nature and evident in biblical stories, mirrors real life. High fantasy is therefore an allegory of our daily struggles to become honorable men and women. It is a struggle that never ends, as Gwydion points out to Taran:

> "Yet Arawn is slain," Taran replied. "Evil is conquered and the blade's work done."
> "Evil conquered?" said Gwydion. "You have learned much, but learn this last and hardest of lessons. You have conquered only the enchantments of evil. That was the easiest of your tasks, only a beginning, not an ending. Do you believe evil itself to be so quickly overcome? Not so long as men still hate and slay each other, when greed and anger goad them. Against these even a flaming sword cannot prevail, but only that portion of good in all men's hearts whose flame can never be quenched." (HK 245/282)

Goryon (GORE-yon), Lord: Goryon is first mentioned by the cowardly giant *Glew. In *The Castle of Llyr,* Glew tells the *Companions that he once joined the battle host of Lord Goryon only to find he couldn't stand the sight of blood (CL 94/119). Goryon does not appear in the *Chronicles until *Taran Wanderer*.

*Taran actually meets Goryon's "border-band" long before he does the Lord. They steal *Melynlas and may have even killed Taran had not the farmer *Aeddan intervened in the scuffle. Aeddan reassures Taran that "the henchmen of Lord Goryon treat steeds better than strangers," so he need not fear for Melynlas (TW 25/39). Taran later travels to Goryon's stronghold to regain his horse.

Goryon's stronghold is not a castle, but a large huddle of buildings circled by a barricade of wooden stakes lashed with osier and chinked up with hard-packed earth. Lord Goryon is a "burly, thickset figure" with a "dark, gray-shot beard" (TW 32–33/48). He is a *cantrev lord of *Cantrev Cadiffor and is under the rule of King *Smoit.

Lord Goryon proves to be a "prickly-tempered" sort who reads insults into the slightest action or word, regularly calling out, "Insolence! Impudence!" (TW 33/48). Goryon is extremely worried about his honor and calls himself "Goryon the Valorous" (TW 34/49). Therefore, he is easily goaded into proving his valor: his own men goad him into trying to tame an indomitable Melynlas, though his heart isn't in it.

Goryon is also quick to save face. Taran helps the cantrev lord preserve his honor by offering him Melynlas as a gift. Goryon conveniently chooses to have no part of a Pig-Keeper's gifts. So Taran gets his horse, and Goryon no longer has to try to break the animal (TW 37/53).

Later, Taran learns from King Smoit that Lord Goryon and his neighbor Lord *Gast (also Taran's acquaintance) have battled one another for years, mainly over the wonderful black cow, *Cornillo. So often has Cornillo changed hands that "neither of them knows whose beast it rightly is" (TW 48/65). While Taran resides with Smoit, the argument erupts anew and threatens full-scale war.

Goryon and Gast choose Aeddan's only field as a battle ground and destroy the farmer's livelihood. Enraged, Smoit will throw the childish lords in his dungeon and keep Cornillo for himself. But Taran wisely suggests that Cornillo be given to Aeddan as partial payment for damages, and that the lords be commanded to labor beside the farmer to restore his crops. Taran's plan includes letting Goryon and Gast take the next calves born to Cornillo, as she always bears twins. Because the herds of Goryon and Gast have become mixed during the fracas, Taran suggests that Goryon split them into two even groups and Gast be allowed to choose first (TW 62/81).

The quarrelsome Goryon puts aside his differences with Gast to fight *Arawn by the side of King Smoit. When the great battle is over, he and Gast come to hail Taran, their new *High King.

The name Goryon is mentioned briefly in the *Mabinogion (M 225). However, *Lady Charlotte Guest recounts another myth in her notes to the Mabinogion that is similar to the story of the feuding lords. The Kings, Nynniaw and Peibiaw (Gast and Goryon), argue over fields and flocks until their feud erupts into a great war. They begin to destroy the countryside as they battle. *Rhitta (here comparable to King Smoit), the giant king of Wales, intervenes to stop their warring and severely punishes the two disobedient lords (M 283). Alexander (1985b) acknowledges that the figures of Gast and Goryon were inspired by the story of Nynniaw and Peibiaw. (CL 94/119; TW 24/38, 31/46, 44/60, 48/65, 60/79; HK 50/65, 82/100, 247/285; M 225, 283)

Govannion (goh-VAN-yon) the Lame: *Annlaw Clay-Shaper tells *Taran of Govannion the Lame, master craftsman of *Prydain:

> "Govannion . . . long ago fashioned all manner of enchanted implements. He gave them to whom he deemed would use them wisely and well, but one by one they fell into the clutches of *Arawn *Death-Lord. Now all are gone.
>
> "But Govannion, too, discovered and set down the high secrets of all crafts," Annlaw went on. "These, as well, Arawn stole, to hoard in *Annuvin." (TW 192/225–226)

Govannion also "forged and tempered *Dyrnwyn at the behest of King *Rhydderch Hael" (HK 22/34).

The *Mabinogion includes passages concerning Govannion (also spelled Govannon), the *son of Don, who was a brother of *Gwydion. Therefore, he is also called the uncle of Dylan, the son of Arianrod, who was the *daughter of Don. Dylan is a child who was baptized in the sea and took its nature, swimming as well as the fishes. Govannion is said to have struck the blow that killed Dylan (M 422).

See also Follin, Iscovan, Menwy.
(TW 192/225; HK 22/34; M 236, 422, 437)

Great Avren (AHV-ren) Harbor: See Great Avren River; Avren Harbor.

Great Avren (AHV-ren) River: The Great Avren River runs generally north and south in *Prydain but turns westward just before it empties into the sea. The *Free Commots border on this river in what is known as the *Valley of the Great Avren (HK 95/114). The *Hill Cantrevs and *eastern strongholds also border the Great Avren.

The river widens at the sea and becomes a natural harbor. The *Companions depart for *Mona from *Great Avren Harbor in *The Castle of Llyr. (BT 23/39, 25/41, 28/45, 31/47, 44/61, 46/63; BC 5/15, 18/32, 28/44; CL 4/18, 5/19; TW 10/23, 46/63, 168/198, 181/213; HK 4/14, 13/24, 35/48, 43/57, 84/102)

Great Belin (BELL-in): "Great Belin" is Fflewddur Fflam's favorite expression or oath.
See also Belin, Fflewddur Fflam, Sons of Don.

Great Hall: Most strongholds have a Great Hall, a meeting or gathering place often called the throne room. The Great Hall of greatest import in the *Prydain Chronicles is the one at *Caer Dathyl. It is in this hall that *Pryderi reveals his traitorous plans to take Caer Dathyl by force and rule *Prydain. The Great Hall of Caer Dathyl is destroyed when the stronghold is leveled by *Cauldron-Born battering rams (HK 128/153).

*Annuvin's Great Hall is the scene of the Chronicles' climax. It is described as "glittering like black, polished marble" (HK 209/242). Just outside the Great Hall, *Taran cleaves in two the serpent that is *Arawn (HK 222/257). Great Halls of *Caer Colur, *Spiral Castle, and other important Prydainian strongholds are also the sites of important occurrences.
(BT 45/63, 180/210; CL 25/42, 30/47, 140/168, 145/173, 153/182; TW 39/55, 45/62, 63/82; HK 115/137, 128/153, 209/242; F 29/33, 54/64)

Greidawl (GREYE-dawl): Greidawl is the father of *Gwythyr, who is a principal player in the story "*Kilhuch and *Olwen." *Medwyn tells part of this story to *Taran in *The Book of Three.

The name Greidawl appears several times in the *Mabinogion. Mostly it is associated with Gwythyr. However, *Lady Charlotte Guest's notes to the Mabinogion tell us that Greidawl (Greidawl Galldonyd) deserves some fame of his own. He was one of the three architects of the Island of Britain, and therefore had the special privilege to go wherever he pleased without breaking the law (M 262).
(BT 120/144; M 223, 229, 249, 262, 313)

Grimgower (GRIM-gauer): Grimgower is the second of Princess *Angharad's suitors. He is a lean, gaunt-faced enchanter with knotted brows and a square black beard twining around his thin lips. He wears iron-shod boots and a black cloak and exudes a menacing aura.

Grimgower seems to think that Queen *Regat and Princess Angharad will accept his proposal of marriage without question. He feels Angharad should be thankful for the opportunity. Not understanding Angharad's free spirit, Grimgower makes the mistake of telling her that though she will be well-treated, he is "the only master" in his household (F 33/38).

In spite of his self-assured attitude, Grimgower must prove his prowess with *magic, for a *daughter of Llyr may only wed an enchanter. He conjures a number of dreadful monsters, but Angharad is neither impressed nor alarmed.

When Angharad chooses *Geraint, who is not truly an enchanter, Queen Regat refuses to allow the union. Grimgower and his fellow suitor, *Gildas, are both incensed at the choice of a charlatan. When Geraint and Angharad run away together, Grimgower tries to stop them with his fearful, conjured monsters, but his enchantments are thrown back by their love.

See also Caer Colur, Castle of Llyr, Characters—fantasy.
(F 33/37)

Guest, Lady Charlotte: See *Lady Charlotte Guest.

**Gurgi (GHUR-ghee): Perhaps the most colorful of the Prydainian figures is Gurgi. He becomes a dynamic character like his kindly master, *Taran. But in the beginning, Gurgi is little more than a wild animal.

> He [Taran] could not be sure whether it was animal or human. He decided it was both. Its hair was so matted and covered with leaves that it looked like an owl's nest in need of housecleaning. It had long, skinny, woolly arms, and a pair of feet as flexible and grimy as its hands. . . .
>
> Taran had just begun to catch his breath. He was covered with Gurgi's shedding hair, in addition to the distressing odor of a wet wolfhound. (BT 26/42–43)

True to his animalistic instincts, Gurgi is always worried about eating, and he always seems to be hungry. Immediately upon his introduction he says, "Then the two strengthful heroes will give Gurgi something to eat? Oh, joyous crunchings and munchings!" (BT 27/43). As primitive as Gurgi seems, the shaggy creature exhibits a sense of humor. He asks Gwydion if he might have Taran as his "crunchings and munchings" (BT 29/45).

Because Taran is repulsed by the creature, *Gwydion explains to him that Gurgi is not really bad at heart. "He would love to be wicked and terrifying, though he cannot quite manage it. He feels so sorry for himself that it is hard not to be angry with him. But there is no use in doing so" (BT 29/46). In the early stages of his development as a character, Gurgi displays a good deal of self-pity, howling and whining constantly.

The trait that most identifies Gurgi is his pattern of speech. He has a delightful habit of using paired rhymings to describe most everything. The most famous of his rhyming phrases is "crunchings and munchings," but there are nearly a hundred different colorful combinations: "smackings and whackings," "whiffings and sniffings," "doings and brewings," "moilings and toilings," "walkings and stalkings," "cooings and mooings," "guttings and cuttings," "squeakings and shriekings," "boatings and floatings," "pawings and clawings," "lotions and potions," "hummings and strummings," "changings and arrangings," "beatings and cheatings," "sloshings and washings," "pinings and whinings," "sighings and dyings," "flyings and spyings," and so on. Gurgi's speech also is characterized by alliteration: "watchful waitings," "dreamful drowsings," "bright blazing," "snoozings and snorings." He also uses phrases that are repetitive, such as "see with lookings!" Even as Gurgi matures he does not abandon his unique patterns of speech.

Throughout the Chronicles, Gurgi continues to have grooming problems. "So many new leaves and twigs had stuck in Gurgi's hair that he had begun to look like a walking beaver dam" (BT 95/117). He continues to look alien, and even the witch, *Orddu, calls him a "whatever-you-call-it" (TW 12/25). Her sister, *Orwen, simply calls him "the gurgi" (TW 13/26). Even as Gurgi helps Taran learn each new trade in *Taran Wanderer, his coat of matted hair is decorated by whatever is at hand. As he pumps the bellows of *Hevydd the Smith, clouds of sparks singe his hair away in patches until "he looked as if a flock of birds had plucked him to make their nests" (TW 178/210). With *Dwyvach Weaver-Woman, Gurgi becomes so covered with dyes he "looked like a rainbow suddenly sprouting hair" (TW 185/217). And when Gurgi helps in the hut of *Annlaw Clay-Shaper, he is so layered with dust, mud, and gritty glaze "that he looked like an unbaked clay pot set on a pair of skinny legs" (TW 196/230).

The course of Gurgi's growth—his psychological and emotional maturing into a being with the best of human qualities—is one of the truly satisfying elements in the *Prydain Chronicles. The maturation process begins when Taran refuses to leave the injured creature in the path of the approaching *Cauldron-Born. Gurgi asks to be killed rather than be left. Even though carrying Gurgi creates a grave risk, Taran chooses to try. The change in the creature is immediate. Gurgi leaves his portion of food for

Taran! This is the ultimate sacrifice for him, and "for the first time they [Taran and Gurgi] smiled at one another" (BT 101/124).

> "Your gift is generous," Taran said softly, "but you travel as one of us and you will need all your strength. Keep your share; it is yours by right; and you have more than earned it."
>
> He put his hand gently on Gurgi's shoulder. The wet wolfhound odor did not seem as objectionable as before. (BT 102/124)

From this point on, Gurgi is totally dedicated to Taran and will not desert him, even in the face of such terrible danger as standing against the Cauldron-Born. "No, no! Faithful Gurgi stays with mighty lord who spared his poor tender head! Happy, grateful Gurgi will fight, too, with slashings and gashings" (BT 103/125). It appears that Gurgi has only needed acceptance and love to trigger his metamorphosis. Later, *Medwyn confirms such when Taran suggests leaving the wounded creature in the safety of *Medwyn's valley.

> "Safer?" asked Medwyn. "Yes, certainly. But you would hurt him grievously were you to turn him away now. Gurgi's misfortune is that he is neither one thing nor the other, at the moment. He has lost the wisdom of animals and has not gained the learning of men. Therefore, both shun him. Were he to do something purposeful, it would mean much to him." (BT 119–120/143)

So Gurgi continues to accompany Taran on his quest, and Taran begins to teach him practical human tasks, such as building a fire and digging a cooking pit (BT 151/178). Finally, Gurgi gets to wear his first weapon, a short sword.

> "Yes, yes!" he cried. "Now bold, valiant Gurgi is a mighty warrior, too! He has a grinding gasher and a pointed piercer! He is ready for great fightings and smitings!" (BT 161/189)

His valor becomes so noteworthy that Gurgi is rewarded by Gwydion with a magical *wallet of food. The wallet will always satisfy Gurgi's hunger, for it is ever full and can never be emptied (BT 181/211). It also provides provisions for the *Companions when none would otherwise be available.

Gurgi's devotion to Taran solidifies as the Chronicles continue. He is crestfallen when he is not allowed to accompany Taran on the quest to destroy the *Black Cauldron. But he and *Eilonwy follow the warriors anyway. Gurgi has become more worried for Taran than for himself and "joins master to keep him from harmful hurtings" (BC 39/56). In *Taran Wanderer, Gurgi is so afraid of being left again that he dares burst into *Dallben's chamber to beg to go along.

"No, no, no!" howled Gurgi at the top of his voice, rocking back and forth and waving his hairy arms. "Sharp-eared Gurgi hears all! Oh, yes, with listenings behind the door!" His face wrinkled in misery and he shook his matted head so violently he nearly sprawled flat on the floor. "Poor Gurgi will be lone and lorn with whinings and pinings!" he moaned. "Oh, he must go with master, yes, yes!" (TW 6–7/19)

Dallben understands Gurgi's need to be with Taran, and he knows that Gurgi is indeed faithful and trustworthy. "Gurgi's staunchness and good sense I do not doubt," he says. "Though before your search is ended, the comfort of his kindly heart may stand you in better stead" (TW 7/19–20).

Even when Taran fears he must stay forever on *Craddoc's rocky farmstead and commands his hairy friend to go, Gurgi refuses to leave. "He threw himself flat on the ground and lay stiff as a poker" (TW 144/172). Gurgi happily stays and becomes Craddoc's shepherd. He calls himself an "Assistant Sheep-Keeper" (TW 147/176). When Craddoc and Taran fall into an icy crevice, Gurgi nurses an incoherent Taran for two weeks. Fflewddur explains to Taran how Gurgi fussed over him like a mother hen.

Gurgi's growing maturity continues to be chronicled in numerous ways. In *The Black Cauldron, Gurgi offers his wallet of food to the witches in exchange for the *Black Crochan. He hopes this will spare Taran from parting with the *Brooch of Adaon. He not only cares more for Taran than himself, but also is willing to sacrifice for any of the Companions. For example, when the cowardly giant, *Glew, threatens the Companions, Gurgi abandons his fearful nature and tells Glew to free them, "or rageful Gurgi will smack your great feeble head!" (CL 102/127). Soon after, Gurgi volunteers to give his life for his friends. Glew demands they choose one of their number to be sacrificed as an ingredient for his latest potion. "'Gurgi will go,' the creature whispered faintly, though he trembled so much he could hardly speak" (CL 106/131).

His valor and wisdom become more and more noticeable. When turned into a gray field mouse by *Morda, Gurgi nevertheless keeps his wits. He saves the day by nibbling through Taran's bonds and retrieving from the floor of Morda's hut the shard of bone that is to be the evil wizard's undoing (TW 97–98/119–120). Using his wits once again, Gurgi rides a great black bull as weapon against *Dorath's Company in the *Commot Isav (TW 206/241). Proud and daring, Gurgi leads the way into battle in *The High King as Taran's banner carrier. It is he who lofts high the *banner of the White Pig. Even though outnumbered and helpless, Gurgi battles to save Eilonwy from shame at the hands of *Dorath, nearly losing his life (HK 164/193). He also pulls the princess from danger during a battle with the Cauldron-Born and likewise rescues the smaller Glew from a fiery death in *Annuvin's treasure chamber (HK 161/189; HK 220/254). Then, showing his kind heart, Gurgi gives Glew the credit for rescuing him (HK 230/266). His hope is to help Glew receive the privilege of traveling with the *Sons of Don to the *Summer Country.

The *Chief Bard of *Prydain, *Taliesin, recognizes the phenomenal growth in Gurgi. "Yours is the wisdom of a good and kindly heart," says Taliesin. "Scarce it is, and its worth all the greater" (HK 113/135).

Another of Gurgi's winning traits is that he is always finding lost objects of importance. In *The Book of Three*, he finds *Hen Wen, and in *The Black Cauldron*, he discovers where the Black Crochan is being kept (BT 143/169; BC 115/147). In *The Castle of Llyr*, he finds the *book of spells of the *House of Llyr (CL 57/76). In *Taran Wanderer*, he spots the missing cow *Cornillo and later the enchanted finger bone of the wizard Morda (TW 58/76, 71–72/91). Gurgi is always pleased with himself. "Crafty Gurgi found it!" (BC 115/147).

As the *Chronicles of Prydain come to an end, Gurgi is invited to travel with the Sons of Don to the Summer Country. However, when Taran announces he will not go, Gurgi decides to stay. But Taran insists he travel to this land of eternal life.

> Taran put a hand on the creature's arm. "You must journey with the others. Do you call me master? Obey me, then, in one last command. Find the wisdom you yearn for. It awaits you in the Summer Country." (HK 237–238/274)

Gurgi says woefully that he has no parting gift to give kindly master, as do the others. But then he remembers something else he found: a chest pulled from Annuvin's treasure trove. The chest contains the secrets of the crafts stolen by *Arawn so many years ago. One last time, Gurgi joyfully calls out, "Gurgi always finds things!" (HK 244/281).

Though Taran and Eilonwy stay behind to rule Prydain, there is little doubt—for those who love happy endings—that one day kindly master and wise, faithful Gurgi will be reunited.

Alexander (Jacobs, 1978:270–271) remembers fondly the creation of Gurgi. The character was furtive and took his time emerging.

> I recall clearly the birth of one particular character; in this case, a diffi-cult delivery.
> Writing *The Book of Three*, the first volume of the Prydain Chron-icles, I was groping my way through the early chapters with that queasy sensation of insecurity that comes when a writer doesn't know what's

going to happen next. I knew vaguely what should happen, but I couldn't figure out how to get at it. The story, at that point, needed another character; whether friend or foe, major or minor, comic or sinister, I couldn't decide. I only knew I needed him and he refused to appear.

The work came to a halt in mid-page. I couldn't go on. I couldn't bypass that section and write around it, since future action depended on what happened now. Day after day, for better than a week, I stumbled into my work room and sat there, feeling my brain turn to concrete. In the course of my research, I had come across an 18th Century account of the various characters in *Celtic mythology. One had stuck in my mind: a creature described only as half-human, half-animal. I had hoped this would give me a clue; but Gurgi, as the text named him, was no help to me.

I was convinced by now that I had suffered severe brain damage, that I would never write again; the mortgage would be foreclosed, Janine carried off to the poor farm; and I—moaning and groaning, sighing and crying, I didn't dare imagine what would become of me. *The Book of Three* promised to be the shortest book in the world, consisting of a couple of chapters and one half-finished page. The would-be author of a hero tale had begun to show his innate cowardice, and I was feeling tremendously sorry for myself.

One morning, I went to my work room for what had become a routine session of sniveling and handwringing. Gurgi still refused to enter the scene. I could see him vaguely in my mind's eye, but I couldn't hear him. If only I could make him speak, if only I could catch the sound of his voice, half the battle would be over. He kept silent.

I sat there, expecting to pass the morning as usual, crying and sighing. Suddenly, for no apparent reason whatever, I heard a voice in the back of my mind, plaintive, whining, self-pitying. It said: "Crunchings and munchings?"

And there, right at that moment, there he was. I could hear his speech pattern, the rhymed phrases that would be his badge of identity. I could see him now, sniveling and wringing his hands, utterly woebegone. Part of him came from research. The rest of him—I have a good idea where that came from.

Though the name Gurgi is used once in the *Mabinogion (the Tribe of Gwrgi, one of the three disloyal Tribes of the Isle of Britain), there is no relationship to Alexander's creature (M 439). Two *Mabinogion* characters, however, are beast-like men. Kynvelyn Keidawd *Pwyll the half-man is briefly introduced, as is Morvian the son of Tegid. Of Morvian the *Mabinogion* says, "No one struck him in the battle of Camlan by reason of his ugliness. . . . Hair had he upon him like the hair of a stag" (M 224). But Alexander

(1985b) makes it plain that neither of these characters was his inspiration for Gurgi.

> Gurgi comes specifically from a book that was written by an 18th Century clergyman named Davies (1809:474, 477). . . . He believed the ark landed in Wales. . . . But in addition to that, he made collections of folklore, mythology, and all that, and I found one of them. And [in it] he lists . . . hundreds of characters . . . with a little description. And he lists Gurgi [Gwrgi] . . . all he says is "hideous and gray, half man, half dog." [Actually, the description reads, "hideous and gray human dog."] And for some reason that struck a spark somewhere in my mind.

In an article concerning Gurgi as an archetypal figure, Nancy-Lou Patterson (1976:24–26) compares Gurgi to Tolkien's Gollum or perhaps the dwarf in Spenser's version of *Saint George*. The archetypal "sidekick"— half human/half animal—often appears in traditional literature as a servant to the hero or the villain. Gurgi's manner of speech, appearance, smell, subservience, and so on make him typical of such characters, yet Patterson feels he is fascinatingly unique, too. Patterson quotes Northrop Frye (1967:196) about such characters:

> The characters who elude the moral antithesis of heroism and villany generally are or suggest spirits of nature. They represent partly the moral neutrality of the intermediate world of nature and partly a world of mystery which is glimpsed but never seen, and which retreats when approached. . . . Such characters are, more or less, children of nature, who can be brought to serve the hero, like Crusoe's Friday, but retain the inscrutability of their origin. As servants or friends of the hero, they impart the mysterious rapport with nature that so often marks the central figure of romance.

Alexander is quick to point out that Gurgi changes and does not "retain the inscrutability" of his origin. But Gurgi is the hero's "sidekick," and as Alexander explains, this is indeed a common motif in myth.

> Don't forget that in most of the myths there is a duality, a hero and his mirror image, his sidekick, his partner, who is usually a clown. The sky hero and the earth clown, two aspects of the same personality. Don Quixote and Sancho Panza, Mr. Pickwick and Sam Weller—these are archetypes. It almost seems that every hero has his comic companion. (Wintle and Fisher, 1974:216–217)

Alexander acknowledges that this type of character combination— shadow figures—generally dictates that the earth clown is not a dynamic character. This character is concerned with creature comforts (eating, sleeping, etc.) and is content to stay the same. Gurgi, however, breaks the mold.

> I wanted to make a difference. . . . Gurgi grows into a full human being. In other words, what Gurgi wants more than anything else is wisdom, and he changes throughout the book[s]. He starts out . . . on a low level of evolution, and he gradually becomes more and more human. . . . And indeed what he wants at the end . . . [is] to be wise, which I think is probably one of the noblest human aspirations. (Alexander, 1985b)

When asked which character seems to be the favorite among children, Alexander answered that Gurgi might have an edge.

> It is probably Gurgi, always fearful for his poor tender head, always hungry for crunchings and munchings. Half-animal, half-human, innocent and questing, cowardly and brave, he yearns for wisdom and, in the course of the adventure, grows up enough to find it. Do children sense a little of themselves in Gurgi? (Alexander, 1970:17–18)

See also Characters—fantasy.

Gwenlliant (gwen-LEE-ant): Gwenlliant is the young daughter of *Llonio and *Goewin. During the time *Taran stays with his family, Llonio sends Gwenlliant to fetch an egg from their moody-natured brown hen. She returns with the single egg granted them by the hen.
(TW 165/195)

Gwybeddin (gwih-BED-in): Gwybeddin is a gnat who volunteers himself and the other gnats in the battle against *Arawn and his *Chief Huntsman. *Kadwyr, the impudent crow, laughs at Gwybeddin's offer, calling him *Prince Flyspeck. As it turns out, the gnats are instrumental in saving Kadwyr's life. As the Chief Huntsman takes aim with his bow at the wounded crow, Gwybeddin and his colleagues swarm around and distract him. This allows Kadwyr to flee.
See also Brynach, Crugan-Crawgan, Edyrnion, Medwyn, Nedir.
(F 43/50, 47/55)

**Gwydion (GWIHD-ion): Gwydion is the war leader of the *High King *Math and is "the mightiest hero in *Prydain" (BT 6/21). He is described as having a wolf-like appearance.

> The stranger had the shaggy, gray-streaked hair of a wolf. His eyes were deep-set, flecked with green. Sun and wind had leathered his broad face,

burnt it dark and grained it with fine lines. His cloak was coarse and travel-stained. (BT 16/31)

His lips drew tightly against his teeth in the lean smile of a stalking wolf. (CL 35/53)

Gwydion is a *Son of Don, the magical race from the *Summer Country who now dwell in Prydain at *Caer Dathyl. Therefore, he has some traces of enchantment in his blood. He has the qualities to possess and draw from its sheath the mighty sword, *Dyrnwyn, which would kill a lesser man. And early in *The Book of Three, Gwydion weaves an enchanted net of grass which he throws at an oncoming foe. "Suddenly the withered wisps grew larger, longer, shimmering and crackling, nearly blinding *Taran with streaks of liquid flame" (BT 41/58). Gwydion's skills of enchantment are limited. But he gains knowledge of the deepest mysteries and secrets of life by overcoming the torments of the Castle *Oeth-Anoeth.

In *The Book of Three*, Taran and the *Companions think Gwydion dead in the ruins of *Spiral Castle. However, *Achren has spirited him away to Oeth-Anoeth, another of *Annuvin's strongholds, in hope she may win him for her cause. This proves fruitless:

> "Raging, she cast me into the lowest dungeon," Gwydion said. "I have never been closer to my death than in Oeth-Anoeth.
>
> "How long I lay there, I cannot be sure," Gwydion continued. "In Oeth-Anoeth, time is not as you know it here. It is better that I do not speak of the torments Achren had devised. The worst were not of the body but of the spirit, and of these the most painful was despair. Yet, even in my deepest anguish, I clung to hope. For there is this about Oeth-Anoeth: if a man withstand it, even death will give up its secrets to him.
>
> "I withstood it," Gwydion said quietly, "and at the end much was revealed to me which before had been clouded. Of this, too, I shall not speak. It is enough for you to know that I understood the workings of life and death, of laughter and tears, endings and beginnings. I saw the truth of the world, and knew no chains could hold me. My bonds were light as dreams. At that moment, the walls of my prison melted." (BT 178/207–208)

Gwydion is never again the same. He discovers that now he can understand the speech of animals. This is how he learns the name of the *Horned King. Speaking directly to the oracular pig, *Hen Wen, Gwydion obtains the name and uses it to overcome *Arawn's war leader and champion. Taran is surprised that merely a name can destroy such as the Horned King. "'Yes,' Gwydion answered. 'Once you have courage to look upon evil, seeing it for what it is and naming it by its true name, it is powerless against you, and you can destroy it'" (BT 179/209). Perhaps Gwydion also learned this great secret concerning good and evil while in the confines of Oeth-Anoeth.

Gwydion is one of Taran's mentors and protectors in the *Prydain Chronicles. Even Taran's steed is a foal of Gwydion's magnificent horse, *Melyngar. A guiding figure such as Gwydion is a hallmark of the classic heroic character, and though Gwydion does not appear on many pages in the story, his inspiration and wisdom are always with Taran. Much of Alexander's wisdom—his philosophy about life—is stated through Gwydion. For example, when Taran is dismayed that the famous Prince Gwydion should look so disheveled, Gwydion answers, "It is not the trappings that make the prince . . . nor, indeed, the sword that makes the warrior" (BT 17/32). And when Taran plaintively complains about not knowing his parentage ("I don't even know who I am."), Gwydion replies, "In a way that is something we must all discover for ourselves" (BT 21/37). The following are further examples of Gwydion's wisdom:

"Do you [Taran] love danger so much?" asked Gwydion. "Before you are a man," he added gently, "you will learn to hate it. Yes, and fear it, too, even as I do." (BC 35/52)

"It is easy to judge evil unmixed," replied Gwydion. "But, alas, in most of us good and bad are closely woven as the threads on a *loom; greater wisdom than mine is needed for the judging." (BC 174/217)

"The destinies of men are woven one with the other, and you can turn aside from them no more than you can turn aside from your own." (CL 162/192)

"It is beyond any man's wisdom to judge the secret heart of another," he said, "for in it are good and evil mixed." (HK 117/139)

"Evil conquered? You [Taran] have learned much, but learn this last and hardest of lessons. You have conquered only the enchantments of evil. That was the easiest of your tasks, only a beginning, not an ending. Do you believe evil itself to be so quickly overcome? Not so long as men still hate and slay each other, when greed and anger goad them. Against these even a flaming sword cannot prevail, but only that portion of good in all men's hearts whose flame can never be quenched." (HK 245/282)

In each volume of the Chronicles, except *Taran Wanderer, Gwydion organizes and leads the quest. He searches for Hen Wen to secure the secret name of the Horned King in The Book of Three. He orchestrates the plan to destroy the *Black Crochan in *The Black Cauldron. In *The Castle of Llyr,

Gwydion leads the party that rescues *Eilonwy from Achren's clutches. Then, in *The High King, Gwydion not only becomes the High King of Prydain when King Math dies but also plans the attack on Annuvin. In each book, Taran is separated from Gwydion but undertakes the tasks necessary to see each quest successfully accomplished.

If Arawn is the perfect example of evil, then Prince Gwydion represents ultimate good. He is pure and wise, partly because he is strong enough to cast aside the temptation of power. Gwydion rejects Achren's promises of power and a chance to control all of Prydain (BT 47/65). A lust for power corrupted many men in the story: *Morgant, *Pryderi, and to some extent *Ellidyr. Morgant recognizes that Gwydion was once offered power such as that of the *Black Cauldron, the very power that corrupted him, and Gwydion refused it (BC 162/203). The *Prince of Don, as Gwydion is often called, has learned to perfectly control his passions and appetites.

As the Chronicles conclude, Gwydion turns the High Kingship over to Taran of *Caer Dallben. He has known all along that Taran might well be the prophesied king who shall rule Prydain after the Sons of Don return to the Summer Country. As *Dallben turns *The Book of Three over to Taran, Gwydion speaks his farewell.

> "The Book of Three is now both history and heritage. For my own gift, I could give you nothing greater. Nor do I offer you a crown, for a true king wears his crown in his heart." The tall warrior clasped Taran's hand. "Farewell. We shall not meet again."
>
> "Take Dyrnwyn, then, in remembrance of me," Taran said.
>
> "Dyrnwyn is yours," Gwydion said, "as it was meant to be." (HK 244–245/281–282)

The character Gwydion plays a major role in the *Mabinogion and in other tales of *Celtic mythology. In some accounts, Gwydion ab Don (the son of Don) is a celebrated enchanter and also a herdsman of cattle for the tribe of Gwynedd (M 273). However, the mythological story concerning Gwydion that relates most closely to the Prydain Chronicles is "The Battle of the Trees." This tale, recounted in *Lady Charlotte Guest's notes to the Mabinogion, comes from another manuscript of Welsh myth, the Myvyrian Archaiology. The following lines, which became Alexander's inspiration for The Book of Three, tell the story.

> These are the Englyns that were sung at the Cad Goddeu (the Battle of the Trees), or, as others call it, the Battle of Achren, which was an account of a white roebuck, and a whelp; and they came from Hell, and

Amathaon ab Don brought them. And therefore Amathaon ab Don, and Arawn, King of Annwn (Hell), fought. And there was a man in that battle, unless his name were known he could not be overcome; and there was on the other side a woman called Achren, and unless her name were known her party could not be overcome. And Gwydion ab Don guessed the name of the man. . . .

"Bran art thou called. . . ." (M 280; WG 49)

So Gwydion was born in Alexander's tale as the one who learned the secret name of the Horned King, a man who could not be overcome unless his name were known. Except for a few similarities in plot, Gwydion is otherwise unrelated to the character from Welsh tales who is somewhat unprincipled and ruthless. The Gwydion of Welsh myth killed Pryderi (a more honorable character than in Prydain) through the use of magical arts, whereby he also defrauded him of special swine sent from Annuvin (M 364; M 418). He also deceives King Math so that his brother (Gilvaethwy ab Don) can steal the king's handmaiden (*Goewin) (M 414). For their deception, King Math turns the brothers into various wild animals. Gwydion and Gilvaethwy live as animals over a span of several years.

In spite of Gwydion's less-than-upright behavior, he is still considered a great Welsh hero. He is one of the three famous tribe-herdsmen of the Island of Britain and was considered "the best teller of tales in the world" (M 415). He was also a great astronomer. In fact, "the Milky-way is after him termed Caer Gwydion" (M 437).

Gwydion ab Don also is the guardian of another well-known mythological character, Llew Llaw Gyffes. He again uses deception to try forcing Gyffes' mother, Arianrod (Arianrhod), to accept her son. One of the deceptions involves disguising himself and Llew Llaw Gyffes as shoemakers or cordwainers (M 423). Prince Gwydion in *The Castle of Llyr* also dons the disguise of a shoemaker but uses the disguise to secretly watch over and protect the Princess Eilonwy (CL 20/36).

Gwydion is said to have learned his *magic from Math. Of his several brothers, *Govannion (Govannon) and Eunydd are listed as celebrated *bards. Gwydion's grave is supposedly located in Morva Dinllev, the scene of one of his adventures with Llew Llaw Gyffes (M 437).

See also Belin; Characters—fantasy; Good versus evil; Heroism; Lady Don, the.

(M 213, 273, 280, 364, 411+, 437, 482; WG 30, 36, 49, 56, 59, 81, 85, 90, 106, 119, 124, 141, 244, 281, 286, 291, 303, 314, 318, 446)

Gwyn (GWINN) the Hunter: Gwyn is a mysterious, almost supernatural being who is never encountered in the *Prydain Chronicles, though the sound of his horn and the baying of his hounds are heard on numerous occasions. His being and purpose are best explained by Prince *Gwydion.

> "Gwyn owes allegiance to a lord unknown even to me," Gwydion answered, "and one perhaps greater than *Arawn. Gwyn the Hunter rides alone with his dogs, and where he rides, slaughter follows. He has foreknowledge of death and battle, and watches from afar, marking the fall of warriors." (BT 36/53)

Soon after Gwydion's instruction, *Taran hears Gwyn's hunting call, and his heart is filled with dread.

> Above the cry of the pack rose the long, clear notes of a hunting horn. Flung across the sky, the sound pierced Taran's breast like a cold blade of terror. Yet, unlike the music itself, the echoes from the hills sang less of fear than of grief. Fading, they sighed that sunlight and birds, bright mornings, warm fires, food and drink, friendship, and all good things had been lost beyond recovery. Gwydion laid a firm hand on Taran's brow.
>   "Gwyn's music is a warning," Gwydion said. "Take it as a warning, for whatever profit that knowledge may be. But do not listen overmuch to the echoes. Others have done so, and have wandered hopelessly ever since." (BT 36–37/53)

The baying of Gwyn's hounds and the call of his horn fill Taran with dread and deep sadness from time to time throughout the Chronicles. Gwyn's horn sounds again just before Gwydion destroys the *Horned King (BT 163/191). It sounds when King *Math perishes under the boots of the *Cauldron-Born (HK 128/153). And perhaps the most poignant example occurs when *Coll dies on the barren stretches of the *Red Fallows (HK 142/168–169).

The name of Gwyn (or Gwynn) appears often in the *Mabinogion and other Welsh tales, with several characters using the name. Gwynn ab Nudd seems to be most like the mythological hunter in the *Prydain Chronicles. Gwynn the son of Nudd is described as one "whom God has placed over the brood of devils in Annwn (*Annuvin), lest they should destroy the present race" (M 241). Therefore, he is also a figure of death. Gwyn ab Nudd (the spelling varies) is also charged with stealing the betrothed of *Gwythyr the son of *Greidawl. He is shown as being extremely cruel: "And he slew Nwython, and took out his heart, and constrained Kyledyr to eat the heart of his father" (M 250–251).

In her notes to the *Mabinogion*, *Lady Charlotte Guest further explains the personage of Gwyn. He is "one of the most poetical characters of Welsh Romance," she says. "He is no less personage than the King of Faerie" (M 263). Gwyn is the sovereign over the *Tylwyth Teg (fairies) and the Elves. He is reportedly given to mischief, such as luring travelers into a bog. The owl is considered to be the bird of Gwyn ab Nudd. Karngrwn is the name of his horse. Guest also notes that the *Triads* (other Welsh tales) commemorate Gwyn as "one of the three distinguished astronomers of the Island of Britain, who by their knowledge of the nature and qualities of the stars, could predict whatever was to be wished to be known to the end of the world" (M 264). He is also sometimes called the King of Annwn (M 264).

Guest also speaks of "The Dogs of Annwn," hounds that are similar to those of Gwyn the Hunter. "It is said that they are sometimes heard at night passing through the air overhead, as if in full cry in pursuit of some object" (M 363). The *Mabinogion* also describes the "death horn for slaying" (M 153). It was common practice to announce or signify death with the sounding of a hunting horn.

Robert Graves in *The White Goddess* makes the most pointed reference to the mythological hunter.

> In Wales the sound of the geese passing unseen overhead at night is supposed to be made by Cwm Annwn ("Hounds of Hell" with white bodies and red ears). . . . The Hunter is called variously Gwyn ("the white one")—there was a Gwyn cult in pre-Christian Glastonbury—Herne the Hunter, and Gabriel. (WG 89)

See also Characters—fantasy.
(BT 36/53, 64/83, 163/191; TW 64/83; HK 128/153, 142/168; M 125, 159, 223, 224, 228, 240, 241, 250, 255, 263, 333, 363, 502; WG 89, 179, 220, 321, 388, 446)

Gwystyl (GWISS-til): Gwystyl of the *Fair Folk maintains a cleverly hidden Fair Folk *way post near the borders of *Annuvin. The way post, concealed in an embankment covered with rocks and brambles, lies to the southwest of *Dark Gate. When the *Companions meet Gwystyl, he appears to be both ill and cowardly.

> The figure heaved a long and melancholy sigh, and the portal opened wider. *Taran saw a creature which, at first glance, looked like a bundle of sticks with cobwebs floating at the top. He realized quickly the strange doorkeeper resembled certain of the Fair Folk he had once seen in

*Eiddileg's kingdom; only this individual seemed in a woeful state of disrepair.

Unlike *Doli, Gwystyl was not of the dwarf kindred. Though taller, he was extremely thin. His sparse hair was long and stringy; his nose drooped wearily above his upper lip, which in turn drooped toward his chin in a most mournful expression. Wrinkles puckered his forehead; his eyes blinked anxiously; and he seemed on the verge of bursting into tears. Around his bent shoulders was draped a shabby, grimy robe, which he fingered nervously. He sniffed several times, sighed again, and grudgingly beckoned Doli to enter. (BC 53–54/72–73)

Gwystyl seems such a pitiful character. He snivels, complains, and sobs constantly. His technique for avoiding uncomfortable situations (and everything seems to be uncomfortable) is to say, "I'm simply not up to [such and such] today. . . . I'm not well, not at all well, really" (BC 54/73). He dislikes visitors and asks the Companions, "When did you say you were leaving?" (BC 56/76). And when Doli threatens to squeeze him to get more information about the *Black Cauldron, Gwystyl faints (BC 62/84).

Gwystyl and his pet crow, *Kaw, know the whereabouts of the missing *cauldron. Kaw hints that the cauldron is in the hands of *Orddu, *Orwen, and *Orgoch. Then wretched Gwystyl is forced to tell all he knows.

As the Companions depart from this first meeting with Gwystyl, the little creature gives the band a black *powder that will mask their footprints, enabling them to travel some distance without being tracked.

Gwystyl's appearance and demeanor are misleading. King *Morgant explains: "Among all who hold the way posts, Gwystyl of the Fair Folk is the shrewdest and bravest. Did you believe King Eiddileg would trust a lesser servant so close to Annuvin? But if you misjudged him, it was his intention that you do so" (BC 158/199). As if to verify those words, Gwystyl appears at the conclusion of *The Black Cauldron to battle against the warriors of the traitorous Morgant. When the battle is won and the *Black Crochan destroyed, Gwystyl gives Taran Kaw as a gift from the Fair Folk. Kaw becomes Taran's trusted comrade throughout the rest of the *Chronicles.

Gwystyl does not appear again until *The High King. As *Eilonwy, *Fflewddur, and *Rhun plan a way to rescue Taran and *Gwydion from the evil *Magg, Gwystyl happens by. Again, he is reluctant to stay around humans. "'How nice to see you again,' he mumbled. 'A pleasure, believe me. I've thought of you often. Good-bye. Now I really must be on my way'" (HK 60/75).

Eilonwy is able to convince the reluctant Gwystyl to help with the rescue plan. Gwystyl's cloak and pack conceal countless tools and tricks to aid them: *magic *eggs that make smoke, magic *powder that hides footprints or blinds if thrown in the eyes, magic *mushrooms that explode into flames, line and grappling hooks.

Gwystyl once again has masked his valor with his whining countenance. He has been on a spying mission and makes his way to the *Realm of the Fair Folk to report to King Eiddileg. Later in *The High King,* Doli appears with a band of Fair Folk warriors just when Taran needs them desperately. "Gwystyl has done his work well," says Taran, acknowledging that Gwystyl is responsible for the Fair Folk reinforcements (HK 151/178).

The last time Gwystyl is mentioned, Doli explains the reason for the valiant creature's unhappy appearance. Because Gwystyl lives so near Annuvin, his digestion and disposition have been adversely affected. Fair Folk will indeed die if they stay long within Annuvin's borders (HK 181/212). This knowledge makes Gwystyl even more of a heroic character.

The name Gwystyl appears several times in the *Mabinogion. However, none of the characters are anything like Gwystyl of the Fair Folk. Gwystyl (Geneir Gwystyl) is listed as a son of Rhun and a knight serving King Arthur (M 82, 225).

Alexander seems to have had a good deal of fun creating Gwystyl. He tells the following story.

> A friend reading *The Black Cauldron* remarked to me: "Oh, I see you've done a very interesting self-portrait here."
> I answered that he must obviously be referring to the brave, kind, wise, noble, handsome Prince Gwydion.
> "Hell, no," he said. "I mean that wretched, miserable Gwystyl!"
> Reluctantly, I admitted he was right, that I was more qualified, even in my own book, to play hypochondriac instead of hero. (Jacobs, 1978:493)

Alexander reveals that he first met "the hopelessly distraught and harassed Gwystyl while sitting, under protest, in a dentist's chair!" (BC 181/224).

Alexander also "confesses to being a confirmed pessimist; and, indeed, his first reaction to anything he is personally connected with is often shrouded in black" (Jacobs, 1978:106). Here again we see a little of Gwystyl.

See also Characters—fantasy.
(BC 51/70, 73/96, 106/137, 136/174, 155/195, 158/199, 172/215, 181/224; HK 60/75, 151/178, 181/212; M 82, 225, 274, 312)

gwythaint (GWITH-aint): Gwythaints are enormous black birds of prey, "greater than the greatest eagle," with "blood-red eyes" and "curving beaks and talons as merciless as daggers" (CWP 78/17; HK 211/244; BT 33/49). *Gwydion explains something of their nature to *Taran.

"They are *Arawn's spies and messengers, the *Eyes of Annuvin, they are called. No one stays long hidden from them. . . .

"The errand of the gwythaints is less to kill than to bring information. . . . Arawn understands their language and they are in his power from the moment they leave the egg." (BT 34/50–51)

But *Medwyn explains that the great birds deserve to be pitied rather than hated:

"Once, long ago, they were as free as other birds, gentle and trusting. In his cunning, Arawn lured them to him and brought them under his power. He built the iron cages which are now their prison house in *Annuvin. The tortures he inflicted on the gwythaints were shameful and unspeakable. Now they serve him out of terror." (BT 119/143)

Armed with this understanding, Taran later rescues a fledgling gwythaint from a thornbush. The *Companions want to kill it, but Taran nurses the creature back to health. Under protest, *Doli builds a cage for the gwythaint with plans to take the bird with them to *Caer Dathyl. Though the fledgling seems to grow accustomed to Taran and even *Eilonwy, it slashes its way out of the cage one night and is gone. All fear that the gwythaint will fly straight to Annuvin and expose their quest to warn Caer Dathyl of the *Horned King (BT 159/186–187). But responding to the kindness, the gwythaint instead finds Prince Gwydion and tells him that the Companions are nearby. Hastening to find them, the *Prince of Don arrives in time to learn the Horned King's secret name from *Hen Wen and thereby destroy Arawn's war leader (BT 179/208–209).

Alexander's mother recalled that he frequently brought home birds and animals, particularly when they were injured or showed signs of neglect. Perhaps this tendency surfaced in the story of the injured gwythaint (Jacobs, 1978:29).

In *The High King, the fledgling gwythaint appears once again and performs another deed that turns the hand of fate toward the *Sons of Don. As Taran clings for life on a crag of *Mount Dragon, a gwythaint plunges toward him. Sure of his death, Taran is overjoyed when the now-grown bird recognizes him. The gwythaint lifts Taran to the mountain peak and then turns to attack the *Cauldron-Born who threaten the *Assistant Pig-Keeper. The noble bird is struck down and killed by the deathless warriors. But he has placed Taran in the exact spot where the enchanted sword, *Dyrnwyn, is hidden (HK 213/247). With the sword, Taran is able to slay the Cauldron-Born and Arawn *Death-Lord.

The other gwythaints in the *Chronicles of Prydain are ruthless enemies to the people of *Prydain. More than once gwythaints attack the Companions. They report to Arawn that Taran and the others are moving the *Black Cauldron to *Caer Dallben (BC 146/185). Gwythaints attack and injure *Kaw as he spies on Annuvin (HK 85–86/103–104). They also attack *Achren as she makes her way to *Dark Gate. Only the intervention of an army of crows led by Kaw saves her life. The crows are so great in number they are able to attack and nearly subdue the giant birds (HK 195–196/227).

As Arawn is slain and Annuvin tumbles, the gwythaints too are destroyed (HK 227/263). The birds apparently do not live to be gentle and free once again.

See also Characters—fantasy.

(BT 33+/49+; BC 5/15, 134/171, 146/185, 156/196, 177/220; TW 38/54, 87/108; HK 35/47, 85/103, 89/108, 194/226, 210/243, 227/262; CWP 78/17; F 42/49)

Gwythyr (GWIH-ther) Son of Greidawl (GREYE-dawl): *Medwyn tells *Taran the story of Gwythyr Son of *Greidawl that is part of the tale of *Kilhuch and *Olwen. In order for Kilhuch to win Olwen's hand in marriage, he must perform several nearly impossible tasks assigned by her father, *Yspadadden the *Chief Giant. One of the tasks is to gather nine bushels of flax seed. Though flax seed is scarce, Gwythyr undertakes this task for his friend. As he wonders how to accomplish the task, Gwythyr hears wailing coming from an anthill surrounded by fire. He extinguishes the flames with his sword, and in gratitude the ants scour every field to collect the nine bushels. But the Chief Giant declares Gwythyr is one seed short, and the seed must be delivered by nightfall. Just as the sun sets, a lame ant hobbles up carrying the last flax seed.

Medwyn uses the story to teach Taran. His analogy is as follows:

> "I have studied the race of men," Medwyn continued. "I have seen that alone you stand as weak reeds by a lake. You must learn to help yourselves, that is true, but you must also learn to help one another. Are you not, all of you, lame ants?" (BT 121/145)

The story of Gwythyr comes directly from the *Mabinogion's tale of "Kilhwch [Kilhuch] and Olwen" (M 249). Medwyn recounts the story exactly as it is told in *Celtic mythology. It is also said that Gwythyr was the father of one of the three Gwenhwyvars (Gwenivere) who were the wives of King Arthur (M 262).

See also Characters—fantasy.

(BT 120/144; M 223, 229, 249, 262)

h

❖

Hall of Bards: The Hall of Bards was located at *Caer Dathyl until the stronghold's destruction by *Pryderi and the *Cauldron-Born. It is located beneath the *Hall of Lore where much of *Prydain's ancient learning is stored. However, the Hall of Bards contains "even richer troves," for the greater parts of the ancient records are kept therein. Only a true *bard may enter this chamber.

See also Chief Bard, Council of Bards, Council Chamber of the Bards, Taliesin.

(HK 113/135, 128/153)

Hall of Lore: According to *Taliesin, *Chief Bard of Prydain, the Hall of Lore is the storehouse for much of *Prydain's ancient learning. "Though *Arawn *Death-Lord robbed men of their craft secrets, he could not gain the songs and sayings of our *bards. Here they have been carefully gathered" (HK 113/134). Yet, beneath this chamber lies the *Hall of Bards where the greater parts of the ancient records are kept.

The Hall of Lore was located in *Caer Dathyl before the stronghold's destruction by *Pryderi and the *Cauldron-Born.

See also *Council of Bards, *Menwy.

(HK 113/134, 114/136, 128/153, 237/273)

Hall of Thrones: The throne room of the *High King, *Math Son of *Mathonwy, is called the Hall of Thrones. It was located at *Caer Dathyl before the stronghold was destroyed by *Pryderi and the *Cauldron-Born.

(HK 107/128, 128/153)

Hall of Warriors: The Hall of Warriors is the building in *Annuvin that houses the *Black Cauldron or the *Black Crochan. "The cauldron stands

on a platform in the Hall of Warriors, which is just beyond *Dark Gate"
(BC 19/32–33). Upon the death of *Arawn, it tumbles to the ground as
does the rest of the *Death-Lord's stronghold.
(BC 19/32–33, 42/60; HK 209/242, 224/259)

Hazel Nuts of Wisdom: On his journey to rescue *Hen Wen from
*Arawn, *Coll eats the nuts of an enchanted hazel tree and suddenly can
understand the speech of animals. He first speaks with *Ash-Wing, an owl
who explains that "only one tree in *Prydain bears" nuts such as these
(CWP 76/11). This enchanted tree grows not too far north of *Caer Dallben, for Coll stumbles upon it shortly after leaving for *Annuvin.

However, the effects of the Hazel Nuts of Wisdom are temporary—a day
of understanding for each nut consumed. Therefore, Coll must hurry if he is
to take advantage of help from Ash-Wing and other animals in his rescue
attempt.

Alexander (1985b) gleaned the idea for his Hazel Nuts of Wisdom
from an explanation given and a tale recounted by Robert Graves in *The
White Goddess*. The Irish story of how Fionn gained wisdom, though much
like that of Little Gwion (M 471–472) and *Dallben (BC 104/135), tells
how he cooks a salmon for a certain Druid, yet is instructed *not* to taste it.
Fionn burns his thumb which he promptly puts in his mouth. As it turns
out, the fish is a salmon of knowledge "that had fed on nuts fallen from the
nine hazels of poetic art" (WG 75). Fionn immediately receives the gift of
inspiration.

As Graves explains, "the ninth tree [in the Celtic-Druid tree-alphabet]
is the hazel, in nutting season. The nut in Celtic legend is always an
emblem of concentrated wisdom: something sweet, compact and sustaining
enclosed in a small hard shell—as we say: 'this is the matter in a nut shell'"
(WG 181–182). It is also interesting to note that the Druid letter represented by the hazel is named Coll (WG 181).

See also Fantastic objects, Oak-Horn, Star-Nose.
(CWP 76/11; WG 75, 181)

Hen (HEN) Rhitta (RIH-ta): *See* *Rhitta.

**Hen Wen (HEN WEN): Hen Wen is "the only oracular pig in *Prydain"
(BT 10/25). Before the story of *Taran begins, *Arawn *Death-Lord sends
his henchmen to steal the marvelous white sow from her owner, *Coll Son
of *Collfrewr. Coll, who loves, "above all, his white pig," goes to *Annuvin
to rescue Hen Wen (CWP 75/7–8). On his journey to the *Land of Death,

Coll learns for the first time that Hen Wen is "no ordinary pig" (CWP 77/11). The owl, *Ash-Wing, explains that Hen Wen knows many deep secrets, and therefore Arawn has stolen her. Arawn hopes to use Hen Wen's secrets in his evil scheme to conquer all Prydain. Coll is able to retrieve the oracular pig and return to his farmstead. At his farm, he finds *Dallben waiting for him. The enchanter stays to protect Hen Wen, and Coll's farm becomes known as *Caer Dallben.

In spite of Dallben's protective shield, Arawn tries to take Hen Wen once again. As *The Book of Three begins, Hen Wen senses that Arawn's champion, the *Horned King, is near Caer Dallben. Because all the farm animals seem fearful, Dallben decides to use the *letter sticks to consult Hen Wen concerning the impending danger. However, Hen Wen is so frightened that she digs her way out of the pen and runs into the woods before Dallben returns with the letter sticks. Young Taran, *Assistant Pig-Keeper, chases after Hen Wen and is therefore launched on his first quest. Hen Wen is the herald who inadvertently calls Taran to adventure (see Heroism).

This time Hen Wen is rescued by the *Fair Folk. Taran finds her in King *Eiddileg's underground kingdom. Soon after, Hen Wen reveals the secret name of the Horned King to Prince *Gwydion, who has recently acquired the ability to understand the speech of animals. Confronting the Horned King and calling his name, Gwydion destroys Arawn's war leader (BT 179/209).

Unless frightened, Hen Wen is extremely good-natured. She is characterized by her grunting, wheezing, and chuckling: "Hwoinch! . . . Hwch! Hwaaw!" (BT 147/173). And those are the only answers Taran gets when he asks Hen Wen to prophesy the outcome of his quest in *Taran Wanderer (TW 8/21). Only through the *ash-wood *letter sticks or one such as Gwydion who understands animal speech can Hen Wen reveal her secrets.

In *The High King, Hen Wen is immortalized on a banner embroidered by the Princess *Eilonwy: a white pig with blue eyes on a field of green. (Eilonwy hadn't noticed that Hen Wen's eyes are brown!) The banner becomes Taran's "battle flag" around which he rallies the men of the *Free Commots to march against Arawn. It is known as the *banner of the White Pig (HK 83/101).

Also in The High King, Hen Wen is asked to reveal how the enchanted sword *Dyrnwyn might be regained from Arawn Death-Lord. Dallben brings the letter sticks to Hen Wen's enclosure. Again, frightened to the point of collapse, the oracular pig can barely read the sticks. It seems strange that Gwydion does not simply talk with her to get the needed answers, as he did to acquire the Horned King's secret name. But Alexander (1985b) explains that Hen Wen "was in such a state of fear and panic that she couldn't communicate in any way." If she could barely point to the symbols on the letter sticks, she would be unable to speak to Gwydion.

However, when Taran calms her, Hen Wen reluctantly points with her snout to symbols on the ash-wood sticks. But the letter sticks shatter before the prophecy is complete. Nevertheless, the message from the first stick answers Dallben's question concerning how Dyrnwyn might be regained: "Ask, sooner, mute stone and voiceless rock to speak" (HK 31/43).

As hopeless as this sounds, the message from the second stick is even less encouraging. It tells of Dyrnwyn's fate.

> Quenched will be Dyrnwyn's flame;
> Vanished, its power.
> Night turn to noon
> And rivers burn with frozen fire
> Ere Dyrnwyn be regained. (HK 31/43)

However, each stipulation is met. Night turns to noon when Eilonwy's *bauble brightens the night landscape of the *Hills of Bran-Galedd, warning Taran of approaching *Huntsmen (HK 171/200). Soon after, *Doli of the *Fair Folk engineers a plan to destroy the Huntsmen. Taran's band lights great brush fires on the surface of a frozen lake at the top of an ice-bound waterfall. As the ice breaks, a cascade of boulders, fiery ice floes, and water rage downward to destroy the Huntsmen of Annuvin (HK 179/208–209). Thus, "rivers burn with frozen fire." Finally, when Taran is perched atop *Mount Dragon, the sound of wind moving past a grotesquely shaped rock is like that of a voice. The wailing alerts Taran to the secret hidden beneath it: Dyrnwyn. "The voiceless stone spoke clearly," says Taran (HK 213/246; HK 221/256).

When each condition is met and Arawn is slain, Dyrnwyn's flame is quenched, and its power is ended. The prophecy of Hen Wen is fulfilled (HK 223/257).

Hen Wen's oracular powers also fade away as the age of enchantment in Prydain comes to an end. Even so, Hen Wen is invited to travel with the *Sons of Don to the *Summer Country. However, Dallben feels she will be happier in Prydain. Indeed, when Taran returns to Caer Dallben he finds the happy sow nursing six new piglets!

Hen Wen plays a significant role in *Celtic mythology. In *Lady Charlotte Guest's notes to the *Mabinogion, a story is recounted concerning Henwen, a marvelous sow belonging to Dadweir Dallpenn and tended by Coll ab

Collfrewi (one of the three powerful swineherds of Britain). Henwen was prophesied to bring evil upon Britain when she bore her young. Therefore, Arthur tried to destroy her. In her flight to escape Arthur, Henwen crossed sea and land, leaving grains of wheat (barley, rye), bees, a piglet, a wolf cub, an eaglet, and a kitten in her wake. Many of these things benefited the areas of Britain where they were left. For example, the best pigs and the finest barley are to this day produced in Dyved. But, in some instances, the things Henwen left behind her brought woe. The kitten became the Palug Cat, one of the three plagues of the *Isle of Mona (M 269).

Robert Graves mentions the same story in *The White Goddess*. However, he maintains that Hen Wen was the Goddess Cerridwen in beast disguise. According to Graves, Hen Wen means "the Old White one" (WG 221). Alexander (1968a:171) agrees with Graves on both counts, explaining that pigs were sacred animals in Wales.

See also Characters—fantasy, Heroism, Llyan, Oak-Horn, Star-Nose. (M 269; WG 51, 67, 221)

Heroism: According to Madsen (1976:52), one of the six motifs of high fantasy is heroism. Fantasy author Natalie Babbitt (1987) also explains that the hero motif is essential to fantasy stories. A hero's quest will always follow an age-old pattern, a pattern that continues to be the backbone of today's fantasy literature. The steps of the classic hero's quest are as follows (Babbitt, 1987:27):

1. *The hero is called to adventure by a "herald."* *Taran is initially called to adventure by *Hen Wen, whom he follows on a wild chase much as Alice does the white rabbit. Prince *Gwydion also serves as herald by setting a course for the particular quest in each novel. However, Gwydion does not function as herald in *Taran Wanderer. Taran is called by his own yearning to determine his parentage. Perhaps one could say his unfulfilled love for *Eilonwy calls him to adventure, for he thinks he may not ask her hand until he knows his heritage.

2. *The hero crosses the threshold into the "other world," which is no longer a place of security.* Taran has lived in the safest place in all *Prydain, *Caer Dallben. When he leaves to chase Hen Wen, he crosses the threshold into a world of danger. Though he returns to Caer Dallben at the conclusion of each novel, he always leaves again to continue his quest.

3. *The hero must survive various trials in his new environment.* Taran struggles against enemies such as *Achren, *Arawn, the *Cauldron-Born, the *Huntsmen of Annuvin, and *Morda. He suffers the pain of long treks through bitter winter weather and of carrying the *Black Cauldron through

marshes and forests. Perhaps the greatest of his trials are trials of the soul. This is best illustrated by Taran's anguish at learning that *Craddoc, a common shepherd, may be his father. When Craddoc falls into an icy crevice, Taran thinks for a moment of leaving him to die. Rescue seems impossible, and freedom from an unwanted heritage could be had. The evil whisperings fill Taran with dark terror and shame. "Then, as if his heart would burst with it, he cried out in terrible rage, 'What man am I?'" (TW 153/181).

4. *The hero is assisted by a protective figure who will aid him through his struggles.* Taran is assisted by *Dallben, by Gwydion, and to some extent by *Coll. Relying on these men, all father figures for Taran, he is able to achieve his destiny.

5. *The hero becomes a "whole person," finding himself, or, perhaps, becoming an adult. He does so by learning the lessons of life that come with surviving and overcoming his trials.* Taran certainly grows to a mature manhood during the course of the *Prydain Chronicles. His wisdom increases immensely in *Taran Wanderer* as he struggles fiercely with his inner self. He has, in fact, matured sufficiently to qualify as the prophesied *High King of Prydain.

6. *The hero returns to the "real world" or returns home.* Within each novel, Taran returns to Caer Dallben, every time a bit older and wiser than when he left. Finally, as the *Chronicles of Prydain come to an end, he chooses a "real world," one devoid of enchantment, rather than the magical world of the *Summer Country.

Marion Carr (1970:509–510) has examined Taran as hero by comparing his story to the characteristics of traditional heroism, as determined by the scholarly work of Jan de Vries. De Vries (1963:510–516) described ten characteristics (motifs) of the hero, but he emphasized that a hero need not exemplify every characteristic. Carr determined that Taran qualifies in eight of the areas. Her rationale follows.

I. *The begetting of the hero.* It is in his wishes rather than in discovered fact that Taran resembles a classic hero within this myth. Nevertheless his hopes and fears until late in the Chronicles are centered on his genealogy. He desperately hopes to learn that he is the offspring of nobility.

II. *The birth of a hero.* The only living person, a swaddled baby hidden among the trees in a forest by one unknown and unknowable, found in the vicinity of a corpse-strewn battlefield, Taran is born—figuratively speaking—from the corpse of his society.

III. *The youth of the hero is threatened.* The exposed child is discovered by Dallben, who hopes that the boy will be the fulfillment of an ancient prophecy. There are many similar tales of abandoned hero-children discovered by shepherds, taken in, and reared by them. Taran is reared by Coll, formerly a warrior, presently keeper of the magical pig Hen Wen for Dallben.

IV. *The way in which the hero is brought up.* (He early reveals unusual characteristics.) Taran very early reveals courage and resourcefulness beyond the expectations of his station in life.

V. *The hero often acquires invulnerability.* Taran does not operate within this motif.

VI. *One of the most common heroic deeds is the fight with a dragon or another monster.* Taran encounters both *gwythaints and the Cauldron-Born, monsters of marvelous invention.

VII. *The hero wins a maiden, usually after overcoming great dangers.* Surely one of the most remarkably satisfying declarations of love in all literature for children (and perhaps in an even broader range) is Eilonwy's decision: "If enchantments are what separates us, then I should be well rid of them!" [HK 245/283].

VIII. *The hero makes an expedition to the underworld.* The storming of *Annuvin is in the classic mold, although often the hero made the journey for information only.

IX. *When the hero is banished in his youth he returns later and is victorious over his enemies.* Taran is not involved with this motif.

X. *The death of the hero.* This is the most fascinating of all of Taran's relationships to the classic motifs; for Taran does not die but the hero does. Presented with the opportunity to join the immortals (after all, that is what heroism is all about), Taran rejects it to assume the responsibilities of mortal life and human promises. (Carr, 1970:509–510)

Alexander feels that the "deepest underlying theme" in all his books is "the process of growing up." Taran is an embodiment of this theme, beginning "as a very pig-headed Assistant Pig-Keeper" and ending up "as an established, almost Promethean, hero" (Wintle and Fisher, 1974:213).

Hevydd (HEH-vid) Son of Hirwas (HEER-wass): Hevydd the Smith resides in the *Commot Cenarth of the *Free Commots. *Taran happens into the smith's yard as he continues his wanderings in *Taran Wanderer.

Taran and *Gurgi had ridden into the outskirts of Commot Cenarth when Taran reined up *Melynlas at a long, low-roofed shed from which rang the sound of hammer on anvil. Within he found the smith, a barrel-chested, leather-aproned man with a stubbly black beard and a great shock of black hair bristly as a brush. His eyelashes were scorched, grime and soot smudged his face; sparks rained on his bare shoulders but he seemed to count them no more than fireflies. In a voice like stones rattling on a bronze shield he roared out a song in time with his hammer strokes so loudly that Taran judged the man's lungs as leathery as his bellows. (TW 175/206–207)

The gruff smith at first will not consent to teach Taran his trade. Taran challenges his skill, and Hevydd deftly forms a perfectly shaped hawthorn blossom from a bar of glowing iron. Taran sees that the smith has great skill as a shaper of metal, the best in *Prydain. Nevertheless, Hevydd acknowledges that the greatest secrets of metal craft were long ago stolen by *Arawn *Death-Lord. Pleased with Taran's praise, Hevydd reassesses the *Wanderer and decides to apprentice him.

Hevydd puts Taran to the task of making a sword to replace the one he lost to the brigand, *Dorath. But the smith starts his apprentice with the most fundamental elements of the process: hauling fuel, smelting ore, etc. When Taran's first attempt at forging a blade fails, Hevydd shows no dismay. "Did you think to gain a worthy blade at first go?" (TW 179/211). After several swords, Taran finally makes one of which the burly smith approves—one that doesn't shatter when struck against a wooden block.

Hevydd asks Taran to stay and become a true swordsmith. However, Taran realizes that smithing is not in his heart. Hevydd presents Taran with the sword he forged as a token of friendship and offers him a bit of parting philosophy. "Life's a forge, say I! Face the pounding; don't fear the proving; and you'll stand well against any hammer and anvil!" (TW 181/213).

Hevydd appears again in *The High King. When Taran is sent to rally the *Commot men to fight against Arawn, Hevydd the Smith is the first to volunteer to fight under the *banner of the White Pig. "The folk of the *Free Commots honor King *Math and the *House of Don," he says. "But they will answer only to one they know as a friend, and follow him not in obligation but in friendship. And so let Hevydd be the first to follow *Taran Wanderer" (HK 92/111). The valiant smith fights fiercely in the losing battle to hold *Caer Dathyl and then chooses to join Taran in an effort to slow the retreat of the *Cauldron-Born to *Annuvin.

As the *Chronicles of Prydain conclude, Hevydd is one of the men who comes to *Caer Dallben to hail Taran, the new *High King of Prydain. It is the common men of Prydain who will be King Taran and Queen *Eilonwy's loyal subjects when the *Sons of Don depart for the *Summer Country.

There are two characters of note in the *Mabinogion who bear the name of Hevydd (Heveydd, Heveidd). Heveidd Unllenn appears in the tale "The Dream of Rhonabwy." A counselor to King Arthur, he is called one of "the best of men and the bravest" (M 312). Heveydd Hen, father of Rhiannon in the story "*Pwyll Prince of Dvyed," is known as "one of the three stranger kings upon whom dominion was conferred for their mighty deeds, and for their praiseworthy and gracious qualities" (M 364).

Alexander (1985b) is known to have tried his hand at forging metal. "I tried that when I was in school. . . . I tried metal casting, metal working, and all. We were forced to. This was a course in junior high school, and I was terrible at it. And I was fascinated with it, but I did badly at it." (TW 175/206, 193/226, 196/230, 217/253; HK 6/16, 91+/110+; M 224, 312, 347, 364, 409)

**High King: As *Taran's story begins, the *High King of *Prydain is *Math Son of *Mathonwy (BT 6/21). When Math is killed by the *Cauldron-Born, Prince *Gwydion is crowned the new High King. Both Math and Gwydion are of the *House of Don.

When the *Sons of Don depart for the *Summer Country at the conclusion of the *Chronicles, Taran of *Caer Dallben is declared the High King of Prydain. As the enchanter *Dallben explains, *The Book of Three* prophesied the possibility of Taran's destiny (HK 239–240/276). It foretold that when the Sons of Don depart Prydain, the new High King would be one who slew a serpent, gained and lost a flaming sword, chose a kingdom of sorrow over a kingdom of happiness, and had no prior station in life. Of course, Taran fulfilled each of these predicted qualifications.

The Foundling reveals the names of several Kings of Prydain before the days of Math: King *Rhych, King *Rhydderch Hael, and King *Rhitta (who bore the sword *Dyrnwyn with dishonor) (F 53/63).

**High King, The: The High King, the fifth of the *Prydain Chronicles, was originally to be the third book of a trilogy. Its title changed from *Little Gwion* to *The High King of Prydain* before becoming simply *The High King*. With the addition of *The Castle of Llyr* to the Chronicles, *The High King* became the fourth book in a series of four. Even after the final book was completed, Ann Durell, Alexander's editor, felt that yet another book was needed—the story of *Taran's maturing. Alexander wrote *Taran Wanderer*, which became book four, and then reworked *The High King* to complete the *Chronicles of Prydain (Jacobs, 1978:284).

The personal experiences of Alexander's days of military service during World War II surfaced in *The High King*. For example, the winter battle scene came from experiencing the terrible winter in Alsace-Lorraine in France when General Patch called for a retreat from Saverne to Luneville. "Alexander's 'having been as cold as the people I was talking about' helped him to shape and give feelings to the scene which he otherwise would not have been able to do" (Jacobs, 1978:492).

The High King concludes the story of Taran. He is sufficiently mature to lead the men of the *Free Commots to battle against *Arawn *Death-Lord. He proves to be of noble worth, drawing *Dyrnwyn to destroy the *Cauldron-Born and Arawn. The novel concludes with Taran's crowning as *High King of *Prydain. He and *Eilonwy stay behind to rule Prydain as the *Sons of Don journey to the *Summer Country.

The final novel in the Prydain series does not pretend that a war for freedom is without its cost. The most poignant moments in all the Chronicles occur in *The High King*. *Rhun gives his life for his friends. *Coll, wise and kind, falls to the blade of a Cauldron-Born. King *Math stands defiantly against the deathless warriors only to be struck down and trampled. The *truthful harp must be sacrificed to build a fire. *Achren dies in an effort to aid the *House of Don. And finally, the *Companions must part forever when Taran and Eilonwy decide they must not travel to the Summer Country.

The High King has been recognized for its quality. It won the 1969 John Newbery Medal, which proclaimed it the best children's book by an American author published in the preceding year (Jones, 1983:186). *The*

Jacket illustration by Evaline Ness

High King was also a National Book Award Finalist (a runner-up award) in 1969 (Jones, 1983:186) and was a National Book Award Finalist in the paperback category in 1981 (Weiss, 1983:420).

Hill Cantrevs (kantrevs): The Hill Cantrevs are located between the River *Ystrad and the *Small Avren. According to the farmer *Aeddan, this area was once noted for its long-fleeced sheep. That was before *Arawn stole the secrets of making the earth yield richly (TW 27/41–42).

When *Taran reaches the Hill Cantrevs, he discovers a sparse land, "grayish and flinty" (TW 66/85). "What might once have been fair pasture-land Taran saw to be overlaid with brush, and the long reaches of forest were close-grown and darkly tangled" (TW 66/85).

*Fflewddur Fflam observes that "the sheep of the Hill Cantrevs—*Great Belin, it's said they had fleece so thick you could sink your arm in it up to the elbow! Nowadays, alas, they tend to be a little scruffy" (TW 66/85). He also notes that "the *cantrev nobles are as glum as their domains" (TW 66/85).

Within the Hill Cantrevs, Taran and his *Companions meet and battle with *Morda, the evil wizard, and with *Dorath's Company. Also, Taran finds in the hill country the shepherd *Craddoc, who misrepresents himself as Taran's father. The Hill Cantrevs nearly become Taran's permanent home as he reluctantly stays to live and work beside his "father." Shortly before his death, Craddoc admits his falsehood and releases Taran to continue on his quest to discover his parentage.
(TW 27/41, 66/85, 80/101, 121/146, 133/158; HK 91/110)

Hills of Bran-Galedd (bran-GAHL-ed): "The *Red Fallows stretch along the Hills of Bran-Galedd, southwestward almost to *Annuvin," says *Coll (HK 136–137/162). He also acknowledges that the hills rise sharper as one goes westward and turn into steep crags. *Mount Dragon, overlooking Annuvin, is the highest of the peaks. For *Taran's army of *Commot men, the Hills of Bran-Galedd provide a shorter though more treacherous path to the *Land of Death. As Taran's assignment is to slow the *Cauldron-Born in their march back to Annuvin, he decides to push the deathless warriors into the hills in hope the terrain may help their cause. The Hills of Bran-Galedd prove, as Coll says, both friend and foe—providing uneven ground for setting traps but making for dangerous and uncomfortable traveling. *Llassar, a young shepherd from the *Free Commots, is invaluable because of his ability to lead Taran's army through the rugged country (HK 144/170).

Within the Hills of Bran-Galedd, one of three Commot men perish at the swords of the Cauldron-Born (HK 147/174). The deep cold and snow and the heavy losses symbolize the rise of dark powers. Indeed, it seems darkest just before the turn of events that secures a victory for the *Sons of Don.

In the *Mabinogion, *Guest notes that Bran-Galedd (Galed) is not a place but an object. The horn of Bran Galed is one of the thirteen precious things of the Island of Britain. "What liquor soever was desired was found therein" (M 286).
(HK 136+/162+; M 286)

Hills of Parys (PAH-riss): The hill country north of River *Alaw on the *Isle of Mona is known as the Hills of Parys. *Glew's cavern is located within these hills.
(CL 44/62, 47/66, 74/96)

Hirwas (HEER-wass): Hirwas was the father of *Hevydd the Smith who apprentices *Taran Wanderer.
(TW 76/207)

Horned King, the: As *The Book of Three opens, *Dallben explains to the young *Taran that "a new and mighty war lord has risen, as powerful as *Gwydion; some say more powerful" (BT 8/22).

> "But he is a man of evil for whom death is a black joy. . . .
> "No man knows his name, nor has any man seen his face. He wears an antlered mask, and for this reason he is called the Horned King."
> (BT 8/22–23)

Prince Gwydion calls the Horned King "*Arawn's avowed champion" (BT 19/35). However, the *Prince of Don knows little about the evil king, whose purpose is "dark and unknown" (BT 19/35). Therefore, Gwydion travels to *Caer Dallben to inquire of *Hen Wen, the oracular pig, concerning the secrets cloaking the mysterious war lord.

Hen Wen senses that the Horned King rides toward Caer Dallben, perhaps to take her. Before Gwydion arrives, Hen Wen flees in panic, and Taran *Assistant Pig-Keeper follows her. Soon after leaving Caer Dallben, Taran comes face to face with the Horned King.

> Taran fell back, terrified. Astride the foam-spattered animal rode a monstrous figure. A crimson cloak flamed from his naked shoulders. Crimson stained his gigantic arms. Horror-stricken, Taran saw not the head of a man but the antlered head of a stag. . . .

The mask was a human skull; from it, the great antlers rose in cruel curves. The Horned King's eyes blazed behind the gaping sockets of whitened bone. . . .

[He] uttered the long cry of a wild beast. (BT 15/30)

Indeed, the Horned King had ridden to Caer Dallben. However, not only was Hen Wen gone when he arrived, but Dallben apparently circled Caer Dallben in fire to ward off Arawn's war lord (BT 29/46).

Traveling with Gwydion, Taran witnesses the cruelty of the Horned King. From a hiding place, the Assistant Pig-Keeper watches the *Antlered King set fire to wicker baskets holding prisoners. The men are burned alive (BT 39/56–57).

As *The Book of Three* draws to a close, Taran finds Hen Wen, who in turn finds Gwydion. Gwydion learns the secret name of the Horned King from the oracular pig and confronts Arawn's champion as he is about to strike down Taran. The *Prince of Don calls a single word, the secret name, and with it destroys the Antlered King.

The Horned King stood motionless, his arm upraised. Lightning played about his sword. The giant flamed like a burning tree. The stag horns turned to crimson streaks, the skull mask ran like molten iron. A roar of pain and rage rose from the Antlered King's throat.

   With a cry, Taran flung an arm across his face. The ground rumbled and seemed to open beneath him. Then there was nothing. (BT 170/199)

"There was the earthquake," *Eilonwy says later, "and the Horned King burning until he just, well, broke apart" (BT 173/202). Taran is amazed that such a little thing like a name could wield such power. "Once you have courage to look upon evil, seeing it for what it is and naming it by its true name," says Gwydion, "it is powerless against you, and you can destroy it" (BT 179/209).

As for the true name of the Horned King, Gwydion tells Taran and Eilonwy that "it must remain a secret" (BT 180/210). And, in spite of all proddings, Alexander will not reveal what is apparently to be an eternal secret.

Kids . . . so often write, and they say, "What was the Horned King's secret name?" And I tell them, "[I] can't tell you; his name must remain a secret," which is a way of dodging out of a question. And yet I want it to be a secret, and I personally don't know what that name is. I can't, in some vague way . . . quite hear what that secret name was except it must have been something pretty powerful and scary. And it's better to leave that a little bit mysterious. You don't want to know too much. It spoils it, because if you say the secret name is "Charlie," it isn't going to work. I mean that very seriously. Whatever name you were to pick, there is no combination of sounds in human language that could convey the mystery, the power . . . once you externalize it, the power goes out of it. (Alexander, 1985b)

"The Battle of the Trees," an ancient tale found in the *Myvyrian Archaiology* and alluded to both by *Lady Charlotte Guest and by Robert Graves, tells a story similar to that of the Horned King (M 280; WG 49). In fact, Alexander (1968a:171–172) was inspired by the following passage to create the basic plot for *The Book of Three*.

These are the Englyns that were sung at the Cad Goddeu (the Battle of the Trees), or, as others call it, the Battle of *Achren, which was on account of a white roebuck, and a whelp; and they came from Hell, and Amathaon ab *Don brought them. And therefore Amathaon ab Don, and Arawn, King of Annwn (Hell), fought. And there was a man in that battle, unless his name were known he could not be overcome; and there was on the other side a woman called Achren, and unless her name were known her party could not be overcome. And Gwydion ab Don guessed the name of the man, and sang the two Englyns following:

> Sure-hoofed is my steed impelled by the spur;
> The high sprigs of alder are on thy shield:
> Bran art thou called, of the glittering
>   branches.
>   And thus,
> Sure-footed is my steed in the day of battle:
> The high sprigs of alder are on thy hand:
> Bran . . . by the branch thou bearest
> Has Amathaon the good prevailed.

(M 280–281; WG 49)

Here the mysterious man who inspired Alexander's Horned King is named: "Bran art thou called." Alexander points out that scholars such as Robert Graves (*The White Goddess*) have shown that "The Battle of the Trees" is not simply the story of a physical battle, but "a battle fought intellectually in the heads and with the tongues of the learned" (WG 38). In other words, the story is symbolic, a riddle of sorts concerning the bardic alphabet, its letters referred to as trees (Beth-Luis-Nion tree alphabet) in the Celtic languages of the time (WG 38, 165). Bran means alder, and the story systematically mentions a variety of trees (WG 43). Graves further explains that "the God Bran possessed an alphabetic secret before Gwydion, with Amathaon's help, stole it from him at the Battle of the Trees in the course of the first Belgic invasion of Britain" (WG 281). Avoiding the deeply involved symbolic meanings in "The Battle of the Trees," Alexander chose to use the events in the story but leave the name as a mystery. He states flatly that Bran was certainly *not* the secret name of his villain. "No, it is not. I can assure you that's not the name. I don't know what the name is, but I know that isn't it" (Alexander, 1985b).

However, the use of secret names seems to be a common mythological element. "The story of the guessing of Bran's name is a familiar one to anthropologists," says Graves. "In ancient times, once a god's secret name had been discovered, the enemies of his people could do destructive *magic against them with it" (WG 49).

A horned king or war leader also is common to many ancient tales. Says Alexander (1966c:6157), "The Horned King figures in many mythologies; there is even a Late Paleolithic sketch of him (not a very good likeness) on a cave wall." Graves also notes antlered headdresses were often worn by Celtic kings and have been unearthed in burial mounds (WG 103).

See also Characters—fantasy, Proud Walkers.
(BT 8+/22+; BC 13/24, 15/28; HK 47/62; M 280; WG 49)

House of Don (DAHN): *See* Sons of Don.

House of Fflam (FLAM): The House of Fflam is the ruling lineage of King *Fflewddur Fflam Son of *Godo. The kingdom of the House of Fflam is found in the *Northern Realms of *Prydain (TW 67/86). It is "several days' journey east of *Caer Dathyl" (BT 88/110). The kingdom is described as being "so small he [Fflewddur Fflam] could almost stride across it between midday and high noon. The fields and pastures grew so near his castle that sheep and cows ambled up to gaze into his bed-chamber" (TH 88/7).
(BT 87/110; TW 67/86; TH 87/7)

**House of Llyr (LEER): The ancestry of the royal House of Llyr goes back to the *Sea People and to *Llyr Half-Speech, the *Sea King (BT 55/73). *Caer Colur, the seat of the House of Llyr (the *Castle of Llyr), was once located on the *Isle of Mona. When Princess *Angharad, daughter of Queen *Regat and mother of *Eilonwy, fled the stronghold to marry against her mother's wishes, *Caer Colur was abandoned. This occurred in part because Angharad took with her two objects of great power that belonged to the *daughters of Llyr: the *book of spells and the *Golden

Pelydryn. Because all daughters of Llyr are enchantresses, the removal of such important objects helped bring about the decay of the kingdom (Alexander, 1986b). The ruins of Caer Colur lie off the shore of *Mona, separated from the larger island during a flood (CL 97/121–122).

The emblem of the House of Llyr is a *crescent moon. Eilonwy wears a silver crescent moon on a silver chain about her neck. Angharad also took with her from Caer Colur a powerful version of the royal emblem. The silver crescent of this pendant holds the *gem of Angharad, a magical *Fair Folk stone that may be used for good or evil (TW 91/112).

Eilonwy is the last *Princess of Llyr and therefore has latent magical powers. "For generations the daughters of the House of Llyr were among the most skillful enchantresses in *Prydain, using their powers with wisdom and kindliness," explains *Gwydion. "In their fastness at Caer Colur were stored all their treasures, magical devices and charmed implements whose nature even I do not know" (CL 129/157). Therefore, in *The Castle of Llyr, the evil enchantress, *Achren, kidnaps Eilonwy in hope of tapping her dormant powers to rule Prydain from what is left of Caer Colur. As Achren's plans are frustrated, Caer Colur is flooded by the sea and totally destroyed (CL 158/187).

*Llyr is a common name in *Celtic mythology. It first appears in the *Mabinogion in the tale, "*Geraint the Son of Erbin." One of the characters is named Caradawc the son of Llyr. Llyr Lediaith, according to *Guest's notes to the Mabinogion, was one of "the three supreme prisoners of the Island of Britain" (M 192). Guest also points out that Shakespeare's King Lear is written "Llyr"in Welsh (M 291). Llyr surfaces often in the Mabinogion, attached to various names, but perhaps the most notable is that of Branwen the daughter of Llyr, who is a heroine of Welsh legend and for whom one of the tales in the Mabinogion is named (M 369). It is in Branwen's story that the *cauldron of rejuvenation appears, the cauldron that inspired Alexander's *Black Crochan.
(M 155, 192, 228, 256, 291, 305, 312, 327, 369, 397)

House of Pwyll (POO-il): See Pwyll.

House of Rhuddlum (ROOD-lum): See Rhuddlum, King.

House of Smoit (SMOYT): See Smoit, King.

Huntsman, Chief: The leader of *Arawn's feared *Huntsmen of Annuvin is called the Chief Huntsman. In the story "The Rascal Crow" from *The

Foundling, the Chief Huntsman is sent "to bait and snare" the animals of *Prydain (F 42/49). He is commanded to capture or slaughter them. *Medwyn organizes the animals to stand against Arawn.

*Kadwyr, the rascal crow, does not take Medwyn's warning seriously and mocks the others who pledge their help. However, he soon learns the Chief Huntsman is to be feared.

> Garbed in the skins of slain animals, a long knife at his belt, a bow and quiver of arrows slung over his shoulder, the hunter had come so stealthily that Kadwyr scarcely had a moment to collect his wits. The hunter flung out a net so strong and finely woven that once caught in it, no creature could hope to struggle free. (F 45/53)

Though Kadwyr dodges the net and subsequent arrows, the crow flies into a tree trunk, breaks a wing, and must scramble along the ground. Each time Kadwyr is about to be captured, the Chief Huntsman is harassed by the very animals earlier mocked by the crow. And when all seems lost for Kadwyr, the turtle *Crugan-Crawgan trips the Chief Huntsman, sending him over a cliff, apparently to his death.

Though the hunter who tracks Kadwyr is never given more than a generic title in the story of "The Rascal Crow," Alexander (1985b) confirms that he indeed is the Chief Huntsman of Annuvin.

The office of Chief Huntsman was a position of honor in the courts of Britain. *Lady Charlotte Guest explains in her notes to the *Mabinogion*:

> In the Laws of Howel Dda, this important personage [chief huntsman] ranks as the tenth officer of the Court, and his duties and immunities are very clearly defined. From Christmas to February he was to be with the king when required, and took the seat appointed for him in the palace, which was "about the recess with the domestic chaplain." After the 8th of February he was to go with his dogs, his horns, and his greyhounds to hunt the young stags until the feast of St. John, which is in the middle of summer; and during that time he was not bound to make compensation (that is, in a Court of Law) to any one who had a claim upon him, except it were one of his fellow-officers. He was to hunt deer from the feast of St. John till the ninth day of winter; and unless he could be taken before he had risen from his bed, and put on his boots, he was not obliged to render compensation to any who had a claim upon him during all that period. From the ninth day of winter to the 1st of December he went to hunt badgers, and was not accountable for his conduct to any except his fellow-officers; and after that he was employed in sharing the skins of the beasts that had been slain, to a portion of which he had himself a right. His lodging was in the kilnhouse, and his allowance was

three hornfuls of liquor and a dish of meat. The value of his horn was one pound, and it was to be of buffalo-horn (beulin). (M 189)

See also Gwybeddin, Nedir.
(F 42/49, 45/53; M 142, 189)

Huntsmen of Annuvin (ah-NOO-vin): The Huntsmen of Annuvin are in the service of *Arawn *Death-Lord. They are a formidable host, as *Gwydion explains.

> "I dread them as much [as the *Cauldron-Born]. They are ruthless as the Cauldron-Born, their strength even greater. They go afoot, yet they are swift, with much endurance. Fatigue, hunger, and thirst mean little to them. . . .
>
> "They are mortal . . . though I scorn to call them men. They are the basest of warriors who have betrayed their comrades; murderers who have killed for the joy of it. To indulge their own cruelty they have willingly chosen Arawn's realm and have sworn allegiance to him with a blood oath even they cannot break.
>
> "Yes . . . they can be slain. But Arawn has forged them into a brotherhood of killers and given them a terrible power. They rove in small bands, and within those companies the death of one man only adds to the strength of all the rest. . . .
>
> "For the more you strike down, the more the others gain in strength. Even as their number dwindles, their power grows." (BC 33–34/50)

Soon after Gwydion's warning, *Taran and the *Companions must battle Arawn's Huntsmen. "They wore jackets and leggings of animal skins. Long knives were thrust into their belts, and from the neck of one warrior hung a curved hunting horn" (BC 45/63). "Each Huntsman bore a crimson brand on his forehead . . . a mark of Arawn's power" (BC 45/63–64). "As they ran, they called out to one another in a weird, wordless cry" (BC 47/66).

During the struggle, *Ellidyr slays one of the Huntsmen. It is then that the Companions witness the horrible power of which Gywdion spoke.

> In the grove there was a sudden moment of silence. Then a long sigh rippled among the attackers as though each man had drawn breath. . . . With a roar, the Huntsmen renewed their attack with even greater ferocity. (BC 46/64)

Under the leadership of the *Chief Huntsman, these warriors have long sought to capture and subdue the animals of *Prydain (F 42/49). In *The Black Cauldron*, as they seek to recover the *Black Crochan, the Huntsmen of Annuvin slay *Adaon, the son of *Taliesin (BC 81/107). Finally, in *The High King*, they are marshaled to aid Arawn in his last and greatest campaign to destroy Prydain. The Huntsmen strip Prince Gwydion of the *magic sword, *Dyrnwyn, giving Arawn the upper hand in the conflict.

"His [Arawn's] Huntsmen will drink their [those who challenge the *Death-Lord] blood," says the evil *Magg (HK 48/63). However, the tables are turned, and the Huntsmen are themselves destroyed. Many perish when Taran and *Doli melt a frozen lake, sending a torrent of water into the ravine where they are camped. At *Medwyn's bidding, wild beasts also stalk and kill the Huntsmen of Annuvin who have long been their enemies (HK 179/208–209). Alexander (1986b) feels that no Huntsmen were left alive as the *Chronicles of Prydain come to an end.

See also Characters—fantasy, Good versus evil.
(BC 33+/49+; TW 11/24, 201/235; HK 12+/23+; F 42/49, 45/53; CWP 15)

✛

Idris (ID-riss): *See* Forest of Idris.

Indeg (IN-deg): When *Taran tries to cloak each of the *Companions' identities from *Orddu, *Orwen, and *Orgoch, he gives *Eilonwy the name Indeg. Orwen only giggles at his effort to lie.

The name of Indeg is found in the *Mabinogion.* *Lady Charlotte Guest explains in her notes to the *Mabinogion* that "Indeg, the daughter of Garwy or Afarwy hir, of Maeleinydd, was one of the three ladies best beloved by Arthur. Her beauty is often the theme of the *bards" (M 279). (BC 100/130; M 229, 279)

Iron Crown of Annuvin (ah-NOO-vin): Even before the days of *Arawn's power, *Achren wore the Iron Crown of Annuvin as a royal symbol of leadership and authority not only in *Annuvin but in all of *Prydain (HK 17/28). During the time of *Taran's story, the Iron Crown is in the possession of Arawn *Death-Lord. However, since the *Sons of Don have become protectors of Prydain, the wearer of the Iron Crown has dominion only over Annuvin.

The crown may not be worn by one who does not have the authority to do so. *Magg is promised by Arawn Death-Lord that the crown will one day be passed to him. But when Magg, the *Chief Steward, finds the Iron Crown abandoned in Arawn's throne room, his lust for power becomes madness. He sets it upon his brow, claiming rule of Annuvin.

> The Chief Steward's triumphant laughter turned to a shriek as he clawed suddenly at the iron band circling his forehead. Taran and *Fflewddur gasped and drew back.

The crown glowed like red iron in a forge. Writhing in agony, Magg clutched vainly at the burning metal which now had turned white hot, and with a last scream toppled from the throne. (HK 218/252)

See also Fantastic objects.
(HK 17/28, 48/63, 217/250)

Iron Portals: The massive Iron Portals, "ugly and brooding," are the gates to *Annuvin (HK 209/242). The shortest roadway to the Iron Portals lies over the treacherous *Mount Dragon. Alexander explains that these gates are literally made of iron. "They are hand-hewn, hand-wrought iron—heavy, massive, gigantic things" (Alexander, 1985b).
(HK 137/163, 206/238, 209/242)

Iscovan (iss-KOH-van): In the days before *Taran's story begins, Iscovan is one of *Prydain's master smiths. His hammer, as with many tools of the day, holds the secrets of its craft and can work any metal into whatever shape its owner desires.

*Arawn *Death-Lord, disguised as a warrior, tricks Iscovan into trading his prized hammer for a conjured tool that appears as gold. Through Arawn's illusions, this hammer seems to have the power to split an anvil. Iscovan succumbs to his greed, makes the trade, and is left with a useless implement made of lead. Much of his skill gone, the poor smith must drudge at his forge the remainder of his days.

The name of Iscovan (Iscovan Hael) appears in the *Mabinogion, though this character does not seem to be a smith (M 224).
(F 65/77; M 224)

Isle of Mona: *Mona is an island off the western coast of *Prydain. Once it had been the kingdom of the *House of Llyr and the site of its stronghold, *Caer Colur. Separated from Mona by a flood, the ruins of Caer Colur were then located on a small island just offshore.

During *Taran's story, the Isle of Mona is the realm of the *House of Rhuddlum ruled by King *Rhuddlum and Queen *Teleria. Upon the death of King Rhuddlum, the kingdom is inherited by his son, Prince *Rhun. Mona's capital is *Dinas Rhydnant, a seaside city and stronghold surrounding the island's chief port, *Mona Haven.

The Isle of Mona is the setting for *The Castle of Llyr. *Eilonwy is sent to the House of Rhuddlum to be schooled in the ways of being a lady and a princess. Soon after arriving, the *Princess of Llyr is kidnapped by *Achren and taken to the ruins of Eilonwy's ancestral home, Caer Colur. Taran and the *Companions search the island to find Eilonwy and in the process discover the cowardly *giant *Glew and the giant mountain cat, *Llyan.

Alexander says that Mona, the background for *The Castle of Llyr*, is the ancient Welsh name of the island of Anglesey. "But this background is not drawn with a mapmaker's accuracy" (CL ix/16). Nevertheless, when his editor, Ann Durell, planned a trip to Wales, Alexander (1965f) advised her to bear in mind certain "famous landmarks." "Mona, of course, is Anglesey," he said.

The Isle of Mona is also mentioned in *Lady Charlotte Guest's notes to the *Mabinogion*. When *Henwen, the marvelous sow of Dadweir Dallpenn (Dallben), was chased across Britain by King Arthur, she left a kitten at Maen Du in Arvon. *Coll ab Collfrewi threw it into the Menai. "But the sons of Palug in Mona (Anglesey), reared this kitten, to their cost; for it became the Palug Cat, which, we are told, was one of the three plagues of the Isle of Mona" (M 268). Of course, the Palug Cat and Llyan are related, both hailing from Mona.

See also book of spells, Rhudd, Alaw.
(CL ix+/16+; TW 3/15, 68/87, 112/136, 141/168; HK 7/17, 20/32, 34/46, 38/52, 46/61, 69/86, 113/135, 153/180, 173/202, 237/273, 241/277; M 268, 439)

Islimach (iss-LIM-ahk): Islimach is the steed of *Ellidyr. She is a powerful roan, as ill-tempered as her master. Islimach is, however, extremely dedicated to Ellidyr. When Ellidyr dies within the *Black Cauldron, Islimach breaks her tether and comes to her master's broken body. Realizing Ellidyr is dead, she goes berserk, galloping through the undergrowth to the brink of a ravine. "Islimach made a mighty leap, hung poised in the air a moment, then plummeted to the rocks below" (BC 173/216). Islimach is buried with Ellidyr in the *barrow raised to her master's honor.
(BC 26+/42+)

K

✛

Kadwyr (KAD-weer): Kadwyr, father of *Kaw (HK 88/107), appears in "The Rascal Crow," a tale from *The Foundling*. He is a cheeky, self-reliant, careless bird who refuses to heed *Medwyn's warning about *Arawn's *Chief Huntsman. Arawn wishes to control all the animals of *Prydain and has sent his *Huntsman to capture or slaughter them. Medwyn calls the animals to council and organizes them to counter the *Death-Lord's attack. But Kadwyr is sure he need not worry or rely on help from other beasts. After all, "a crow's a match for any hunter" (F 42/49).

The impudent crow even ridicules the other animals as they pledge their support to Medwyn's plan. He especially makes fun of the smaller, slower beasts. Kadwyr laughs at *Gwybeddin the gnat, calling him *Prince Flyspeck. He tells *Nedir the spider to "keep to your knitting" (F 43–44/51). *Crugan-Crawgan the turtle is so slow in speech that Kadwyr can't be bothered to stay and hear him out. "Gnats and spiders! Turtles! What an army!" Kadwyr laughs to himself. "I'll have to keep an eye on all of them" (F 45/52).

When the Chief Huntsman stalks Kadwyr, the silly crow taunts him. Dodging the hunter's net and arrows, Kadwyr flies straight into a tree trunk, breaking his wing. But Gwybeddin and his swarm of gnats distract the Huntsman as he draws his bow to send an arrow into Kadwyr's breast. Scrambling across the forest floor, Kadwyr cannot escape. But again, before the Huntsman can catch the crow, he stumbles into the heavy webs of Nedir the spider. Finally, when all seems lost for Kadwyr, the Chief Huntsman of *Annuvin is tripped by a rock that is in fact Crugan-Crawgan. The evil hunter plunges over a cliff to his death.

Saved by those he thought useless, Kadwyr learns never to "scorn a spider . . . taunt a turtle . . . [or] annoy a gnat" (F 50/58). But nevertheless, he takes the credit for ridding the forest of the Chief Huntsman. "But—but, come to think of it . . . if it hadn't been for me—yes, it was I! I who led that hunter a merry chase! I who saved all in the forest!" (F 50/58).

Kadwyr (Kadwr) is a character of honor in the *Mabinogion and, of course, not a crow. Kadwr, Earl of Cornwall, had the duty of arming King Arthur on days of battle (M 306). *Lady Charlotte Guest tells more of Kadwr in her notes accompanying the tale "The Dream of Rhonabwy." When Arthur died or, rather, was conveyed to the *magic Island of Avalon, the crown descended to Cystennin, the son of Kadwr (M 324). Also, Kadwr was one of the three knights "who fled neither for spear, nor arrow, nor sword, and who never shamed their leader in the day of conflict" (M 330).

See also Brynach, Edyrnion.
(HK 88/107; F 41/47; M 306, 324, 329, 330)

Kaw (KAW) Son of Kadwyr (KAD-weer): Kaw is a large crow belonging to *Gwystyl of the *Fair Folk. He first appears in *The Black Cauldron* when the *Companions take refuge in Gwystyl's *way post. "The crow resembled more a humpy ball with straggling tail feathers, feathers as wispy and disordered as Gwystyl's cobwebby hair. But its eyes were sharp and bright" (BC 56/76). Gwystyl explains that the bird is named Kaw, "because of the noise he makes" (BC 57/77).

Kaw has some power of human speech. In fact, it is Kaw who reveals to the Companions through single word hints that the *Black Cauldron is in the hands of *Orddu, *Orwen, and *Orgoch.

As *The Black Cauldron* concludes, Gwystyl brings Kaw to the battle against King *Morgant's forces. Afterwards, Gwystyl presents the crow to *Taran as a gift from the Fair Folk for service rendered. (Taran located and retrieved the *Black Crochan.) However, it seems as if Kaw has already chosen to remain with the *Assistant Pig-Keeper. He happily croaks, "Taran" (BC 176/220).

Kaw remains as a faithful companion to Taran throughout the Chronicles. When not perched on Taran's shoulder, the pesky crow serves as an aerial spy for the Companions. In *The Castle of Llyr, Kaw is sent to search for the kidnapped *Eilonwy and returns croaking, "Eilonwy" and "*Alaw"—again, one word hints indicating that he spotted the princess along the River *Alaw (CL 72–73/94–95). He also comes to the Companions' rescue, "dive-bombing" the giant mountain cat *Llyan. Kaw tweaks Llyan's whiskers, luring the cat away from Taran and the others (CL 77/99–100).

Kaw's service proves helpful and indeed invaluable. He retrieves Eilonwy's *bauble when it is apparently lost in the sea (CL 168/198).

*Dallben uses him to deliver a shrinking potion to the cowardly *giant *Glew (TW 5/17) and later to deliver a message to Taran that Eilonwy had returned to *Caer Dallben (HK 4/14). When *Fflewddur and Llyan are lost in a blizzard they are found and guided to safety by Kaw (TW 158/187). The crow is sent to spy on *Annuvin in *The High King but is injured by *gwythaints (HK 86/104). He makes his way to *Medwyn's valley and is able to alert Medwyn and all the animals of Annuvin's rise. Later, as a part of Medwyn's call to all animals to rally against *Arawn, Kaw leads an army of crows that attacks and drives away gwythaints trying to kill *Achren (HK 196–197/228). Finally, Kaw brings word to Taran that Prince *Gwydion has at last arrived for his assault on Annuvin (HK 209/242).

In spite of his usefulness, Kaw may be irritating. His father, *Kadwyr, was no less a scamp (HK 88/107; F 40/47). Kaw seems to especially enjoy tormenting Fflewddur Fflam. In *Taran Wanderer, he steals the *bard's harp key.

> "He's brazen as a magpie!" cried Fflewddur, setting off after the crow. "He's thieving as a jackdaw!"
>
> No sooner did Fflewddur come within half a pace of him than Kaw nimbly hopped away again, bearing the key in his beak. Squawking merrily, the crow stayed always out of Fflewddur's grasp, and Taran could not help laughing at the sight of the long-shanked bard vainly racing in circles, while Kaw danced ahead of him. (TW 69/88–89)

Yet, even Kaw's playfulness is beneficial. When the Companions find a strange shard of bone carefully stowed in a chest and placed in the crotch of a tree, Fflewddur insists the thing is enchanted. They agree to leave it alone, but later Kaw shows up with the bone in his beak. "A sour jest, you magpie!" exclaims Fflewddur, angrily (TW 84/105). But the bone soon proves to be the key to destroying the evil wizard *Morda, and Fflewddur has Kaw to thank for freeing him from Morda's spell which had turned him into a rabbit (TW 106/129).

As the *Chronicles of Prydain conclude, Kaw must return with *Doli to the *Realm of the Fair Folk. The age of enchantments has come to an end, and the passages to King *Eiddileg's kingdom will be barred to all humans (HK 229/264).

> "Farewell," Kaw croaked. "Taran! Farewell!"
>
> "Farewell to you," Taran answered, smiling. "If I have despaired of teaching you good manners, I have rejoiced in your bad ones. You are a rogue and a scamp, and a very eagle among crows." (HK 242/278)

The name Kaw (or Caw) is used frequently in the *Mabinogion, usually in relation to one of the many sons of Kaw (who was, of course, not a crow)

(M 228). For example, *Gildas the son of Caw was a scholar of Arthur's court (M 153; M 198).

The *Mabinogion* also tells of an army of ravens called the Ravens of Owain. As with Kaw's army of crows, the Ravens of Owain were a formidable host. They were reportedly three hundred strong and would attack and slay whomever their lord commanded. In one instance, the ravens attacked King Arthur's pages and attendants (M 311).

See also Characters—fantasy.
(M 153, 198, 228, 271, 291, 303, 307, 331)

Kilhuch (KILL-uhk): *Medwyn tells *Taran a tale from what he calls "a long history" (BT 120/144). The tale concerns the quest of a young man named Kilhuch to win the hand of *Olwen in marriage. Olwen's father, *Yspadadden the *Chief Giant, gives Kilhuch a number of tasks he must accomplish to win his daughter. However, each of the tasks is nearly impossible to complete.

Only one of the tasks is related by Medwyn. Yspadadden demands that nine bushels of flax seed be gathered, though there is scarcely that much in all the land. Out of true friendship, *Gwythyr Son of *Greidawl accepts this challenge on behalf of Kilhuch.

The entire tale of "Kilhuch (Kilhwch) and Olwen" is found in the *Mabinogion.* Kilhwch was a cousin to King Arthur. Because his mother became wild during her pregnancy and wandered aimlessly, Kilhwch was born in the mountains among the swine (M 217). Yet he was returned to the palace, then "put out to nurse" (M 217). As Kilhwch matures, he is sent for and instructed to take a wife. His step-mother tells him he must marry no other but Olwen, the daughter of Yspaddaden (Yspadadden) Penkawr. Kilhwch travels to Arthur's court to enlist the king's aid in winning Olwen.

Kilhwch is eventually assigned thirty-seven tasks by Olwen's father. All of the tasks are related to the acquisition of some item for the wedding feast and ceremony (if it occurs). Though each task is seemingly impossible to complete, Kilhwch states, "It will be easy for me to compass this, although thou mayest think that it will not be easy" (M 236). The first task is to root up a hill, burn the grubbings for manure, and plow and plant the ground all in one day. Then, the grain must ripen in one day (M 235). The wheat will be used for food and to make drink for the wedding. The story of Gwythyr and the nine bushels of flax seed is also part of "Kilhwch and Olwen" and is found later in the tale (M 249).

See also Characters—fantasy.
(BT 120/144; M 217, 364)

King of Cadiffor (ka-DIF-for): *See* Smoit.

King of Madoc (MA-dok): *See* Morgant.

King of Mona: *See* Rhuddlum; Rhun.

King of Prydain (prih-DANE): In the days before the *Sons of Don journeyed to *Prydain, rulers of Prydain were presumably given this title rather than that of *High King. The ancient Kings of Prydain named in the Prydain books are *Rhitta, *Rhych, and *Rhydderch Hael.
   See also Amrys, barrow, Dyrnwyn, Govannion the Lame, Spiral Castle. (F 53/63)

King of Stones: *See* Glew.

King of the Sun: *See* Belin.

King of the West Domains: *See* Pryderi.

Kingdom of Tylwyth Teg (TILL-with TEG): *Tylwyth Teg may be roughly translated as *Fair Folk (BT 137/162). Therefore, the Kingdom of Tylwyth Teg means the Kingdom of the Fair Folk. The *Companions enter this realm by way of *Black Lake, one of many entrances. Black Lake, however, is designed to suck anyone who enters its waters down a whirlpool and into the underground world of the Tylwyth Teg, thereby catching intruders. Though the Kingdom of Tylwyth Teg is where most of the Fair Folk live, many Fair Folk *way posts and mines are located across *Prydain.
   This subterranean kingdom is a marvel to *Taran and the Companions, and they find it difficult to realize that they are indeed underground.

> The corridors soon broadened into wide avenues. In the great domes far overhead, gems glittered as bright as sunshine. There was no grass, but deep carpets of green lichen stretched out like meadows. There were blue lakes, glistening as much as the jewels above; and cottages and small farmhouses. (BT 146/172)

Blustery and overly dramatic, yet kind and wise, King *Eiddileg rules the Fair Folk. Though humans who blunder into his kingdom are seldom allowed to leave, Eiddileg releases the Companions to continue their quest against *Annuvin and the *Horned King (BT 145–146/172). Eiddileg proves to be an ally in the battle against *Arawn up until the *Death-Lord is destroyed.

The Companions leave the Kingdom of Tylwyth Teg through a passage that exits from behind a high waterfall (BT 148/175). Never do they return to Eiddileg's realm. As the *Chronicles of Prydain conclude, *Dallben explains that no man shall see the *Realm of the Fair Folk again. The age of enchantments has ended, and Eiddileg must bar the passages to his kingdom (HK 229/264).

*Lady Charlotte Guest writes of Tylwyth Teg in her notes to the *Mabinogion, explaining that Tylwyth Teg is a race of "beneficent and joyous beings" often called "Family of Beauty." They "dance in the moonlight on the velvet sward, in their airy and flowing robes of blue or green, or white or scarlet, and . . . delight in showering benefits on the more favoured of the human race" (M 263). *Gwyn ab Nudd is their sovereign.

The description of these "fairies" is similar to that of the *Children of Evening, a part of the Fair Folk peoples who sing rather than dance in the nighttime forests of Prydain (BT 138–139/163–165).

Alexander has the location of Eiddileg's kingdom pinpointed in Wales. In a letter to his editor, Ann Durell, he asks her to watch for it when she takes a Welsh vacation. "Black Lake and Eiddileg's realm would be around Lake Bala" (Alexander, 1965f).
(BT 137/162, 146/172; HK 229/264; M 263)

Kynvael (KIN-vale): Kynvael is a river running from somewhere near *Caer Dathyl northwestward to the sea. The *Valley of Kynvael that follows the river is of gentle terrain and is therefore easily traveled.

The *Sons of Don keep ships hidden in a secret harbor near the mouth of Kynvael, the location of which is known only by *Gwydion and *Math. These ships, the same that brought them from the *Summer Country to *Prydain, have been maintained in case of need. They are used to take Gwydion close to *Annuvin in *The High King and later to carry the Sons of Don back to their homeland.
(HK 132/157)

L

✛

Lady Charlotte Guest: Lady Charlotte Guest translated a number of Welsh tales from ancient manuscripts. Her translations were published under the title of the *Mabinogion in 1838–1849. Though strictly speaking there are but four tales of the Mabinogi, *Guest expanded her book to include twelve (McGovern, 1980:10).

Alexander estimates that he read Guest's Mabinogion no less than twelve times as he prepared to write the *Chronicles of Prydain and attributes the inspiration for *Prydain to her work (Jacobs, 1978:266). He feels that Guest was more of a folklorist and an antiquarian than an historical scholar like Robert Graves or Gwyn Jones (Alexander, 1986b). She was primarily interested in translating and telling the Celtic tales; Graves was more concerned with the deeper symbolic meanings the stories may hold, as is evident in The White Goddess. Graves's in-depth analysis of "The Battle of the Trees" is an example of their differing orientations. Graves and others maintain that the account was not describing a physical battle, but instead (quoting Rev. Davies) "a battle fought intellectually in the heads and with the tongues of the learned" (WG 38). Graves discovered that this tale, upon which Alexander loosely based *The Book of Three, is in truth a riddle of sorts concerning the bardic alphabet (WG 38+). Guest's single reference to "The Battle of the Trees" appears in her notes to the Mabinogion, and Alexander (1985b) suggests that she only considered this and other tales basically legendary.

Lady Don (DAHN), the: The Lady Don and her consort, *Belin (*King of the Sun), are the ancestral parents of the *Children of Don. The Sons and *Daughters of Don voyaged from the *Summer Country, a land of never-ending life and joy, to *Prydain. They built a stronghold named

*Caer Dathyl in the *Eagle Mountains and there stood as guardians against the threat of *Annuvin.

Alexander (1985b) explains, however, that the Lady Don and Belin did not voyage to Prydain. They remained in the Summer Country where they still dwell today.

See also Characters—fantasy, Gwydion, Math.
(BT 7/22)

Lake Llew (LOO): When *Taran goes to the witches of the *Marshes of Morva (*Orddu, *Orwen, *Orgoch) to inquire of his parentage, Orwen suggests he might ask the *salmon of Lake Llew. "I've never met a wiser fish," she says (TW 19/33). However, Orgoch informs everyone that the salmon is "long gone" (TW 19/33).

The Salmon of Llyn Llyw (llyn means lake in Welsh) is told of in the *Mabinogion*. The wise fish, probably one of the oldest of the animals, led Arthur's knights to the secret prison of Mabon. This was a part of fulfilling the quest of *Kilhuch (Kilhwch) to obtain *Olwen's hand in marriage (M 248).
(TW 19/33; M 248)

Lake of Llunet (LOO-net): The witches *Orddu, *Orwen, and *Orgoch suggest that *Taran find the *Mirror of Llunet, an oracular pool that may tell him of his parentage. The Mirror of Llunet is to be found in the *Llawgadarn Mountains. *Doli of the *Fair Folk tells Taran that he has never heard of such a "mirror." However, he knows of a Lake Llunet that is also in the Llawgadarn Mountains. Indeed, as *Taran Wanderer* concludes, Taran finds the lake and the mirror in close proximity to one another.
(TW 112+/136+)

Lake Sprites: Lake Sprites are one of the many types of beings that make up the *Fair Folk. They are mentioned only once in the *Chronicles of Prydain when King *Eiddileg is complaining about how taxing it is to run the *Kingdom of Tylwyth Teg.

> "The Lake Sprites have been quarreling all day; now they're sulking. Their hair's a mess. And who does that reflect on? Who has to jolly them along, coax them, plead with them? The answer is obvious." (BT 138/164)

It could be supposed that Lake Sprites are a part of the *Children of Evening, the Fair Folk singers. Eiddileg complains of both in the same breath. However, Alexander (1985b) explains that Lake Sprites are definitely *not* singers. Dwarves, Lake Sprites, and Children of Evening are all separate branches of the Fair Folk.

See also Characters—fantasy.
(BT 138/164)

Land of Death: *See* Annuvin.

Land of the Dead: *See* Annuvin.

letter sticks: *Dallben's letter sticks, three "long rods of *ash wood carved with spells," are used to receive prophecies from the oracular pig, *Hen Wen (BT 12/27). In *The Book of Three*, Hen Wen runs away before the enchanter can bring the rods to her pen. However, in *The High King*, Dallben uses the letter sticks with Hen Wen to determine where the *magic sword, *Dyrnwyn, is hidden and how it may be retrieved. He plants the letter sticks upright in the ground and whispers the questions to the pig. Hen Wen is frightened and reluctant to answer. Finally, calmed by *Taran, she begins to point to the ancient symbols carved on the rods while Dallben records them on parchment. But before she can read the third stick, "the ash-wood rods shook and swayed like living things. They twisted as though to uproot themselves, and with a sound that ripped the air like a thunder clap, they split, shattered, and fell to earth in splinters" (HK 28/40).

In *The Book of Three*, *Gwydion communicates with Hen Wen without the use of letter sticks. Because of his ordeal in the stronghold of *Oeth-Anoeth, Gwydion is able to understand the speech of animals. He asks Hen Wen the name of the *Horned King and receives the answer. One wonders why he did not do the same thing when the letter sticks shatter, thereby completing the message. Alexander explains that Hen Wen is "in such a state of fear and panic that she couldn't communicate in any way." If she could barely communicate with the ash rods, "she . . . couldn't speak to him [Gwydion] and answer him" (Alexander, 1985b).

Though the letter sticks are destroyed, most of the message has been given, and Dallben translates it. Hen Wen's response to the first stick answers the question, how might Dyrnwyn be recovered: "Ask, sooner, mute stone and voiceless rock to speak" (HK 31/43). The second stick spells out Dyrnwyn's fate.

> *Quenched will be Dyrnwyn's flame;*
> *Vanished, its power.*
> *Night turn to noon*

And rivers burn with frozen fire
Ere Dyrnwyn be regained. (HK 31/43)

The cryptic messages are prophecies to be fulfilled. Indeed, each comes to pass. Night turns to noon when *Eilonwy lights the nighttime landscape of the *Hills of Bran-Galedd with her *bauble (HK 171/200). It truly becomes as bright as day. *Doli engineers a plan to drown an army of the *Huntsmen of Annuvin by lighting brush fires on a frozen lake. The eventual cascade of water, boulders, and flaming brands fulfills another part of the prophecy: "And rivers burn with frozen fire" (HK 178/208–209). Finally, when Taran clambers to the peak of *Mount Dragon trying to escape the *Cauldron-Born, an oddly shaped rock makes a keening sound as the wind passes. It is much like a human voice calling. The "voiceless rock" draws his attention to a stone that hides Dyrnwyn (HK 221/255–256).

When the Cauldron-Born are destroyed and *Arawn is slain, both by the blade of Dyrnwyn, the sword's flame flickers and extinguishes. Thus is the prophecy from the second letter stick completely fulfilled (HK 223/257–258). Later, Dallben reveals what must have been the message from the third letter stick.

> "It is clear to me now why the ash rods shattered. They could not withstand such a prophecy, which could only have been this: Not only shall the flame of Dyrnwyn be quenched and its power vanish, but all enchantments shall pass away, and men unaided guide their own destiny." (HK 229/264)

Indeed, Dallben loses his powers of enchantment. He and all the *Sons of Don must leave the world of men and travel to the mythic land of eternal life, the *Summer Country.

Ash rods play a prominent role in *Celtic mythology, as does ash wood in general. Nion, the ash tree, was the sacred tree of the god, Gwydion (WG 244). *Lady Charlotte Guest describes in her notes to the *Mabinogion three ash rods upon which were inscribed all knowledge and science. The "bardic rods" were taken by the *bard *Menwy, who learned all that was written upon them and then taught the knowledge to others (M 269).

See also Fantastic objects.

(BT 12/27; HK 24/36, 229/264; M 269)

Llamrei (LAM-ray): Llamrei is the foal of *Melynlas and *Lluagor. The sorrel mare is ridden by *Coll during the last great battles between *Arawn and the *Sons of Don.

As recorded in the *Mabinogion, Llamrei was the mare of King Arthur (M 251). *Lady Charlotte Guest writes in her notes accompanying the Welsh tales that the "mare of Arthur's was very celebrated. Her name implies bounding or curvetting" (M 291).
(HK 37/50, 44–45/59; M 251, 258, 291)

Llassar (LASS-ar) Son of Drudwas (DRUD-was): Son of the shepherd *Drudwas of the *Commot Isav, Llassar is "a tall, eager-faced boy scarcely older than *Taran had been when *Coll first dubbed him *Assistant Pig-Keeper" (TW 202/236). When Taran proposes a plan to defeat the raiders of *Dorath's Company, Llassar volunteers to help by standing guard in the sheepfold with Taran. Llassar illustrates his bravery and sense of duty when he says, "The flock is in my charge" (TW 203/237). Later, when the battle ensues, the young shepherd plunges between Taran and the outlaw, *Gloff, saving Taran's life and being wounded himself (TW 205–206/240).

In *The High King, Taran returns to the *Free Commots to rally troops for the *Sons of Don. Drudwas is dead now, and an older Llassar throws in his lot with Taran, choosing to fight under the *banner of the White Pig (HK 96/116). Llassar's skills as a shepherd prove invaluable to Taran's troops. He is able to lead them away from the ruins of *Caer Dathyl, over the snow-swept mountains, and into the lowlands (HK 134/160). Later, he becomes the "shepherd to a . . . grimmer flock" as he leads the battered army of *Commot men through the treacherous *Hills of Bran-Galedd (HK 144/170).

As the *Chronicles of Prydain conclude, Llassar is among the people of *Prydain who come to hail Taran, their new *High King (HK 247/285).

The name of Llassar appears in the *Mabinogion. Llassar, the son of Llaesar Llaesgygwyd, was one of the seven knights left to protect Britain while King Bendigeid Vran attacked Ireland to avenge the ill treatment of his sister, Branwen (M 377).
(TW 202/236; HK 96+/116+; M 377)

Llawgadarn (law-GAD-arn) Mountains: The Llawgadarn Mountains rise in eastern *Prydain, "in the land of the *Free Commots" (TW 46/63). These peaks, located along the *Commots' northern border, cradle the *Mirror of Llunet. The magical pool, located near *Lake Llunet, is said to have oracular powers, and the witch *Orddu suggests to *Taran that it might reveal to him his parentage (TW 19/34). It is within the Llawgadarn Mountains that Taran fights with the mercenary leader, *Dorath, for the third and final time (TW 214/250).
(TW 19+/34+)

Llonio (LAHN-io) Son of Llonwen (LAHN-wen): As *Taran looks for someone who will give *Craddoc's sheep a home, he happens upon a low-roofed cottage and sheds near the banks of the *Small Avren. The place is neat and well-kept, yet strange. Woven baskets are set all about the cottage, trees by the river hold wooden platforms, and stakes support fishing nets and lines drifting in the river's current. Soon Taran meets the owner of the unusual dwelling and finds a home for the sheep.

> The man who stood before Taran was thin as a stick with lank hair tumbling over his brow and blue eyes bright as a bird's. Indeed, his narrow shoulders and spindly legs made him look like a crane or stork. His jacket was too short in the arms, too long in the body, and his garments seemed pieced together with patches of all sizes, shapes, and colors.
>
> "I am Llonio Son of *Llonwen," he said, with a friendly grin and a wave of the hand. "A good greeting to you, whoever you may be." (TW 164/194)

Llonio is the eternal optimist. He believes in luck and good fortune. For example, he builds a sheepfold and clears a pasture when he has no sheep. Taran thinks such was work in vain.

> "Was it now?" asked Llonio, winking shrewdly. "If I hadn't, would you be offering me a fine flock in the first place; and in the second, would I have the place to keep them? Is that not so?"
>
> "But you couldn't have known," Taran began.
>
> "Ah, ah," Llonio chuckled, "why, look you, I knew that with any kind of luck a flock of sheep was bound to come along one day. Everything else does!" (TW 165/195)

The terribly cheerful fellow places the baskets in his yard to catch or attract whatever will come: bees, goosefeathers, etc. The fishing nets are to catch whatever may float down the Small Avren. "Small it [the river] is," says Llonio, "but sooner or later whatever you might wish comes floating along" (TW 168/198). Also, a weir of branches in the river is used to "strain and sift the current" (TW 169/199). This then is Llonio's philosophy of life: "Life's a matter of luck. Trust it, and a man's bound to find what he seeks, one day or the next. . . . If I fret over tomorrow, I'll have little joy today" (TW 169/199).

Nevertheless, there is a "secret" to Llonio's luck. "Have you not already guessed?" he asks Taran. "Why, my luck's no greater than yours or any man's. You need only sharpen your eyes to see your luck when it comes, and sharpen your wits to use what falls into your hands" (TW 174/205). Everything Llonio finds is eventually put to some good and usually creative use: an old bridle makes belts and a cart wheel becomes a spinning wheel.

Llonio's cottage is near the *Free Commots. He dwells there peacefully with his wife, *Goewin, and a half-dozen children. (*Gwenlliant is the only of Llonio's children whose name is given.)

In *The High King, Llonio rides up to join Taran's forces under the *banner of the White Pig. He is outfitted in the most outlandish armor: bits of metal stitched to his shirt, a cookpot fashioned into a helmet, and a makeshift scythe for a weapon (HK 93/112–113). But Llonio fights fiercely as *Pryderi seeks to overthrow *Caer Dathyl. "The man's makeshift helmet bobbed over his eyes, his long legs were drawn up high in the stirrups, and he looked like nothing so much as a scarecrow come to life; yet, where Llonio passed, attackers fell as wheat to a scythe" (HK 124/148).

Llonio perishes in the battle to preserve *Caer Dathyl (HK 129/154–155). Sadly, the reader lays him to rest and thinks uncomfortably of Goewin and the children.

The name of Llonnio Llonnwen is mentioned in *Lady Charlotte Guest's notes to the *Mabinogion. This Llonnio received from *Henwen, Dadweir Dallpenn's marvelous sow, a grain of barley and a piglet. Dyved, the area where Llonnio lived, produced the best barley and pigs from that time forth (M 268).

Also, in the story titled "Taliesin" in the Mabinogion, a character named Gwyddno uses a weir like that of Alexander's Llonio. Gwyddno "catches" the infant Taliesin in his weir (M 473).
(TW 163/193, 217/253; HK 93/112, 124/148, 129/154, 237/273; M 268)

Llonwen (LAHN-wen): Father of the cheerful optimist, *Llonio. The name of Llonwen (Llonnio Llonnwen) is found in *Lady Charlotte Guest's notes to the *Mabinogion (M 268).
(TW 164/194; HK 93/113, 129/155; M 268)

**Lluagor (lew-AH-gore): This bay mare was the steed of *Adaon. Foreseeing his own death, Adaon wills Lluagor to *Taran. When Adaon is slain, *Eilonwy rides Lluagor because she has lost her own horse (BC 84/110). Taran, of course, still has *Melynlas. Soon Eilonwy comes to prefer Lluagor above all other steeds (CL 4/19). Later, a foal is born of Melynlas and Lluagor and given the name *Llamrei (HK 37/50).

*Lady Charlotte Guest's notes to the *Mabinogion tell of a Welsh hero named Caradawc who had a horse named Lluagor. "Lluagor is recorded as one of the three battle horses of the Island [of Britain]" (M 328).
(M 328)

Llyan (lee-AHN): In an abandoned hut on the *Isle of Mona, the *Companions find *Glew's diary. *Fflewddur reads that Glew captured a small mountain cat on which to try his potions for growing larger. The book gives the cat's name as Llyan and reports that she grew so large as to need a new cage. However, the last pages of Glew's diary are nibbled away by mice, and both Glew and Llyan seem to have vanished (CL 59/79).

Suddenly, Llyan makes her debut in the *Chronicles of Prydain. It seems her lair is not far from Glew's hut.

> Though Glew had written of Llyan's growth, *Taran had never imagined a mountain cat so big. The animal stood as tall as a horse but leaner and longer; her tail alone, thicker than Taran's arm, seemed to take up much of the room in the hut. Heavily and sleekly furred, the cat's body was golden-tawny, flecked with black and orange. Her belly was white with black splotches. Curling tufts sprouted from the tips of her ears, and shaggy handfuls of fur curved at her powerful jaws. Her long whiskers twitched; her baleful yellow eyes darted from one companion to another. Judging from the white points of her teeth, glittering as her lips drew back in a snarl, Taran was certain Llyan could gulp down anything that suited her fancy. (CL 62/82)

The wild and angry Llyan does indeed seem ready to devour the Companions, but Fflewddur soothes her with his harping while the others escape. Llyan is lulled to sleep, and Fflewddur is able to sneak away from her. However, the *giant cat is so enamored by the *bard's music that when awakened, she stalks him. Llyan catches Fflewddur by the banks of the River *Alaw, but *Kaw manages to distract her by tweaking the cat's whiskers. Llyan angrily chases Kaw into the forest while Fflewddur escapes on a raft.

The Companions do not realize that Llyan has been tamed by Fflewddur's *truthful harp. This taming is indeed fortunate, for Llyan later saves each of them from a certain death. When the evil *Magg opens the sea gates and floods *Caer Colur, Llyan pulls the Companions from the sea.

> Fflewddur turned . . . to Taran. "We have to thank Llyan for a great deal. Everything, in fact. She fished us all out of the surf after the sea had washed us up. If she hadn't, I'm afraid we should still be there. . . .
> "I did have a start when I came to my senses with Llyan sitting beside me," said Fflewddur. "She had my harp between her paws, as though she couldn't wait for me to wake up and begin again. The creature is mad about my music! That's why she tracked us all the way here. . . . She's really been quite gentle," he added, as Llyan began to rub her

head against him with such vigor the bard could hardly keep his balance. (CL 159–160/189)

A lasting companionship begins at this point between Fflewddur Fflam and Llyan. "'I think I shall keep her. Or,' he [Fflewddur] added, while Llyan nuzzled her whiskers on his neck and gripped the bard with her powerful paws, 'perhaps I should put it the other way around'" (CL 160/190).

Llyan becomes Fflewddur's mount and is faster and more durable than a horse. Many times, Llyan proves to be a formidable ally when the Companions are in danger. When the Companions are threatened by the wizard, *Morda, Llyan uses her tremendous strength to bound over Morda's impenetrable *wall of thorns. Her great strength makes her deadly on the battlefield.

As the *Chronicles of Prydain draw to a close, Llyan accompanies Fflewddur Fflam and the *Sons of Don to the land of eternal life, the *Summer Country.

Lloyd Alexander is himself a devoted cat lover. However, he did not care for them before he met and married his wife, Janine. He was a dog man, so he thought, until circumstances brought a cat into his home. The cat, named Rabbit, "completely converted Lloyd to feline worship." Soon, as many as four cats (Heathcliff being Alexander's favorite) roamed the Alexander household (Jacobs, 1978:248–250). Soon cats started appearing in his writing: My Five Tigers (Alexander, 1956), Park Avenue Vet (Alexander, 1962), Time Cat (Alexander, 1963), The Cat Who Wished to Be a Man (Alexander, 1977a), The Town Cats (Alexander, 1977b), The Remarkable Journey of Prince Jen (Alexander, 1991), The House Gobbaleen (Alexander, 1995), Gypsy Rizka (Alexander, 1999), How the Cat Swallowed Thunder (Alexander, 2000), and The Rope Trick (Alexander, 2002). Llyan was a welcome feline addition. In a letter to Ann Durell, his editor, Alexander says that his cats (Solomon, Sylvester J. Meissel, and a Siamese) all claimed that the cover painting for *The Castle of Llyr shows a picture not of a fictitious cat (Llyan), but of them. Of course, each cat claims that the artist, Evaline Ness, meant to show him or her (Alexander, 1965h).

There appear two unusual cats in the *Mabinogion. In the story, "The Lady of the Fountain," a large black lion (referred to by the proper noun Lion) is rescued from a serpent by Owain. Lion serves Owain faithfully from that moment forward—as a hunter, as a guardian, and as a battle companion (M 25).

Alexander (1985b) says that Owain's lion was not an inspiration for Llyan. Instead, she was inspired by the Palug Cat of the Isle of Mona. *Lady

Charlotte Guest writes of the Palug Cat in her notes to the *Mabinogion.
When *Henwen, the marvelous sow of Dadweir Dallpenn, was chased
across Britain by King Arthur, she left a kitten at Maen Du in Arvon. The
sons of Palug in *Mona (the Isle of Anglesey) reared the kitten. It became
the dreaded Palug Cat, one of the three plagues of the Isle of Mona (M 268).
Robert Graves also relates the story of the Palug Cat in The White Goddess
(WG 221).

Alexander humorously claims that Llyan was "inspired by the letters of
two literary-minded cats, denizens of the household of a certain editor.
They insisted that in a land like *Prydain, the prototype of cat-greatness
must exist—and it turned out they were right" (CL 173/204).
(M 25, 268; WG 221, 409)

Llyr (LEER): *See* House of Llyr.

Llyr (LEER) Half-Speech: This ancient *Sea King is a distant relative of
*Eilonwy. "'My ancestors,' she said proudly, 'are the *Sea People. I am of
the blood of Llyr Half-Speech, the Sea King'" (BT 55/73).

Alexander (1985b) says that "mythologically . . . he [Llyr Half-Speech]
was a sea god. He was Neptune, in effect." Robert Graves, in The White
Goddess, writes that the British god, *Llyr (Lludd, Nudd), was indeed a god
of the sea. He seems to be associated with the Roman god Janus, who was
two-headed and the patron of the New Year (WG 177–178).

See also Characters—fantasy.
(BT 55/73; WG 177)

loom: Two looms of importance are in the *Chronicles of Prydain. The first
is the loom of the three witches, *Orddu, *Orwen, and *Orgoch. When
the *Companions visit the cottage of the witches, *Eilonwy is warned not
to touch the fabric on their loom. "Nasty prickles if you do. It's full of
nettles," says Orddu (BC 102/133). Taran visits the witches again in *Taran
Wanderer. Again he notices the work on their loom.

> The work on the frame had gone forward somewhat, but it was far from
> done; knotted, twisted threads straggled in all directions, and what
> looked like some of Orgoch's cockleburs were snagged in the warp and
> weft. *Taran could make out nothing of the pattern, though it seemed to
> him, as if by some trick of his eyes, that vague shapes, human and animal,
> moved and shifted through the weaving. (TW 12–13/26)

As *The High King* concludes, the three witches, now beautiful women, appear to Taran and present him with the tapestry they have been weaving on their loom.

> Puzzled, Taran looked more closely at the fabric and saw it crowded with images of men and women, of warriors and battles, of birds and animals. "These," he murmured in wonder, "these are of my own life."
>
> "Of course," Orddu replied. "The pattern is of your choosing and always was."
>
> "My choosing?" Taran questioned. "Not yours? Yet I believed . . ." He stopped and raised his eyes to Orddu. "Yes," he said slowly, "once I did believe the world went at your bidding. I see now it is not so. The strands of life are not woven by three hags or even by three beautiful damsels. The pattern indeed was mine. But here," he added, frowning as he scanned the final portion of the fabric where the weaving broke off and the threads fell unraveled, "here it is unfinished."
>
> "Naturally," said Orddu. "You must still choose the pattern, and so must each of you poor, perplexed fledglings, as long as thread remains to be woven." (HK 234/270)

Indeed, the young *Dallben understands the symbolic meaning of the witches' weaving, when he says, "These are no threads, but the lives of men" (F 8/6).

The second loom of importance in the Chronicles is that of *Dwyvach Weaver-Woman. Taran apprentices under Dwyvach and learns to weave at her loom, described as "a high loom standing like a giant harp of a thousand strings" (TW 182/214). The products of Dwyvach's skill are without rival in all *Prydain. After his time with the *Weaver-Woman, Taran prophetically wonders if he is but a thread on Orddu's loom or is truly weaving his own pattern in life (TW 188/221). Dwyvach turns her loom to the service of the *Sons of Don by weaving clothing for the armies of Prydain (HK 96/116).

See also Fantastic objects.
(BC 102/132; TW 12/26, 18/32, 182/214; HK 96/116, 233/269; F 8/6)

Lord of Annuvin (ah-NOO-vin): *See* Arawn.

Lord of Death: *See* Arawn.

Lord Swineherd: Lord Swineherd is the mocking title *Dorath gives to *Taran, *Assistant Pig-Keeper.
(TW 118/142, 124/149, 129/155, 213/248; HK 164/192)

M

✛

Mabinogion: In *The White Goddess*, Robert Graves explains the origin and history of the *Mabinogion*, which he calls the most famous Welsh collection of romances. The *Mabinogion* is often known as "Juvenile Romances," and all apprentice minstrels in ancient Wales were to know these stories. The *Mabinogion* is contained in the *Red Book of Hergest*, though most of the incidental verses were lost. Graves also explains that some of the romances were updated by the minstrels, to be more current in their language and description of manners and morals (WG 27).

*Lady Charlotte Guest translated the Welsh Romances from the *Red Book of Hergest* and from other sources (*Tales from the White Book of *Rhydderch*), which were published in her version of the *Mabinogion* between 1838 and 1849 (McGovern, 1980:10). The *Mabinogion* by Guest was then updated by subsequent editions. Alexander estimates he read Guest's *Mabinogion* at least twelve times as he prepared to write the *Chronicles of Prydain (Jacobs, 1978:266) and says Guest's notes at the conclusion of each tale proved perhaps most valuable (Alexander, 1985a). However, it is important to note that Alexander's work is very loosely based upon *Welsh mythology and is *not* a retelling of the *Mabinogion*.

The word *Mabinogion* is the plural of *Mabinogi*, which may be interpreted to mean "tale of a hero's childhood" (McGovern, 1980:10). Strictly speaking, only four of Guest's twelve tales are considered a part of the *Mabinogion*: "*Pwyll Prince of Dyved," "Branwen the *Daughter of Llyr," "Manawyddan the Son of *Llyr," and "*Math the Son of *Mathonwy" (McGovern, 1980:10). The other tales in Guest's the *Mabinogion* are "The Lady of the Fountain," "Peredur the Son of Evrawc," "*Geraint the Son of Erbin," "*Kilhwch and *Olwen," "The Dream of Rhonabwy," "The Dream of Maxen Wledig," "The Story of Lludd and Llevelys," and "*Taliesin."

Gwyn Jones disagrees that the word Mabinogion means "juvenile romances" or "tales of a hero's childhood." He feels it means "tales of the son of a virgin mother" and therefore applies only to the four romances in which *Pryderi, the son of Rhiannon, appears (WG 95). These four tales are the same four mentioned above.

The individual tales—especially the stories of Pwyll, Math, Branwen, and Manawyddan—grew from oral tradition and eventually took their present form somewhere between A.D. 1000 and 1250 (Gantz, 1976:21).

The *Mabinogion* has its roots firmly embedded in *Celtic mythology. McGovern (1980:15–16) explains that the ancient Celts were highly superstitious, and their traditional myths were well developed but localized. His account of Celtic bardic tradition follows.

> The Celtic storytellers had two broad categories from which to draw: myth and folklore on one hand, and history and pseudo-history on the other. Since the Celts were escapist by nature these categories often overlapped. Celtic mythology didn't contain the well organized pantheons found in Egypt, Greece or Rome, instead they had a mixture of local gods, epic heroes and borrowed deities. "What remains is an imbroglio of anecdotes, allusions, motifs and characters which under close scrutiny reveal the outlines of a number of mythological paradigms within a British setting" (McCana, 1970:18). Many of the characters found in the *Mabinogion* have almost marginal identities, bordering between the heroic mortal and the *magic wielding god.

McGovern explains that the list of various gods in *Celtic mythology is virtually endless, though there are several characters and motifs that seem common to most localities and thus "suggest a unifying theme." "One such theme is concerned with the invasion and replacement of one family of gods for another . . ." (McGovern, 1980:16).

> The two major families of Welsh mythology are the *children of Don and the children of Llyr, both of whom appear throughout the *Mabinogion* at various times involved in a myriad of adventure.
> Other common elements of Welsh mythology which are significant:
>
> 1. The Celtic otherworld which was not a Christian hell but a place of happiness and abundance. . . .
>
> 2. The partnership of a man with . . . *Arawn Lord of the Underworld.
>
> 3. The yearning for a Golden Age when peace will reign supreme.
>
> 4. The use of magic by the family of *Don, i.e., *Gwydion turning moss into horses.

5. The importance of certain magical things.

6. The use of zoomorphic representation, the most common animals used are the boar, the bull and the horse.

7. The belief in an afterlife which made the Celts especially good soldiers since they were not afraid to die. (McGovern, 1980:16–17)

(WG 27, 95)

Madoc (MA-dok): Madoc is the name of the kingdom ruled by King *Morgant. Though it could be the name of Morgant's father as well, Alexander (1985b) says that we simply "don't know who his father was." Alexander (1985b) found the name Madoc in the *Mabinogion, liked it, and chose it for Morgant's realm.

The name Madoc or Madawc is assigned to several characters in the Mabinogion. Madawc was one of King Arthur's foresters (M 142). Madoc, the son of Modron, is listed as one of the three supreme prisoners of the Isle of Britain (M 192). Madawc, the son of Maredudd, "was a prince of more than common talent, and was highly extolled by contemporary *bards and historians" (M 316–317). *Lady Charlotte Guest explains that this Madawc was indeed a real figure in Welsh and British history (M 316). Also, Guest's notes to the Mabinogion list the names of the three "Baptismal Bards of the Isle of Britain." Merddin the son of Madoc Morvryn is one of these most famous of bards (M 498).
(BC 13/25, 174/217; M 142, 192, 255, 299, 316, 498)

Magg (MAG): Magg is introduced as the *Chief Steward of the *House of Rhuddlum on the *Isle of Mona. However, Magg has an insatiable need for power and recognition. Even as Chief Steward, he makes himself prominent by adorning himself in finery. "He wore one of the finest cloaks *Taran had ever seen, its rich embroidery almost surpassing King *Rhuddlum's garment" (CL 15/31). In order to attain rank, Magg allies himself with the evil enchantress, *Achren, and secretly plans to kidnap the Princess *Eilonwy. If Achren's plan succeeds, she will rule *Prydain once again, this time through Eilonwy and the enchantments of *Llyr. Magg has been promised the rule of *Dinas Rhydnant, capital of the House of Rhuddlum, when Achren controls Prydain. Indeed, Magg abducts Eilonwy and takes her to *Caer Colur, the ancestral home of Llyr, which lies in ruin just off the shore of *Mona. It is from Caer Colur that Achren envisions ruling Prydain.

"Spiderlike" in his movements, Magg embodies all the despicable qualities of a traitor and a villain (CL 33/51). He is concerned only with his own comfort and glory. *Gwydion explains that Magg's "vanity and ambition have made him Achren's willing creature" (CL 127/154).

When it seems as if Achren has triumphed, Magg gleefully calls himself King Magg and Magg the Magnificent. *Fflewddur, however, calls him King Magg the Maggot, ever referring to him as a spider. But Achren's plans are frustrated, and her power is destroyed. Magg is scorned by the enchantress. He seeks revenge by secretly opening the sea gates and flooding Caer Colur, in hope of drowning Achren and the *Companions (CL 157/186).

Magg reappears in *The High King* as a servant and ally of *Arawn *Death-Lord. With Arawn's forces, he takes *Caer Cadarn, the stronghold of *Smoit, and is sitting on the good King's throne when the Companions arrive. Still thin and spider-like, the evil Magg grins "like a skull" (HK 45/60). He boasts to the Companions that he devised the ruse that lured Gwydion into the clutches of Arawn's *Huntsmen so that *Dyrnwyn might be stolen. (The Death-Lord changed his shape to appear as Taran in distress.) Magg also boasts that Arawn has promised he will one day wear the *Iron Crown of Annuvin and thus rule in the Death-Lord's stead.

Magg's control of Caer Cadarn is brief. Eilonwy, Fflewddur, and *Rhun arrive at Smoit's stronghold a half a day later than Taran and Gwydion and sense something is amiss. Exercising caution, they discover what has happened and devise a scheme to free their friends and Smoit's guards.

Magg slips away from Caer Cadarn and makes his way back to *Annuvin. On the journey, he and his war band happen upon Achren. The once powerful enchantress travels to Annuvin to seek revenge against Arawn. Magg is no less vengeful, attacking Achren and leaving her for dead (HK 205/237). However, Achren lives to see Magg suffer a horrible death.

When Annuvin is about to fall to the *Sons of Don, Arawn deserts his throne room, leaving behind the Iron Crown of Annuvin, symbol of his power. Remembering and believing Arawn's promise, Magg finds the crown and, in his madness, claims it for his own. Calling himself Magg the Magnificent and Magg Death-Lord, he sets the Iron Crown on his brow.

> The Chief Steward's triumphant laughter turned to a shriek as he clawed suddenly at the iron band circling his forehead. Taran and Fflewddur gasped and drew back.
>
> The crown glowed like red iron in a forge. Writhing in agony, Magg clutched vainly at the burning metal which now had turned white hot, and with a last scream toppled from the throne.
>
> Eilonwy cried out and turned her face away. (HK 218/252)

Thus ended the vain dreams of glory entertained by the Chief Steward Magg. Though the *Mabinogion contains no character named Magg, it does include those of similar rank: Chief Steward, or Steward of the Household (M 141). In her notes to the Mabinogion, *Guest refers to the ancient Welsh Laws, which explain that Stewards of the Household were important members of the royal court.

> He was the chief of all the officers of the Court, who had each to pay him a fee of twenty-four pence upon their installation. On him devolved the important care of providing food for the kitchen, and liquor for the mead-cellar; and he had the charge of the king's share of booty, until the king desired to dispose of it, when he was allowed to choose from it a steer, as his own share. It was his particular duty "to swear for the king." Besides his clothes, and four horse-shoes, and various perquisites of the skins of beasts, he was entitled to a "male hawk, from the master of hawks, every feast of St. Michael." (M 186)

(CL 15+/31+; HK 45/60, 205/237, 216/250; M 141, 186)

Magic: Magic is fantasy literature's most essential and basic element and draws upon the deepest wellsprings of our culture (Madsen, 1976:43–44). Colwell (1968:178), quoting Eleanor Farjeon, expresses its fundamental importance by saying: "Magic had its feet under the earth and its hair above the clouds . . . in the beginning, Magic was everywhere and nowhere." Magic is the power fueling the struggle between good and evil, and "although it is never stated, Christians might equate the powers of magic with the powers possessed by God and Satan to order and control the physical aspects of the universe" (Madsen, 1976:45).

The magic in fantasy is part of the natural world and often explains otherwise unexplainable events. But the magic of each mythical world operates under a strict set of rules. As Alexander (1965e:143) explains, to break the rules spells death for a fantasy story.

> True enough, the writer of fantasy can start with whatever premises he chooses. . . . In the algebra of fantasy, A times B doesn't have to equal B times A. But, once established, the equation must hold throughout the story. You may set your own ground rules and, in the beginning, decree as many laws [laws of magic, laws of the universe] as you like—though in practice the fewer departures from the "real" world the better. A not very serious breach and the fantasy world explodes just as surely as if a very real hydrogen bomb had been dropped on it.

In much the same way, an overuse of magic may weaken a fantasy tale. A flick of the magic wand or a quickly muttered incantation cannot take the place of human initiative in solving the major problems people encounter. Too much of the struggle occurs in the hearts of men and women. Alexander explains:

> It seems to me that I am a very hard-headed realist and by virtue of that particular turn of mind I tend not to rely on mysticism as any kind of resolution. Possibly one of the driving ideas in all the *Prydain Chronicles is the uselessness of magic—the books end with the end of magic in the world. Magic can't help us. It's very nice to imagine that it might have been like that at one point, but if it ever existed it's gone. We are stuck with our own human resources. (Wintle and Fisher, 1974:217–218)

Maibon (MAY-bon): Maibon is a cottager who lived in the days before *Taran's story begins. He frees *Doli of the *Fair Folk from a fallen tree, and therefore Doli must grant him a wish. Maibon fears growing older, and so he requests one of the legendary Fair Folk *stones that can keep anything from aging. Doli discourages his choice, but Maibon will not be dissuaded. However, when the cottager gets the stone home, he soon discovers that nothing around him will change: his beard doesn't grow, the eggs won't hatch, the field won't sprout, the baby won't teethe, and so on.

Alarmed, Maibon tries to rid himself of the stone, but it only finds its way back. At last, Doli returns and explains to Maibon that he must truly desire to be rid of the stone before it will disappear. The cottager decides firmly that this is what he wishes, and Doli tells him to leave the stone and return home. Maibon has learned to be content with the normal course of human life.

It is interesting to note that Maibon's fear of growing old is sparked by his offering a ride to a decrepit old man. This old man is *Dallben, who has just been aged overnight by reading *The Book of Three.

Alexander (1985b) borrowed the names for Maibon and his wife, *Modrona, from a single character in the *Mabinogion: Mabon, the son of Madron. Finding Mabon's secret prison is one of the many tasks Kilhwch (*Kilhuch) must complete in order to win *Olwen's hand in marriage (M 240). Part of this story is told to Taran by *Medwyn (BT 120/144). (F 17/19; M 240)

Marshes of Morva (MORE-va): The Marshes of Morva are first mentioned by *Kaw. The wily crow croaks the single word "Morva" as a hint to

the *Companions concerning the whereabouts of the *Black Cauldron
(BC 64/86). The marshes are the dwelling place of the three witches *Orddu,
*Orwen, and *Orgoch. *Fflewddur Fflam describes them as "dreadful, smelly,
ugly-looking fens" (BC 65/87). The *bard's opinion proves well-founded.

> Ropes of fog, twisting and creeping like white serpents, had begun to rise
> from the reeking ground . . . huge growths of thorny furze rose up. At the
> far side, Taran distinguished meager clumps of wasted trees. Under the
> gray sky, pools of stagnant water flickered among dead grasses and broken
> reeds. A scent of ancient decay choked his nostrils. A ceaseless thrum-
> ming and groaning trembled in the air. (BC 92/120)

The Companions are able to find their way safely and speedily across the
Marshes of Morva only because *Taran wears the *Brooch of Adaon, a
curious pin that grants its wearer special insight. The *Huntsmen of Annuvin pursuing the Companions are not so fortunate and are swallowed by the
marsh (BC 93/121).

Within the Marshes of Morva, the Companions find the cottage of
Orddu, Orgoch, and Orwen. The Black Cauldron is in the witches' possession, and Taran must sacrifice dearly to acquire it. Unable to destroy the
cauldron on the spot, the Companions must haul it through the marshes as
they travel for *Caer Dallben.

Taran returns to the Marshes of Morva in *Taran Wanderer. He hopes
the witches may reveal to him his parentage. Again, the marshes are un-
inviting and are described as "bleak, ugly, untouched by spring" (TW 11/24).
The witches reveal nothing but send Taran to find the oracular *Mirror of
Llunet for possible answers.

The infant *Dallben was found floating in a basket in the Marshes of
Morva (F 5/3). He was raised in the marshes by Orddu, Orwen, and Orgoch
until he acquired too much wisdom and knowledge and had to be sent on
his way.

The name Morva appears several times in the *Mabinogion. *Guest
mentions in her notes to the Mabinogion a meadow near Romney called
Morva Yvor (M 201). Alexander (1985b) admits that he took the name for
the Marshes of Morva from this entry in Guest's notes. "I didn't hesitate if
there were names that as names themselves had a sound that somehow
appealed to me. I would swipe them! I didn't hesitate."

Guest's notes indicate that *Gwydion is said to have been buried in
Morva Dinlley, the scene of one of his adventures with Llew Llaw Gyffes
(M 437). Also, the text of the Mabinogion tells of Morva Rhiannedd, a

place where King Maelgwn and Elphin raced horses in the story of "*Taliesin" (M 490).
(BC 64+/86+; TW 9/22, 78/98, 188/221; HK 232/268; F 5/3, 11/10; M 201, 437, 490)

Master of Horse: Master of Horse, a title given to a noble's horse trainer and stable master, is used in two instances in the *Prydain Chronicles. King *Rhuddlum of the *Isle of Mona maintains a Master of Horse in his court. When *Eilonwy is abducted, Rhuddlum places Prince *Rhun, his cheerful but incompetent son, in command of the search party. However, the King tells *Taran privately that his Master of Horse, a skilled tracker, will in truth direct the search (CL 44/63).

Lord *Goryon of *Cantrev Cadiffor also keeps a Master of Horse, one unable to sit astride the stolen *Melynlas. In fact, Goryon's Master of Horse carries one arm in a sling from his encounter with Taran's steed (TW 33/48).
(CL 44/63, 46/65, 49/68, 52/71, 68/90, 73/95; TW 32/47, 36/52)

Math (MATH) Son of Mathonwy (math-ON-wee): Math is the *High King above all the other lesser kings of *Prydain (BT 6/21). One of the *Sons of Don, Math rules with a just hand, and through his leadership *Arawn *Death-Lord is at least partly held in check. He dwells in the stronghold of *Caer Dathyl, "far north in the *Eagle Mountains" (BT 7/22). Math makes rare appearances in the *Prydain Chronicles, once at the conclusion of *The Book of Three and then briefly in *The High King.

When *Taran first meets Math, the elderly king is described as a "white-bearded monarch, who looked as old as *Dallben and as testy . . . [but] was even more talkative than *Eilonwy" (BT 180/210–211). However, Taran notices a distinct change in Math when they meet again in The High King.

> Not since the battle between the Sons of Don and the armies of the *Horned King had Taran been in the presence of Math Son of *Mathonwy, and he saw the years had borne heavily upon the monarch of the Royal House. The face of Math was even more careworn and more deeply furrowed than Dallben's; upon his brow the *Gold Crown of Don seemed a cruel burden. Yet his eyes were keen and filled with stern pride. More than this, Taran sensed a sorrow so profound that his own heart grieved and he bowed his head.
>
> "Face me, *Assistant Pig-Keeper," Math commanded in a quiet voice. "Fear not to see what I myself know. The hand of death reaches toward mine and I am not loath to clasp it. I have long heard the horn of

*Gwyn the Hunter, that summons even a king to his *barrow home." (HK 107–108/128–129)

Math tells Taran that he is deeply disturbed by the war that rages in Prydain. "What grieves me is not my death; but at the end of my life to see blood spilled in the land where I sought only peace" (HK 108/129).

But hatred and death only intensify. When *Pryderi arrives at Caer Dathyl, it is thought he has come to strengthen the forces of the Sons of Don. But the traitorous king has aligned himself with Arawn and demands the surrender of King Math. Blinded by pride, Pryderi declares he will see done what the Sons of Don could never do: "Make an end of endless wars among the *cantrevs, and bring peace where there was none before" (HK 119/142). Pryderi will see obedience achieved by force. Math sadly answers, "Is there worse evil than that which goes in the mask of good?" (HK 119/142).

Pryderi's forces, along with Arawn's *Cauldron-Born, level an assault upon Caer Dathyl that cannot be turned aside. When the deathless warriors batter down the gates, Math Son of Mathonwy stands alone and defiant before them. The deathless warriors pause "as if at the faint stirring of some clouded memory" (HK 127/152). Then they stride forward, knocking Math's sword aside and striking him down.

King Math staggered and dropped to one knee. The mass of mute warriors pressed forward, their weapons thrusting and slashing. Taran covered his face with his hands and turned away weeping, as Math Son of Mathonwy fell and the iron-shod boots of the Cauldron-Born pressed their relentless march over his lifeless body. From the dark hills then there rose the long notes of a hunting horn, trembling, echoing among the crags, and a shadow seemed to brush the sky above the fortress. (HK 128/152–153)

The Cauldron-Born turn their battering rams to the walls of Caer Dathyl, and Math is buried by the rubble of his once proud stronghold. *Taliesin, *Chief Bard of Prydain, consecrates the ruined mountain valley as Math's barrow. "Each broken stone of Caer Dathyl shall be a mark of honor, and the whole valley a resting place for Math Son of Mathonwy and all our dead" (HK 130/155).

Math ab Mathonwy is a principal character in the *Mabinogion. One of the tales bears his name and is one of the original branches of the Mabinogi (McGovern, 1980:10). Math was one of the principal enchanters of Welsh myth, "who were styled Men of Illusion and Phantasy" (M 213). He is to have "declared his illusion to Gwdion [*Gwydion] the son of Don" (M 213).

Math was lord of Gwynedd and dwelt at Caer Dathyl in Arvon. He could not exist unless his feet were in the lap of a maiden (a virgin), except when he was at war (M 413). The maiden who cradled his feet was named *Goewin. Gwydion and Gilvaethwy conspire to take Goewin from their uncle, for Gilvaethwy covets her. By means of deception through enchantment, Gwydion takes the swine of *Annuvin from Pryderi, thus beginning a war that takes Math from his chamber. When Math is gone, Gilvaethwy enters his chamber and forces his affections on Goewin (M 417). Math returns to find his maiden no longer a virgin. He punishes Gwydion and Gilvaethwy by turning them into deer, wild hogs, and wolves. The treacherous brothers live as each type of animal for a full year (M 419–421).

According to *Guest's notes to the *Mabinogion*, Math's *magic seems to have excelled all the enchanters of Welsh fiction except Merlin and perhaps Gwydion (M 434). Yet, the name of Math has a meaning unrelated to enchantments, that being "treasure" (WG 51).

See also Characters—fantasy.
(BT 6/21, 180/210; BC 17/30, 178/221; CL 21/37; TW 6/18, 9/22, 47/64; HK 17/28, 92/111, 107/128, 115/137, 127–128/152, 130/155, 132/157; M 213, 364, 413, 434; WG 50, 97, 303)

Mathonwy (math-ON-wee): Mathonwy is the father of the *High King *Math. His name also accompanies that of Math (Math the son of Mathonwy) in the *Mabinogion*.

Medwyn (MED-win): "There is an ancient dweller in the foothills of *Eagle Mountains," *Gwydion tells *Taran. "His name is Medwyn, and it is said he understands the hearts and ways of every creature in *Prydain. . . . I have never seen him. Others have sought him and failed" (BT 36/52).

In spite of Medwyn's secret nature, Taran and the *Companions are granted a visit to his secret valley. *Gurgi is severely injured, and *Melyngar, Gwydion's steed, takes him to Medwyn to be healed. As he enters *Medwyn's valley, Taran is impressed by its peaceful aura.

> Mountains, seemingly impassable, rose on all sides. Here the air was gentler, without the tooth of the wind; the grass spread rich and tender before him. Set among tall hemlocks were low, white cottages, not unlike those of *Caer Dallben. . . .
> The valley was the most beautiful he had ever seen. Cattle grazed peacefully in the meadow. Near the hemlocks, a small lake caught the sky and sparkled blue and white. The bright plumage of birds flashed among

the trees. Even as he stepped across the lush green of the turf, Taran felt exhaustion drain from his aching body. (BT 115–116/138–139)

Medwyn is "a strange-looking figure, broad and muscular, with the vigor of an ancient but sturdy tree. His white hair reache[s] below his shoulders and his beard [hangs] to his waist. Around his forehead he [wears] a narrow band of gold, set with a single blue jewel" (BT 113/136–137). He wears a coarse brown robe and is as powerful as he appears to be. Medwyn lifts Gurgi as if he weighs no more than a squirrel, and stones do not bother his bare feet.

Indeed, Medwyn and the animals that dwell in his valley (or come and go) speak to and understand one another. Wolves and fawns live together in harmony in Medwyn's valley, and it is not uncommon for bears to come to dinner in Medwyn's cottage. Fruits and vegetables seemingly grow year round. "This is a place of peace," Medwyn tells Taran, "and therefore not suitable for men, at least, not yet. Until it is, I hold this valley for creatures of the forests and the waters. In their mortal danger they come to me, if they have the strength to do so—and in their pain and grief" (BT 121/145). "Every living thing deserves our respect . . . be it humble or proud, ugly or beautiful" (BT 119/142).

Against the face of a slope behind Medwyn's cottages, Taran notices the "weather-worn ribs and timbers of a long ship" that is overgrown with vegetation (BT 115/139). He inquires of Medwyn concerning the ship.

> "*Dallben," said Taran, "taught me that when the black waters flooded Prydain, ages ago, *Nevvid Nav Neivion built a ship and carried with him two of every living creature. The waters drained away, the ship came to rest—no man knows where. But the animals who came safe again into the world remembered, and their young have never forgotten. And here," Taran said, pointing toward the hillside, "I see a ship, far from water. Gwydion called you Medwyn, but I ask . . ."
>
> "I am Medwyn," answered the white-bearded man, "for all that my name may concern you." (BT 121–122/145–146)

Medwyn is certainly the Noah figure from Prydain's legendary past. Nevvid Nav Neivion is also the name of the Noah figure from *Celtic mythology. *Guest's notes to the *Mabinogion explain that one of "the three great exploits of the Island of Britain" was "the ship of Nevydd Nav Neivion, which carried in it a male and female of all things living, when the Lake of floods burst forth" (M 134). In *The High King, when Medwyn makes his second appearance in the *Chronicles of Prydain, he states plainly who he really is. He has just tended to the wounded *Kaw and listened to the crow's story of *Annuvin's rise. Medwyn speaks then to the animals that dwell with him, particularly *Edyrnion the eagle and *Brynach and *Briavael the wolves, and instructs them to warn and rally the animals of Prydain against the *Death-Lord.

> "Speak to them in my name and tell them: such are the words of one who built a ship when the dark waters flooded Prydain, of one who bore their ancient sires to safety. Now, against this flood of evil, each nest, each lair, must be a stronghold. Let every creature turn tooth, beak, and claw against all who serve *Arawn Death-Lord." (HK 90/109)

Medwyn had rallied the animals of Prydain against Arawn earlier in the history of Prydain. In *The Foundling, the story of "The Rascal Crow" tells how Medwyn warns and organizes all the creatures to fight against the *Chief Huntsman of Annuvin. At this time, he also speaks plainly of having built the ship that carried the animals' forefathers to safety (F 41–42/47–49).

While in Medwyn's valley, Taran learns many things. Medwyn explains that the vicious *gwythaints were once gentle birds until captured and tortured by Arawn. Taran also learns why Gurgi needs his acceptance. Then, through the story of *Gwythyr Son of *Greidawl, he comes to understand his need to accept aid and companionship from Gurgi and others. "I have studied the race of men," Medwyn says. "I have seen that alone you stand as weak reeds by a lake. You must learn to help yourselves, that is true; but you must also learn to help one another" (BT 121/145).

As the Chronicles of Prydain draw to a close, the age of enchantments in Prydain ends. The *Sons of Don leave for the *Summer Country. King *Eiddileg of the *Fair Folk bars the passages to the *Kingdom of Tylwyth Teg. And Medwyn closes his valley forever to the race of men (HK 227–229/263–265).

See also Characters—fantasy, Crugan-Crawgan, Gwybeddin, Kadwyr, Kilhuch, Nedir, Olwen.
(BT 36/52, 113/136; HK 88/106; F 41/47, 49/58; M 134, 284)

Medwyn's valley: See Medwyn.

Melyngar (MELIN-gar): This white mare is the steed of Prince *Gwydion. She is a war horse and exhibits her fighting spirit when Gwydion and *Taran are attacked by warriors of the *Horned King.

> Melyngar now had entered the fray. Her golden mane tossing, the white mare whinnied fearsomely and flung herself among the riders. Her mighty flanks dashed against them, crowding, pressing, while the steeds

of the war party rolled their eyes in panic. One warrior jerked frantically at his reins to turn his mount away. The animal sank to its haunches. Melyngar reared to her full height; her forelegs churned the air, and her sharp hoofs slashed at the rider, who fell heavily to earth. Melyngar spun about, trampling the cowering horseman. (BT 42/59)

Melyngar also aids the *Companions by guiding them to *Medwyn's secret valley when *Gurgi is seriously injured (BT 114/137). Taran's mount, presented to him at the conclusion of *The Book of Three, is of the lineage of Melyngar and is appropriately named *Melynlas.

*Guest's notes to the *Mabinogion tell us that the steed of Llew Llaw Gyffes, a nephew of Gwydion, was named Melyngan (Melyngar) mangre and was "one of the chief war-horses of the island" (M 438). (BT 20+/36+; BC 26/41, 35/51; TW 33/48; HK 35+/48+; M 438)

Melynlas (MELIN-lass) Son of Melyngar (MELIN-gar): "*Gwydion had given each of the *companions a handsome steed; to *Taran he had given the finest: the gray, silver-maned stallion, Melynlas, of the lineage of *Melyngar and as swift" (BT 183/213).

Melynlas continues as Taran's faithful steed throughout the *Chronicles of Prydain. In *Taran Wanderer, Melynlas is stolen from Taran by Lord *Goryon's men. However, he cannot be ridden by any of Goryon's people, including Goryon himself and his *Master of Horse. The stable boy calls Melynlas a "gray dragon" (TW 31/46).

Melynlas has a foal by *Lluagor named *Llamrei. *Coll rides Llamrei during the campaign against *Arawn in *The High King.

In *Guest's notes to the *Mabinogion, a steed named Meinlas appears. This was the horse of Caswallan (M 393). (M 393)

Menwy (MEN-wee) Son of Teirgwaedd (TEER-gwed): Menwy was a *bard in the days when *Arawn was stealing the secrets of craftsmanship from the artisans of *Prydain. He owned a harp that played of itself, knowing the secrets of its craft. The harp's music was so filled with beauty that it lifted the hearts of all who heard it (F 65/77).

Arawn *Death-Lord desired Menwy's harp and devised a ruse to trick the bard into parting with it. Arawn conjured the most beautiful golden harp, which he offered as a trade for Menwy's instrument. Menwy challenged the disguised Death-Lord to play his golden harp first, but Arawn could not play an illusion. Menwy, being "a poet and used to seeing around the edge of things," recognized Arawn and saw that the golden harp was truly made from dry bones with strings of poisonous serpents (F 71–72/86). Even though the true visage of Arawn Death-Lord was terrifying, the bard faced him and played a joyful tune. Arawn could not bear this, and he struck the enchanted harp with his sword, destroying it. But the birds and the winds and all of nature picked up the melody, driving Arawn away. "And the *Lord of Death fled in terror of life" (F 72/87).

We learn from the witch, *Orddu, that Menwy Son of *Teirgwaedd, "first of the bards," fashioned the *Brooch of Adaon long ago (BC 127/162). He "cast a mighty spell on it and filled it with dreams, wisdom, and vision" (BC 127/162). Of course, it is Menwy's ornament Taran must trade to the witches for the *Black Cauldron, though it breaks his heart.

Menwy the son of Teirgwaedd appears in the *Mabinogion. He was indeed a great bard, and according to *Guest's notes to the Mabinogion, he was one of the principal enchanters of Welsh legend who taught his illusion to Uthyr Pendragon, father of Arthur (M 213). He is called one of the three men of "Phantasy and Illusion in the Island of Britain" (M 269). Kilhwch (*Kilhuch) requests of King Arthur Menwy's aid in his quest to obtain *Olwen's hand in marriage (M 223).

However, Menwy holds an even greater place of honor among the heroes of Welsh tales, for he is credited with discovering the bardic alphabet. The original vision revealing the *bardic symbol, from which the alphabet is derived, was seen by the bard, Einigan Gawr. The three radiating lines (arranged like an arrowhead) forming the symbol had inscribed upon them all knowledge and science. The tale tells that Einigan transcribed the knowledge to three ash rods, and the people who later saw the rods deified them. Upset by the people's reaction, Einigan destroyed the ash rods and soon after died. A year later in a vision, Menwy "saw three rods growing from the mouth of Einigan" (M 269). He took the rods, learned all that was written upon them, and then taught the knowledge to others. Menwy discovered that the three lines of the bardic symbol contain all the elements of the bardic alphabet, "as there is not a single letter in it that is not formed from them" (M 269).

A reader of Alexander's Prydain may get the impression that the author is partial to bards or, in other words, writers and musicians. After all, other craftsmen (*Iscovan, *Follin) are unable to "see around the edge of things" and avoid Arawn's trickery. Alexander's bards seem to be wiser and more intelligent than most other men. Is this his opinion of writers and artists even today?

I'd like to think so, but it isn't true. . . . [A]s much as I would like it to be the case, writers aren't always wise. Bards were [however] wiser than, let's say, your average wandering minstrel or something. Put it this way: realistically speaking, I could only wish wisdom came with the territory of being an artist. . . . A few artists happen also to be extremely wise . . . [but] I wouldn't say flat out they were wiser. I would say that they have more insight than some others. . . . I think . . . that [it is] realistically true that a good poet has a sort of vision that non-poets don't have. (Alexander, 1985b)

See also ash-wood, Characters—fantasy.
(BC 127/162; F 65/77, 70/84; M 213, 223, 269, 292, 313)

Mirror of Llunet (LOO-net): The Mirror of Llunet is an oracular pool of water hidden in the *Llawgadarn Mountains. Knowing nothing more about the mirror than its general location, *Taran sets out at the suggestion of the witch, *Orddu, to find it. It is his quest in *Taran Wanderer* to discover his parentage, and Orddu thinks the Mirror of Llunet may reveal something significant.

When Taran eventually meets *Annlaw Clay-Shaper, he is told by the old potter that the mirror is in a cave at the foot of *Mount Meledin, a high peak in the Llawgadarn Mountains near *Lake Llunet. Following Annlaw's directions, Taran has little trouble finding the enchanted pool.

Within [the cave], a shallow basin hollowed in the floor of smooth stones, lay the Mirror of Llunet like a shield of polished silver, gleaming of itself despite the shadows. Taran slowly knelt at the rim. The basin held no more than a finger's depth of water, fed drop by drop from a thread of moisture twining down the rocky wall. The passing of countless years had not filled it to the brim. Yet shallow though it was, the water seemed a depthless crystal whose facets turned one upon the other, each catching brilliant beams of white. (TW 212/247–248)

Taran looks in the mirror and he cries out in disbelief at what he sees. Only moments later, the Mirror of Llunet is destroyed by the mercenary, *Dorath, who follows Taran to the cavern suspecting hidden treasure. Angry because no treasure exists, Dorath stamps his heavy boot in the pool, and the water spurts from the basin. It will take untold centuries for the magical waters to gather again. Taran returns to Annlaw's cottage and tells the old man what the mirror has shown him.

"I saw myself," Taran answered. "In the time I watched, I saw strength—and frailty. Pride and vanity, courage and fear. Of wisdom, a little. Of folly, much. Of intentions, many good ones; but many more left undone. In this, alas, I saw myself a man like any other.

"But this, too, I saw," he went on. "Alike as men may seem, each is different as flakes of snow, no two the same. You told me you had no need to seek the Mirror, knowing you were Annlaw Clay-Shaper. Now I know who I am: myself and none other. I am Taran. . . .

"There was no enchantment. . . . It was a pool of water, the most beautiful I have seen. But a pool of water, no more than that. . . .

"As for my parentage," he added, "it makes little difference. True kinship has naught to do with blood ties, however strong they be. I think we are all kin, brothers and sisters one to the other, all children of all parents. And the birthright I once sought, I seek it no longer." (TW 216–217/252–253)

See also Fantastic objects.
(TW 19+/34+)

Modrona (moh-DROH-nah): Modrona is the wife of the cottager, *Maibon. She exhibits a good deal more common sense than her husband, who worries about growing older. She wisely demands Maibon get rid of an enchanted *stone he receives for helping *Doli of the *Fair Folk. The stone magically impedes the aging process. Maibon will not listen to his wife at first, but when nothing he owns will change one whit (crops won't mature, eggs won't hatch, baby won't teethe, etc.), the silly cottager decides Modrona was right all along. However, being rid of such a stone is not a simple task.

Alexander (1985b) borrowed the names for Modrona and Maibon from a single character in the *Mabinogion*: Mabon, the son of Modron (M 240). (F 17/19)

Mona: *See* Isle of Mona.

Mona Haven: The crescent-shaped harbor of *Dinas Rhydnant on the *Isle of Mona is called Mona Haven. It is the major port of the *House of Rhuddlum and is described as having piers, jetties, and a stone seawall, and as being clustered with ships. Also, steep cliffs rise from near the water's edge.
See also Rhuddlum, Rhun, Teleria.
(CL 13/28, 126/153; HK 7/18, 19/30)

Morda (MORE-dah): Morda is alluded to in *The Castle of Llyr*. *Glew tells of obtaining the *book of spells of the *House of Llyr from a certain wizard (CL 97/122). Morda does not appear in the *Chronicles until his confrontation with the *Companions in *Taran Wanderer*.

While traveling through the *Hill Cantrevs, the Companions find a dehydrated frog, far from any source of water. The frog is *Doli of the *Fair Folk, bewitched by the evil wizard, Morda. After Doli has been soaked in water, he tells *Taran and the others that Morda's power is vast, for he can do something no other enchanter has ever had the power to do: cast a spell on one of the Fair Folk. And Morda is so heartless that he prefers seeing Doli perish slowly in the dry hills rather than killing him outright (TW 82/102).

Morda's dwelling is not far from where the Companions find Doli. It is surrounded by a tall, impenetrable *wall of thorns Morda has himself conjured. Inside the thorns, it appears as the lair of a wild beast but is in reality "a rambling, ill-shaped dwelling of low, squat walls roofed with sod" (TW 87–88/109).

In an effort to see Doli restored to proper form, Taran and the others finally confront the wizard. Morda's gaunt face is "the color of dry clay, eyes glittering like cold crystals deep set in a jutting brow as though at the bottom of a well" (TW 89/110–111). His skull is hairless, and his mouth is little more than "a livid scar stitched with wrinkles" (TW 89/111). Clad in a "grimy, threadbare robe," it is plain that Morda's body is wasted (TW 90/112). His neck is withered, his lips bloodless, and his hands bent like claws. But Morda's most unnerving feature is his unblinking stare. "Even in the candle flame the shriveled eyelids never closed; Morda's cold stare never wavered" (TW 90/112).

Taran notices that Morda wears around his neck a silver chain suspending the *crescent moon emblem of the *House of Llyr. Though similar to the one worn by *Eilonwy, this is larger and holds a carved gem, clear as water, in the horns of the crescent. Though Morda is certain Taran comes for the emblem of *Llyr with its stone, he is also certain that he is invulnerable. Therefore, Morda tells his story before working his evil spells on the Companions.

Morda tells how Princess *Angharad (Eilonwy's mother) wandered into his keep on a winter's night, ill yet searching for her abducted infant daughter. She traded the emblem of the House of Llyr for refuge, then died during the night. Angharad told Morda that the emblem with its stone has power to "lighten burdens and ease harsh tasks" (TW 93/115).

Not long after the princess died, Morda received a visit from Glew. He sold the little man an empty book also left by Angharad. Little did Morda know this was the book of spells of the House of Llyr. The spells are only visible under the light of the *Golden Pelydryn (Eilonwy's *bauble). It was Morda's plan to teach the "sniveling upstart" a lesson, so he warned Glew "not to open it [the book] or look upon it until he had traveled far from here lest the spells vanish" (TW 92/114).

The enchanter then worked with *Angharad's gem until he learned its ways and perverted its power. At first, he used it to dwindle "the heaviest fagots to no more than piles of twigs," to locate hidden streams of water, and to raise his enclosure of thorns (TW 93/115). Then he searched for and found Fair Folk treasure troves, turning their guardians into wild creatures. Morda was looking for the Fair Folk *stones that grant endless life, but he found none of them.

The evil wizard now holds the entire human race in contempt. Morda even holds *Dallben in contempt, calling him a "gray-bearded dotard" (TW 95/117). He hints that he is no longer human, that he has transcended humanity.

> "I had gained power even beyond what I sought. Who now would disobey me when I held the means to make men into the weak, groveling creatures they truly are! Did I seek only a gem? The whole kingdom of the Fair Folk was within my grasp. And all of *Prydain! It was then I understood my true destiny. The race of men at last had found its master." (TW 94/116)

*Fflewddur and *Gurgi are then disposed of by the power of Morda's gem. Fflewddur is transformed into "a dun-colored hare," a fact that bothers him immensely long after his shape is restored. Gurgi becomes a gray field mouse (TW 95–96/118). Gurgi the mouse nibbles through Taran's bonds as Morda deliberates about Taran's fate. Taran grasps his sword and drives it deep into the wizard's breast. What follows is perhaps the most terrifying and bizarre incident in the Chronicles.

Taran rips the blade free, and Morda is unharmed. He does not bleed from the wound. His harsh laughter mocks Taran and all mankind. "My life is not prisoned in my body," Morda boasts. "No, it is far from here, beyond the reach of death itself" (TW 99/121–122). Indeed, Morda has used Angharad's gem to place his life force in a secret hiding place.

Morda then decides to turn Taran into a spineless, limbless worm. But his enchantment does not work! Unknowingly, Taran has the vessel of Morda's life force in his pocket, and it blocks the wizard's spell. It is the bone of Morda's little finger, the bone Gurgi found in a small chest hidden in the crotch of a tall tree. Pesky *Kaw had retrieved it, though the Companions had wanted to leave the obviously enchanted fragment alone.

"My life! Poured into my finger!" cries Morda, as Taran shows him the bone. "With a knife I cut it from my own hand. Give! Give it back to me!"

(TW 101/123). The mighty wizard sobs and begs for his life, and Taran real-izes that breaking the bone will destroy Morda. Taran makes the mistake of allowing the wizard to live, and Morda quickly uses his reprieve to attack. Swinging the emblem of Llyr, he knocks Taran backward. The shard of bone flies from Taran's fingers, and Angharad's gem dislodges from its mounting. Despite Morda's emaciated appearance, he has the strength of many. He is at Taran's throat and would have killed him had not *Llyan suddenly appeared. The giant cat leaps over the wall of thorns to rescue Fflewddur. But Morda has the strength to grapple with and subdue Llyan, rendering the cat unconscious.

Taran is able to retrieve the bone and with great effort snap it in two. It makes "a sound sharper than a thunderclap," which is followed by "a horrible scream" (TW 106/129). Morda crumples to the ground "like a pile of broken twigs" and perishes (TW 106/129). With Morda dead, his spells are broken. The wall of thorns falls and each of the Companions, including Doli, is restored to his true shape. Angharad's gem, a gift from the Fair Folk to the House of Llyr, is given to Doli to return to the *Kingdom of Tylwyth Teg.

Alexander explains that "Morda's life secret . . . is familiar in many mythologies" (TW ix/14). He gives several examples including Kaschkei the Deathless from Slavic mythology. "Kaschkei the Deathless had his life hid-den in an egg. . . . The monstrous characters seem to be the ones who have their lives hidden in strange places" (Alexander, 1985b). Alexander (1985b) does not count the myth of Achilles, for his secret was not hidden elsewhere.

In the *Mabinogion, Morda was a blind man who kindled the fire for the hag Caridwen's (Cerridwen) cauldron of Inspiration and Science (M 472). The potion of this cauldron was much like that brewed by *Orddu, *Orwen, and *Orgoch. (See Dallben.)

See also Characters—fantasy, Fantastic objects, Magic.
(CL 97/122; TW 81/101, 116/140, 141/168, 145/173; M 472)

Morgant (MORE-gant) of Madoc (MA-dok), King: Morgant appears in *The Black Cauldron. He apparently joins with the *Sons of Don in the quest to destroy the *Black Crochan. Of Morgant, *Fflewddur says, "[He is] the boldest war leader in *Prydain, second only to *Gwydion himself. He owes allegiance to the *House of Don. . . . They say he once saved Gwydion's life. I believe it. I've seen that fellow in battle. All ice! Absolutely fearless!" (BC 13–14/25).

Morgant is described as a "dark warrior" who is richly attired. "His high-bridged nose was falconlike, his eyes heavy-lidded but keen. Only to Gwydion did he bow" (BC 13/25).

Assigned by Gwydion to lead a different band than that of *Taran, Morgant does not surface again until *The Black Cauldron* concludes. At this time, the Black Crochan, found and acquired by the *Companions, is stolen from them by *Ellidyr. But Ellidyr stumbles into Morgant's men, and it seems that the *cauldron is safe at last.

However, Morgant of *Madoc succumbs to the evil temptations of the *Black Cauldron. When the Companions arrive at Morgant's camp, he binds them as he has done with Ellidyr. Morgant reveals his plan to use the cauldron to gain power over Prydain. He will create his own *Cauldron-Born and march them against even his own kinsmen.

> "What," Taran cried, "will you set yourself to rival *Arawn?"
>
> "To rival him?" Morgant asked with a hard smile. "No. To surpass him. I know my worth, though I have chafed in the service of lesser men than I. Now I see the moment is ripe. There are few," he continued haughtily, "who understand the uses of power. And few who dare use it when it is offered them." (BC 162/203)

Because Morgant judges Taran to be of good mettle, he offers the *Assistant Pig-Keeper an opportunity to serve with him and eventually become his second in command. But the offer has an alarming alternative. "I shall leave you with this to consider: will you be first among my warriors—or first among my Cauldron-Born?" (BC 163/204–205).

Morgant's lofty but evil dreams are thwarted when Ellidyr throws himself into the cauldron. The only way to destroy the Black Crochan is if a man willingly climbs inside it, sacrificing his life. The *Crochan splits asunder, and Ellidyr's broken body lies amid the jagged shards. Concurrently, Gwydion's men attack the traitorous forces of Morgant. The *King of Madoc is slain by the mighty onslaught of King *Smoit.

> Eyes unhooded and blazing, his teeth bared, Morgant fought savagely amid the shattered pieces of the cauldron, as though he sought defiantly to claim them. His sword had broken under the force of Smoit's attack, yet he slashed and thrust again and again with the jagged blade, the grimace of hatred and arrogance frozen upon his features, his hand still clutching the bloodstained weapon even as he fell. (BC 173/215)

Even though Morgant ended his life as a traitor, Gwydion says he will still raise a *barrow above the King of Madoc.

> "King Morgant served the Sons of Don long and well," he went on. "Until the thirst for power parched his throat, he was a fearless and noble lord. In battle he saved my life more than once. These things are

part of him and cannot be put aside or forgotten. And so shall I honor Morgant for what he used to be." (BC 174/217–218)

The name of Morgant appears briefly several times in the *Mabinogion* (Morgant Hael, Morgant ab Adras, Rhyawd the son of Morgant). *Guest's notes to the *Mabinogion* also mention Morgant as the name of the Bishop of Caer Vudei (Silchester) during the reign of Arthur (M 203).
(BC 13+/25+; M 203, 225, 267, 312, 334)

mounds of honor: The mounds of honor were located in *Caer Dathyl. "Within its bastions, in the farther reaches of one of its many courtyards, grew a living glade of tall hemlocks, and among them rose mounds of honor to ancient kings and heroes" (HK 109/131). The *Cauldron-Born level the hemlock grove near the mounds of honor when Caer Dathyl is destroyed (HK 129/154).
(HK 109/131, 129/154)

Mount Dragon: Mount Dragon is a mountain peak in *Annuvin that is the sentinel marking the *Land of Death.

> The summit had been well named, for *Taran saw its peak was in the rough shape of a monstrous, crested head with gaping jaws, and on either side the lower slopes spread like outflung wings. The great blocks and shafts of stone that rose to form its jagged bulk were dark, mottled with patches of dull red. (HK 208/240)

*Achren reveals that the treacherous peak is indeed the "very road-way to the *Iron Portals of Annuvin. To reach it there is a hidden trail" (HK 206/238). It is atop Mount Dragon that *Arawn has hidden the *magic sword, *Dyrnwyn, and there that Taran slays the deathless *Cauldron-Born (HK 214/247).
(BT 23/39; BC 19/32; HK 204/236, 230/266)

Mount Kilgwyry (kil-GWEE-ree): *Orddu, *Orwen, and *Orgoch suggest to *Taran other oracular sources that may help him discover his parentage. One of these, suggested by Orwen, is a brown-and-orange *ousel that comes once a year to sharpen his beak on Mount Kilgwyry. The ousel knows all that has ever happened. Unfortunately, Orddu informs Orwen that she lives too much in the past. "Mount Kilgwyry has been worn down long ago with his pecking and the little darling has flown elsewhere" (TW 19/33).

Such an oracular ousel appears in the *Mabinogion. The Ousel of Cilgwri was sought by Arthur's knights so that they might learn from it the whereabouts of the secret prison of Mabon. The ousel does not know and sends them to the older, wiser Stag of Redynvre (M 246). The finding of Mabon was one of the tasks assigned Kilhwch (*Kilhuch) in the story of "Kilhwch and *Olwen." *Lady Charlotte Guest also explains in her notes to the Mabinogion that Cilgwri is in Flintshire in Wales (M 291).

See also Characters—fantasy.
(TW 19/33; M 246, 291)

Mount Meledin (mehl-AY-din): Mount Meledin is a high peak in the *Llawgadarn Mountains. At the foot of Mount Meledin is located the cave which holds the *Mirror of Llunet. *Taran seeks the Mirror of Llunet, hoping it may reveal to him his parentage.
(TW 211/246)

mushrooms, magic: Acquired by *Eilonwy, *Fflewddur, and *Rhun from the reluctant *Gwystyl, these mushrooms produce fire when broken. "Beware, beware!" warns Gwystyl of the *Fair Folk. "Break them, and they'll singe your hair off! They make a handsome puff of flame, if you should ever need such a thing" (HK 66/82). The three *Companions and Gwystyl use the mushrooms, along with smoke-producing *eggs and blinding *powder, in a successful attempt to rescue *Gwydion, *Taran, *Smoit, and the others from imprisonment in *Caer Cadarn at the hand of *Magg.

See also Fantastic objects.
(HK 66/82)

n

✥

Nedir (NEH-deer): Nedir is the spider who pledges her help in the battle against *Arawn and his *Chief Huntsman of *Annuvin. However, *Kadwyr, the impudent crow, ridicules Nedir for thinking she has anything to offer. "Take my advice, Granny," Kadwyr says, "and keep to your knitting. Be careful you don't get your arms and legs mixed up, or you'll never untangle them" (F 43–44/51). But when the crow is injured and stalked by the Chief Huntsman, Nedir and her kind prove their worth. They spin their heaviest webs among the trees to trap and delay the hunter, allowing Kadwyr to escape momentarily.

See also Brynach, Crugan-Crawgan, Edyrnion, Gwybeddin, Medwyn. (F 43/51, 48/56)

Nevvid (NEV-id) Nav (NAV) Neivion (NAYV-yon): *Taran hears from *Dallben the story of Nevvid Nav Neivion, who long ago built a ship and carried with him two of every animal when the black waters covered *Prydain. In *Medwyn's valley Taran finds the ancient remains of a ship far from water. He wonders if *Medwyn, who has a special relationship with all animals, might be the legendary Nevvid (BT 121–122/145).

This Noah figure indeed appears in *Celtic mythology. *Guest's notes to the *Mabinogion explain that one of "the three great exploits of the Island of Britain" was "the ship of Nevydd Nav Neivion, which carried in it a male and female of all things living, when the Lake of floods burst forth" (M 134). The "Lake of Floods" mentioned in Welsh myth bears reference to "the universal Deluge" (M 284).

See also Characters—fantasy. (BT 121/145; M 134, 284)

northern domains: *See* Northern Realms.

Northern Realms: *Fflewddur Fflam's kingdom is located in the region of *Prydain known as the Northern Realms, which lie north of *Caer Dathyl and the *Eagle Mountains. The Northern Realms and the *northern domains are synonymous terms (Alexander, 1986b). *Arianllyn, the betrothed of *Adaon, also lives in this part of the land (BC 28/44).

See also *House of Fflam.
(BC 28/44; TW 67/86; HK 81/99)

O

✥

Oak-Horn: On his way to rescue *Hen Wen from *Annuvin, *Coll frees a tall stag whose antlers are entangled in a thorn bush. The stag, Oak-Horn, warns Coll that the *Huntsmen of Annuvin are riding abroad that night and offers to bear the farmer on his back so that he will not be captured. It is vital that Coll travel swiftly to Annuvin. The effects of the *Hazel Nuts of Wisdom, which have given the farmer ability to speak with animals, are temporary. Coll must communicate with several animals, including Oak-Horn, if Hen Wen's rescue is to be realized (CWP 78/15).

When the rescue is attempted, Oak-Horn (though stags are not noted for bravery) lures away the Huntsmen who guard Hen Wen (CWP 80/21).

The *Mabinogion also tells of a stag who provides aid to men in need. In the story of "Kilhwch [*Kilhuch] and *Olwen," the Stag of Redynvre, one of the oldest and wisest animals in the world, helps the knights of Arthur find the secret prison of Mabon (M 246). Finding Mabon is essential in fulfilling Kilhwch's quest to obtain Olwen for his wife.

See also Ash-Wing, Star-Nose.
(CWP 78+/15+)

Oeth-Anoeth (eth-AHN-eth): The stronghold of Oeth-Anoeth once belonged to *Arawn *Death-Lord. It is located not far from *Spiral Castle and was built when Arawn "held wider sway over *Prydain" (BT 177/207). *Achren controls Oeth-Anoeth as the *Chronicles of Prydain begin. She imprisons *Gwydion there and submits him to its unmentionable tortures. Prince Gywdion calls Oeth-Anoeth "a place of death, its walls . . . filled with human bones" (BT 177/207).

"Raging, she [Achren] cast me into the lowest dungeon," Gwydion said. "I have never been closer to my death than in Oeth-Anoeth.

"How long I lay there, I cannot be sure," Gwydion continued. "In Oeth-Anoeth, time is not as you know it here. It is better that I do not speak of the torments Achren had devised. The worst were not of the body but of the spirit, and of these the most painful was despair. Yet, even in my deepest anguish, I clung to hope. For there is this about Oeth-Anoeth: if a man withstand it, even death will give up its secrets to him." (BT 178/207–208)

Gwydion indeed withstands the torments of Oeth-Anoeth, and therefore much is revealed to him.

"I understood the workings of life and death, of laughter and tears, endings and beginnings. I saw the truth of the world, and knew no chains could hold me. My bonds were light as dreams. At that moment, the walls of my prison melted." (BT 178/208)

The experience in Oeth-Anoeth also gives Gwydion the ability to understand "the speech of any living creature" (BT 179/209). He uses this newly acquired skill to speak with *Hen Wen, thereby discovering the secret name of the *Horned King.

*Guest's notes to the *Mabinogion explain that King Arthur suffered three imprisonments, one of which was a three-night incarceration in the Castle of Oeth and Anoeth (M 192). "And I have been in Caer Oeth and Annoeth [Anoeth]," says Arthur in the story of "Kilhwch [*Kilhuch] and *Olwen" (M 221). In The White Goddess, Graves also notes this castle as the prison of both Gwair and Arthur (WG 109).

See also Fantastic objects.
(BT 177/207; CL 22/38; M 192, 221, 361; WG 109)

Old Writing: The inscription upon *Dyrnwyn's scabbard is engraved in symbols of the "Old Writing" (BT 85/106). *Taran and *Fflewddur are unable to read the words, but *Eilonwy is able to decipher most of the message, except for the symbols that have been marred. Indeed, King *Rhitta of old had scratched away some of the runes, for their meaning seared his conscience (F 59–60/70). The full meaning of the ancient words is not revealed in the *Chronicles of Prydain until the conclusion of *The High King. Moments before the enchanted sword's power wanes, the Old Writing comes clear under the light of Eilonwy's *bauble, the *Golden Pelydryn. *Taliesin, *Chief Bard of *Prydain, reads the inscription before it fades forever.

"Draw Dyrnwyn, only thou of noble worth, to rule with justice, to strike down evil. Who wields it in good cause shall slay even the *Lord of Death." (HK 223/258)

(BT 85/106; HK 22/34, 223/258; F 59–60/70)

Olwen (OHL-wen): *Medwyn tells *Taran part of an ancient story, that of *Kilhuch and Olwen (BT 120/144). Kilhuch sought Olwen for his bride. But her father, the *Chief Giant *Yspadadden, assigned to Kilhuch a number of nearly impossible tasks prerequisite to receiving his daughter's hand in marriage.

The story "Kilwch [Kilhuch] and Olwen" is recounted in the *Mabinogion. Olwen, the daughter of Yspaddaden (Yspadadden) Penkawr, was destined to be the wife of Kilhwch. Nevertheless, Kilhwch had to complete thirty-seven difficult assignments in order to win Olwen's hand (M 219). With the help of King Arthur and many other comrades, Kilhwch met Yspaddaden's requirements and married Olwen.

Because Olwen does not appear in the *Chronicles of Prydain, she is not described. Therefore, the following description from the Mabinogion is here provided.

> The maiden was clothed in a robe of flame-coloured silk, and about her neck was a collar of ruddy gold, on which were precious emeralds and rubies. More yellow was her head than the flower of the broom, and her skin was whiter than the foam of the wave, and fairer were her hands and her fingers than the blossoms of the wood anemone amidst the spray of the meadow fountain. The eye of the trained hawk, the glance of the three-mewed falcon was not brighter than hers. Her bosom was more snowy than the breast of the white swan, her cheek was redder than the reddest roses. Whoso beheld her was filled with her love. Four white trefoils sprung up wherever she trod. (M 233)

See also Characters—fantasy, Gwythyr.
(BT 120/144; M 219)

Orddu (OR-doo): Orddu and her sisters, *Orwen and *Orgoch, are first mentioned by *Kaw at *Gwystyl's *Fair Folk *way post. The *Companions discover from Kaw that the *Black Cauldron is in the hands of the three witches (BC 63/84).

The witches' cottage is located in the middle of the *Marshes of Morva, a dangerous stretch of land. The best description of Orddu's dwelling is found in *Taran Wanderer*, when *Taran returns to visit the three sisters.

> Built against the side of a high mound, half hidden by sod and branches, it seemed in even greater disrepair than Taran had remembered. The thatched roof, like a huge bird's nest, straggled down to block the narrow windows; a spiderweb of mold covered the walls, which looked ready to tumble at any moment. (TW 11/24–25)

Orddu herself looks in a state of disrepair, as do her sisters, and the Companions are surprised by her appearance.

> Facing him [Taran] was a short and rather plump little woman with a round, lumpy face and a pair of very sharp black eyes. Her hair hung like a clump of discolored marsh weeds, bound with vines and ornamented with bejeweled pins that seemed about to lose themselves in the hopeless tangle. She wore a dark, shapeless, ungirt robe covered with patches and stains. Her feet were bare and exceptionally large. (BC 95/123–124)

It is soon evident that Orddu is the spokesman for the trio and that she is always jolly, even when speaking of gruesome things. "I've never met a person who could talk about such dreadful things and smile at the same time," says *Eilonwy (BC 97/127). Orddu also addresses the Companions with endearing yet demeaning terms such as "dear mice" (BC 100/130). More often than not, she will address them as some species of bird: my goslings, my ducklings, poor chickens, etc.

The three weird sisters have the amazing ability of trading bodies with one another. It seems that they literally take turns being Orddu.

> "I remember very distinctly, my dear," replied the first enchantress, "but you were Orddu then. And when you're being Orddu, you can do as you please. But I'm Orddu today, and what I say is . . ."
> "That's not fair," interrupted Orgoch. "You always want to be Orddu. I've had to be Orgoch three times in a row, while you've only been Orgoch once." (BC 99/128–129)

Orddu and her sisters are extremely powerful enchantresses. Shifting shape is a minor trick for them. When the Companions peer into the windows of the hags' cottage, they watch instead three beautiful women at work carding, spinning, and weaving (BC 117/149). And at the conclusion of *The High King, the sisters come to Taran in like form.

> Light filling the chamber dazzled him [Taran], but as his vision cleared he saw three tall and slender figures; two garbed in robes of shifting colors, of white, gold, and flaming crimson; and one hooded in a cloak of glitter-

ing black. Gems sparkled in the tresses of the first, at the throat of the second hung a necklace of shining white beads. Taran saw their faces were calm, beautiful to heartbreak, and though the dark hood shadowed the features of the last, Taran knew she could be no less fair. (HK 232/268)

Orddu speaks of their power when she explains to the Companions that the three sisters retrieved the Black Cauldron from *Arawn. The *cauldron was theirs to begin with, says Orddu. They only lent it to the *Death-Lord. "Even Arawn had to be allowed to have his chance" (BC 107/138). But Arawn did not return it when his time had elapsed, so the sisters took it from him. *Fflewddur is aghast, wondering aloud how the three hags were able to challenge the *Lord of Death and carry the cauldron away from *Annuvin.

> Orddu smiled. "There are a number of ways, my curious sparrow. We could have flooded Annuvin with darkness and floated the cauldron out. We could have put all the guards to sleep. Or we could have turned ourselves into—well, no matter—let us say we could have used a variety of methods." (BC 108/139)

More of their power is revealed when Orddu and her sisters explain that they found and raised "dear little *Dallben" (BC 101/131). The tale of Dallben's infancy and childhood is recounted in *The Black Cauldron by Orddu and told in more detail in the title story of *The Foundling. As the young Dallben watches the daily activities of his surrogate mothers, he discovers they indeed wield powerful *magic. The sisters control nature from the confines of their cottage.

> Now he [Dallben] understood that the leather bellows lying by the hearth commanded the four winds; the pail of water in the corner, the seas and oceans of the world. The earthen floor of the cottage held the roots of all plants and trees. The fire showed him the secrets of its flame, and how all things come to ashes. (F 8/6)

Young Dallben comes to this knowledge because he inadvertently tastes a potion he stirs for the witches. It spatters on his hands, burning his fingers. When he pops his fingers into his mouth, Dallben suddenly understands all things (BC 105/135; F 7–8/6). Orddu explains that it was then impossible to have Dallben stay any longer: "You can't have that many people knowing that much all under the same roof" (BC 105/135). So they let him choose of several enchanted items lying around the cottage and send him on his way. Dallben chooses *The Book of Three. When Dallben is surprised that the sisters will give him such a book, Orddu answers him mysteriously.

"Give? Only in a manner of speaking. If you know us as well as you say you do, then you also know we don't exactly *give* anything. Put it this way: We shall *let* you take that heavy, dusty old book if that's what you truly want. Again, be warned: The greater the treasure, the greater the cost. Nothing is given for nothing; not in the Marshes of Morva—or anyplace else, for the matter of that." (F 11/10)

Indeed, the price for gaining wisdom is anguish. What is revealed to him in *The Book of Three* so fills him with sorrow that Dallben ages in a single night. The weight of the world is a heavy burden (F 13/13).

Orddu, Orwen, and Orgoch indeed give nothing away. A price is always set and must be paid. Orddu explains that even Arawn "paid dearly" for the use of the Black Cauldron. When the Companions ask for the cauldron, the answer is the same: "*Give* you the [*Black] Crochan? Oh, goodness no! We never *give* anything" (BC 122/155). The Companions must trade something for it. Though Fflewddur offers his *truthful harp, *Gurgi his *wallet of food, and *Eilonwy her *bauble, Taran must eventually part with his most valued possession, the *Brooch of Adaon. It is the only object for which the enchantresses will bargain, though they would gladly take from Taran the memory of the nicest summer day he can recall.

Though Orddu and her sisters seem unconcerned about Arawn's threat, they are not siding with the Death-Lord. "We're neither good nor evil," says Orddu. "We're simply interested in things as they are." Orwen adds, "We care. . . . It's that we don't care in quite the same way you do, or rather *care* isn't really a feeling we can have" (BC 120–121/154). The witches are indeed neutral, says Alexander (1985b). "They are sort of observers. . . . They're not choosing sides."

Orddu, Orwen, and Orgoch set the stage, and humans play the parts as the witches see fit. They place the cauldron where Taran and the Companions will happen upon it. Why? "To find out what you'd do when you did find it," says Orddu. "They [the witches] were simply working out a destiny," says Alexander (1985b). He explains that the weird sisters realize Taran may indeed become the *High King, yet they are not sure he will fulfill his destiny. "The end is not predetermined" (Alexander, 1985b). Yet, Orddu and her sisters know more of Taran's possibilities than even Dallben. "I see the three weird sisters as being some notches above Dallben," says Alexander. "They are on a different, higher level" (Alexander, 1985b). The sisters know of Taran's destiny, whereas Dallben only suspects (Alexander, 1985b).

In *Taran Wanderer*, when Taran returns to Orddu's cottage to ask of his parentage, Orddu and the others refuse to dabble in his future by revealing his past. However, Taran is the first person to have ever returned to the

Marshes of Morva to see the witches, a fact that seems to please Orddu. Therefore the sisters send him to find the *Mirror of Llunet, an oracular pool that may answer his question. But the witches know that the Mirror will tell him nothing he has not already discovered on his own. The search is designed to either temper or shatter the prospective High King. Orddu hints at this when she says to Taran, "Has the darling robin ever scratched for his own worms? That's bravery of another sort" (TW 14/27). When Taran finally reaches the Mirror of Llunet, he has experienced many trials. He looks into the pool and realizes that Orddu has sent him to see nothing more than a clear reflection of himself (TW 216–217/253).

The tapestry Orddu and her sisters weave at their *loom may seem to control people's destinies. Young Dallben says of their weaving, "The threads you spin, and measure, and cut off . . . these are no threads, but the lives of men" (F 8/6). However, when Orddu presents Taran with a tapestry of his life scenes, she makes it clear that "the pattern is of your choosing and always was" (HK 234/270). Indeed, the tapestry is unfinished because there is more of his life to be woven.

Orddu, Orwen, and Orgoch depart as the *Chronicles of Prydain conclude. Taran wonders if they too travel to the *Summer Country. Orddu replies, "We are journeying, but not with you. . . . We travel to—well—anywhere. You might even say everywhere" (HK 233/269). Alexander (1985b) feels the nature and whereabouts of the three enchantresses is better left a mystery. Before they disappear, Taran requests one final boon, to know why his joy is shadowed by a strange grief. Orddu's answer is true to form. "'Dear chicken,' said Orddu smiling sadly, 'when, in truth, did we really give you anything?'" (HK 234/270).

Orddu appears in the *Mabinogion. In the tale, "Kilhwch [*Kilhuch] and *Olwen," Arthur must obtain "the blood of the witch Orddu, the daughter of the witch Orwen, of Penn Nant Govid, on the confines of Hell" (M 257–258). This was one of the tasks assigned Kilhwch in his quest to win Olwen's hand in marriage.

Alexander admittedly drew the three witches from mythology. "Orddu, Orwen, and Orgoch have appeared in other guises (as might well be expected of them): the Three Norns, the Moirae, the Triple Goddess, and very likely some other transformations they decline to admit" (TW ix/14). Alexander (1985b) agrees that even the three witches from *Macbeth* are related. The three goddesses recur "so often in so many mythologies" (Alexander, 1985b). The Three Norns are from Scandinavian mythology. The Moirae or Three Fates appear in Greek myth and are named Clotho, Lachesis, and Atropos (Alexander, 1968a:171). Indeed, King Arthur was taken to Avalon in a ship and there cared for by three queens (M 45). Alexander (1985b) feels this must be yet another guise of Orddu, Orgoch, and Orwen.

In *The White Goddess*, Robert Graves explains that the Triple Muse of *Celtic mythology was born from the cauldron of knowledge owned by the hag, Cerridwen (WG 76). Cerridwen herself is a goddess of nature, a representation of Graves's White Goddess (WG 68). Graves also points to several appearances of triple goddesses in other mythologies. Indeed, Greek myth contains several examples: the Three Nymphs from the story of Perseus, the Triple Goddess Ana, the Three Daughters of the West who gave golden apples to Hercules (Melon), etc. (WG 229; WG 374; WG 257).

Cerridwen (Caridwen) is related to Alexander's Orddu because their stories are similar. Cerridwen, who may also be a Triple Goddess, prepared a potion stirred by Gwion. Gwion is burned by spattering brew, pops his scorched fingers into his mouth, and immediately gains knowledge of all things (M 471–472). Unlike Orddu, who sends the young Dallben away with a blessing, Cerridwen tries to kill Gwion.

See also Characters—fantasy.
(BC 63+/84+; TW ix/14, 9–10/22, 56/74, 78/98, 110/133, 188/221, 210/245, 216/253; HK 232/268; F 5/3; M 257, 471)

Orgoch (OR-gock): As with her sisters, *Orddu and *Orwen, Orgoch is first mentioned by *Kaw in *Gwystyl's *Fair Folk *way post (BC 63/84). She makes her first appearance when the *Companions arrive at the weird sisters' cottage in the *Marshes of Morva as they search for the *Black Cauldron (BC 97/126). She resembles Orddu, except she wears a black cloak with the hood pulled up, nearly concealing her face. She speaks little and then with a hoarse, gruff voice. Her temperament is more melancholy than that of her sisters. She is the most threatening of the three. She and her sisters imply that Orgoch is given to eating her victims.

"I love babies," said Orgoch, smacking her lips. (BC 103/134)

"With Orgoch it is difficult to keep pets about." (BC 123/157)

"Orgoch . . . was the one who wanted to keep him [the infant *Dallben]. In her own fashion, which I doubt he would have liked." (BC 105/135)

"A sweet morsel [the infant Dallben]," croaked the one named Orgoch from the depths of her hood. "A tender lamb. I know what I should do."
    "Please be silent, Orgoch," said the one named Orddu. "You've already had your breakfast." (F 5/3)

Even when the three hags appear to *Taran as beautiful women, Orgoch is still hooded in black (HK 232/268). And her temperament seems no better. Orddu comments one last time concerning Orgoch's appetites when she says they will not travel across the sea to the *Summer Country. "Salt air makes Orgoch queasy, though it's very likely the only thing that does" (HK 233/269).

Elizabeth Lane (1973:27) explains that Orgoch "may mean the 'blood-red sorceress,' as *coch* in Welsh is 'red,' modified to *goch* by a preceding consonant."

> The name also suggests, along with the hood Orgoch wears . . . , the carnivorous Morrigu of Irish legend. The Morrigu, herself a Triple Goddess figure, haunted battle sites in the form of a raven or hooded crow. Orgoch's desire to eat everything, even Taran and his friends . . . may be an echo of the Morrigu—or she may represent the all-devouring Past in the threesome of Past, Present, and Future. (Lane, 1973:27)

In the years just after Orgoch was created in the *Prydain Chronicles, Alexander seems to have had great fun expanding on her personality outside of his books. When his editor, Ann Durell, sent Alexander a wood carving of Orgoch, he replied, "It's a gorgeous piece of work. I've never seen such a variety of textures in a wood carving; parts of that hood look actually moss-covered, and the coloring is unbelievable. And that face—well, I think I'd better put it back in the box" (Alexander, 1964d). Thereafter, in correspondence between Alexander and Durell, Orgoch receives constant billing. The following examples come from Alexander's letters.

> Orgoch, temporarily back in her box, has been making disagreeable, gnashing noises. (Alexander, 1964e)

> Orgoch, however, will stand for no nonsense, so I will soon have to get down to business. (Alexander, 1965d)

> Tomorrow being Halloween, Orgoch is going out begging. Begging? Hardly the word for it. When Orgoch says trick or treat, it's like OR ELSE! (Alexander, 1965g)

> The crabs disagreed with Orgoch (it's risky for anything to disagree with her) and she has turned her attention to me, gifting me with a cyst, tumor, syncretion, ossification or some such in my left wrist. (Alexander, 1966b)

> Virginia Beach? Orgoch favors White Sulfur Springs as more invigorating. (Alexander, 1966b)

[Concerning Durell's back surgery] WHAT HATH ORGOCH WROUGHT? . . .

Orgoch has really gone too far this time. She must be drunk with power and will definitely have to be restrained in some way. (Alexander, 1967c)

You're right. Orgoch has warped my mind. (Alexander, 1967d)

Alexander (1985b) says he could always have great fun with Orgoch. "She lends herself to it marvelously."

For a full description of the three enchantresses and their role in the Prydain Chronicles, see "Orddu."

See also Characters—fantasy.
(BC 63+/84+; TW 9–10/22; HK 232/268; F 5/3)

Orwen (OR-wen): Orwen is one of the three witches encountered by the *Companions during their search for the *Black Cauldron. Her name, along with those of her sisters, is first mentioned by *Kaw in *Gwystyl's *Fair Folk *way post (BC 63/84). Orwen makes her first appearance when the Companions arrive at the witches' cottage in the *Marshes of Morva (BC 97/126). Orwen looks much like her sister, *Orddu, except she wears a necklace of milky white stones.

Though Orddu is the spokesperson for the three weird sisters, Orwen speaks more than *Orgoch. She will normally elaborate on Orddu's statements. For example, when Orddu explains that the sisters are neither good nor evil, *Eilonwy accuses them of not caring. Orwen extends Orddu's explanation by saying that they do indeed care. "It's that we don't care in quite the same way you do, or rather *care* isn't really a feeling we can have" (BC 120–121/154). In another instance, Orwen follows Orddu's lead and suggests *Taran trade his memories of Eilonwy for knowledge of his parents (TW 17/31). And when the witches appear to Taran as beautiful women, Orddu explains that their former appearance was when "we were hardly at our best" (HK 233/268). Orwen giggles and says, "You mustn't think we look like ugly old hags *all* the time. Only when the circumstances seem to require it" (HK 233/269).

For a full description of the three enchantresses and their role in the *Prydain Chronicles, see "Orddu."

Orwen is briefly mentioned in the *Mabinogion. She is listed as the mother of the witch Orddu. King Arthur sought the blood of Orddu in order to help fulfill the quest of Kilhwch [*Kilhuch] in the story "Kilhwch and *Olwen" (M 257).

See also Characters—fantasy.
(BC 63+/84+; TW 9–10/22; HK 232/268; F 5/3; M 257)

Other worlds: In high fantasy literature a special geography or universe is established wherein *magic may freely operate (Madsen, 1976:46). Tolkien (1966:60) names this process "subcreation." Such imaginary worlds may include prehistoric realms, recognizable worlds with imaginary histories, imaginary worlds with real histories, or simply long, long ago. Each place must be whole and perfect by itself. Subcreative or secondary worlds may be introduced in fantasy tales in one of the following ways (Madsen, 1976:47):

1. The action may take place entirely in the imaginary world, as with Middle Earth in *The Fellowship of the Ring* by J. R. R. Tolkien (1954) or *Prydain in the *Chronicles of Prydain.

2. Characters may move into the imaginary world from the real world, usually at the beginning of the story. This occurs in *The Lion, the Witch and the Wardrobe* by C. S. Lewis (1950).

3. The imaginary world may enter into the realm of the real world, as occurs in *The Dark Is Rising* by Susan Cooper (1973).

Alexander's subcreative world of Prydain is a mixture of the real and the imaginary. He had in mind's eye the landscape of Wales as he created *Taran's world. Yet, Alexander says, "Prydain is not Wales—not entirely, at least. The inspiration for it comes from that magnificent land and its legends; but, essentially, Prydain is a country existing only in the imagination" (BT viii/15).

ousel: *See* Mount Kilgwyry.

p/q

⁜

Parys (PAH-riss): *See* Hills of Parys.

Pebyr (PEH-bir): Pebyr is the father of *Drudwas, the shepherd of *Commot Isav who battled against *Dorath and his mercenaries. The name, Pebyr, surfaces in the *Mabinogion in the tale "Kilhwch [*Kilhuch] and *Olwen." One of the many men who aided Kilhwch in his quest was named Ruawn Pebyr, the son of Dorath (M 223).
(TW 201/235; M 223)

Pen-Llarcau (pen LAHR-kow): Pen-Llarcau is the father of *Ellidyr. *Dallben refers to him as "old Pen-Llarcau in the northern lands" (BC 22/36). Pen-Llarcau's kingdom is not one of wealth. Dallben explains that Ellidyr, though he carries the title of prince, has no inheritance. "His elder brothers have inherited what little there was of family fortune, and even that is gone" (BC 22/36). Pen-Llarcau is also mentioned in the *Mabinogion and is also named as the father of Ellidyr (Eiladyr) (M 228).
(BC 6/16, 34–35/20–21; M 228)

powder, magic: Acquired by the *Companions from a reluctant *Gwystyl of the *Fair Folk, this black, loamy, yet powdery, earth can hide tracks or cause blindness. "Put this on your feet, and no one can see your tracks—that is, if someone's looking for your tracks," says Gwystyl. "That's really what it's for. But if you throw it into someone's eyes, they can't see anything at all—for a short while at least" (HK 67/83).

Gwystyl provides this *magic powder on two occasions. The first occurs when the Companions are leaving Gwystyl's *way post in *The Black Cauldron. He gives them the powder to cloak their footprints from the *Huntsmen of Annuvin. In *The High King, Gwystyl gives up his supply of powder to *Eilonwy. She, *Fflewddur, and *Rhun use it in their plan to rescue *Taran and *Gwydion from imprisonment at the hand of *Magg.

See also Fantastic objects.

(BC 62/83, 68/91, 72/96; HK 67/83, 72/89)

Prince of Don (DAHN): *See* Gwydion.

Prince of Mona: *See* Rhun.

Prince of Pen-Llarcau (pen LAHR-kow): *See* Ellidyr.

Princess of Llyr (LEER): *See* Eilonwy; Angharad.

Princess Vixen: This is the name *Dorath uses for *Eilonwy when he captures her in the *Hills of Bran-Galedd. "Welcome, Princess Vixen," says Dorath. "You are a choicer prize than any ransom. A long score lies between Dorath and your pig-keeper" (HK 164/192).

(HK 164/192)

Proud Walkers: Hidden in the forest undergrowth, *Taran and *Gwydion watch a pagan war ritual conducted by the *Horned King. The ceremony is stirring and brutal.

> Around the fiery circle, warriors on high stilts beat upraised swords against their shields.
> "What are those men?" Taran whispered. "And the wicker baskets hanging from the posts?"
> "They are the Proud Walkers," Gwydion answered, "in a dance of battle, an ancient rite of war from the days when men were no more than savages. . . ."
> Before Gwydion could speak again, the Horned King, bearing a torch, rode to the wicker baskets and thrust the fire into them. Flames seized the osier cages; billows of foul smoke rose skyward. The warriors clashed their shields and shouted together with one voice. From the baskets rose the agonized screams of men. Taran gasped and turned away.
> (BT 39/56–57)

Alexander discovered the Proud Walkers when reading about a Celtic archeological find (possibly in *National Geographic*). "In rituals and ceremonies . . . (ancient, barbaric customs) indeed there were people walking around on stilts. I saw the term Proud Walkers, and it suddenly connected in my mind with that old folk song, 'Green Grow the Rushes-o'" (Alexander,

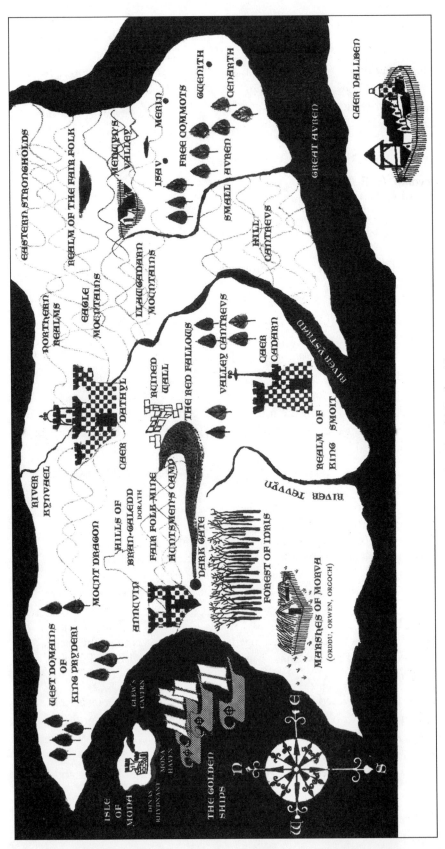

Map of Prydain by Evaline Ness

1986b). Alexander goes on to explain that one line in the song speaks of the Proud Walkers. From these sources were born the Proud Walkers in *The Book of Three*. Alexander (1986b) also explains that human sacrifice, including burnings, was practiced by the ancient Celts.
(BT 39/56)

**Prydain (prih-DANE): Alexander modeled *Prydain, the imaginary world of the *Chronicles, after his memories of Wales, where he was stationed for a brief time during World War II. Alexander found Wales a magical place.

> The beauty of this ancient, rough-hewn country fascinated me. To my eyes, it was still a realm of *bards and heroes; the *Companions of Arthur might have galloped from the mountains with no surprise to me. I seemed to recognize faces from all the hero tales of my childhood. Not until years later did I realize I had glimpsed another enchanted kingdom. (Alexander, 1972:5)

However, Alexander is quick to point out that "Prydain is not Wales—not entirely, at least" (BT viii/15). He explains that the inspiration indeed comes "from that magnificent land and its legends; but essentially, Prydain is a country existing only in the imagination" (BT viii/15). It is Wales "more as it never was" (HK ix/12). Alexander broadened what he had seen of Wales and what he had read in the *Mabinogion and other collections of *Celtic mythology in an attempt to make a land of fantasy relevant to a land of reality (HK ix/12).

*Dallben says, "But in Prydain evil is never distant" (BC 15/28). Indeed, Alexander sees the central conflict in the Chronicles as the struggle between good and evil. The background for the conflict "implies a feudalistic society based on hierarchy, rank, and lineage, contrasting with the independent yeomanry of the *Free Commots" (Alexander, 1972:5). Alexander (1985b) sees Prydain as a primitive land. There were no inns for the wayfarer, for example. "When you traveled you took your food and slept on the ground" (Alexander, 1985b).

Prydain has a carefully drawn geography. Landmarks become familiar to the Prydain reader, providing confident guidance across the mythical realm again and again. The realm is divided in half by the River *Ystrad, flowing north to south. Its eastern border is the *Great Avren River, which turns and flows to the western sea. The eastern half of Prydain contains the *Northern Realms and the *eastern strongholds to the extreme north. Here the *Eagle Mountains cover the land, harboring the *Realm of the

Fair Folk. Farther south are the *Llawgadarn Mountains and *Medwyn's hidden valley. The *Hill Cantrevs lie in the south, bordered by the River Ystrad to the west and the *Small Avren River to the east. Between the Small Avren and the Great Avren, in the southeast, are located the Free Commots. *Caer Dallben lies still farther south, across the Great Avren as it turns westward and just below the *Commots.

The western half of Prydain is bordered to the north by the sea. *Caer Dathyl lies northward in the Eagle Mountains near the River Ystrad. From this region the River *Kynvael flows to the northern sea. The *West Domains of King *Pryderi are found in the northwest. *Annuvin, *Mount Dragon, and the *Hills of Bran-Galedd are located below Pryderi's kingdom. Running from north to south along the River Ystrad are the *Red Fallows, the *Valley Cantrevs, and the realm of King *Smoit. The River *Tevvyn lies between Smoit's realm and the southwestern region which contains the *Forest of Idris and the *Marshes of Morva. Prydain's western boundary is the sea. The *Isle of Mona, home of Prince *Rhun, is tucked in the crescent limned by the coastline.

Tongue in cheek, Alexander (1986c) gives partial credit for the creation of Prydain to his high school social studies teacher, "Miss Gorgon," who failed him in geography. "Unable to comprehend the natural resources of Venezuela, was I thus compelled, long after, to create my own geographies?"

The name for Alexander's subcreative or secondary world comes from the *Mabinogion*. Prydain or Prydein is used numerous times in conjunction with the names of various characters: Culfynawyt Prydein, Ardderchawg Prydain, Iddawc Cordd Prydain, and Prydain ab *Aedd Mawr. Iddawc Cordd Prydain was the messenger sent between King Arthur and Madrawd (Mordred) at the battle of Camlan (M 302). It is said he betrayed Arthur (M 323). According to *Guest's notes to the *Mabinogion*, Prydain ab Aedd Mawr was one of the three Kings of Britain "who gave stability to sovereignty by the excellence of their system of government" (M 386).

The Island of the Mighty, one of several titles bestowed by the Welsh upon Britain, was known by many other ancient names. When conquered by Brut, the island's name was changed from Vel Ynys, as it had been known, to Ynys Prydain or the Isle of Brut. However, Guest's notes explain that some authorities attribute the name Ynys Prydain to Britain's conquest by Prydain, the son of Aedd the Great (M 390).

See also Good versus evil, Other worlds.

(M 56, 226, 302, 323, 386, 390, 438)

Prydain (prih-DANE) Chronicles: *See* Chronicles of Prydain, the.

Pryderi (prih-DEH-ree) Son of Pwyll (POO-il): Pryderi is known as a mighty and noble king. *Gwydion says of him, "Our greatest help will come from King Pryderi of the *West Domains. No lord in *Prydain commands a mightier army. His allegiance to the *House of Don is firm, and between us are strong bonds of friendship" (HK 81/99). In *The High King, when Pryderi arrives at *Caer Dathyl, he seems all Gwydion has described.

> He was as tall as Gwydion himself, and his rich raiment glittered in the torchlight. He wore no helmet; what *Taran had seen [from a distance] was his long hair that shone like gold about his brow. At his side hung a naked sword, for it was Pryderi's custom, as *Fflewddur whispered to Taran, never to sheathe his blade until the battle was won. Behind him followed falconers with hooded hawks on their gauntleted wrists; his war-leaders, with the *crimson hawk emblem of the *House of Pwyll broidered on their cloaks; and spearmen flanking his banner-bearer. (HK 116/138)

Yet, Pryderi proves far less honorable than Gwydion has assessed. The *King of the West Domains demands the surrender of the House of Don, for he has aligned himself with *Arawn *Death-Lord. Blinded by his pride, Pryderi commands the *High King, *Math Son of *Mathonwy, to bow to his will.

> "I chose what is best for Prydain. . . . I do not serve Arawn. Is the axe the woodcutter's master? At the end, it is Arawn who will serve me."
> With horror, Taran listened to the words of Pryderi as he spoke to the High King.
> "Lay down your arms. Abandon the weaklings who cling to you for protection. Surrender to me now. Caer Dathyl shall be spared, and yourself, and those I deem worthy to rule with me."
> Math raised his head. "Is there worse evil?" he said in a low voice, his eyes never leaving Pryderi's. "Is there worse evil than that which goes in the mask of good?" (HK 119/142)

Math does not accept Pryderi's offer. The next day the great battle between the House of Don and the armies of Pryderi is launched. The battle is costly for both sides. At one point Taran tries to engage Pryderi in combat, but he will pay the *Assistant Pig-Keeper no mind. "It was Pryderi's scornful glance that stung Taran more sharply than the blade which swung up from the mass of foemen to lash across his face" (HK 124–125/148).

When it seems as though Pryderi may be defeated, his armies move aside to make way for Arawn's *Cauldron-Born and other fresh fighting men from *Annuvin. Caer Dathyl falls under this renewed assault, and the High King Math is killed and then trampled beneath the iron-shod boots of the deathless warriors.

Later, Pryderi travels to *Caer Dallben on a two-fold mission. However, *Dallben foresees his coming and uses *magic to dissuade him. Great winds and earthquakes send Pryderi's men running, but the determined King of the West Domains presses onward to Dallben's cottage.

Pryderi's first task is to kill the enchanter. He swings his sword which shatters against Dallben's *ash-wood staff. But Pryderi reveals that Arawn has given him the secret of Dallben's vulnerability. Dallben has a ban placed upon him: he cannot kill. Pryderi has also been given a *black dagger that has the power to penetrate Dallben's spells, thus allowing him to strike a fatal blow. His second task is to take *The Book of Three.

Dallben informs Pryderi that Arawn has told him only half-truths. *The Book of Three* has already marked Pryderi for death. Though Pryderi may indeed take Dallben's life, he will not leave Caer Dallben alive. At that moment, a wall of flames encircles the cottage and will immediately engulf Caer Dallben as the enchanter dies.

Pryderi falters, realizing Arawn has led him to his death. Flinging the dagger aside, he grasps *The Book of Three*. Lightning blazes from the ancient tome, striking Pryderi dead (HK 190/221).

Pryderi is a prominent figure in the *Mabinogion*. He is the son of *Pwyll and Rhiannon. However, Pwyll's infant son is stolen one night, and the nursemaids, afraid for themselves, smear blood on Rhiannon's face and lay bones at her feet while she sleeps. They claim Rhiannon has devoured her own son. Later, Teirnyon Twryv Vliant finds a baby boy, apparently stolen from his parents by a monster. As the boy matures, Teirnyon sees he resembles Pwyll and therefore realizes he is Pwyll's lost child. Teirnyon returns the boy, thus ending Rhiannon's punishment. The child is then named Pryderi, which means anxiety (M 353–357).

As an adult, Pryderi takes over and adds to his father's realm. He is known as a prosperous and beloved leader (M 358–359). *Guest's notes to the *Mabinogion* also reveal that Pryderi is known as one of the chief swineherds of the Island of Britain (M 364). However, Gwydion ab *Don steals from Pryderi the highly regarded swine from Annuvin. Gwydion then trades what appear to be fine horses and greyhounds for the pigs. In truth, he has conjured them from fungus, and of course, the spell is only tempo-

rary (M 415–416). Gwydion is also accused of using his magic to kill Pryderi (M 364).
(HK 81+/99+; M 353, 364, 381, 399, 413; WG 56, 95, 107, 109)

Pwyll (POO-il): Pwyll is the father of *Pryderi, *King of the West Domains and the *House of Pwyll. Alexander (1985b) explains that a "house"—such as the House of Pwyll—is not renamed after a ruler dies and his son assumes leadership. Pwyll was probably also the name of an ancient ancestor—the founder of the House of Pwyll.

Though Pwyll does not appear in the *Chronicles of Prydain, he is a prominent figure in *Celtic mythology, particularly in the *Mabinogion. There are primarily two characters who share the name Pwyll. The name of the first, Kynnelyn Keudawd Pwyll, the Half Man, appears only briefly. The second and most prominent is Pwyll Prince of Dyved, the father of Pryderi. Indeed, one of the tales in the Mabinogion bears his name. Pwyll was "lord of the seven *Cantrevs of Dyved" (M 339). He exchanged places with *Arawn, one of the Kings of Annwvyn (*Annuvin), and lived in his stead for one year in order to help defeat Arawn's rival, Havgan. Indeed, Pwyll conquers Havgan and combines the two kingdoms of Annwvyn into one. Arawn, a noble and kindly lord in the Mabinogion, is extremely grateful. He and Pwyll remain great friends (M 343).

Pwyll, Prince of Dyved, married Rhiannon. Later their son is stolen from them one night, and the nursemaids, fearing for themselves, smear blood on the face of the sleeping Rhiannon and place bones at her feet. They accuse her of devouring her own child. However, Teirnyon Twryv Vliant finds a child apparently taken from its parents by a monster. The child so resembles Pwyll as it matures that Teirnyon knows it to be Pwyll's missing son. He returns the boy to Pwyll thus ending Rhiannon's punishment. The child is named Pryderi which means anxiety (M 353–357). The name Pwyll means prudence (M 360).
(HK 116/138, 117/140, 119/143, 124/148, 186/216; M 228, 278, 339, 409, 413; WG 107, 109, 216, 385)

Queen of Prydain (prih-DANE): *See* Achren, Eilonwy.

R

Realm of the Fair Folk: *See* Kingdom of Tylwyth Teg.

Red Fallows: *Taran and his army make a stand against the *Cauldron-Born on the barren landscape of the Red Fallows. They defend an old, ruined wall that crosses the Fallows and indeed turn the deathless warriors away toward the *Hills of Bran-Galedd.

The Red Fallows is a cheerless place. It is "a broad, winding belt of wasteland" (HK 135/161). Grassless earth stretches as far as one can see.

> The dead ground was broken, rutted as though ill-plowed, slashed with deep ditches and gullies. No tree, no shrub rose from the dull red earth, and nowhere did Taran see the faintest sign that any growing thing had ever flourished there. He looked at it uneasily, chilled not only by the bitter wind but by the silence that hovered like frozen mist about the lifeless land. (HK 135/161)

Taran had thought the Red Fallows a mere travelers' tale. But *Coll assures him the stories told about this desert are true.

> "Men have long shunned it, yet once it was the fairest realm in *Prydain. The land was such that all manner of things would grow, as if overnight. Grains, vegetables, fruits—why, in size and savor the apples from the orchards here would have made mine look like shriveled windfalls beside them. A prize it was, to be won and held, and many lords fought for its possession. But in the fighting over it, year after year, the hooves of steeds trampled the ground, the blood of warriors stained it. In time the land died, as did those who strove to claim it from their fellows, and soon its blight crept far beyond the battle grounds." Coll sighed. "I know this land, my boy, and it does not please me to see it again. In my younger days I, too, marched with the battle hosts, and left not a little of my own blood in the Fallows." (HK 136/162)

Coll's words are almost prophetic. Though the Cauldron-Born are turned aside, Coll receives his death wound. He bleeds his life away on the cursed soils of the Red Fallows. Taran buries the noble old farmer and warrior in the dark red earth (HK 142/169).

Taran later speaks of making the Red Fallows once again a fruitful place. It is one of the goals he sets when deciding to remain in Prydain rather than traveling to the *Summer Country (HK 237/273).
(HK 135+/161+)

Regat (REH-gat): Queen Regat of the *House of Llyr is the mother of *Angharad and the grandmother of *Eilonwy. Regat appears in the tale from *The Foundling* entitled "The True Enchanter." She oversees the selection of a husband for Princess Angharad. Regat is serious about affairs of state, such as the marriage of a princess, and is therefore concerned that the selected suitor be a qualified enchanter. It is forbidden that a *daughter of Llyr marry anyone other than an enchanter. "Rules are to be obeyed, not questioned," says Regat to her daughter. "You may wed the one your heart desires, and choose your husband freely—among those, naturally, with suitable qualifications" (F 29/33).

Nevertheless, Angharad falls in love with *Geraint, who does not possess powers of wizardry. Regat refuses to allow the union, and Angharad runs away from her ancestral home, *Caer Colur, to be with the man she loves (F 37/44).

*Gwydion explains to the *Companions that Caer Colur was soon abandoned after Angharad left (CL 129/157). The Princess took with her the *book of spells of the *enchantresses of Llyr and the *Golden Pelydryn, both items essential to the *magic that maintained the House of Llyr. The ultimate fate of Queen Regat is unknown.

See also Characters—fantasy, Gildas, Grimgower.
(BT 55/73; CL 129/157; TW 91/112, 109/133; HK 163/192; F 29/33)

Rhitta (RIH-ta) Son of Rhych (RIK): In *The Book of Three* *Taran and *Eilonwy happen upon the *barrow of King *Hen Rhitta Son of *Rhych as they wander in the maze of tunnels beneath *Spiral Castle. The corpse of the ill-fated king lies on a great slab of stone. "Rich raiment clothed the body; polished stones glowed in his broad belt. The clawed hands still grasped the jeweled hilt of a sword, as if ready to unsheathe it" (BT 71/91). The sword is the enchanted blade, *Dyrnwyn.

In *The High King*, *Gwydion explains what is known of Rhitta and his connection to Dyrnwyn.

"King Rhitta, grandson of *Rhydderch [who had Dyrnwyn forged by *Govannion the Lame], was the last to hold the blade. He was lord of Spiral Castle before it became the stronghold of Queen *Achren. He met his death, in a way unknown, with Dyrnwyn clutched in his hands. From that time on the sword was seen no more, forgotten as it lay buried with him in Spiral Castle's deepest chamber." Gwydion turned to Eilonwy. "Where you, Princess, found it." (HK 23/34)

In *The Foundling, the entire story of King Rhitta and his fate is told in the story entitled "The Sword." Rhitta was indeed given Dyrnwyn as a token of his kingship in the days before the *Sons of Don arrived in *Prydain (Alexander, 1986b). The *King of Prydain began his reign as a just and noble monarch.

One day, while on the royal hunt, Rhitta breaks the sheepfold gate of the old shepherd *Amrys. He promises it will be mended but forgets to have it done. When Amrys comes a second time to the castle to urge the king to keep his word, Rhitta draws Dyrnwyn in a rage and slays the old man (F 55/65). This act begins Rhitta's steady march toward his destruction. Dyrnwyn is stained by Amrys's blood, slowly growing darker until it turns black, Rhitta's heart darkening with it.

Rhitta's ability to rule justly diminishes as guilt and suspicion plague his mind. Soon he turns against his own trusted nobles and wages war on them. But the ghost of Amrys appears to the king as he makes battle on what was once the poor shepherd's land. Rhitta is driven back to his castle by the vision (F 58/68). However, Amrys appears in the king's bedchamber, warning Rhitta that the path he follows leads him astray (F 59/69).

Soon Rhitta tries to draw Dyrnwyn, but he cannot. He realizes the words inscribed on the sword's scabbard speak to him: "Draw Dyrnwyn, only thou of noble worth" (F 59/70). In his shame and anger, Rhitta tries to scratch the *Old Writing from the scabbard, but the words remain to mock him.

The "nightmares" continue, Amrys returning to plead with Rhitta to alter his ways. Instead, the king orders killed all who even vaguely seem a threat to his power. His paranoia deepens until Rhitta commands new chambers be dug deep underneath the castle—winding, twisting hallways with endless galleries and rooms. This is the birth of Spiral Castle (F 61/71–72).

Finally, in a room of solid rock far below the castle, Rhitta barricades himself with his most trusted guards. Yet Amrys appears again, and Rhitta tries to draw Dyrnwyn to strike the apparition. He is able to unsheathe "a hand's-breadth of the blade when tongues of white flame burst crackling from the hilt and all the length of the scabbard" (F 62/74).

Like a lightning bolt, the flame filled the chamber in an instant, striking down even the guards who staggered to their feet. Then, as suddenly as it had risen, the flame was quenched. Still gripping the blackened sword in his lifeless hands, King Rhitta fell back on the couch. And all was silent. (F 62/74)

No one could find a way through his maze of passages, so Rhitta lay as he had fallen. "And only the shepherd Amrys ever grieved for him" (F 62/74).

*Lady Charlotte Guest's notes to the *Mabinogion* tell of Rhitta, the *Giant, who was the King of Wales. Rhitta is said to have stopped the bloody feud between the Kings Nynniaw and Peibiaw. (See *Gast; *Goryon.) When attacked by the twenty-eight kings of the Island of Britain, who sought to avenge Nynniaw and Peibiaw, Rhitta defeats and dishonors them by "disbearding" each one. Guest says that Rhitta (Rhitta Gawr) was indeed King Ryons of North Wales (M 283–284).
(BT 71/90; HK 23/34; F 53/63; M 283)

Rhudd (ROOD): Rhudd was the father of King *Rhuddlum of the *Isle of Mona and grandfather of Prince *Rhun.
(CL 4/18)

Rhuddlum (ROOD-lum) Son of Rhudd (ROOD): King Rhuddlum Son of *Rhudd is the monarch of the *House of Rhuddlum on the *Isle of Mona. His queen is *Teleria; his stronghold, *Dinas Rhydnant. *Dallben says that Rhuddlum and Teleria "are kindly and gracious" (CL 4/18). *Eilonwy is given to their care so she may be schooled in the ways of being a lady and a princess.

King Rhuddlum's son is Prince *Rhun. Rhun is sent to accompany Eilonwy across the sea to *Mona. When arriving on Mona, the *Companions notice that "King Rhuddlum ha[s] the same round and cheerful face as Prince Rhun" (CL 14/29). However, the king is not a clumsy, feckless individual like his son. In fact, his greatest concern is that Rhun will somehow learn the responsibility needed to someday rule in his stead.

When Eilonwy is kidnapped by *Achren and *Magg, *Taran is assigned to a search party apparently led by Prince Rhun. However, Rhuddlum approaches Taran privately and explains that in truth his *Master of Horse will lead, though Rhun will think it is his own task. Then the king asks Taran to swear an oath to protect Rhun and not let him make too great a fool of himself. Taran swears the oath, even though Rhuddlum reveals that he plans for Eilonwy and Rhun to marry (CL 44–45/62–63).

King Rhuddlum does not appear again in the *Chronicles of Prydain. As *The High King begins, Rhun, now *King of Mona, reports sadly that his father died last summer (HK 7/17).

*Guest's notes to the *Mabinogion tell of Rhuddlwm the *Giant (Rhuddlwm Gawr). He was one of the principal enchanters of Welsh legend and is said to have learned his illusions from *Eiddileg the Dwarf and from *Coll, the son of Collfrewi (*Collfrewr) (M 213). In another instance, Guest's notes say that Coll learned his *magic from Rhuddlwm Gawr (M, 269). (See Coll.) Also, Rhuddlwm Gawr is said to have taught magic to Iddawc Cordd *Prydain, who used it to betray King Arthur (M 323). (CL 4+/18+; HK 7/17; M 213, 269, 323)

Rhun (ROON): Rhun is the son of King *Rhuddlum and Queen *Teleria of the *Isle of Mona. He is a cheerful, lovable, well-meaning young man, but terribly awkward and irresponsible. His introduction in *The Castle of Llyr accentuates these traits. He has sailed to *Prydain to accompany *Eilonwy to *Mona, where she will live with Rhuddlum and Teleria at *Dinas Rhydnant and learn the ways of being a lady and a princess.

> [The *Companions] cantered down the slope and dismounted at the water's edge. Seeing them, the sailors ran a plank out from the vessel to the shore. No sooner had they done so than a young man clambered onto the plank and hastened with eager strides toward the companions. But he had taken only a few paces along the swaying board when he lost his footing, stumbled, and with a loud splash pitched headlong into the shallows.
>
> *Taran and *Coll ran to help him, but the young man had already picked himself up and was awkwardly sloshing his way ashore. He was of Taran's age, with a moon-round face, pale blue eyes, and straw-colored hair. He wore a sword and a small, richly ornamented dagger in a belt of silver links. His cloak and jacket, worked with threads of gold and silver, were now sopping wet; the stranger, however, appeared not the least dismayed either by his ducking or the sodden state of his garments. Instead, he grinned as cheerfully as if nothing whatever had befallen him.
>
> "Hullo, hullo!" he called, waving a dripping hand. (CL 6/20–21)

"Hullo, hullo!" becomes another of Rhun's trademarks, one that at first irritates Taran. Taran decides early that Rhun is "scatterbrained" and "feckless" (CL 7/22, 10/25). Further observation only cements Taran's opinion. Taran notices that Rhun happily barks orders to the sailors, who indulgently go about their business of sailing the ship while ignoring him. When Rhun draws his sword to salute the Captain of the Guard, he snags Taran's cloak and tears it. Taran begins to feel that Rhun is not worthy of being a true prince.

When Eilonwy is kidnapped by *Achren and *Magg, Rhun is given command of one of the search parties. King Rhuddlum privately acknowledges to Taran that the command is in name only. His *Master of Horse will in truth direct the search. Rhuddlum then asks Taran to swear an oath to protect Rhun from danger and from making too great a fool of himself. Though the king reveals that he plans for Eilonwy and Rhun to marry, Taran still swears to do as Rhuddlum has requested (CL 43–45/62–64).

After causing all sorts of mishaps, including getting the Companions separated from the search party, Rhun accidentally pulls them down into *Glew's cavern. However, when Glew, the cowardly *giant, wants the Companions to choose one of their number to be sacrificed to his latest shrinking potion, Rhun volunteers.

> "I've thought a great deal about this since we've been in the cavern, and there's no sense not facing facts. I—I don't see that I've been any help whatever. On the contrary, I've brought nothing but ill luck. Not that I meant to, but it seems that's the way of it with me. So, if any one of us can be dispensed with, why, I should have to say that person is— myself. . . .
>
> "There's not one of you who wouldn't give up his life for a companion," Rhun added. . . . "Can a Prince do less? I doubt I should ever really be able to measure up to being a true Prince. Except in this." (CL 107/132–133)

Instead, Taran and *Fflewddur vote to lift Rhun to a ledge that promises freedom. He is to take Eilonwy's *bauble that the Companions found earlier and continue the search for the princess. But Rhun circles back and arrives in time to save his friends from Glew. Caring more for the others than himself, Rhun is able to make the bauble blaze brilliantly, blinding the giant who has long lived in the dark. The Companions are then able to escape.

The ability to light Eilonwy's bauble indicates a leap in maturity for Prince Rhun. Earlier in *The Castle of Llyr, he had asked to see the bauble, only to have it wink out when he touched it. The light of the bauble seems to be like a meter that will measure a man's quality. Alexander (1985b) says that it was indeed a turning point in Rhun's character development when he is finally able to make it glow.

Rhun accompanies Taran, Fflewddur, and *Gurgi on to *Caer Colur, the ancient castle where Eilonwy is being held captive. He participates in her rescue and proves further that he may yet qualify to rule Mona.

Rhun appears again in *The High King*. This time Rhun is taller and leaner, but he still seems a little careless and disheveled. "His handsomely embroidered cloak looked as though it had been water-soaked, then wrung out to dry. His bootlacings, broken in several places, had been retied in large, straggling knots" (HK 7/17).

Rhun is now *King of Mona. His father, King Rhuddlum, died during the last summer. The new king strives to serve his people. One task he assumes is building a much-needed seawall at *Mona Haven. But poor Rhun starts the wall at both ends and tries to meet in the middle—unsuccessfully (HK 19/30–31). After Rhun finishes serving the *Sons of Don in the battle against *Arawn, he plans to return and try building the wall once more.

Sadly, Rhun never sees Mona again. Eilonwy, Fflewddur, and Rhun execute a plan to rescue Taran and others from imprisonment at the hand of Magg. When the plan seems to have gone awry, Rhun charges into the fray calling commands to nonexistent reinforcements. The ruse works, and the tide of battle is turned. But Rhun receives his death wound.

> "Hullo, hullo!" Rhun murmured and waved a hand. His face was deathly white.
>
> "The day is ours," Taran said. "Without you, it would have gone differently. Don't move," he cautioned, loosening the young King's blood-stained jacket. Taran frowned anxiously. An arrow had sunk deep in Rhun's side and the shaft had broken.
>
> "Amazing!" Rhun whispered. "I've never been in battle before, and I wasn't sure of—of anything at all. But, I say, the oddest things kept running through my head. I was thinking of the seawall at Mona Haven. Isn't it surprising? Yes, your plan will work very well," Rhun murmured. His eyes wandered and suddenly he looked very young, very lost, and a little frightened. "And I think—I think I shall be glad to be home." He made an effort to raise himself. Taran bent quickly to him.
>
> Fflewddur had come up with *Llyan loping at his heels. "So there you are, old boy," he called to Rhun. "I told you we'd have more than our share of trouble. But you pulled us out of it! Oh, the *bards will sing of you . . ."
>
> Taran lifted a grief-stricken face. "The King of Mona is dead." (HK 79/96–97)

The Companions, silently and with heavy hearts, raise a burial mound close to King *Smoit's stronghold, *Caer Cadarn. "The warriors of Smoit joined them; and at dusk, horsemen bearing torches rode slowly circling the mound, to honor the King of Mona" (HK 79/97). Taran pledges to his dead companion that the seawall will be completed, even if he must build it himself. Indeed, Taran makes good on his pledge (HK 237/273).

There are several characters in the *Mabinogion named Rhun: *Gwystyl, the son of Rhun; Rhun Rhudwern; Rhun mab Einiawn (Rhuawn Pebyr); Rhun, the son of Maelgwn Gwynedd. However, Alexander (1969:10) states that the *Prince of Mona was inspired by a single sentence concerning Rhun, the son of Maelgwn Gwynedd: "Now Rhun was the most graceless man in the world" (M 478). Rhun, the son of Maelgwn Gwynedd, was sent by his father to discredit the adopted parents of *Taliesin and was ruthless in completing his assigned task. Though this character was brutal, Alexander's became a "feckless, goodhearted, accident-prone blunderer" (Alexander, 1969:10).

*Lady Charlotte Guest also includes in her notes to the Mabinogion several lines from the Myvyrian Archaiology, another collection of ancient Celtic tales, that links a certain Rhun with Rhydnant. (*Dinas Rhydnant is the capital city of the Isle of Mona.) However, Rhydnant seems to be a river rather than a city or stronghold.

> Whose is the grave on the banks of the Rhydnant?
> Rhun was his name, of the steady progress,
> He was a king; Rhiogan slew him. (M 332)

See also House of Rhuddlum.
(CL 6+/20+; HK 7+/17+; M 225, 266, 274, 313, 332, 478; WG 74)

Rhych (RIK): Rhych was an ancient *King of Prydain who wielded the sword, *Dyrnwyn. His father was *Rhydderch Hael, who had *Govannion the Lame forge the enchanted sword. His son was King *Rhitta, the infamous ruler who died with Dyrnwyn in his hand.
(F 53/63)

Rhydderch (RID-erk) Hael (HALE): Rhydderch Hael is the ancient *King of Prydain who commanded *Govannion the Lame, the master craftsman, to forge and temper *Dyrnwyn as a weapon of great power and as a protection for the land. He is the father of King *Rhych and the grandfather of King *Rhitta, the infamous ruler who was struck down by the power of Dyrnwyn.

According to *Guest's notes to the *Mabinogion, one of the four Northern (Northumberland) princes was named Rhydderch Hael (M 34). Also, the sword Dyrnwyn, listed as one of the thirteen precious things of the Island of Britain, was owned by Rhydderch Hael (M 285). "If any man drew

it except himself, it burst into a flame from the cross to the point, and all who asked it received it; but because of this property all shunned it: and therefore was he called Rhydderch Hael" (M 285).
(HK 23/34; F 63; M 34, 285)

River Alaw (AH-law): *See* Alaw.

River Kynvael (KIN-vale): *See* Kynvael.

River Tevvyn (TEV-in): *See* Tevvyn.

River Ystrad (ISS-trad): *See* Ystrad.

Royal House of Don (DAHN): *See* Sons of Don.

Royal House of Llyr (LEER): *See* House of Llyr.

S

❖

salmon of Lake Llew (LOO): *Orwen suggests to *Taran that he ask the salmon of Lake Llew for answers concerning his parentage. "I've never met a wiser fish," she says. However, *Orgoch reminds her sister that the salmon is "long gone" (TW 19/33).

The Salmon of Llyn (lake) Llyw is a figure in *Celtic mythology. In the *Mabinogion*, this wise fish, probably one of the oldest of all animals, gives Arthur's knights directions to the secret prison of Mabon (M 248). Freeing Mabon is one of the many tasks Kilhwch (*Kilhuch) must complete in order to win *Olwen for his wife.

Alexander (1985b) explains that wisdom embodied in fish and other animals is a common mythological motif. In fact, in the tale "Kilhwch and Olwen," Arthur's knights consult an *ousel, an owl, an eagle, and a stag before conversing with the Salmon of Llyn Llyw (M 246–247). In *The White Goddess*, Graves relates the Irish myth of Fionn or Finn, who gains wisdom by tasting a certain salmon. The fish had fed on the nuts of the nine hazels of poetic art, thus passing its knowledge and wisdom through its flesh (WG 75).

See also Hazel Nuts of Wisdom.
(TW 19/33; M 248; WG 75)

Sea King: *See* Llyr Half-Speech.

Sea People: *See* Llyr Half-Speech.

Small Avren (AHV-ren): The Small Avren is a wide, rapidly flowing river that begins in the *Llawgadarn Mountains and flows southward to empty into the *Great Avren (TW 163/193). It forms a natural boundary between the *Free Commots and the *Hill Cantrevs. This river runs by *Llonio's

cottage. His weirs and nets strain the Small Avren of whatever treasures float in its waters.
(TW 163/193, 168/198, 174/205, 180/212; HK 91/110)

Smoit (SMOYT): Smoit is the *King of Cadiffor. His stronghold is *Caer Cadarn. The banner of the *House of Smoit is crimson with a *black bear emblem (TW 45/62).

Of King Smoit, *Fflewddur says, "You can always hear him before you can see him" (BC 14/25). Indeed, such is *Taran's introduction to the boisterous ruler of *Cantrev Cadiffor.

> A bellow of laughter resounded beyond the chamber, and in another moment a giant, red-headed warrior rolled in at the side of *Adaon. He towered above all in the chamber and his beard flamed around a face so scarred with old wounds it was impossible to tell where one began and another ended. His nose had been battered to his cheekbones; his heavy forehead was nearly lost in a fierce tangle of eyebrows; and his neck seemed as thick as Taran's waist. (BC 14/25–26)

"What a bear," says Fflewddur. "But there's not a grain of harm in him" (BC 14/26). Indeed, King Smoit is good-natured, kindhearted, and generous. However, he is a fierce warrior when angered or when the need arises.

King Smoit is noted for his colorful expressions. He calls the calculating *Morgant an icicle and Fflewddur Fflam a butter-headed harp-scraper (BC 14/26–27). And when *Gwydion rallies support for finding and destroying the *Black Cauldron, Smoit shouts, "Any whey-blooded pudding-guts who fears to stand with you will have me to deal with!" (BC 17/30–31). As *The Black Cauldron concludes, Smoit leads the attack against Morgant's host. He personally engages Morgant, striking down the traitorous king and slaying him (BC 172–173/215).

Smoit loves to eat. When the *Companions arrive at Caer Cadarn in *Taran Wanderer, Smoit has just finished his supper. Nevertheless, he will hear nothing of Taran's news "until the companions had eaten and the King had downed another full meal" (TW 46/63). Once, when Smoit nearly drowns, he is revived only to speak of food. "'Give me to eat!' gasped Smoit. 'I may be half-drowned, but I'll not be half-starved'" (TW 56/74).

Perhaps Smoit receives fullest exposure in *Taran Wanderer* when the ongoing feud between Lord *Goryon and Lord *Gast erupts once again. The two lords have argued over possession of the marvelous cow, *Cornillo, for so many years that neither knows who owned her originally. Smoit shouts of breaking heads and locking them in his dungeon, and then rides forth to make good on his threats. Though Taran tries to suggest other, more reasonable solutions, Smoit is so busy blustering and fuming that he doesn't pay attention. "'The dungeon!' cried Smoit. 'I'll have Gast and Goryon in it before the squabble gets further out of hand'" (TW 53/71).

Taran saves Smoit from drowning, and the king claps a "red-furred" hand to the *Assistant Pig-Keeper's shoulder and grants him any favor. Taran eventually asks that King Smoit restore the field of the farmer *Aeddan, which was destroyed by Goryon and Gast. He also pleads that the two feuding lords be spared from the dungeon and instead be made to labor in Aeddan's behalf (TW 59–64/77–82). So impressed is Smoit with the wisdom of these and subsequent suggestions by Taran that he offers the Assistant Pig-Keeper the opportunity to be his heir. But Taran, who longs to accept, feels he must continue to seek his own parentage (TW 64/83–84).

Smoit also appears in *The High King*. He is imprisoned in his own dungeons (now converted to larders after the Goryon/Gast incident) by the villainous *Magg (HK 49/64). Taran, *Gwydion, *Gurgi, and *Coll soon join him. Smoit and the others are freed through the intelligence of *Eilonwy and the daring of King *Rhun, with help from Fflewddur and *Gwystyl. Gwydion then asks Smoit to muster every loyal warrior in Cantrev Cadiffor and neighboring dominions to fight against *Arawn *Death-Lord (HK 81/99).

As the *Chronicles come to an end, Smoit arrives at *Caer Dallben for feasting and celebrating (HK 227/262). He is there to hail the new *High King of *Prydain—Taran, Assistant Pig-Keeper (HK 247/285).

The name of Smoit surfaces on one occasion in the *Mabinogion: Selyf, the son of Smoit (M 223). However, Alexander (1969:10) reveals "that a good deal of the personality of King Bran went into the making of King Smoit!" In the *Mabinogion*, King Bran, known also as Bendigeid Vran, was the brother of the heroine, Branwen, in the tale, "Branwen the *Daughter of Llyr" (M 369). He was a large, good-natured individual when not angered beyond control.

A story similar to the incident with Lords Goryon and Gast is also found in the *Mabinogion* in *Guest's notes. Nynniaw and Peibiaw were quarreling kings who fought over lands and flocks. *Rhitta, the *giant King of Wales, put a stop to their feuding before the entire countryside was destroyed (M 283). Alexander (1985b) acknowledges that Goryon and Gast grew from the story of Nynniaw and Peibiaw, with King Smoit playing the role of Rhitta. (BC 14/25, 172/215; TW 22/36, 32/47, 38/54, 45/62, 54/73; HK 33/45, 42/56, 44/59, 55/70, 70/87, 74/91, 99/119, 227/262, 247/285; M 223, 369)

Sons of Don (DAHN): The offspring of the *Lady Don and her consort, *Belin, *King of the Sun, are known as the Sons of Don. Long ago, the Sons of Don voyaged in *golden ships from their home in the *Summer Country to *Prydain (HK 108/129). They built *Caer Dathyl in the *Eagle Mountains and have stood for years "as guardians against the lurking threat of *Annuvin" (BT 7/22). They also rule Prydain from Caer Dathyl. As the *Chronicles begin, *Math Son of *Mathonwy is the *High King of Prydain. He wears the *Gold Crown of Don and rules under the emblem of the *Golden Sunburst (HK 107/128; HK 105/126). *Gwydion is also of the *House of Don. Even *Fflewddur Fflam is a distant relation of this noble line (TW 67/86).

The Sons of Don (*Children of Don) are not entirely human. They hold some powers of enchantment and therefore must depart from Prydain and return to the Summer Country when the age of enchantment is at an end (HK 228/263). Alexander (1985b) explains that the Sons of Don are nearly demigods or are "almost like the elves in *The Lord of the Rings*." They are "up-scaled humans" and therefore have deeper understandings.

> [The Sons of Don] are larger than life. They are not a race of man. They are more than men. . . . Can I call them epic figures? They are bigger, stronger, smarter than the ordinary man on the street. (Alexander, 1985b)

The family of *Don is very prominent in the *Mabinogion*. Many Sons of Don appear in the tales, including Gwydion and Math (M 414). *Guest explains in her notes to the *Mabinogion* that the Sons of Don were honored by having constellations named after them: Llys Don (Cassiopeia), Caer Arianrod (Corona Borealis), Caer Gwydion (Milky Way) (M 436).

Robert Graves in *The White Goddess* explains the origin of the Sons of Don. They were originally called the Tuatha dé Danaan, a confederacy of tribes, some of which invaded Ireland from Britain in the middle Bronze Age. They were "the folk of the God whose mother is Danu" (WG 50). "The Goddess Danu was eventually masculinized into Don, or Donnus, and is regarded as the ancestor giving the name to the confederacy" (WG 50). In the "Romance of Math the Son of Mathonwy," she appears as Math's sister and as the mother of Gwydion and Amathaon. The Tuatha dé Danaan, according to Irish tradition, had been driven northward from Greece because of a Syrian invasion. They arrived in Ireland by way of Denmark and North Britain (WG 50).

See also Characters—fantasy.

(BT 7/22, 40/57, 75/95, 82/103, 90/112, 119/143, 173/203, 180/210; BC 14/26, 174/217; CL 21/37; TW 67/86, 204/239; HK 17/28, 48/63, 55/70, 80/98, 87/106, 92/111, 105/126, 107/128, 115/137+; M 236, 280, 413, 436; WG 50, 57, 61, 81, 90, 93, 119, 304)

Spiral Castle: Located near *Annuvin, Spiral Castle is the abode of *Achren. It is "a tall, gray fortress" looming on the crest of a hill (BT 45/62). *Taran and *Gwydion are imprisoned in Achren's dungeons early in *The Book of Three*. It is in the bowels of Spiral Castle that Taran meets *Eilonwy and learns from her about the nature of his prison.

> "There are hundreds of [chambers] under Spiral Castle, and all kinds of galleries and little passages, like a honeycomb. Achren didn't build them; this castle, they say, once belonged to a great king." (BT 54/73)

Eilonwy helps Taran escape by traveling through the maze of passageways. Along the way, they stumble upon the *barrow of an ancient king and take from his death grasp a sword (BT 73/93). It is *Dyrnwyn, the enchanted blade that will become *Arawn *Death-Lord's nemesis. When Dyrnwyn is removed from Spiral Castle, the stronghold tumbles to the ground. "In a violent explosion that seemed ripped from the very center of the earth, Spiral Castle crumbled in on itself" (BT 72/92). Later, Gwydion confirms that the stronghold could not withstand the removal of so powerful an object as Dyrnwyn (BT 176/206).

In *The High King*, Gwydion reveals that King *Rhitta was lord of Spiral Castle before the evil enchantress, Achren. He was the last to possess Dyrnwyn, taking it to his death with him. It was Rhitta's barrow Taran and Eilonwy found beneath Spiral Castle (HK 23/34).

The Foundling reveals that King Rhitta constructed the endless maze of passages and galleries beneath the castle, thus giving Spiral Castle its name (F 61/72). Because Rhitta brought dishonor upon himself and Dyrnwyn, he felt the need to protect himself against supposed treachery. He hid among the tunnels and chambers until the ghost of *Amrys, a poor shepherd Rhitta murdered, visited him in the room that became his barrow. Rhitta tried to draw Dyrnwyn to strike the apparition, but he was unworthy to wield the blade. Dyrnwyn's fire destroyed the king and all his guards. Rhitta lay in his secret barrow until Taran and Eilonwy happened upon his remains.

Robert Graves, in *The White Goddess*, explains that the castle of Arianrhod, one of the *daughters of Don, was called Spiral Castle. Arianrhod supposedly had several castles or her stronghold was known by several names:

Caer Arianrhod, Caer Sidi (Revolving Castle), *Caer Colur. However, the castle (or castles) was still designated as Spiral Castle (WG 103–104). The idea of a mazelike construction was associated with her strongholds.

Graves believes Spiral Castle was symbolic of death. The constellation Corona Borealis was also called Caer Arianrhod or Caer Sidi by the ancient Celts (WG 98). It swirls in a spiraling pattern, and Graves explains that the ancients probably thought the constellation to be the place where the dead sojourned (WG 103). Many unearthed barrows have a maze-like spiral pattern carved in stone slabs or on doors and walls (WG 102). One such archeological find is New Grange, a barrow discovered in Ireland (WG 101). Graves postulates that the pagan Irish could have called New Grange "Spiral Castle," and "revolving a forefinger in explanation, could say, 'Our king has gone to Spiral Castle,' in other words, 'he is dead'" (WG 103). The revolving forefinger would refer to Corona Borealis or Caer Sidi (WG 103).
(BT 24/41, 45/62, 50/68, 54/73, 61/80, 69/88, 72/91, 79/100, 94/116, 172/201, 176/206; CL 22/38, 130/157, 143/171; HK 23/34; F 61/72; WG 97, 329)

Star-Nose: On his way to *Annuvin to rescue *Hen Wen, *Coll saves Star-Nose, the *Chief Mole of Prydain, from a *gwythaint. Star-Nose repays the kindly farmer by helping rescue Hen Wen. When all seems lost, the floor of the pit in which Coll and Hen Wen are trapped miraculously opens. Star-Nose, leading thousands of moles, tunnels Coll and his marvelous pig to safety.
    See also Ash-Wing, Oak-Horn.
(CWP 79+/17+)

Steward, Chief: The role of a Chief Steward in the *Chronicles of Prydain is like that of the Steward of the Household, as explained by *Guest in her notes to the *Mabinogion. "He was the chief of all the officers of the Court. . . . On him devolved the important care of providing food for the kitchen, and liquor for the mead-cellar; and he had the charge of the king's share of booty, until the king desire to dispose of it. . . . It was his particular duty 'to swear for the king.' Besides his clothes, and four horse-shoes, and various perquisites of the skins of beasts, he was entitled to a 'male hawk, from the master of the hawks, every feast of St. Michael.'—Welsh Laws" (M 186).

    *Magg, the evil steward of King *Rhuddlum and Queen *Teleria of the *Isle of Mona, is the principal Chief Steward in the *Prydain Chronicles.

Other than Magg, the Chief Steward of Lord *Gast is briefly mentioned in
*Taran Wanderer.
(CL 15+/31+; TW 38/54; HK 46/60, 205/237, 216/250; M 141, 186)

stone, magic: In *The Foundling, the cottager, *Maibon, frees *Doli of the
*Fair Folk from a fallen tree. Doli must grant him a wish, and Maibon asks
for one of the Fair Folk stones that will keep him from aging. But such magical stones, as Doli warns, don't mix well with humans. Maibon finds that
everything around him remains forever unchanged: eggs won't hatch, fields
don't sprout, the baby won't teethe, and his beard will not grow. Though
Maibon tries to rid himself of the stone, it always returns. He learns that
the stone cannot be discarded or destroyed unless the owner truly desires
the aging process to continue. Finally, Maibon has a change of heart, and
his life is returned to normal.

In *Taran Wanderer, the evil wizard, *Morda, unsuccessfully searches for
these "life-giving" stones in a Fair Folk treasure trove (TW 93/115).

See also Fantastic objects, Magic, Modrona.
(TW 93/115; F 20/23)

Summer Country: The *Sons of Don (*Children of Don) voyaged from
the Summer Country to *Prydain long before the story of *Taran begins
(BT 7/22). *Taliesin, the *Chief Bard, explains that the Summer Country
is an enchanted land.

> "But know that the Summer Country is a fair land, fairer even than Pry-
> dain, and one where all heart's desires are granted. . . .
> "Know this, too," Taliesin added. "All men born must die, save those
> who dwell in the Summer Country. It is a land without strife or suffering,
> where even death itself is unknown." (HK 228/263–264)

As the *Chronicles of Prydain conclude, *Gwydion announces that the
Sons of Don must board the *golden ships on which they came to Prydain
and return to the Summer Country (HK 228/263). As the age of enchantment ends in Prydain, the Children of Don, and all others with *magic in
their blood, must leave its boundaries.

A reference to the Summer Country is made in the *Mabinogion. However, it does not seem to be an extraordinary place. Arthur summons warriors from far and wide, including those from the Summer Country
(M 253). *Guest's notes to the Mabinogion quote an ancient commentator
who described the Summer Country as "that part of the East now called

Constantinople" (M 285). The designation, "Summer Country," may also have been intended to allude to Somersetshire (M 292).

Alexander says that his idea for the Summer Country came from a combination of many mythical places. "It's [some of] Tolkien . . . and it's the Islands of the Blessed, and maybe it's Avalon or Atlantis or who knows what. But it was someplace that was evocative enough for me that I wanted to use it" (Alexander, 1985b).

See also Other worlds.
(BT 7/22; HK 132/157, 228/263; M 253, 285, 292)

Sword Maidens: "Among my people in the olden days," says *Eilonwy, "the Sword Maidens did battle beside the men" (BT 88/109). With this statement, the *Princess of Llyr tries to convince *Taran that it is acceptable for her to carry *Dyrnwyn.
(BT 88/109)

T

❖

Taliesin (tally-ESS-in): Taliesin, the *Chief Bard of *Prydain, does not appear in the Chronicles until *The High King. However, he is mentioned in *The Book of Three by *Fflewddur Fflam. Taliesin was the one who presented Fflewddur with the *truthful harp when the would-be *bard failed to pass the bardic exam (BT 89/110). The story of this event is told in more detail in *The Truthful Harp. The Chief Bard, who is never called Taliesin in the picture book, sees the quality of Fflewddur's soul and does not send him away empty-handed. Fflewddur later returns to the *Council of the Bards after learning that the harp will not allow him to "color the facts." Taliesin compares the deeds of kindness and bravery performed by Fflewddur to his stretchings of the truth. "Yet those deeds were far more worthy than all your gallant fancies, for a good truth is purest gold that needs no gilding" (TH 94/30).

Taliesin is also mentioned in *The Black Cauldron. His son, *Adaon, joins the quest to destroy the *Black Cauldron and arrives at *Caer Dallben with greetings to Fflewddur Fflam from his father. Adaon says that Taliesin asks how Fflewddur fares with the harp (BC 12/23). The Chief Bard of Prydain loses his son to a *Huntsman's dagger as the quest unfolds (BC 81/107).

In the final volume of the Chronicles, before Taliesin appears, *Gwydion shares the known history of the enchanted sword, *Dyrnwyn, a tale he has received from the Chief Bard (HK 22/33). Finally, the *Companions visit *Caer Dathyl, and Taliesin makes his first appearance.

> He was tall, his face deeply weathered; white hair fell straight to his shoulders. The coarse cloak of a warrior was flung loosely about him, but neither sword nor dagger hung at his unadorned leather belt. . . .
>   *Taran at first had seen Taliesin as a man of many years; now he could not guess the Chief Bard's age. Taliesin's features, though heavily lined, seemed filled with a strange mixing of ancient wisdom and youthfulness.

He wore nothing to betoken his rank; and Taran realized there was no need for such adornment. Like Adaon, his son and Taran's companion of long ago, his eyes were gray, deep-set, seeming to look beyond what they saw, and there was, in the Chief Bard's face and voice, a sense of authority far greater than a war-leader's and more commanding than a king's. (HK 110–111/132–133)

Taliesin and the members of the Council of Bards dwell in Caer Dathyl. Caer Dathyl, the stronghold of the *Sons of Don, houses the *Council Chamber of the Bards, the *Hall of Lore, and the *Hall of Bards.

As Taliesin and Fflewddur meet once again, the Chief Bard says of the truthful harp, "I have thought often of that gift. Indeed, it has been a little on my conscience" (HK 111/132–133). It is true that he had known the harp's "nature" and suspected Fflewddur would have trouble with the strings. Taliesin then allows Fflewddur to choose any of his harps in exchange, but Fflam chooses to keep "the old pot" (HK 112/133).

Taliesin has always understood the make-up of Fflewddur's heart. At this Caer Dathyl meeting, he also peers into the hearts of each of the other Companions. Of *Gurgi, who longs for wisdom, he says, "Do you believe you have none? . . . Of wisdom there are as many patterns as a *loom can weave. Yours is the wisdom of a good and kindly heart. Scarce it is, and its worth all the greater" (HK 113/135). Taliesin remarks that *Coll possesses similar wisdom, plus "the wisdom of the earth, the gift of waking barren ground and causing the soil to flourish in a rich harvest" (HK 113/135). When *Eilonwy comments that she learned nothing of wisdom on the *Isle of Mona—only needlework and curtsying, Taliesin laughs. "Learning is not the same as wisdom. . . . In your veins, Princess, flows the blood of the *enchantresses of Llyr. Your wisdom may be the most secret of all, for you know without knowing; even as the heart itself knows how to beat" (HK 114/136). Indeed, Eilonwy takes the Chief Bard's advice and listens with her heart when the wolves, *Brynach and *Briavael, rescue her from *Dorath. She is able to understand the wolves, perhaps by "feeling" the meaning of their message, and thus communicate with them (HK 166–167/195).

Taran is certain any wisdom he might have possessed came and went with his brief possession of the *Brooch of Adaon. Saddened by the thought of his son, Taliesin answers Taran thoughtfully and foreshadows Taran's rise to the High Kingship.

"There are those," he said gently, "who must first learn loss, despair, and grief. Of all paths to wisdom, this is the cruelest and longest. Are you one who must follow such a way? This even I cannot know. If you are, take heart nonetheless. Those who reach the end do more than gain wisdom. As rough wool becomes cloth, and crude clay a vessel, so do they change and fashion wisdom for others, and what they give back is greater than what they won." (HK 114/136)

Taliesin's final words in the *Chronicles of Prydain are spoken to Fflewddur Fflam. He tries to help Fflewddur understand that they both must leave Prydain and travel to the *Summer Country.

"It is not for you to choose, Son of *Godo. But know that the Summer Country is a fair land, fairer even than Prydain, and one where all heart's desires are granted. *Llyan shall be with you. A new harp you shall have. [The truthful harp was destroyed.] I myself shall teach you the playing of it, and you shall learn all the lore of the bards. Your heart has always been the heart of a true bard, Fflewddur Fflam. Until now, it was unready." (HK 228/263–264)

Taliesin is a prominent figure in *Celtic mythology. One of the tales of the *Mabinogion is entitled "Taliesin," and tells the story of the most famous of bards.

In his tale, Taliesin is originally called Gwion Bach. He is set to stirring a cauldron of Inspiration and Science prepared by the hag, Caridwen (Cerridwen). The brew is for her son, but Gwion accidentally tastes it first. The potion spatters onto his hand, burning him. Gwion sucks his scorched fingers and immediately gains "knowledge of the mysteries of the future state of the world" (M 471). This parallels the experience of the young *Dallben. However, unlike the witches in Dallben's story, Caridwen tries to destroy Gwion. The cauldron splits asunder after Gwion Bach tastes the brew, thereby depriving Caridwen's son of limitless knowledge.

As Caridwen chases Gwion, he turns himself into various animals and objects in order to escape her. Finally, he turns himself into a grain of wheat. Caridwen changes herself into a hen and swallows him. Eating the seed causes Caridwen to become pregnant; she carries Gwion nine months, delivers him, and then has not the heart to kill the child. She casts him into the sea in a leathern bag that will float, to survive as God wills. Gwion is found by one named Elphin, who names him Taliesin, which means "Radiant Brow." Taliesin develops into a great bard, even as a child, and foresees that he will be the Chief of the Bards of the West (M 473–474).

*Guest's notes to the Mabinogion explain that Taliesin was indeed a Welsh bard of the sixth century. He was reportedly the son of Henwg, but little is known of his true history (M 495).

Taliesin, fictional or factual, was indeed the Chief of the Bards. He was "the highest of the most exalted class, either in literature, wisdom, the science of vocal song, or any other attainment, whether sacred or profane" (M 498). He was one of the three "Baptismal Bards of the Isle of Britain" (M 498). He was also the "chair-president" of the "Nine Impulsive Stocks of the Baptismal Bards of Britain" and was thus known as the Chief Bard of the West. He was supposedly buried near Aberystwyth (M 499).

Taliesin, Chief of the Bards, is said to have possessed the "thirteen Rarities of Kingly Regalia of the Isle of Britain" (M 54). For example, he is said to have had a ring that would cause the wearer to become invisible when the stone was clutched within the hand (M 13, 54).

Alexander (1985b) agrees with Robert Graves concerning the likelihood that the Taliesin of Celtic lore was indeed a real person. Graves, in The White Goddess, does not confuse "the miraculous child Taliesin of the 'Romance of Taliesin' with the historic Taliesin of the late sixth century, a group of whose authentic poems is contained in the Red Book of Hergest" (WG 74). The sixth-century poet spent time with many chiefs and princes, writing complimentary poems about them, but was then killed in a drunken quarrel. Many mythic names were also those of men he rubbed shoulders with: *Rhydderch Hael, Elidir (*Ellidyr) Mwynfawr, *Rhun, etc. These great names seem to have been adopted by leaders and bards as the centuries rolled by. A later poet calling himself Gwion wrote some six centuries after the original historic Taliesin. Gwion proclaimed himself a master-poet and took the name of Taliesin, "as an ambitious Hellenistic Greek poet might have taken the name of Homer" (WG 75).

It seems that Alexander's version of Taliesin paints the bard as being superior to all other men. "There was, in the Chief Bard's face and voice, a sense of authority far greater than a war-leader's and more commanding than a king's" (HK 111/133). But Alexander does not feel Taliesin is the ultimate of characters.

> If I had thought that, I'd have done more with him. . . . [However,] Taliesin was one of the greatest of the bards. Now a bard encompasses much more than an ability to compose poetry, play the harp, and so on. [Being a bard] encompass[es] knowledge of everything—of medicine, of philosophy, of governance. . . . [Taliesin] is the most admirable. In other words, he knows all of these things, but he does not necessarily use them actively. . . . He'd be the wisest of kings, if he chose to be. (Alexander, 1985b)

Alexander says Taliesin perhaps could have been the wisest of enchanters, if he had so decided, for he has more potential than anyone.

"[Taliesin] could have been any one of those things, but he chose not to be" (Alexander 1985b).

See also Characters—fantasy.
(BT 89/110, 129/153; BC 11/23; HK 22/33, 110+/132+; TH 88/13, 93/26; M 35, 54, 224, 281, 471, 495; WG 43, 74, 92, 120, 158, 420)

Tannwen (TAN-wen): Tannwen is the mother of Queen *Teleria of the *Isle of Mona. The name is mentioned briefly in the *Mabinogion*: Tannwen, the daughter of Gweir Datharweniddawg (M 228). Kilhwch (*Kilhuch) asks Arthur to allow Tannwen to aid him in his quest of obtaining *Olwen's hand in marriage.

See also Rhuddlum.
(CL 7/21; M 228)

**Taran (TAH-ran): Taran of *Caer Dallben is the central figure in the *Chronicles of Prydain. His rise from assistant pig-keeping to the High Kingship of *Prydain follows the developmental pattern of classic *heroism. His growing maturity is examined here in each of the five successive novels.

*The Book of Three

Taran is a young and impulsive boy as the Chronicles of Prydain begin. He is anxious for glory and adventure and shows his impatience on the first page of *The Book of Three* when *Coll is trying to teach Taran to make horseshoes. Taran wants to make a sword. And later, when *Dallben warns of an unknown danger that is abroad in the land, Taran is dismayed that he is ordered not to leave Caer Dallben for the time being. "'For the time being!' Taran burst out. 'I think it will always be for the time being, and it will be vegetables and horseshoes all my life!'" (BT 8/23). Then, when he burns his fingers trying to secretly read the magical *Book of Three,* Taran decides he has no real future.

> "What is the use of studying much when I'm to see nothing at all?" Taran retorted. "I think there is a destiny laid on me that I am not to know anything interesting, or do anything interesting. I'm certainly not to *be* anything. I'm not anything even at Caer Dallben!"
>
> "Very well," said Coll, "if that is all that troubles you, I shall make you something. From this moment, you are Taran, *Assistant Pig-Keeper." (BT 10/25)

In spite of Dallben's directive, Taran chases *Hen Wen into the forest and is launched on his first great adventure. There he meets *Gwydion, the

*Prince of Don. However, Taran challenges Gwydion's identity because his boyish ideal of the famous war leader does not match the prince's appearance. Gwydion answers Taran's disappointment by giving him his first lesson in heroism. "'It is not the trappings that make the prince,' he said gently, 'nor, indeed, the sword that makes the warrior'" (BT 17/32). Nevertheless, Taran holds to his basic assumptions about heroism and is astounded to learn that Coll once entered the depths of *Annuvin, the *Land of Death, to rescue Hen Wen. "'But . . . but . . . ,' Taran stammered. 'Coll? A hero? But . . . he's so bald!'" (BT 24/40).

Taran's youth and inexperience are also mirrored in his disregard for danger. Of the dreaded *Horned King he says, "I would not fear him" (BT 18/34). Gwydion answers flatly, "Then you are a fool" (BT 18/34). Yet, Taran indeed shows courage, if foolhardy courage. He jumps into the bushes to catch something or someone who lurks near their camp, only to find *Gurgi. He later stands against the *Cauldron-Born with Gwydion, though the Prince of Don orders him to flee (BT 44/61).

From the very beginning, Taran is concerned about his parentage. "I have always lived at Caer Dallben," he tells Gwydion. "I don't think I have any kinsmen. I don't know who my parents were. Dallben has never told me. I suppose . . . I don't even know who *I* am" (BT 21/36–37). Later, Taran defends his lineage by saying to *Eilonwy, "I wasn't *born* an Assistant Pig-Keeper" (BT 87/108). But Gwydion seems to know (or guess) something of Taran's potential and foreshadows his ascension to the High Kingship of Prydain with these rhetorical questions: "'Is there a destiny laid on me that an Assistant Pig-Keeper should help me in my quest?' He hesitated. 'Or,' he mused, 'is it perhaps the other way around?'" (BT 21/37).

The young Taran also exhibits a temper. When Gwydion chastises him for leaping upon and shaking Gurgi, he exclaims hotly, "Save your own life next time" (BT 37/54). He rashly passes judgment on Eilonwy and angrily calls her "a traitor and liar" (BT 75/96).

His rashness gets Taran into a good deal of trouble. When Taran foolishly tries to cross the *Great Avren without knowing how to swim, he blames *Melyngar, Gwydion's steed, for the mishap that nearly drowns him. Gwydion points out that Taran "must learn to answer for [his] own folly" (BT 32/48). Slowly, Taran learns to think before he acts and speaks.

Taran's growth is most evident during the time when he thinks Gwydion dead and feels he must continue the war leader's quest alone. The burden of leadership is placed upon his shoulders; he is responsible for Eilonwy, *Fflewddur Fflam, and Gurgi. Responsibility has a strange way of tempering the young hero. He becomes less prone to impatience and quick anger. He is able to feel compassion for Gurgi, whom he earlier despised, and steadily comes to care for the miserable creature. Taran also realizes that he indeed cannot stand against the evil of Prydain alone and is able to accept the friendship and support of his *Companions. The role of hero starts to lose its mystique for Taran as he begins to understand its complexities. "He yearned for the peacefulness of Caer Dallben, yearned even to weed the vegetable gardens and make horseshoes" (BT 83/104).

As Taran and his Companions pursue Hen Wen and make their way toward *Caer Dathyl, they find the dwelling place of *Medwyn. The ancient Noah figure usually allows no humans in his hidden valley. Already weary of heroism, Taran says to Medwyn that he could be tempted to stay forever in this peaceful place. Again, Taran's destiny is foreshadowed when the ancient one replies. "'Your heart is young and unformed,' Medwyn said. 'Yet, if I read it well, you are of the few I would welcome here. Indeed, you may stay if you choose'" (BT 124/149). Medwyn indeed recognizes the quality of Taran's character.

Taran fulfills his quest in *The Book of Three*. Hen Wen is found, and the Horned King is destroyed. However, Taran is seriously injured when he tries to draw *Dyrnwyn. The enchanted blade's blue flame stuns and scorches him, for only one of "noble worth" may wield Dyrnwyn. Nevertheless, Taran has grown tremendously from his experiences. Humbly, the Assistant Pig-Keeper admits that he has no cause to be prideful of his accomplishments.

> "It was Gwydion who destroyed the Horned King, and Hen Wen helped him do it. But Gurgi, not I, found her. *Doli and Fflewddur fought gloriously while I was wounded by a sword I had no right to draw. And Eilonwy was the one who took the sword from the *barrow in the first place. As for me, what I mostly did was make mistakes." (BT 185/215)

However, Dallben recognizes that Taran held the Companions together and led them. This alone is a cause for pride in a job well done.

Taran desires nothing more than returning to Caer Dallben. He has had enough of adventures for the time being. Yet, home does not seem the same.

> "I asked for nothing better than to be at home, and my heart rejoices. Yet it is a curious feeling. I have returned to the chamber I slept in and found it smaller than I remember. The fields are beautiful, yet not quite as I recalled them. And I am troubled, for I wonder if I am to be a stranger in my own home."
>
> Dallben shook his head. "No, that you shall never be. But it is not Caer Dallben which has grown smaller. You have grown bigger. That is the way of it." (BT 185–186/216)

The growing relationship between Eilonwy and Taran solidifies during the final pages of *The Book of Three*, when Taran asks Dallben if she might stay at Caer Dallben. "You're to stay!" Taran cries happily (BT 186/216). Eilonwy is pleased, though she upbraids Taran for not bothering to ask her first. It is obvious staying is just what she wants to do.

*The Black Cauldron

Though Taran has grown much during the course of his last quest, he still struggles to curb his pride as *The Black Cauldron* begins. *Ellidyr, the angry and prideful *Prince of Pen-Llarcau, tests him sorely. Upon their first meeting, Taran hurls back insults at the sharp-tongued Ellidyr. Gwydion reprimands Taran. "You have repaid anger with a childish insult. I had thought better of you" (BC 21/35).

However, Ellidyr's insults stir Taran's unrest about his unknown parentage. "Whose son are you?" the Prince of Pen-Llarcau asks sarcastically. Taran later says to Dallben, "Ellidyr spoke the truth. . . . Whose son am I? I have no name but the one you gave me" (BC 22/36).

Dallben does not dwell on Taran's self-pity. Instead he produces for the Assistant Pig-Keeper a sword, Taran's first. Taran is to accompany the warriors of Gwydion on the quest to seek and destroy the *Black Cauldron of *Arawn. He is certain the sword must have some magical powers, but Dallben assures him that the sword's powers, as with all weapons, are "only those held by him who wields it" (BC 23/38). Taran rushes to Eilonwy to have her gird the weapon on him. Though he really wants her to be the one to do the honors, Taran makes the clumsy blunder of saying, "After all, you're the only girl in Caer Dallben" (BC 24/38). Needless to say, Eilonwy is insulted, but seems to understand Taran's ineptitude with women. She girds the sword on him, and Taran reverts to his glorified ideas of manhood and the glory of war. "'Yes,' he cried, 'this is a weapon for a man and a warrior!'" (BC 24/39).

Taran is assigned to the same band as that of Ellidyr, who calls him pigboy. Taran's maturity is furthered as he learns to cope with the arrogant, self-centered prince. Even when Ellidyr forces Taran off the trail and down a steep embankment, Taran does not refute the prince's lies to Gwydion about the "accident." He quietly takes the blame. However, when Eilonwy follows the band unbidden, Ellidyr insultingly reproves her. This Taran will not abide! Nevertheless, Taran continues to otherwise bridle his temper and does not rise to the many abusive attacks leveled at him by Ellidyr.

*Adaon, the son of *Taliesin (*Chief Bard of Prydain), leads Taran's band. Adaon is wise and noble. He possesses great insight and understanding, partially due to the enchanted *brooch he possesses. When Adaon begins to see his imminent death, he wills all his possessions to Taran. "I have watched you closely, Taran of Caer Dallben. In all my journeys I have met no one else to whom I would rather entrust them" (BC 75/99). Again, this foreshadows Taran's special nature, one that will qualify him to rule Prydain. Indeed, Adaon is slain by a *Huntsman's dagger. His death dispels any of Taran's misconceptions concerning the glories of war.

Taran then possesses the *Brooch of Adaon, and he, too, experiences visions of prescience. He feels the power of being "wise"; it promises him the glory he seeks. Therefore, the greatest test of his character comes because of the brooch. The Black Cauldron—now in the hands of the witches, *Orddu, *Orwen, and *Orgoch—is located by the Companions. However, the witches will not part with it unless they receive something deemed of value in trade. Each of Taran's friends tries to give his or her most valued possession. Eilonwy offers her *bauble; Fflewddur, his *truthful harp; and Gurgi, his enchanted *wallet of food. Each hopes to keep Taran from offering the Brooch of Adaon. But the witches will accept nothing except the brooch, and Taran indeed offers it. Orddu makes his decision no easier by saying, "With such a clasp, a duckling could win much glory and honor. Who can tell? He might rival all the heroes of Prydain, even Gwydion Prince of Don" (BC 127/162). Grateful for and humbled by the willingness of his Companions to sacrifice on his behalf, Taran makes the trade. At least, "this [gaining the *Cauldron] much have I done," Taran says to comfort himself, but privately he weeps at the brooch's loss (BC 133/170).

But Taran's sacrifice does not end here. As the Companions labor to move the Black Cauldron to Caer Dallben, they drop it into the River *Tevvyn. Ellidyr, who has forsaken them long before their journey to the witches' dwelling, suddenly appears. He is angry beyond control because the pig-boy has stolen his glory by finding the cauldron. The Companions are unable to remove the cauldron from the water without Ellidyr's help. He will assist only if the Companions swear an oath that they will give Ellidyr credit for finding and obtaining the cauldron. Though Eilonwy will hear nothing of this, Taran sets aside personal aggrandizement for the good of all Prydain. He agrees to swear Ellidyr's oath, saying, "We do not speak of rightness. We speak of a task to be finished" (BC 148/189).

Ellidyr goes mad and steals the cauldron from the Companions, even trying to kill them. Later, as the Companions dejectedly make their way homeward, Taran examines his search for honor.

> "Adaon once told me there is more honor in a field well plowed than in a field steeped in blood. . . . I see now that what he said was true above all.

I do not begrudge Ellidyr his prize. I, too, shall seek honor. But I shall seek it where I know it will be found." (BC 156/196)

Still, Taran is tested again. King *Morgant, who leads another of the parties assigned by Gwydion, finds the Companions. He has in his possession the Black Cauldron and Ellidyr. But Morgant is a traitor and has decided to use the cauldron to create his own army of Cauldron-Born. Thereby, he plans to rule Prydain. Morgant judges Taran's mettle to be of high quality and offers him the eventual position of second in command. Taran answers, "You would know I scorn to serve an evil traitor" (BC 163/204).

Morgant is destroyed, as is the Black Cauldron. Taran's quest again ends successfully. Yet, he sadly realizes that all he has longed for may only be a source of unhappiness. "I had longed to enter the world of men. Now I see it filled with sorrow, with cruelty and treachery, with those who would destroy all around them." Gwydion answers, "Yet, enter it you must for it is a destiny laid on each of us" (BC 177/221).

*The Castle of Llyr

Alexander explains in the Author's Note accompanying *The Castle of Llyr* that this book is in a sense more romantic than the preceding novels because "Taran is noticeably aware of his feelings toward Eilonwy" (CL viii/15). Dallben directs Eilonwy to live, at least for a time, on the *Isle of Mona with King *Rhuddlum and Queen *Teleria. She is to learn the art of being a princess and a lady. Taran's heart is "suddenly and strangely heavy" when the decision is announced (CL 3/17).

Taran is allowed to accompany Eilonwy to *Mona. They are met on Prydain's shore by Prince *Rhun, the good-natured but bumbling son of King Rhuddlum. On the voyage to the Isle of Mona, Taran seems jealous of Rhun, reacting to his gentlemanly though awkward gestures of politeness toward Eilonwy. In a fit of self-pity, Taran complains to the princess that he can never compete with one of royal title.

> "An Assistant Pig-Keeper," Taran snapped. "Yes, that's to be my lot in life. I was born to be one, just as the Princeling of Mona was born to his rank. He's a king's son and I—I don't even know the names of my parents." (CL 10/25)

Soon after arriving on Mona, Eilonwy is kidnapped by the evil sorceress, *Achren. Taran is assigned to a search party that is to be led by Rhun. Rhun, however, is not competent, and King Rhuddlum knows it. Secretly, he calls Taran aside and explains that Rhun will lead in name only. In truth the king's *Master of Horse will be in charge. King Rhuddlum then asks

Taran to swear an oath that he will watch over Rhun, to protect him from harm and from making too big a fool of himself. Rhuddlum reveals that he hopes Rhun and Eilonwy will marry. The news causes Taran to grieve, but he still swears to do as the king asks. Taran honors his pledge to the end.

Much later, Rhun succeeds in getting the Companions separated from the Master of Horse and then trapped in the cavern of *Glew, the *giant. They have with them Eilonwy's bauble, lost in her struggle with *Magg, Achren's wicked servant. None of them has power to light the bauble so that they may illuminate the cavern. It is a measure of Taran's worth that he is finally able to make it shine. However, he must turn his thoughts away from his own plight to that of the princess before it is possible (CL 85/109).

Taran falls into a pool of luminescent water, making him visible to Glew. He tells the others to run and save themselves while Glew pursues him. It is another example of Taran's honorable character. Later, when Fflewddur suggests killing the unconscious Glew, Taran will not allow it, even though the giant would have taken their lives. "'Leave him,' said Taran, staying Fflewddur's arm. 'I know he tried to do us ill, but I still pity the wretched creature and mean to ask Dallben if he can help him'" (CL 117/143). Indeed, compassion is one of Taran's blossoming attributes.

Finally, Taran and the Companions find and rescue Eilonwy. Taran would have given his life, and almost does, to see her safe. As *The Castle of Llyr* ends, Taran must return to Caer Dallben while Eilonwy stays on Mona as intended. But she makes it plain that she shall not wed Rhun. Taran and Eilonwy pledge not to forget one another while they are separated. She gives to Taran as a token of her pledge an ancient *battle horn. As Taran has nothing tangible to give, she happily accepts "the word of an Assistant Pig-Keeper" (CL 170/201).

*Taran Wanderer

Taran's unrest concerning his parentage comes to a head in *Taran Wanderer*. He decides to ask Eilonwy to marry him, but must first know his true background. If he is not of noble birth, then Taran feels he must not ask her hand. Dallben cannot answer Taran's question, so the Assistant Pig-Keeper asks the enchanter's leave to search for his roots. During his journey, Taran passes from boyhood to manhood.

First, Taran travels to the *Marshes of Morva to inquire of the witches Orddu, Orwen, and Orgoch. They also can be (or choose to be) of no help, suggesting Taran find the *Mirror of Llunet. The Mirror of Llunet is an oracular pool of water that may reveal what Taran wishes to know (TW 19/34). Orddu foreshadows Taran's upcoming tests of manhood when she says, "Has the darling robin ever scratched for his own worms? That's brav-ery of another sort" (TW 14/27).

On his way to search for the Mirror, Taran travels to *Cantrev Cadiffor, the realm of King *Smoit. Before reaching Smoit's stronghold, Taran is attacked by the henchmen of Lord *Goryon. Though Taran is aided by the stout farmer, *Aeddan, *Melynlas is stolen. Taran and Gurgi stay awhile with Aeddan and help him work his only field. It is the first of his experi-ences with the skills and trades of the world, even though he had farmed some with Coll. Aeddan offers Taran a place on his farm, but Taran must continue his quest.

Taran travels to the stronghold of Lord Goryon to retrieve Melynlas. His growing talents of leadership are evidenced as he uses diplomacy to con-vince Goryon to return his steed. Wisely, Taran does not antagonize Goryon but capitalizes on his weakness: Goryon worries excessively about his honor. His men have goaded Goryon into breaking Melynlas. This is not an easy task, yet Goryon's honor will not allow him to quit. Taran offers Goryon a way out. He offers Melynlas to the lord as a gift.

> "What?" shouted Goryon at the top of his voice, his face turning livid.
> "Insults! Impertinence! Insolence! How dare you! I take no gifts from
> pig-keepers! Nor will I lower myself to mount the beast again." He flung
> up an arm. "Begone! Out of my sight—your nag, your monster [Gurgi],
> and his pony along with you!" (TW 37/53)

Taran finally arrives at *Caer Cadarn, the stronghold of Smoit. While visiting with the good King Smoit, the ongoing feud between Lords Goryon and *Gast erupts once again. Smoit explains angrily that the two have fought over the marvelous cow, *Cornillo, for so long that neither knows who possessed her in the beginning. Smoit rages about, threatening to knock heads and throw the two into his dungeon. Taran tries to suggest alternate solutions, but Smoit is too angry to listen.

When the battle is over, Aeddan's only field is ruined, and Smoit is bent on keeping Cornillo for himself this time. However, Taran saves the burly king from drowning during the chase, and Smoit grants him any favor. Taran asks that Smoit heed his suggestions for solving the multiple prob-lems created by the feuding lords.

With the wisdom of Solomon, Taran suggests Goryon and Gast be set free "to labor beside Aeddan and strive to mend what they have destroyed" (TW 61/80). He asks that Smoit give Cornillo to Aeddan, for his need is greatest. Yet, Goryon and Gast shall be allowed her next calves. Also, the lords' herds have been mixed during the fracas. Taran suggests that Goryon divide the animals, and Gast be the first to choose his half. "The lad has a better head on his shoulders than I do," exclaims King Smoit, "and his judgment is wiser. Kinder, too, for my choice would have been the dungeon" (TW 61/80–81).

Smoit honors Taran by asking him to stay at Caer Cadarn and become his heir—the future *King of Cadiffor (TW 63–64/83). Taran's heart leaps at the thought, for he could then ask Eilonwy to marry him. But he knows he will not be satisfied until he discovers his true heritage. Taran continues his quest.

The Companions meet and challenge the evil wizard, *Morda, not long after leaving Smoit's realm. Taran and the others risk their lives to save Doli of the *Fair Folk from Morda's spell, an enchantment that has changed the dwarf to a frog. Taran unknowingly carries the secret of Morda's life in his pocket: the fingerbone from Morda's hand. Gurgi had found it hidden in the crotch of a tall tree. When Morda's spells will not work on Taran, he realizes that the bone has protected him. Taran's compassion nearly brings disaster, however. Morda pleads that Taran not break the bone, thus killing him. Taran decides to let the evil one live. In a moment of confusion, Morda attacks. Taran is barely able to snap the bone and end Morda's dreadful existence (TW 106/129).

Morda's power had come from the *gem of Angharad, a Fair Folk *stone that once belonged to the *House of Llyr. Though Taran has rightful claim to the stone, he willingly returns it to Doli. Again, Taran does not violate his code of honor, though the temptation is great. He is certain Orddu would have traded the knowledge of his parentage for the enchanted gem (TW 110/133–134).

After leaving Morda's dwelling, the Companions meet *Dorath's Company, a band of ruthless mercenaries, and Taran is pressed into combat with *Dorath himself. It is a hand-to-hand battle with no weapons, Taran's first carefully described fight. He does well against the larger man and might have won. But Dorath does not fight fairly, and Taran loses. His sword, the one given him by Dallben, is lost to the outlaw (TW 128–131/154–157).

The turning point in Taran's life occurs when the Companions happen upon the shepherd, *Craddoc. Craddoc claims that he left his infant son in Dallben's care many years ago, and that Taran is therefore his son. Taran's honor forces him to stay with Craddoc. But he is bitter and unhappy and cannot call Craddoc father. Taran is convinced that he will never marry Eilonwy. Fiercely proud, Taran says Eilonwy must not learn of his parentage. "Bid her my farewell," says Taran to Fflewddur. "She and I must never meet again. It were better the Princess forget the shepherd boy, better that all of you forget me" (TW 144/171).

Taran and Gurgi stay to work Craddoc's farmstead. Taran even begins to feel some pride in his work. Still, he is unable to accept his lot in life. When Craddoc saves Taran from a rampant fire while they are burning brush, he calls a reluctant thanks. "But in his voice there was as much bitterness as gratitude, for the man who had saved his life was the same man who had broken it" (TW 146/174).

However, Taran's moment of truth comes that winter, when Craddoc slips into an icy gorge. It seems the shepherd may be dead, and Taran involuntarily feels a wild sense of freedom. But Craddoc is alive, though rescue is nearly impossible. Taran begins to rationalize that the risk of saving him might be too great—that all their lives might be lost.

> It was not despair that filled him, but terror, black terror at the thoughts whispering in his mind. Was there the slimmest hope of saving the stricken herdsman? If not, even Prince Gwydion would not reproach Taran's decision. Nor would any man. Instead, they would grieve with him at his loss. Free of his burden, free of the valley, the door of his cage opened wide, and all his life awaited him; Eilonwy, Caer Dallben. He seemed to hear his own voice speak these words, and he listened in shame and horror.
>
> Then, as if his heart would burst with it, he cried out in terrible rage, "What man am I?" (TW 152–153/181)

Taran leaps into the pit and expends all he has to save Craddoc, nearly losing his life in the cause. He learns from the dying shepherd that though Dallben did come years ago, he took no child away with him. Craddoc is not Taran's father. He wanted Taran for a son and for his strength to rebuild his farmstead. When he learned to care for Taran, he was too ashamed to tell the truth. Despite the deception, Taran feels no anger or bitterness—he has been cleansed of those emotions. He then uses the single call left in the Fair Folk battle horn given to him by Eilonwy. The call summons Fair Folk to the rescue, and Taran loses consciousness. Only when he is safe and healing does he discover that Craddoc is dead. He is filled with anguish (TW 155–156/184–185).

Sickened and shamed by his attitude concerning noble birthright, Taran no longer seeks his parentage. "If I do find pride, I'll not find it in what I was or what I am, but what I may become. Not in my birth, but in myself" (TW 160/190). He knows it is time to scratch for his own worms.

Taran gives himself the name *Wanderer when later pressed by *Llonio for a longer name. Llonio and his family, who live by the *Small Avren River, adopt Craddoc's sheep and teach Taran to be optimistic and creative in his approach to life. Taran is at peace with himself once again when he leaves Llonio to travel into the *Free Commots (TW 174/204–205).

In the *Commots, Taran apprentices with *Hevydd the Smith, *Dwyvach Weaver-Woman, and *Annlaw Clay-Shaper. He learns much from Hevydd and Dwyvach but realizes in both instances that smithing and weaving are not to be his path. But Taran feels a special joy in the craft of clay-shaping and a special attraction to the *Commot Merin where Annlaw dwells. He thinks Eilonwy will like Merin, too. "We may have come to the end of our journey," Taran tells Gurgi (TW 196/230).

Over time, both Taran and Annlaw begin to realize that Taran does not have the gift to be a potter. Taran is devastated. "Must the one skill I sought above all be denied me?" he asks (TW 198/232). Annlaw gently explains that it is fortunate Taran has learned this now and not spent years "in vain hope" (TW 198/232).

Taran stays to aid Annlaw, delivering clay vessels to nearby commots. In the *Commot Isav, Taran's leadership abilities are given opportunity to develop. Dorath's Company has been raiding defenseless commots, including Isav. Taran organizes the shepherds and formulates a plan to take the raiders by surprise. Indeed, he leads the men of Isav to victory (TW 207/242).

Yet, Taran still feels a stranger to himself. He has found no niche in life. "What use am I? To myself, to anyone? None that I can see," he laments to Annlaw (TW 208/244). The old potter then offers Taran a startling suggestion.

"The Commot lore tells how one may see himself for what he is. Whether it be true or no more than an old wives' tale I will not judge," the potter went on slowly. "But the lore says that he who would know himself need only gaze in the Mirror of Llunet." (TW 209/244)

Annlaw knows the way to the Mirror of Llunet and feels that looking into the enchanted pool may put Taran's heart at ease, though Taran is reluctant. The Assistant Pig-Keeper begins his journey the next day. The Mirror of Llunet reveals much to Taran.

"I saw myself," Taran answered. "In the time I watched, I saw strength— and frailty. Pride and vanity, courage and fear. Of wisdom, a little. Of folly, much. Of intentions, many good ones; but many more left undone. In this, alas, I saw myself a man like any other.

"But this, too, I saw," he went on. "Alike as men may seem, each is different as flakes of snow, no two the same. You told me you had no need to seek the Mirror, knowing you were Annlaw Clay-Shaper. Now I know who I am: myself and none other. I am Taran. . . .

"There was no enchantment. . . . It was a pool of water, the most beautiful I have seen. But a pool of water, no more than that.

"At first," he went on, "I thought Orddu had sent a fool on a fool's errand. She did not. She meant me to see what the Mirror showed me. Any stream, any river, would have given me the same reflection, but I would not have understood it then as I understand it now.

"As for my parentage," he added, "it makes little difference. True kinship has naught to do with blood ties, however strong they be. I think we are all kin, brothers and sisters one to the other, all children of all parents. And the birthright I once sought, I seek it no longer. The folk of the Free Commots taught me well, that manhood is not given but earned." (TW 216–217/252–253)

Thus ends the quest of *Taran Wanderer. Taran returns to Caer Dallben ready to ask Eilonwy's hand in marriage and to establish his rightful place in the world of men.

*The High King

Eilonwy is waiting for Taran when he reaches Caer Dallben. She immediately senses his new maturity. "Unless you told someone they'd never guess you were an Assistant Pig-Keeper" (HK 5/16). Coll adds, "He left us a pigkeeper and comes back looking as if he could do all he set his hand to, whatever" (HK 6/16). Dallben also has an opinion. "You found more than you sought," he says to Taran, "and gained perhaps more than you know" (HK 6/17).

Taran is on the verge of asking Eilonwy to marry him, when Fflewddur Fflam bursts into Dallben's cottage to announce danger and launch the final quest of the Chronicles. Fflewddur brings a wounded Gwydion with him, and Taran takes charge, using Adaon's herbs to treat the Prince of Don. Taran realizes he is commanding under Dallben's roof and is embarrassed. But Dallben says, "Nor should you fear to command under any roof, since you have learned to command yourself. I trust your skill as I see you trust it" (HK 12/23).

The Companions depart for Caer Cadarn to accompany Gwydion part way to Annuvin. He seeks the stolen sword Dyrnwyn. Eilonwy will hear nothing of being left behind, and Taran, grinning, says he has long since given up trying to talk her out of things (HK 44/59).

Taran sets out on this adventure with a different perspective than in earlier days. "For the boy I was, this would have been a bold adventure, full of glory. This much have I learned: A man's life weighs more than glory, and a price paid in blood is a heavy reckoning" (HK 38/51). His statement is prophetic, for many of Taran's closest friends must die to assure Prydain its freedom.

Rhun is the first of Taran's associates to lose his life. He dies freeing Taran and Gwydion from imprisonment at the hand of Magg. Taran vows to finish the seawall Rhun has begun on Mona (HK 80/97).

Seeing that Arawn means to make his final assault against Prydain, Gwydion sends Taran to the Free Commots to raise an army. Eilonwy attaches to a spear the embroidered banner of Hen Wen she made while living on Mona. It becomes Taran's standard around which the *Commot men rally. Though Taran has long desired to be a war leader, the prospect is no longer appealing. "My heart . . . will be easier when I am once more an Assistant Pig-Keeper" (HK 99/119).

The second of Taran's friends to die is Annlaw Clay-Shaper, who is killed by marauders. Taran blames himself for not better protecting the innocent inhabitants of the Free Commots. He feels the first agonies of true leadership. *Llassar, the shepherd youth from Commot Isav, says of Taran, "The Wanderer has not stirred from the potter's hut. It is harsh enough for each man to bear his own wound. But he who leads bears the wounds of all who follow him" (HK 103/124). Coll answers, "Leave him where he chooses to be. In the morning he will be well, though likely never healed" (HK 103/124).

Taran takes his troops and marches northwestward to Caer Dathyl to meet Gwydion and the others who will fight against Arawn. There Taran meets Taliesin, Chief Bard and father of Adaon. As Taliesin assesses the qualities of each of the Companions, he foreshadows Taran's destiny by alluding to his various apprenticeships. "There are those . . . who must first learn loss, despair, and grief. Of all paths to wisdom, this is the cruelest and longest. . . . Those who reach the end do more than gain wisdom. As rough wool becomes cloth, and crude clay a vessel, so do they change and fashion wisdom for others, and what they give back is greater than what they won" (HK 114/136).

Though the first days at Caer Dathyl are peaceful, soon *Pryderi arrives and demands the *High King *Math surrender. The traitorous Pryderi has aligned himself with Arawn and attacks Caer Dathyl with Cauldron-Born to aid his troops. For the first time, Taran must face a true battlefield and "an odd impatience, mixed with fear, drew him taut as a bowstring" (HK 122/146). Suddenly Taran realizes that he may not return, and he did not take the opportunity to tell Eilonwy of his love for her. "Regret for his unspoken words was an iron hand gripping his throat" (HK 123/147).

Though Caer Dathyl falls to Pryderi and Math is slain, Taran and Eilonwy are spared. Taran is assigned by Gwydion to delay the Cauldron-Born in their march back to Annuvin, thus allowing the *Sons of Don to attack a more vulnerable Arawn. With his army of Commot men, Taran accepts the task.

On the barren plains of the *Red Fallows, Taran suffers his greatest personal loss: Coll perishes at the hands of the deathless warriors. The stout farmer is a father figure to Taran, raising him from infancy. Taran insists on hollowing a shallow grave alone. The Companions raise a mound with the tumbled stones of an old wall, then Taran sends them on toward the *Hills of Bran-Galedd. He stays to mourn the grower of turnips, catching up with the others later (HK 142/169).

The weight of command increases yet again. One out of three of Taran's Commot men perish in the Hills of Bran-Galedd at the swords of the Cauldron-Born. Also, Eilonwy and Gurgi are missing after the battle with the deathless warriors. Taran wants the others to go on while he searches for them, but Fflewddur sadly reminds him of his duty (HK 148/174–175). Taran must ride with his army. But Eilonwy finds her way back to Taran, and his heart leaps when he learns she is alive (HK 175/204). "Taran stepped quickly to Eilonwy's side, put his arms about her, and drew the Princess close to him" (HK 179/209). This is the first recorded instance of overt affection between Taran and Eilonwy.

Taran makes a final push to slow the Cauldron-Born. Learning the secret way to Annuvin's *Iron Portals, he drives his troops through the mountains. Doli of the Fair Folk tries to accompany them, but Fair Folk cannot survive in the Land of Death. As Doli weakens, Taran decides to take him back to a safe region. Doli chastises Taran, for time and personnel cannot be spared. "Are you a war-leader or an Assistant Pig-Keeper," cries Doli. Taran answers, "Need you ask, old friend? I'm an Assistant Pig-Keeper" (HK 193/225). But Taran's compassion need not have its price, for Doli discovers his invisibility shields him from Annuvin's evil spell. Invisibility is bothersome for Doli, and the irritable dwarf gives Taran the highest praise when he says, "I'd not do this willingly—oh, my ears—for any mortal in Prydain—oh, my head—but you!" (HK 194/226).

However, Taran's compassion does pay great dividends. In *The Book of Three*, he rescues and nurses to health a young *gwythaint, against everyone's advice. As Taran's band approaches Annuvin, this same great bird rescues Taran from falling to his death and takes him to the peak of *Mount Dragon (HK 211–212/244–245). Here Taran finds Dyrnwyn hidden beneath a stone, slays the Cauldron-Born with the enchanted blade, and descends to Annuvin to find and destroy Arawn himself (HK 213–223, 246–257). No longer need he fear Dyrnwyn's flame; Taran is proven to be "of noble worth."

Now that the threat of Arawn is gone, the Sons of Don must return to their ancestral home, the *Summer Country. All of the Companions are invited to travel with them. Eilonwy and Fflewddur are required to go, for the age of enchantment is ended in Prydain and the blood of enchantment flows in the veins of them both. It is a time for great rejoicing, and Taran finally asks Eilonwy to be his bride (HK 230/265–266).

The night before their departure, Taran is troubled and cannot sleep. With help from Orddu, Orwen, and Orgoch, who appear in his chamber, Taran begins to realize that he cannot leave Prydain. The next day he announces to all his friends that he must stay, though it will break his heart to be separated from them. "Never had he loved each of them more than at this moment" (HK 236/272). Of course, being separated from Eilonwy will be nearly unbearable.

Dallben urges Taran to think carefully, for once he has decided, the choice may not be recalled. But Taran says he must stay to build what has been destroyed: he must tend Coll's garden, finish Rhun's seawall, restore the Red Fallows, aid the widows and fatherless children of the Free Commots (HK 237/273). Again, Dallben asks Taran to reconsider, for the tasks he has chosen are cruelly difficult and the rewards likely to be few.

> Taran nodded. "So be it," he said. "Long ago I yearned to be a hero without knowing, in truth, what a hero was. Now, perhaps, I understand it a little better. A grower of turnips or a shaper of clay, a Commot farmer or a king—every man is a hero if he strives more for others than for himself alone. Once," he added, "you told me that the seeking counts more than the finding. So, too, must the striving count more than the gain." (HK 238/274)

Taran says he is content being an Assistant Pig-Keeper. But Dallben answers, "Even that contentment shall not be yours. . . . No longer are you Assistant Pig-Keeper, but High King of Prydain" (HK 238/275). Dallben explains that *The Book of Three* prophesied that a new High King would rule Prydain in the days after the Sons of Don departed. However, the man who would be king must meet certain specified conditions: he would slay a serpent (the shape-changed Arawn), gain and lose a flaming sword (Dyrnwyn, whose power fades), choose a kingdom of sorrow over one of happiness (Prydain versus the Summer Country), and be of no station in life (HK 239–240/276). Indeed, Taran meets all these requirements. Dallben reveals that he found Taran in a forest near a battlefield. All were slain, even women and children, except for a lone infant. "Here, surely, was one of no station in life, an unknown babe of unknown kin," says Dallben

(HK 240/277). The enchanter, who had long searched for the prospective High King, felt the child might be the chosen one. "Until now, my boy . . . you were always a great 'perhaps'" (HK 241/277).

As Taran's friends prepare to depart for the Summer Country, each leaves him with a parting gift: a gem from Glew's cavern, a Fair Folk axe from Doli, a melted harpstring from Fflewddur's truthful harp, *The Book of Three* from Dallben, and the bauble from Eilonwy. But Eilonwy falters as she presents her gift.

> Eilonwy was about to turn away, but suddenly her blue eyes flashed furiously and she stamped her foot. "It's not fair!" she cried. "It's not my fault I was born into a family of enchantresses. I didn't ask for magical powers. That's worse than being made to wear a pair of shoes that doesn't fit! I don't see why I have to keep them!" (HK 245/282–283)

Indeed, Dallben is waiting for Eilonwy to say those words. He explains that there is a way to give up her heritage of enchantment and stay in Prydain. The ring upon her finger, given her long ago by Gwydion, holds the power to change her. "Turn the ring once upon your finger," says Dallben. "Wish with all your heart for your enchanted powers to vanish" (HK 246/283). Eilonwy happily complies, and as she does, the light in her bauble winks out. Then Dallben performs his last official act in Prydain. "Come, clasp hands the two of you, and pledge each other your troth" (HK 246/284).

King Taran and Queen Eilonwy walk outside to greet their waiting subjects, including old friends and acquaintances: Hevydd, Llassar, Aeddan, King Smoit, many folk of the Free Commots, and even Lords Goryon and Gast.

> And so they lived many happy years, and the promised tasks were accomplished. Yet long afterward, when all had passed away into distant memory, there were many who wondered whether King Taran, Queen Eilonwy, and their companions had indeed walked the earth, or whether they had been no more than dreams in a tale set down to beguile children. And, in time, only the *bards knew the truth of it. (HK 248/285)

The name Taran briefly appears in the *Mabinogion*: Glinneu, the son of Taran and Gluneu Eli Taran (M 251, 381). Gluneu Eli Taran was one of the seven men of the Isle of the Mighty (Britain) who were left alive after a terrible war against the Irish. It was this war in which the cauldron of renovation, Alexander's pattern for the Black Cauldron, was destroyed. Gluneu Eli Taran appears in the tale "Branwen the *Daughter of Llyr" (M 381).

Another character in the *Mabinogion* may show some relationship to Alexander's Taran. Llew Llaw Gyffes was an unclaimed child raised by Gwydion ab *Don (M 438). Gwydion was a protective figure for Gyffes, much as with Taran, and Gyffes also emerged as a great hero. However, Alexander says there is little if any connection between these two. "If there is a thread [of similarity] it is very slight . . . because he [Gyffes] was a much more vigorous, athletic, different type of hero" (Alexander, 1985b).

Another character from the *Mabinogion*, Manawyddan, the son of *Llyr, shares with Taran a common experience. Manawyddan travels about the land learning and mastering a number of crafts including the making of saddles, shields, and shoes (M 399–401).

Alexander himself has shared emotions and experiences with Taran. Like the young Taran, the young Alexander was a romantic. He joined the army during World War II in order "to distinguish himself in the glories of war. That Alexander never had the least inclination toward the battle-cry aspect of life made no difference. He was more than willing to enter the action without a doubt that he was perfectly suited to strike a significant blow for victory as a modern Rogers' Ranger" (Jacobs, 1978:125). But when he was sworn in, the romantic bubble burst. "All at once he sensed that the army was a real organization, and not one of swashbuckling, carefree adventurers" (Jacobs, 1978:126).

Alexander also had his experiences with the crafts of metal forging, weaving, and pottery making.

> Lloyd's sister, Florence, inadvertently helped prepare him for *Taran Wanderer* in those lean years in the late 1940's when she taught him how to weave and make pottery. When Lloyd took Taran on his wanderings, the scenes with Dwyvach the weaver and Annlaw the potter came from his experience as well as his creativity. (Jacobs, 1978:492)

Alexander tried working metal in a junior high school course. It fascinated him, but he says he was never good at it (Alexander, 1985b). However, upon completing each of the five Prydain novels, Alexander designed a medallion which he commissioned a silversmith to produce.

> The spiral pattern for *The Book of Three* suggests beginnings, endings, and beginnings again. Then I designed another when *The Black Cauldron* was finished. On this one, the three bars stand for wisdom, truth, and love. By the time the third volume was published, I was really caught in these medallions. For *The Castle of Llyr*, I combined symbols for man and woman in a circle of eternity. The design for *Taran Wanderer* is

supposed to suggest a bird in flight. And finally, for *The High King,* the five connected links stand for the five books. (Alexander, 1974)

Alexander also experienced disappointment similar to that Taran felt when discovering he had not the talent to be a master potter. Alexander wanted to master the violin, but he started too late in life. After a few years of lessons and hard work, Alexander was gently told by his instructor that, though he had done amazingly well, there was no point in continuing the instruction (Jacobs, 1978:304).

Taran is the Prydainian character with which Alexander identifies most, though he feels Taran is far more heroic than he could ever be (Jacobs, 1978:494). "I have been racked up by indecision just as much as poor Taran, and I certainly have physically gone through, to some small extent, the same kinds of miseries" (Jacobs, 1978:494). In part, Alexander is describing the struggles of maturation. The universal theme of growing up, which is as important as any theme in the Chronicles, speaks to every reader (Alexander, 1966c:6158). Taran, classic hero though he may be, is very human. "His destiny is not predetermined," says Alexander (1985b). "I guess we'd always have to say Taran has free agency. . . . I don't think there can be any morality without decision." The human condition is most important to Alexander, and Taran is a vehicle through which this is expressed. Alexander (1985b) calls Taran's choice to stay in Prydain "a kind of commitment to the human condition." Even though Taran had a way to escape living and dying, he didn't accept it. "I think I was trying to say we are human beings and must therefore live like human beings" (Alexander, 1985b).

See also Characters—fantasy.

(M 251, 381)

Taran (TAH-ran) Threadbare: This is the name given Taran by Dwyvach Weaver-Woman when she notices his well-worn cloak. She then suggests he learn to weave a new one.

See also Dwyvach Weaver-Woman.

Taran Wanderer: This is the name *Taran gives himself as he travels through the *Free Commots in *Taran Wanderer. He first speaks the name to *Llonio, shortly before crossing the *Small Avren and entering the *Commots.

See also Annlaw Clay-Shaper, Drudwas, Dwyvach Weaver-Woman, Hevydd, Llassar.

(TW 164+/194+; HK 92+/111+)

**Taran (TAH-ran) Wanderer: *Taran Wanderer* is the fourth book in the Prydain series. The last of the novels, **The High King,* was actually written before *Taran Wanderer,* and was thought to have been the fourth and final book of the Prydain cycle. However, Alexander's editor, Ann Durell, was troubled by *The High King,* until she suddenly realized one whole book was missing in the series.

> As Ann reviewed the book [*The High King*] and made her notes, she turned the situation over and over in her mind. Something was not right, but she could not put her finger on it. . . .
>
> Ann went to bed on a Friday evening in August, 1965. At 2:00 a.m. she suddenly awoke with what seemed to be the solution to the problem: an entire book was missing between **The Castle of Llyr* and *The High King of *Prydain* [working title]. Allusions were made in *The High King of Prydain* to **Taran's* period of maturing which occurred between books three and four but was never detailed in either volume. It needed to be developed more fully for the reader. At the end of *The High King of Prydain,* Taran chooses to remain on earth, rejecting the offer to return to the eternal peace of the **Summer Country.* The reader needs to feel more deeply his connection with the common folk of Prydain. In short,

Jacket illustration by Evaline Ness

he "is the link between the faery and the mundane" and needs to be established more firmly in the mundane. (Jacobs, 1978:286)

Alexander agreed, of course, and *Taran Wanderer* was added to the *Chronicles of Prydain. Its plot and theme revolve solely around Taran's initiation into manhood. He leaves *Caer Dallben to discover the secret of his parentage. Instead, he finds himself. Taran apprentices with the craftsmen of the *Free Commots and grows to know and love the common folk of his country. Indeed, when the time comes to raise an army of *Commot Folk, Taran is one of the few outsiders around whom they will rally.

Teirgwaedd (TEER-gwed): Teirgwaedd is the father of the *bard, *Menwy, who is noted for fashioning the *Brooch of Adaon. Teirgwaedd is also listed in the *Mabinogion* as the father of Menwy, who was one of the principal enchanters of Welsh legend and is credited with discovering the bardic alphabet.
(BC 127/162; M 213, 223, 228, 269, 313)

Teleria (tel-EH-ree-ah) Daughter of Tannwen (TAN-wen): Teleria Daughter of *Tannwen is Queen to King *Rhuddlum of the *Isle of Mona. She is also mother to Prince *Rhun. *Dallben describes the king and queen as "kindly and gracious" (CL 4/18). *Eilonwy lives with them for a time so that she may learn the ways of being a lady and a princess.

Teleria appears early in *The Castle of Llyr*. "The Queen was a stout, pleasant-looking woman dressed in fluttering white garments; a golden circlet crowned her braided hair, which was the same straw color as Prince Rhun's" (CL 14/29–30).

The good queen habitually interrupts herself to give motherly advice as she speaks. "'Welcome, *Daughter of Angharad,' Queen Teleria began, returning to Eilonwy. 'Your presence honors—don't fidget, child, and stand straight—our Royal House'" (CL 15/30). Her favorite expression is "*Good Llyr," an oath comparable to *Fflewddur's "*Great Belin" (CL 15/30).

See also Dinas Rhydnant, House of Rhuddlum.
(CL 4+/18+; HK 55/70, 69/86, 106/127)

Tevvyn (TEV-in), River: This river runs north to south through the *Forest of Idris and is a tributary of the *Great Avren. It is in the River Tevvyn that the *Companions drop the *Black Crochan. They are unable to free the *cauldron from the river's waters until *Ellidyr offers his ill-given aid. The River Tevvyn is described as turbulent and brown (BC 137/174).
(BC 137/174, 158/199)

**truthful harp: *Fflewddur Fflam's truthful harp is introduced in *The Book of Three* when the would-be *bard pretends to understand the *Old Writing on *Dyrnwyn's scabbard.

> "It says, oh, something like 'Beware My Wrath'—the usual sentiments."
> At that moment there was a loud twang. Fflewddur blinked. One of his harp strings had snapped. (BT 86/107)

The harp's repeated behavior of breaking strings finally forces Fflewddur to explain its unusual qualities and how he came to possess it. He begins by explaining that he had once tried to become a bard. However, Fflewddur had miserably failed the bardic examination.

> "The *Council [of the Bards] were very nice to me," continued Fflewddur. "*Taliesin, the *Chief Bard himself, presented me with this harp. He said it was exactly what I needed. I sometimes wonder if he was really doing me a favor. It's a very nice harp, but I have such trouble with the strings. I'd throw it away and get another, but it has a beautiful tone; I should never find one as good. If only the beastly strings . . ."
> "They do seem to break frequently," *Eilonwy began.
> "Yes, that's so," Fflewddur admitted, a little sheepishly. "I've noticed it usually happens when—well, I'm an emotional sort of fellow, and I do get carried away. I might, ah, readjust the facts slightly; purely for dramatic effect, you understand." (BT 89/110–111)

Soon after his explanation, Fflewddur throws caution to the wind and begins once again to embellish the truth. "'Forward, then!' the bard cried. 'And if we must give battle, so be it! Why, I've carved my way through walls of spearmen. . . .'" (BT 93/115). Suddenly, six strings break at once, and many others seem to be on the verge of snapping.

However, the truthful harp does more than remind Fflewddur he's stretching the truth. Its music is beautiful, enchanted. When Fflewddur first plays for *Eilonwy and *Taran, the melody is gentle and haunting.

> Then the harp fell silent. Fflewddur sat with his head bent close to the strings, a curious expression on his long face. "Well, that was a surprise," said the bard at last. "I had planned something a little more lively, the sort of thing my war-leader always enjoys—to put us in a bold frame of mind, you understand. The truth of the matter is," he admitted with a slight tone of discouragement, "I don't really know what's going to come out of it next. My fingers go along, but sometimes I think this harp plays of itself." (BT 129/153)

The harp develops a personality of sorts as the *Chronicles of Prydain unfold, becoming as real a character as some boasting flesh and blood.

Fflewddur never seems to bridle his passion for expanding upon the facts, and the truthful harp bows and bends, snapping strings throughout each adventure.

> No sooner were the words past his lips than the harp bent like an overdrawn bow and a string broke with a loud twang. "Drat the thing!" muttered the bard. "Will it give me no peace? I swear it's getting worse. The slightest bit of color added to the facts and it costs me a string." (TW 41/57)

No matter how Fflewddur complains, he loves the harp as a dear friend. In *The High King, Fflewddur meets Taliesin once again, and the Chief Bard offers to trade any of his harps for the one he gave to the would-be bard. At first Fflewddur cries joyfully at the sight of Taliesin's beautiful instruments, but then he looks carefully at the truthful harp.

> "Ah—yes, well, you honor me," he murmured in some confusion, "but this old pot is quite good enough for me. . . . Not to belittle these, but what I mean is that somehow we're used to each other. Yes, I'm most grateful. But I would not change it." (HK 112/134)

However, the time comes when Fflewddur must part from his dear friend, the truthful harp. On their trek toward *Annuvin, the *Companions are caught in a terrible blizzard. They can find neither shelter nor wood for a fire. Eilonwy and *Gurgi have already fallen into the chilled sleep of death when Fflewddur realizes he must burn the harp.

> For a long moment he held the harp lovingly in his hands and gently touched the strings, then with a quick motion raised the beautiful instrument and smashed it across his knee.
> Taran cried out in anguish as the wood shattered into splinters and the harp strings tore loose with a discordant burst of sound. Fflewddur let the broken fragments drop from his hands.
> "Burn it," he said. "It is wood well-seasoned." (HK 201/233–234)

Taran thinks the bard foolish to destroy the harp for the moment's warmth that so little wood will bring. But the magical wood burns bright and warm. "The bits of wood seemed hardly to be consumed, yet the fire burned all the more brightly" (HK 201/234). Eilonwy awakens, tears filling her eyes when she understands Fflewddur's sacrifice.

> "Don't give it a second thought," cried Fflewddur. "The truth of the matter is that I'm delighted to be rid of it. I could never really play the thing, and it was more a burden than anything else. *Great Belin, I feel light as

a feather without it. Believe me, I was never meant to be a bard in the first place, so all is for the best."

In the depths of the flame several harp strings split in two and a puff of sparks flew into the air.

"But it gives a foul smoke," Fflewddur muttered, though the fire was burning clear and brilliant. "It makes my eyes water horribly."

The flames had now spread to all the fragments, and as the harp strings blazed a melody sprang suddenly from the heart of the fire. Louder and more beautiful it grew, and the strains of music filled the air, echoing endlessly among the crags. Dying, the harp seemed to be pouring forth all the songs ever played upon it, and the sound shimmered like the fire.

All night the harp sang, and its melodies were of joy, sorrow, love, and valor. The fire never abated, and little by little new life and strength returned to the companions. And as the notes soared upward a wind rose from the south, parting the falling snow like a curtain and flooding the hills with warmth. Only at dawn did the flame sink into glowing embers and the voice of the harp fall silent. (HK 202/234–235)

Alexander confirms that the harp did more than protect the Companions from the storm. Indeed, it "caused a weather change" (Alexander, 1985b).

All that remains of the truthful harp the next morning is a single string, the one unbreakable string *Gwydion had given Fflewddur long ago. The fire had caused the string to twist and coil around itself, yet it glittered like pure gold. When Fflewddur departs for the *Summer Country, as the Chronicles conclude, he presents Taran with the melted harp string as a token of remembrance (HK 242/279).

The story of Fflewddur's acquisition of the magical harp is also told in the *Prydain picture book, *The Truthful Harp (and now in The Foundling).

There appears in the *Mabinogion a magical harp with qualities similar to that of the truthful harp. The harp of Teirtu, though its strings did not break at stretchings of the truth, did produce magical music. "When a man desires that it should play, it does so by itself, and when he desires that it should cease, it ceases" (M 237).

Alexander (1985b) admits that the harp of Teirtu "triggered the idea" for his truthful harp. However, the true inspiration came from the real thing. Alexander found an ancient Irish lap harp in Joseph Primavera's violin workshop in Philadelphia. The harp had a small stand that kept it upright on its own. Its age was uncertain, and it had a deep crack running through the dark wood. Though Alexander was hard-pressed at this point in his life for the money to purchase the harp, he eventually gave in to his desires and bought it (Jacobs, 1978:245–246).

> A few weeks later, in the middle of the night, Alexander discovered another quirk about his new acquisition. Janine and he were sleeping soundly when they heard what sounded like a shot. An investigation revealed nothing. The mystery remained until the next day when Lloyd noticed a broken string on his harp. The humidity, or lack of it, played havoc with the harp which continued the unnerving practice of snapping a string, usually in the neighborhood of 3:00 a.m. The crack also deepened and lengthened until Alexander gave up the occasional playing. The harp now serves as a mantel decoration, a complex reminder of times past, and even . . . as inspiration for [some] of his books. (Jacobs, 1978:246)

See also Fantastic objects.
(M 237, 287)

Jacket illustration by Evaline Ness

**Truthful Harp, The: *The Truthful Harp*, a picture book illustrated by Evaline Ness, is a tale that predates the story of *Taran. Alexander wrote the text for this picture book after finishing the first draft of *Taran Wanderer (Jacobs, 1978:287).

The tale introduces King *Fflewddur Fflam at the time in his life when he decides to become a *bard. Leaving his tiny kingdom, Fflewddur journeys to *Caer Dathyl to meet with the *Council of the Bards. However, Fflam has not prepared for the bardic examination, and he miserably fails it. Nevertheless, the *Chief Bard gifts Fflewddur with a wonderful harp. "The beautiful instrument seemed to play of itself. He needed only touch his fingers to the strings and melodies poured forth in a golden tide" (TH 89/13).

The harp, however, will not allow Fflewddur to stretch the truth. The first time he tries to "color the facts," the *truthful harp breaks a string. On a freezing day, Fflewddur gives his cloak to an old man, saying, "'Take it and welcome. For the truth of the matter is, I find the day uncomfortably hot!' No sooner had he spoken these words than the harp shuddered as if it were alive, bent like an overdrawn bow, and a string snapped in two with a loud twang" (TH 89–90/14–17).

Fflewddur Fflam performs other kind and valiant deeds as he travels *Prydain. But he cannot curb his tongue, and his new harp loses many strings. "Dismayed at the state of his harp strings," Fflewddur returns to Caer Dathyl. As he comes before the Chief Bard, Fflewddur suddenly realizes why he cannot keep his harp strung. "I can't help adding a little color [to the facts]," he says. "Poor things, they need it so badly" (TH 93/29).

"Yet those deeds were far more worthy than all your gallant fancies," said the Chief Bard, "for a good truth is purest gold that needs no gilding. You have the modest heart of the truly brave; but your tongue, alas, gallops faster than your head can rein it."

"No longer!" Fflewddur declared. "Never again will I stretch the truth!"

The harp strings tightened as if ready to break all at once.

"That is to say," Fflewddur added hastily, "never beyond what it can bear. A Fflam has learned his lesson. Forever!"

At this, a string snapped loudly. But it was only a small one. (TH 94/30)

The picture book is no longer in print, but the story of *The Truthful Harp* has been added to the collection of Prydain short stories in the current edition of *The Foundling*.

See also Fantastic objects, Taliesin.

Tylwyth (TILL-with) Teg (TEG): *See* Kingdom of Tylwyth Teg.

V

‏✦

Valley Cantrevs (kantrevs): These are the *cantrevs that are located along the River *Ystrad (TW 22/36), specifically in the *Valley of Ystrad. *Cantrev Cadiffor, the realm of King *Smoit, is one of the Valley Cantrevs. The farmer, *Aeddan, tells *Taran that the "the Valley Cantrevs . . . were known far and wide for the finest oats and barley, and Cantrev Cadiffor itself for wheat bright and heavy as gold" (TW 27/41). Unfortunately, *Arawn *Death-Lord stole not only the plows and enchanted tools that worked by themselves, but also the secrets of making the earth yield richly. The Valley Cantrevs are now only minimally productive. Aeddan's crops have failed two years in a row.
(TW 22/36, 27/41, 66/85; HK 82/100)

Valley of Great Avren (AHV-ren): *See* Great Avren River.

Valley of Kynvael (KIN-vale): *See* Kynvael.

Valley of Ystrad (ISS-trad): *See* Ystrad, River.

wall of thorns: With *magic acquired from the *gem of Angharad, the evil wizard, *Morda, raised an impenetrable wall of thorns around his dwelling. The wall of thorns snags all who try to breach it, including the *Companions. *Llyan, however, is powerful enough to leap over the evil barrier. The wall of thorns is destroyed as its creator is slain.
(TW 87/108, 108/131, 111/135)

wallet of food: *Gwydion presents each of the *Companions a gift at the conclusion of *The Book of Three. "To faithful and valiant *Gurgi shall be given a wallet of food which shall be always full. Guard it well; it is one of the treasures of *Prydain" (BT 181/211).

Gurgi's wallet of food comes to the rescue of the Companions many times when food is scarce or time is limited. But, despite its marvelous powers of providence, the wallet has its shortcomings, as *Eilonwy points out.

> "It's certainly a magical wallet . . . it never seems to get empty. The food is really quite nourishing, I'm sure, and wonderful to have when you need it. But the truth of the matter is, it's rather tasteless. That's often the trouble with magical things. They're never what you'd expect."
> (BC 40/58)

In *The Black Cauldron, Gurgi tries to trade the wallet of food to the witches, *Orddu, *Orwen, and *Orgoch, for the *Black Cauldron. He had hoped to spare Taran the anguish of parting with the *Brooch of Adaon. However, the witches decline Gurgi's offer.

When the age of enchantment comes to an end in Prydain, Gurgi's wallet of food loses its *magic. Gurgi, who will travel to the *Summer Country with the *Sons of Don, had hoped to leave it with *Taran as a gift of remembrance. "'Alas, alas!' wailed Gurgi. 'Poor Gurgi has nothing to give kindly master for fond rememberings. Woe and misery! Even wallet of crunchings and munchings now is empty!'" (HK 242–243/279).

Gurgi's wallet of food is similar in properties to three of the thirteen precious things of the Island of Britain, as described in *Guest's notes to the *Mabinogion. The first is the basket of Gwyddno Garanhir. If food for one man were put in it, when opened the basket would contain food for a hundred. The pan and the platter of Rhengynydd Ysgolhaig are items two and three. Whatever food was required could be found either in the magical pan or on the enchanted platter (M 286).

See also Fantastic objects.
(BT 181/211; BC 40/58, 74/98; CL 27/44, 87/111, 124/151; TW 8/21, 111/135, 138/164; HK 38/51, 166/195, 204/236, 243/279; M 286, 502)

Wanderer: *See* Taran Wanderer.

way post: The *Fair Folk maintain way posts all around *Prydain. *Gwystyl of the Fair Folk keeps the way post closest to *Annuvin. Such places are apparently hidden; Gwystyl's is beneath ground (BC 54–55/74–75). *Doli of the Fair Folk mentions a way post maintained near the cottage of the sorcerer, *Morda. Its guardian was never heard from again for he was bewitched by the evil wizard (TW 80–81/101–102). Doli also speaks of Fair Folk way posts kept in the *Free Commots (TW 112/135).
(BC 53/72; TW 80/101, 93/115, 112/135; HK 62/77)

Weaver-Woman: *See* Dwyvach.

Welsh mythology: *See* Mabinogion.

West Domains: The realm of King *Pryderi is located in the West Domains, which are north and west of *Annuvin. Alexander (1985b) explains that west domains is better stated as a common noun, even though it is capitalized in *The High King.
(HK 81/99, 109/130)

White Horses of Llyr (LEER): *Eilonwy speaks of a childhood memory about the sea. "The waves break against the cliffs and churn into foam, and farther out, as far as you can see, there are the white crests, the White

Horses of Llyr, they call them; but they're really only waves waiting their turn to roll in" (BT 129/154).

See also House of Llyr.

(BT 129/154)

White Pig: *See* banner of the White Pig; Hen Wen.

Yspadadden (iss-pah-DAH-den): Yspadadden, the *Chief Giant, is the father of *Olwen. As *Medwyn relates to *Taran, Yspadadden gives *Kilhuch several nearly impossible tasks to complete before he may win Olwen's hand in marriage (BT 120/144).

The story of Kilhwch (Kilhuch) and Olwen is a tale found in the *Mabinogion. Yspaddaden (Yspadadden) Penkawr is indeed Olwen's father and assigns many tasks to Kilhwch, just as Medwyn explains in *The Book of Three*. However, in the *Mabinogion* it is told that Yspaddaden Penkawr's life will only last until Olwen is espoused. With the help of many allies, Kilhwch is able to complete all of Yspaddaden's tasks and is given Olwen for his wife. Yspaddaden's life is then forfeit. "Then Goreu, the son of *Custennin, seized him by the hair of his head and dragged him after him to the keep, and cut off his head and placed it on a stake on the citadel. Then they took possession of his castle, and of his treasures" (M 258).

See also Gwythyr.
(BT 120/144; M 219, 223, 231, 249, 258, 280)

Ystrad (ISS-trad), River: This river flows north to south, dividing *Prydain in half. It is a tributary of the *Great Avren. *Caer Dathyl, stronghold of the *Sons of Don, lies near the River Ystrad's source in the *Eagle Mountains. The *Valley of Ystrad, surrounding the river to the south, holds the *Valley Cantrevs, a once rich and productive farming region.

The name Ystrad appears several times in the *Mabinogion. Ystrad Towi is a town or perhaps a stronghold controlled by Gruffudd ab Rhys, Prince of South Wales (M 213). Ystrad Yw is yet another place, town or stronghold, and is mentioned in the tale "Kilhwch (*Kilhuch) and *Olwen" (M 256). *Math, the son of *Mathonwy, possessed the three *Cantrevs of Ystrad

Tywi (M 413). There is also reference to the Cistercian Abbey of Ystrad Marchell (M 321).
(BT 23/39, 44/62, 94/116, 108/130, 160/188; BC 29/45; TW 66/85; HK 87/106, 99/119; M 213, 256, 293, 321, 358, 362, 413)

$\mathcal{A}$PPENDIX

Categories of Entry Headings

❖

animals: Ash-wing, Briavael, Brynach, Cornillo, Crugan-Crawgan, Edyrnion, Gwybeddin (Prince Flyspeck), gwythaints, Hen Wen (White Pig), Islimach, Kadwyr, Kaw, Llamrei, Lluagor, Llyan, Melyngar, Melynlas, Nedir, Oak-Horn, ousel, salmon of Lake Llew, Star-Nose (Chief Mole)

bardic objects and terms: bardic symbol, Council of Bards, Council Chamber of the Bards, Hall of Bards, Hall of Lore, letter sticks, Old Writing, truthful harp

bards: Adaon, Council of Bards, Fflewddur Fflam, Menwy, Taliesin (Chief Bard)

birds: Ash-wing, Edyrnion, gwythaints, Kadwyr, Kaw, ousel

books: *The Black Cauldron*, book of spells, *The Book of Three*, *The Castle of Llyr*, Celtic mythology (Welsh mythology), Chronicles of Prydain, *Coll and His White Pig*, *The Foundling*, Lady Charlotte Guest, *The High King*, *Mabinogion*, *Taran Wanderer*, *The Truthful Harp*

castles: Annuvin, Caer Cadarn, Caer Colur, Caer Dathyl, Dinas Rhydnant, Oeth-Anoeth, Spiral Castle

castle-related terms: Council Chamber of the Bards, Great Hall, Hall of Bards, Hall of Lore, Hall of Thrones, Hall of Warriors, Iron Portals

characters—fantasy: Achren, Adaon, Arawn, Ash-Wing, Belin, Briavael, Brynach, Cauldron-Born, Children of Evening, Crugan-Crawgan, Dallben, Daughters of Don, Doli, Edyrnion, Eiddileg, Eilonwy, enchantresses of Llyr, Fair Folk, Fflewddur Fflam, Geraint, giant, Gildas, Glew, Govannion the Lame, Gurgi, Gwybeddin, Gwydion, Gwyn the Hunter, Gwystyl, gwythaints, Hen Wen, Horned King, Huntsmen of Annuvin, Kadwyr, Kaw, the Lady Don, Lake Sprites, Llyan, Llyr Half-Speech, Math, Medwyn, Morda, Nedir, Nevvid Nav Neivion, Oak-Horn, Orddu, Orgoch, Orwen, ousel, Regat, salmon of Lake Llew, Sons of Don, Yspadadden

cities: Dinas Rhydnant

common folk: Aedd, Aeddan, Alarca, Amrys, Annlaw Clay-Shaper, Coll, Collfrewr, Commot folk, Commot men, Craddoc, Custennin, Dorath, Drudwas, Dwyvach Weaver-Woman, Follin, Free Commots, Gloff, Goewin, Gwenlliant, Hevydd, Llassar, Llonio, Llonwen, Maibon, Modrona, Pebyr

companions: Doli, Eilonwy, Fflewddur Fflam, Gurgi, Kaw, Llyan, Lluagor, Melynlas, Rhun, Taran

craftsmen or craftswomen: Annlaw Clay-Shaper, bard, Dwyvach Weaver-Woman, Follin, Geraint, Govannion the Lame, Hevydd the Smith, Iscovan, Menwy

"Daughter of . . .": Angharad, Don, Goewin, Regat, Tannwen

dwellers of Cantrev Cadiffor: Aedd, Aeddan, Alarca, Amren, Gast, Goryon, Smoit

dwellers of the Free Commots: Annlaw Clay-Shaper, Drudwas, Dwyvach Weaver-Woman, Hevydd the Smith, Llassar, Pebyr

dwellers of the Isle of Mona: Angharad, enchantresses of Llyr, Geraint, Gildas, Grimgower, Regat, Rhudd, Rhuddlum, Rhun, Teleria

Eilonwy's names: Daughter of Angharad, Indeg, Princess of Llyr

emblems (symbols): Angharad's gem, banner of the White Pig, bardic symbol, black bear (House of Smoit), crescent moon (House of Llyr), crimson hawk (House of Pwyll), Gold Crown of Don, Golden Sunburst of Don, Iron Crown of Annuvin

enchanters: Arawn (Death-Lord), Dallben, Eiddileg, Geraint, Gildas, Govannion the Lame, Grimgower, Medwyn, Morda

enchantresses: Achren, Angharad, Eilonwy, enchantresses of Llyr, Orddu, Orgoch, Orwen, Regat

Fair Folk: Children of Evening, Doli, Eiddileg, Gwystyl, Lake Sprites, way post

fantasy motifs: Characters—fantasy, Fantastic objects, Good versus evil, Heroism, Magic, Other worlds

farmers: Aedd, Aeddan, Alarca, Amren, Coll, Maibon, Modrona

female characters: Achren, Alarca, Arianllyn, Eilonwy, Goewin, Gwenlliant, the Lady Don, Modrona, Olwen, Orddu, Orgoch, Orwen, Regat, Sword Maidens, Tannwen, Teleria

giants: Glew, Llyan, Yspadadden (Chief Giant)

harbors: Avren Harbor, golden ships, Mona Haven

horses: Islimach, Llamrei, Lluagor, Master of Horse, Melyngar, Melynlas

huntsmen: Chief Huntsman, Gwyn the Hunter, Huntsmen of Annuvin

kings: Arawn, Belin (King of the Sun), Eiddileg (Dwarf King), Fflewddur Fflam, Godo, Gwydion, High King, Horned King (Antlered King), King of Stones (Glew), Llyr Half-Speech (Sea King), Math (High King), Mathonwy, Morgant (King of Madoc), Pryderi (King of the West Domains), Pwyll, Rhitta (King of Prydain), Rhuddlum (King of Mona), Rhun (King of Mona), Rhych (King of Prydain), Rhydderch Hael (King of Prydain), Smoit (King of Cadiffor), Taran

lakes (pools): Black Lake, Lake Llew, Lake of Llunet, Marshes of Morva, Mirror of Llunet

legendary Prydainian characters: Belin, Govannion the Lame, Gwyn the Hunter, Gwythyr, Kilhuch, the Lady Don, Llyr Half-Speech, Nevvid Nav Neivion (Medwyn), Olwen, Proud Walkers, Rhitta, Rhych, Rhydderch Hael, Sword Maidens, Yspadadden

legendary Prydainian places: Caer Colur, Medwyn's valley, Mirror of Llunet, Summer Country

lords: Death-Lord (Arawn), Gast, Goryon, Lord of Annuvin (Arawn), Lord Swineherd

magic objects: Angharad's gem, ash-wood, battle horn, bauble (Golden Pelydryn), Black Cauldron (Black Crochan), black dagger, Black Lake, book of spells, *The Book of Three*, Brooch of Adaon, Dyrnwyn, eggs—magic, fantastic objects, Hazel Nuts of Wisdom, Iron Crown of Annuvin, letter sticks, Mirror of Llunet, mushrooms—magic, powder—magic, stone—magic, truthful harp, wall of thorns, wallet of food

memorials: barrow, mounds of honor

mountains: Dark Gate, Eagle Mountains, Llawgadarn Mountains, Mount Dragon, Mount Kilgwyry, Mount Meledin

oaths (expressions): Good Llyr, Great Belin

people of Don: Belin, Daughters of Don, Fflewddur Fflam, Gwydion, the Lady Don, Math, Mathonwy, Sons of Don (House of Don)

people of Llyr: Angharad, Daughters of Llyr, Eilonwy, Llyr Half-Speech, Regat, Sea People, Sword Maidens

peoples of Prydain: cantrev, Commot folk, Fair Folk, Free Commots, House of Don (Sons of Don), House of Fflam, House of Llyr (Sea People), House of Pwyll, House of Rhuddlum, House of Smoit

potters: Annlaw Clay-Shaper

princes: Ellidyr (Prince of Pen-Llarcau), Flyspeck, Glessic, Gwydion (Prince of Don), Rhun (Prince of Mona)

princesses: Angharad, Eilonwy, Princess of Llyr, Princess Vixen

queens: Achren, Eilonwy, Queen of Prydain, Regat, Teleria

realms (kingdoms): Annuvin (Land of the Dead, Land of Death), cantrev, Cantrev Cadiffor, Cantrev Dau Gleddyn, Cantrev Mawr, Cantrev Rheged, Commot Cenarth, Commot Gwenith, Commot Isav, Commot

Merin, eastern strongholds, Free Commots, Isle of Mona, Kingdom of
Tylwyth Teg (Realm of the Fair Folk), Madoc, Medwyn's valley, north-
ern domains, Northern Realms, Prydain, Summer Country, Valley
Cantrevs, West Domains

regions, geographical: eastern strongholds, Forest of Idris, Free Commots,
Hill Cantrevs, Hills of Bran-Galedd, Hills of Parys, Isle of Mona, Land
of Death (Annuvin), Marshes of Morva, Northern Realms (northern
domains), Red Fallows, Valley Cantrevs, West Domains

rivers (streams): Alaw River, Fernbrake Stream, Great Avren River,
Kynvael, Small Avren, Tevvyn, Ystrad

royal blood (ruling class): Achren, Adaon, Angharad, Arawn, Arianllyn,
Belin, Daughters of Don, Daughters of Llyr, Eiddileg, Eilonwy, Ellidyr,
Fflewddur Fflam, Gast, Godo, Goryon, Gwydion, Horned King, the Lady
Don, Llyr Half-Speech, Math, Mathonwy, Morgant, Pen-Llarcau, Pryderi,
Pwyll, Regat, Rhitta, Rhudd, Rhuddlum, Rhun, Rhych, Rhydderch
Hael, Smoit, Sons of Don, Tannwen, Taran, Teleria

sea: golden ships, White Horses of Llyr

shepherds: Amrys, Craddoc, Custennin, Drudwas, Llassar, Pebyr

smiths: Hevydd the Smith, Iscovan

"Son of . . .": Aedd, Collfrewr, Custennin, Don, Drudwas, Godo, Greidawl, Hirwas, Kadwyr, Llonwen, Mathonwy, Pebyr, Pen-Llarcau, Pwyll,
Rhudd, Rhych, Rhydderch, Taliesin

stewards: Chief Steward, Magg

strongholds: Annuvin, Caer Cadarn, Caer Colur (Castle of Llyr), Caer
Dallben, Caer Dathyl, Dinas Rhydnant, Marshes of Morva, Medwyn's
valley, Oeth-Anoeth, Spiral Castle, Tylwyth Teg, wall of thorns, way
post

Taran's names: Assistant Pig-Keeper, High King, Lord Swineherd, Taran
Threadbare, Taran Wanderer (Wanderer)

Taran's war party: Coll, Commot men, Doli, Eilonwy, Fflewddur Fflam,
Glew, Gurgi, Hevydd, Kaw, Llamrei, Llassar, Llonio, Lluagor, Llyan,
Melynlas, Taran

valleys: Medwyn's valley, Valley of the Great Avren, Valley of Kynvael,
Valley of Ystrad

villains: Achren, Arawn, Cauldron-Born, Chief Huntsman, Dorath,
Dorath's Company, Ellidyr, Gloff, gwythaint, Horned King, Huntsmen
of Annuvin, Magg, Morda, Morgant, Proud Walkers, Pryderi

war leaders: Adaon, Gwydion, Horned King, Morgant, Pryderi, Taran

weapons: black dagger, Dyrnwyn, eggs—magic, mushrooms—magic,
powder—magic

weavers: Dwyvach Weaver-Woman, Follin, loom, Orddu, Orgoch, Orwen

REFERENCES

✤

(Note: In order to facilitate locating the numerous Alexander references, they are arranged chronologically rather than alphabetically by title.)

Alexander, Lloyd. My *Five Tigers*. New York: Crowell, 1956.

Alexander, Lloyd. *Park Avenue Vet*. New York: Holt, Rinehart and Winston, 1962.

Alexander, Lloyd. *Time Cat*. New York: Holt, Rinehart and Winston, 1963. (Reissued by Henry Holt and Company, 2003.)

Alexander, Lloyd. *The Book of Three*. New York: Holt, Rinehart & Winston, 1964. (Reissued by Henry Holt and Company, 1999.)

Alexander, Lloyd. Letter to Ann Durell, 23 September 1964.

Alexander, Lloyd. Letter to Ann Durell, 10 November 1964.

Alexander, Lloyd. Letter to Ann Durell, 12 December 1964.

Alexander, Lloyd. Letter to Ann Durell, 15 December 1964.

Alexander, Lloyd. *The Black Cauldron*. New York: Holt, Rinehart and Winston, 1965. (Reissued by Henry Holt and Company, 1999.)

Alexander, Lloyd. *Coll and His White Pig*. New York: Holt, Rinehart & Winston, 1965. (Included in the reissue of *The Foundling*, Henry Holt and Company, 1999.)

Alexander, Lloyd. Letter to Ann Durell, 13 March 1965.

Alexander, Lloyd. Letter to Ann Durell, 31 March 1965.

Alexander, Lloyd. "The Flat-heeled Muse." *The Horn Book Magazine*, April 1965, 141–146.

Alexander, Lloyd. Letter to Ann Durell, 12 May 1965.

Alexander, Lloyd. Letter to Ann Durell, 29 October 1965.

Alexander, Lloyd. Letter to Ann Durell, 20 December 1965.

Alexander, Lloyd. *The Castle of Llyr*. New York: Holt, Rinehart & Winston, 1966. (Reissued by Henry Holt and Company, 1999.)

Alexander, Lloyd. Letter to Ann Durell, 26 July 1966.

Alexander, Lloyd. "Substance and Fantasy." *Library Journal* 91 (December 15, 1966): 6157–6159.

Alexander, Lloyd. *Taran Wanderer*. New York: Holt, Rinehart & Winston, 1967. (Reissued by Henry Holt and Company, 1999.)

Alexander, Lloyd. *The Truthful Harp*. New York: Holt, Rinehart & Winston, 1967. (Included in the reissue of *The Foundling*, Henry Holt and Company, 1999.)

Alexander, Lloyd. Letter to Ann Durell, 30 June 1967.

Alexander, Lloyd. Letter to Ann Durell, 24 July 1967.

Alexander, Lloyd. "The Truth About Fantasy." *Top of the News* 24 (January 1968): 168–174.

Alexander, Lloyd. *The High King*. New York: Holt, Rinehart & Winston, 1968. (Reissued by Henry Holt and Company, 1999.)

Alexander, Lloyd. "Letter to the Editor." *Orcrist* 4 (January 1969): 10.

Alexander, Lloyd. "No Laughter in Heaven." *The Horn Book Magazine*, February 1970, 11–19.

Alexander, Lloyd. Untitled, unpublished chapter on fantasy written for Dr. Shelton Root, University of Georgia, 1972.

Alexander, Lloyd. *The Foundling and Other Tales of Prydain*. New York: Holt, Rinehart & Winston, 1973. (Reissued by Henry Holt and Company, 1999.)

Alexander, Lloyd. "Meet the Newbery Author—A Series." Filmstrip and cassette. New York: Miller Brody, 1974.

Alexander, Lloyd. *The Cat Who Wished to Be a Man*. New York: Dutton, 1977.

Alexander, Lloyd. *The Town Cats*. New York: Dutton, 1977.

Alexander, Lloyd. Telephone interview, 19 March 1985.

Alexander, Lloyd. Personal interview, 24 November 1985.

Alexander, Lloyd. Letter to author, 13 January 1986.

Alexander, Lloyd. Personal interview, 13 April 1986.

Alexander, Lloyd. "Reading as a High-Risk Activity." International Reading Association, Philadelphia, Pennsylvania, 15 April 1986.

Alexander, Lloyd. Letter to author, 22 November 1986.

Alexander, Lloyd. *The Remarkable Journey of Prince Jen*. New York: Dutton, 1991.

Alexander, Lloyd. *The House Gobbaleen*. New York: Dutton, 1995.

Alexander, Lloyd. *Gypsy Rizka*. New York: Dutton, 1999.

Alexander, Lloyd. *How the Cat Swallowed Thunder*. New York: Dutton, 2000.

Alexander, Lloyd. *The Rope Trick*. New York: Dutton, 2002.

Babbitt, Natalie. "Fantasy and the Classic Hero." *School Library Journal* 34, no. 2 (October 1987): 25–29.

Carr, Marion. "Classic Hero in a New Mythology." *The Horn Book Magazine*, October 1971, 508–513.

Colwell, Eileen. "Folk Literature: An Oral Tradition and An Oral Art." *Top of the News* 24 (January 1968): 175–180.

Cooper, Susan. *The Dark Is Rising*. New York: Atheneum, 1973.

Davies, the Rev. Edward. *Mythology and Rites of British Druids*. London: J. Booth, 1809.

Durell, Ann. "Who's Lloyd Alexander?" *The Horn Book Magazine*, August 1969, 382–384.

Frye, Northrop. *Anatomy of Criticism*. New York: Atheneum, 1967.

Gantz, Jeffrey, trans. *The Mabinogion*. New York: Penguin, 1976.

Graves, Robert. *The White Goddess: A Historical Grammar of Poetic Myth*. First American revised and enlarged edition. New York: Farrar, Straus and Giroux, 1966.

Guest, Lady Charlotte. *The Mabinogion*. 1877 ed. Chicago: Academy, 1978.

Jacobs, James S. "Lloyd Alexander: A Critical Biography." Ed.D. diss., University of Georgia, 1978.

Jones, Dolores Blythe. *Children's Literature Awards and Winners: A Directory of Prizes, Authors, and Illustrators*. Detroit: Neal-Schuman, 1983.

Lane, Elizabeth. "Lloyd Alexander's Chronicles of Prydain and Welsh Tradition." *Orcrist* 7 (1973): 25–29.

Lewis, C. S. *The Lion, the Witch and the Wardrobe*. New York: Macmillan, 1950.

Madsen, Linda Lee. "Fantasy in Children's Literature: A Generic Study." Master's thesis, Utah State University, 1976.

McCana, Proinsias. *Celtic Mythology*. London: The Hamlin Publishing Group, 1970.

McGovern, John Thomas. "Lloyd Alexander—Bard of Prydain: A Study of the Prydain Cycle." Ed.D. diss., Temple University, 1980.

Patterson, Nancy-Lou. "Homo monstrosus: Lloyd Alexander's Gurgi and Other Shadow Figures of Fantastic Literature." *Mythlore* 3, no. 11 (1976): 24–26.

Sullivan, Anita. "Ray Bradbury and Fantasy." *English Journal* 61 (December 1972): 1314.

Tolkien, J.R.R. *The Fellowship of the Ring*. New York: Houghton Mifflin, 1954.

Tolkien, J.R.R. *The Tolkien Reader*. New York: Ballantine, 1966.

Vries, Jan de. *Heroic Song and Heroic Legend*. London: Oxford University Press, 1963.

Weiss, Jacqueline Shachter. *Prizewinning Books for Children: Themes and Stereotypes in U.S. Prizewinning Prose Fiction for Children*. Lexington, Mass.: Lexington Books, 1983.

Wintle, Justin, and Emma Fisher. "Lloyd Alexander," *Pied Pipers*. New York: Paddington Press, 1974.

LLOYD ALEXANDER
A Biographical Sketch

✣

Lloyd Alexander was born in Philadelphia in 1924 and now lives on a quiet street in Drexel Hill, Pennsylvania, only a few blocks from his boyhood home. He lived briefly in Europe during and after World War II (he served as a member of U.S. Army Intelligence), and it was in France that he met and married his wife, Janine. Otherwise, Alexander has never strayed far from the Philadelphia area for long, and there he has done virtually all his writing.

More than fifty years ago Lloyd Alexander's writing career was launched with English translations of French works by authors such as Jean-Paul Sartre. During the 1950s and early 1960s, he wrote several well-received adult novels. However, in the late 1950s, Alexander began creating books for young readers and eventually left a successful career writing for adults to write full-time for children. Since that time, he has produced thirty-six children's books, most of which have won awards or appeared on "best books" lists, and now calls writing for children "the happiest discovery of all." Most notable are the books of the Chronicles of Prydain, the stunning, Newbery Award–winning high fantasy series that is the topic of this book and that has now enjoyed brisk readership for more than thirty years.

Books by Lloyd Alexander

Translations
Eluard, Paul. *Selected Writings of Paul Eluard*. Norfolk, Conn.: New Directions, 1951.
Sartre, Jean-Paul. *Nausea*. New York: New Directions, 1949.

Sartre, Jean-Paul. *The Wall and Other Stories*. New York: New Directions, 1949.

Vialar, Paul. *The Sea Rose*. London: Peter Nevill, 1951.

Adult Audience

And Let the Credit Go. New York: Crowell, 1955.

Fifty Years in the Doghouse. New York: Putnam, 1964.

Janine Is French. New York: Crowell, 1959.

My Five Tigers. New York: Crowell, 1956 (also for young readers).

My Love Affair with Music. New York: Crowell, 1960.

Park Avenue Vet. New York: Holt, Rinehart & Winston, 1962 (with Dr. Louis J. Camuti).

Young Audience

The Arkadians. New York: Dutton, 1995.

The Beggar Queen. New York: Dutton, 1984.

The Black Cauldron. New York: Holt, Rinehart & Winston, 1965. (Reissued by Henry Holt and Company, 1999.)

The Book of Three. New York: Holt, Rinehart & Winston, 1964. (Reissued by Henry Holt and Company, 1999.)

Border Hawk: August Bondi. New York: Farrar, Straus and Cudahy, 1958.

The Castle of Llyr. New York: Holt, Rinehart & Winston, 1966. (Reissued by Henry Holt and Company, 1999.)

The Cat Who Wished to Be a Man. New York: Dutton, 1973.

Coll and His White Pig. Illustrated by Evaline Ness. New York: Holt, Rinehart & Winston, 1965. (Included in the reissue of *The Foundling*, Henry Holt and Company, 1999.)

The Drackenberg Adventure. New York: Dutton, 1988.

The El Dorado Adventure. New York: Dutton, 1987.

The First Two Lives of Lukas-Kasha. New York: Dutton, 1978.

Flagship Hope: Aaron Lopez. New York: Farrar, Straus and Cudahy, 1960.

The Fortune-tellers. Illustrated by Trina Schart Hyman. New York: Dutton, 1992.

The Foundling and Other Tales of Prydain. New York: Holt, Rinehart & Winston, 1973. (Expanded edition by Henry Holt and Company includes *Coll and His White Pig* and *The Truthful Harp*, 1999.)

The Four Donkeys. Illustrated by Lester Abrams. New York: Holt, Rinehart & Winston, 1972.

The Gawgon and The Boy. New York: Dutton, 2001.

Gypsy Rizka. New York: Dutton, 1999.

The High King. New York: Holt, Rinehart & Winston, 1968. (Reissued by Henry Holt and Company, 1999.)

The House Gobbaleen. Illustrated by Diane Goode. New York: Dutton, 1995.

How the Cat Swallowed Thunder. Illustrated by Judith Byron Schachner. New York: Dutton, 2000.

The Illyrian Adventure. New York: Dutton, 1986.

The Iron Ring. New York: Dutton, 1997.

The Jedera Adventure. New York: Dutton, 1989.

The Kestrel. New York: Dutton, 1982.

The King's Fountain. Illustrated by Ezra Jack Keats. New York: Dutton, 1971.

The Marvelous Misadventures of Sebastian. New York: Dutton, 1970.

My Five Tigers. New York: Crowell, 1956.

The Philadelphia Adventure. New York: Dutton, 1990.

The Remarkable Journey of Prince Jen. New York: Dutton, 1991.

The Rope Trick. New York: Dutton, 2002.

Taran Wanderer. New York: Holt, Rinehart & Winston, 1967. (Reissued by Henry Holt and Company, 1999.)

Time Cat. New York: Holt, Rinehart & Winston, 1963. (Reissued by Henry Holt and Company, 2003.)

The Town Cats and Other Tales. New York: Dutton, 1977.

The Truthful Harp. Illustrated by Evaline Ness. New York: Holt, Rinehart & Winston, 1967. (Included in the reissue of *The Foundling*, Henry Holt and Company, 1999.)

Westmark. New York: Dutton, 1981.

The Wizard in the Tree. New York: Dutton, 1975.

About the Author

MICHAEL O. TUNNELL has written everything from picture books and middle-grade novels to educational books in the field of children's literature. He co-authored *Lloyd Alexander*, a "bio-bibliography," and has contributed articles on Prydain to *The New Advocate* and *School Library Journal*. A professor of children's literature at Brigham Young University, Mr. Tunnell lives in Orem, Utah, with his wife, Glenna, an elementary school librarian.